BUNNY DROP

yumi unita

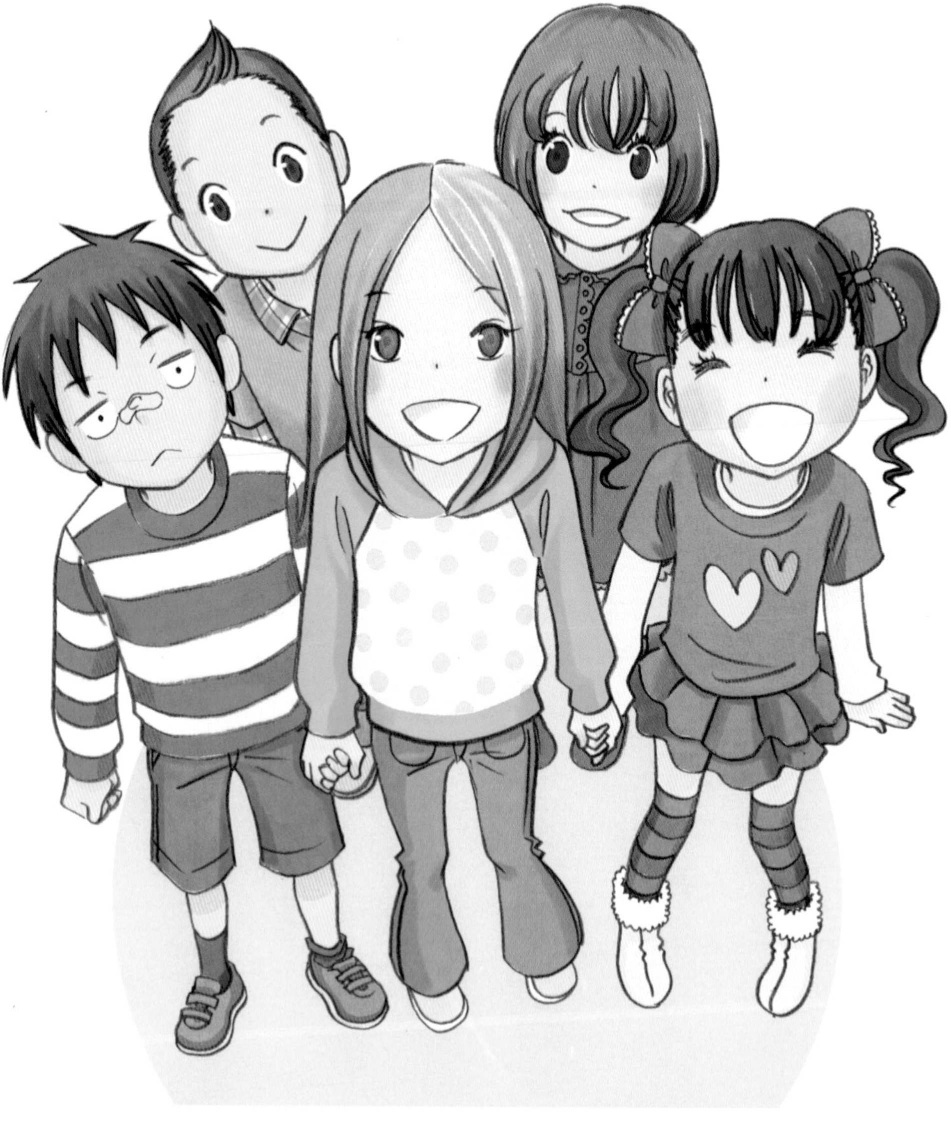

BUNNY**DROP** 10

yumi unita

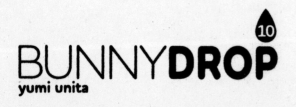

STORY

Ten years have passed since Daikichi, a single guy with no experience in child-rearing, made the decision to take in Rin, a little girl thought to be his grandfather's love child. Supported and kept afloat by the help of family and friends, Daikichi faced the numerous challenges resulting from his decision head-on.

After living together for more than ten years, Rin has finally accepted her romantic feelings for Daikichi, and the two have made a promise to marry after her high school graduation...

MAIN CHARACTERS

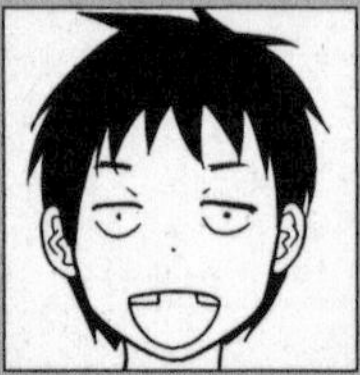

Ten years later

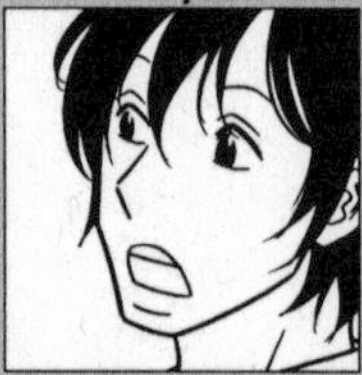

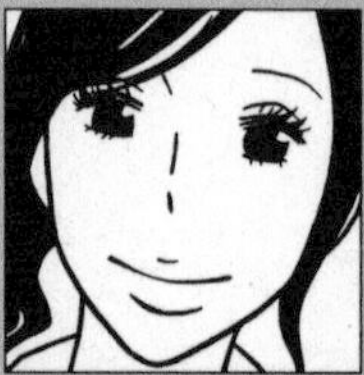

KOUKI NITANI
Rin's childhood friend from day care. Because of one thing after another, he was rejected by Rin.

KOUKI'S MOM
Kouki's mother and a single mom. Remarried while Kouki was in high school.

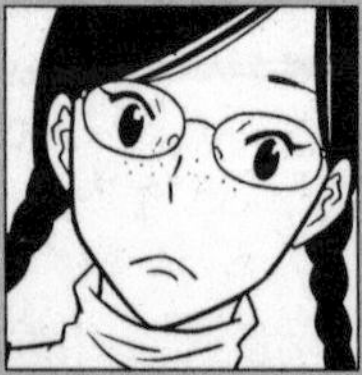

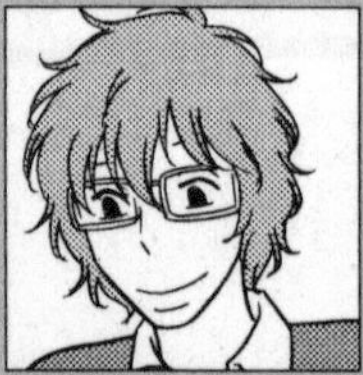

MASAKO YOSHII
Rin's birthmother. Chose her career as a manga artist over parenthood and was an absent mother, but recently reestablished a relationship with Rin.

MASAKO'S HUSBAND
Also Masako's chief assistant at work. The father of Masako's second child.

Ten years later

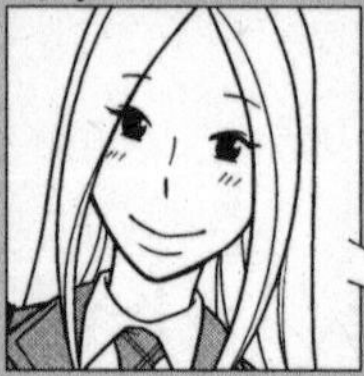

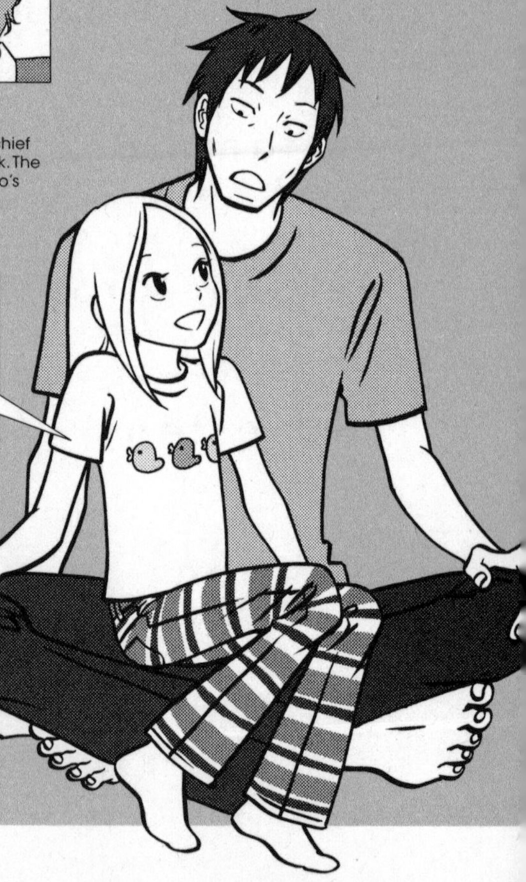

DAIKICHI KAWACHI
Used to be like a fish out of water around women and kids but now has an impressive decade of being Rin's guardian under his belt.

RIN KAGA
Taken in by Daikichi when she was six. Began to realize she had feelings for him when she got to high school.

contents

extra.1

little heart

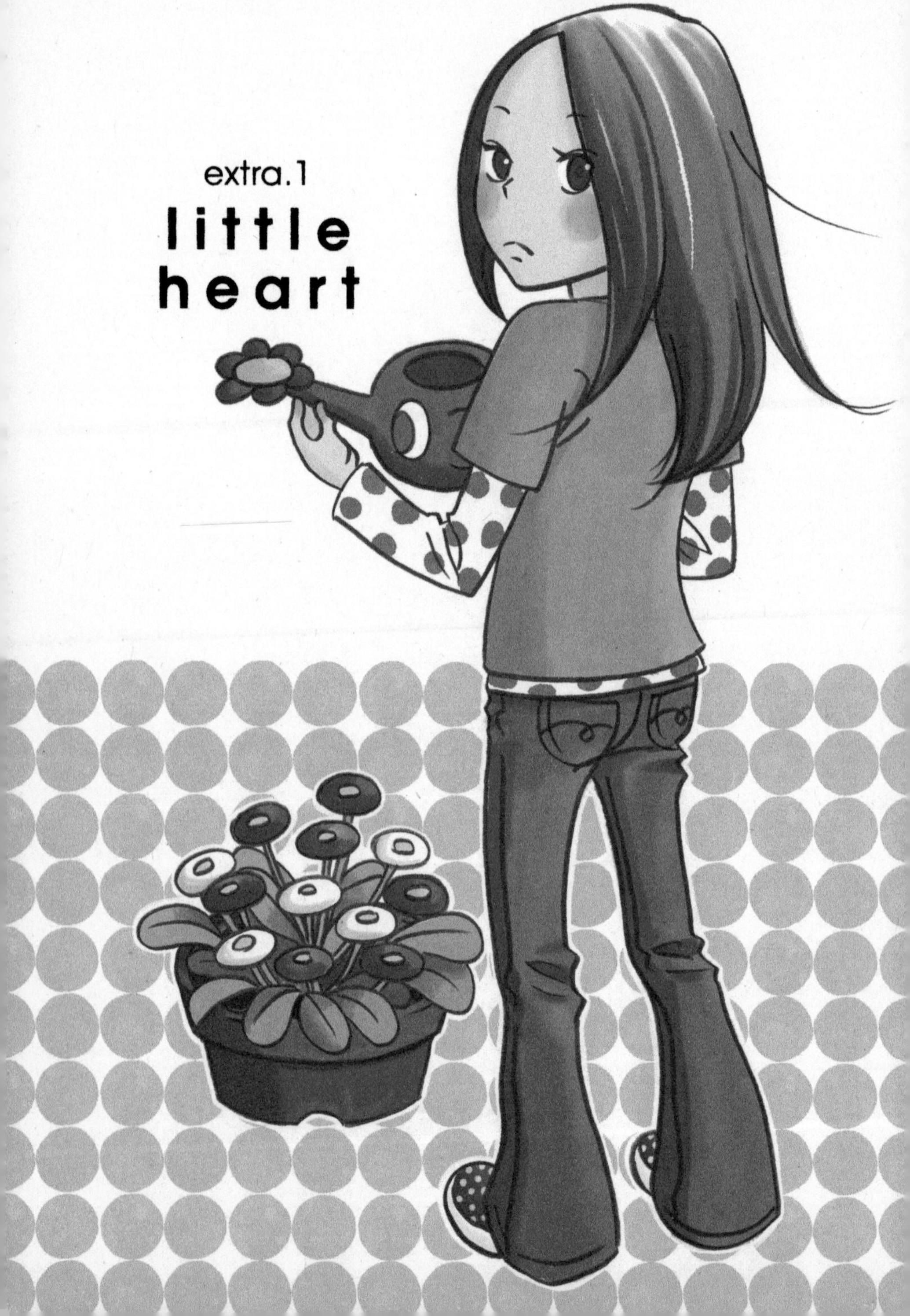

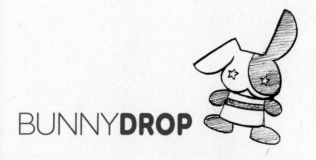

BUNNY**DROP**

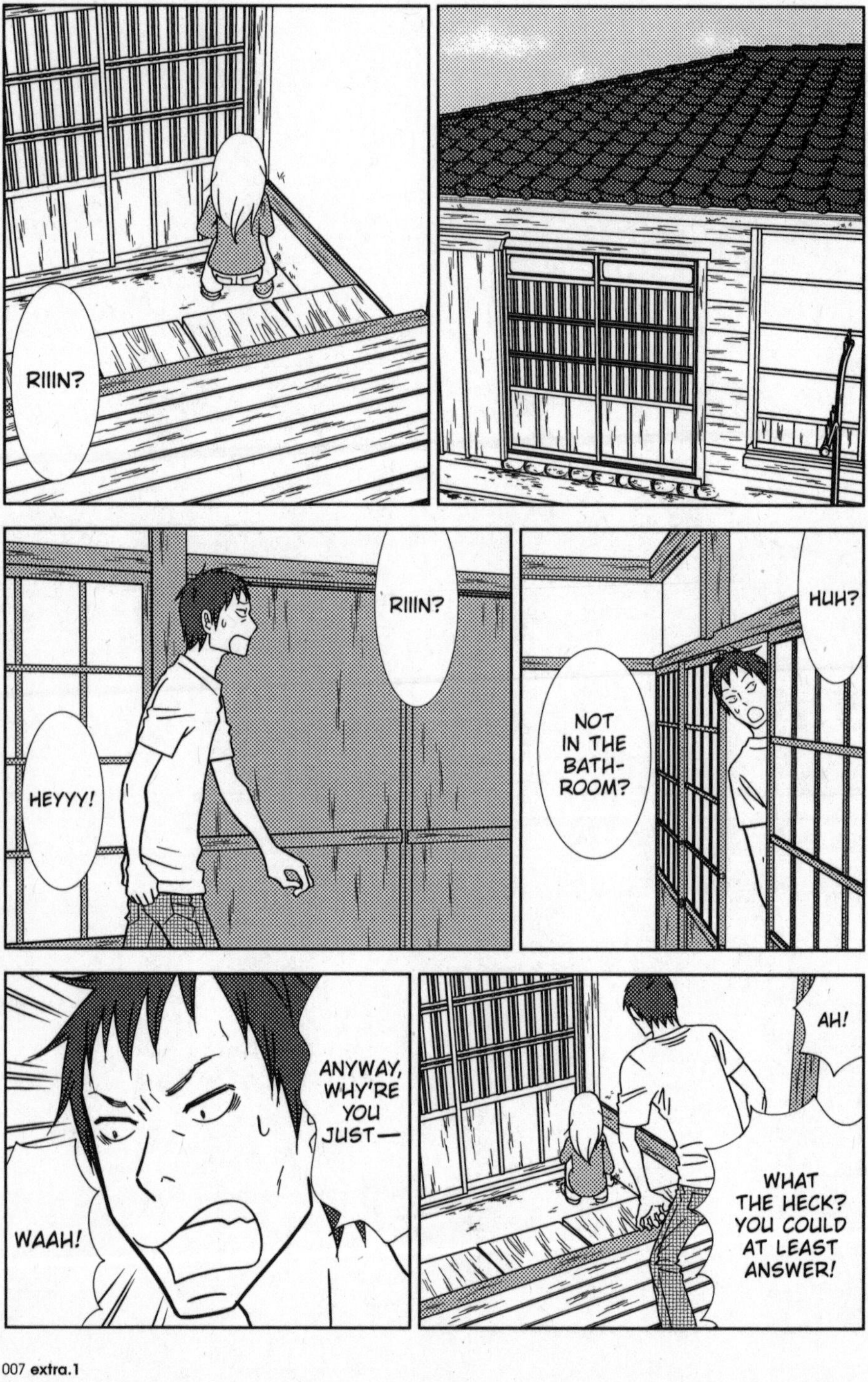
RIIIN?
HUH?
NOT IN THE BATH-ROOM?
RIIIN?
HEYYY!
AH!
WHAT THE HECK? YOU COULD AT LEAST ANSWER!
ANYWAY, WHY'RE YOU JUST—
WAAH!

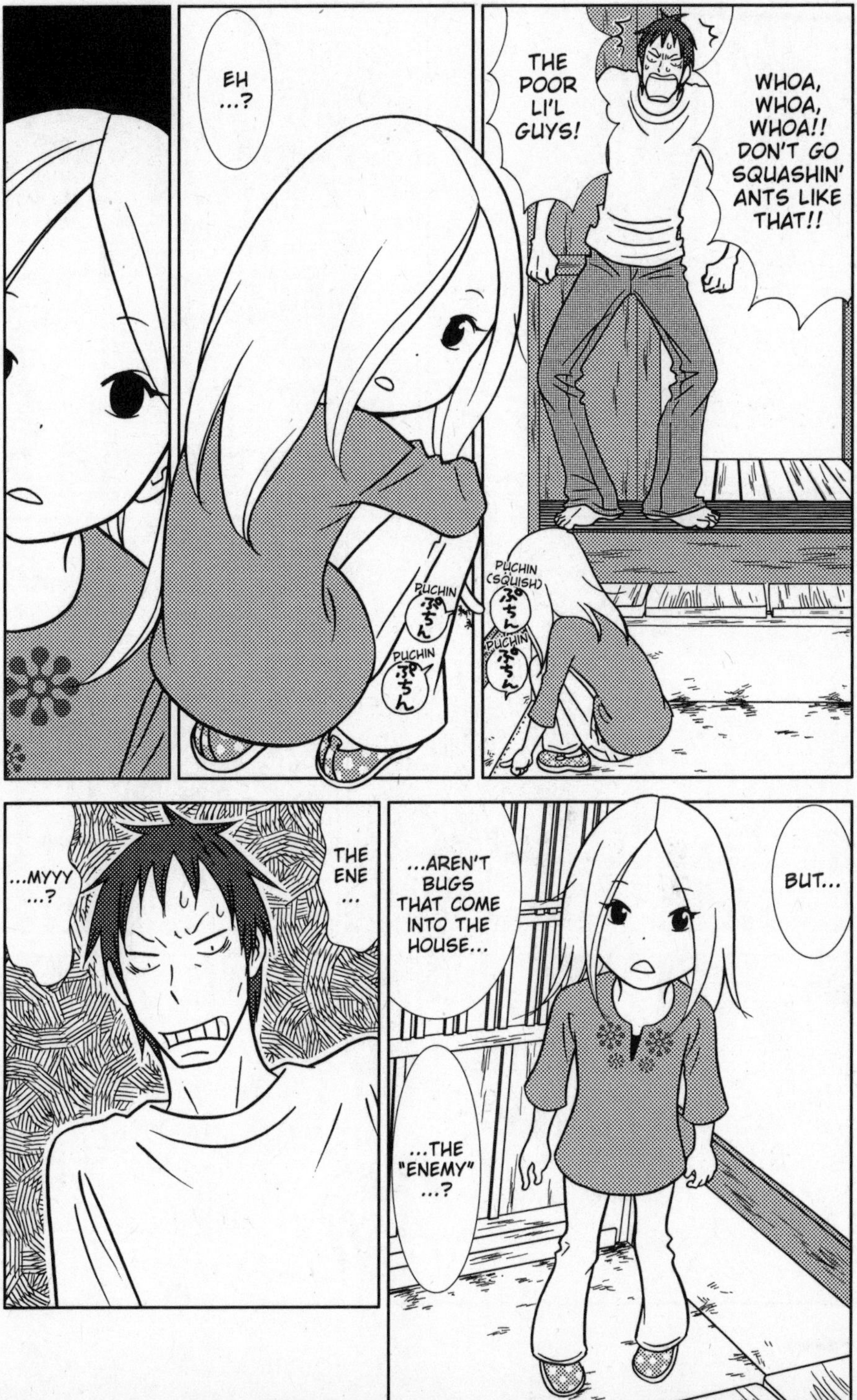
WHOA, WHOA, WHOA!! DON'T GO SQUASHIN' ANTS LIKE THAT!!
THE POOR LI'L GUYS!
PUCHIN (SQUISH) ぷちん
PUCHIN ぷちん
EH ...?
PUCHIN ぷちん
PUCHIN ぷちん
BUT...
...AREN'T BUGS THAT COME INTO THE HOUSE...
...THE "ENEMY" ...?
THE ENE ...
...MYYY ...?

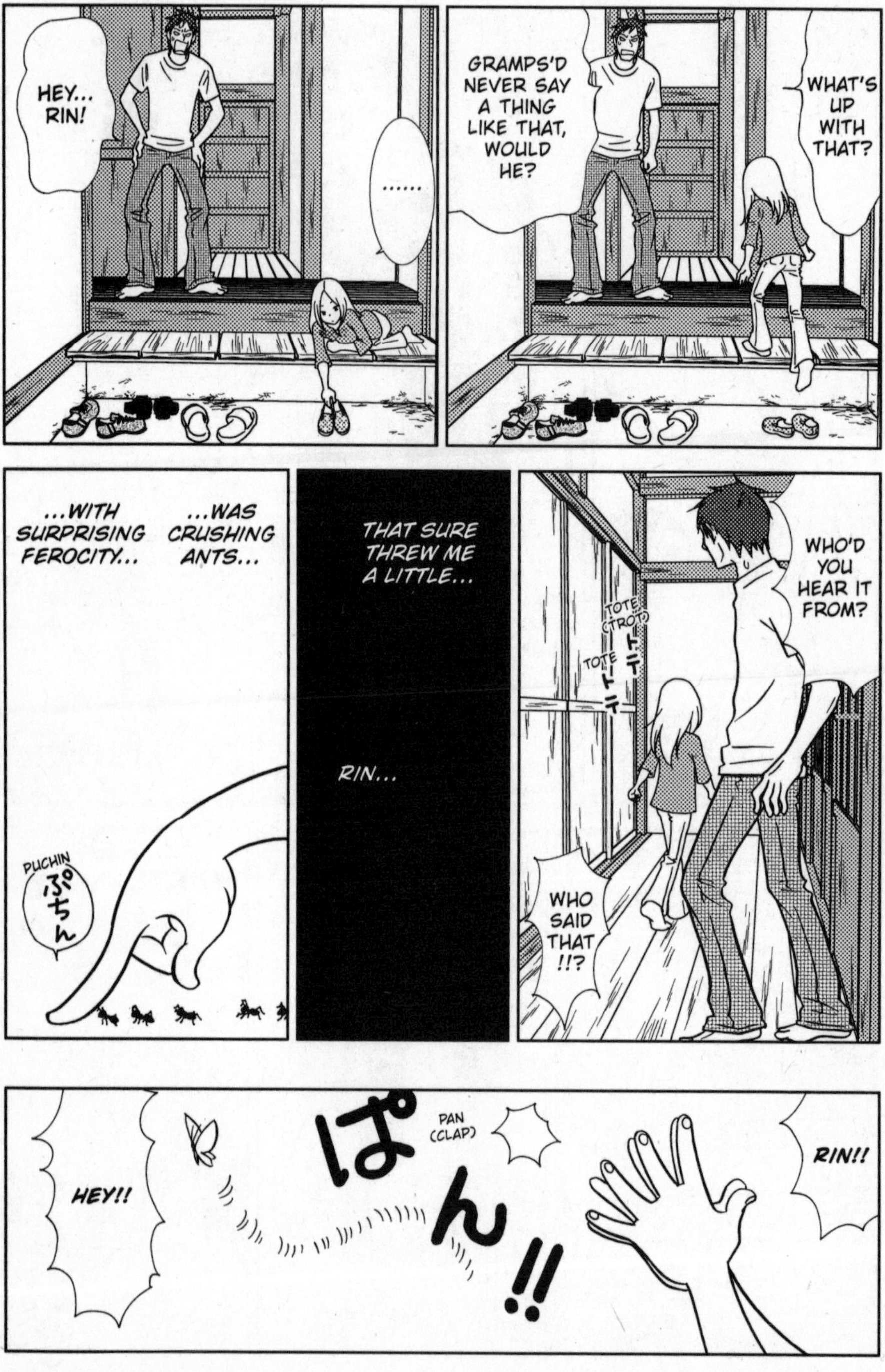
WHAT'S UP WITH THAT?
GRAMPS'D NEVER SAY A THING LIKE THAT, WOULD HE?
HEY... RIN!
......
WHO'D YOU HEAR IT FROM?
TOTE (TROT) トテ
TOTE トテ
WHO SAID THAT !!?
THAT SURE THREW ME A LITTLE...
RIN...
...WAS CRUSHING ANTS...
...WITH SURPRISING FEROCITY...
PUCHIN
ぷちん
RIN!!
PAN (CLAP)
ぱん!!
HEY!!

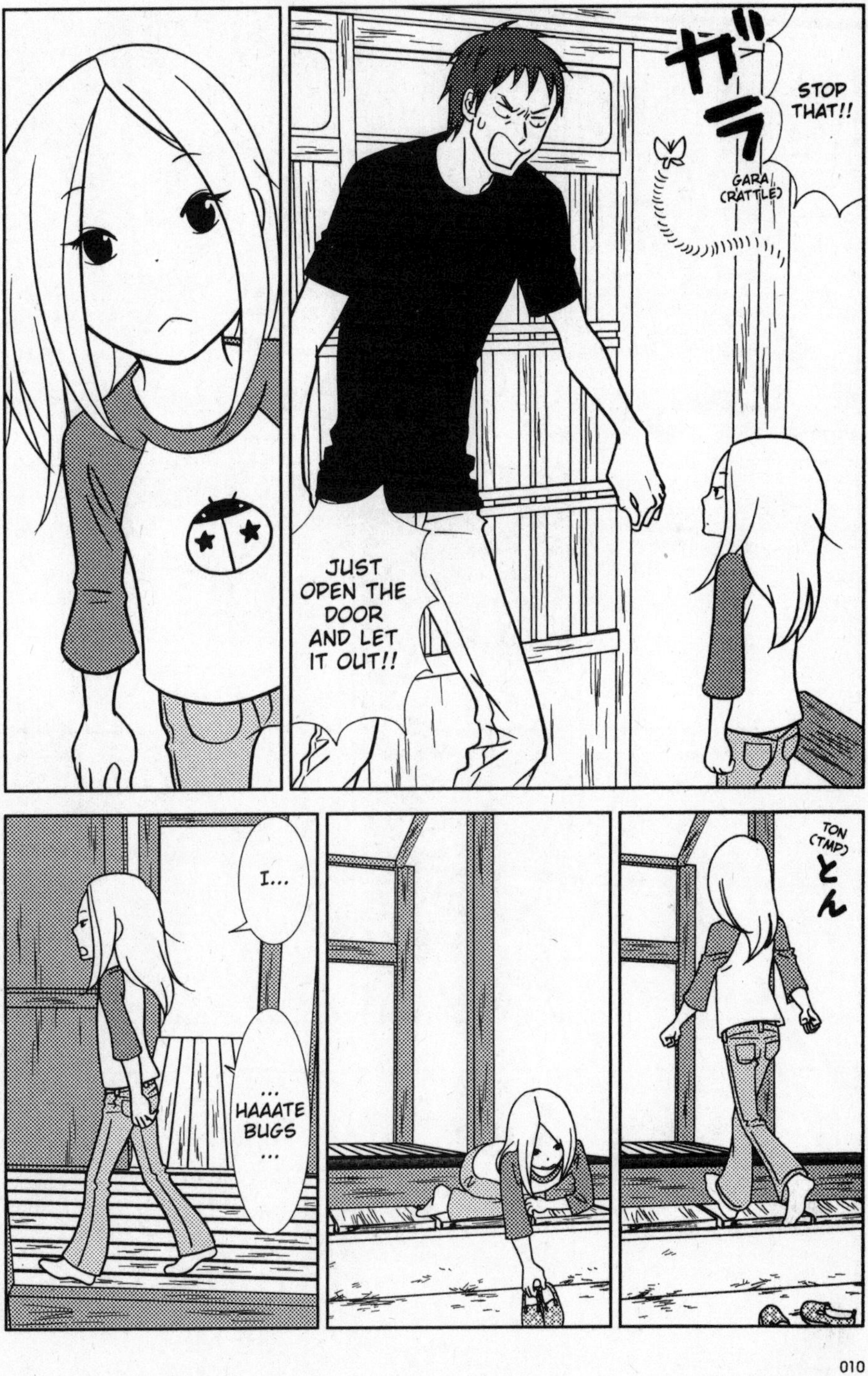
STOP THAT!!
ガラ
GARA (RATTLE)
JUST OPEN THE DOOR AND LET IT OUT!!
TON (TMP)
とん
I...
...HAAATE BUGS...

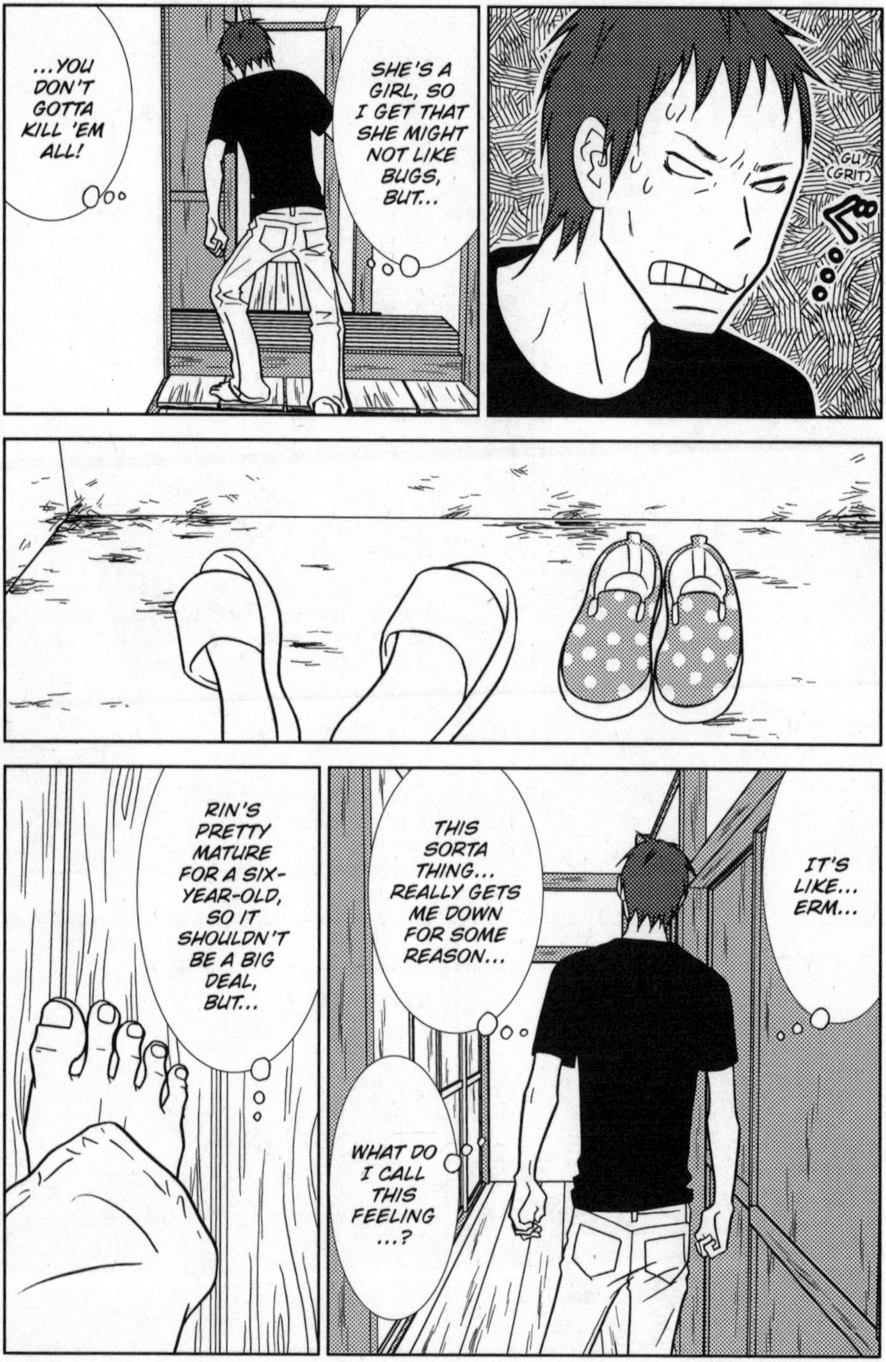
GU (GRIT)
SHE'S A GIRL, SO I GET THAT SHE MIGHT NOT LIKE BUGS, BUT...
...YOU DON'T GOTTA KILL 'EM ALL!
IT'S LIKE... ERM...
THIS SORTA THING... REALLY GETS ME DOWN FOR SOME REASON...
WHAT DO I CALL THIS FEELING ...?
RIN'S PRETTY MATURE FOR A SIX-YEAR-OLD, SO IT SHOULDN'T BE A BIG DEAL, BUT...

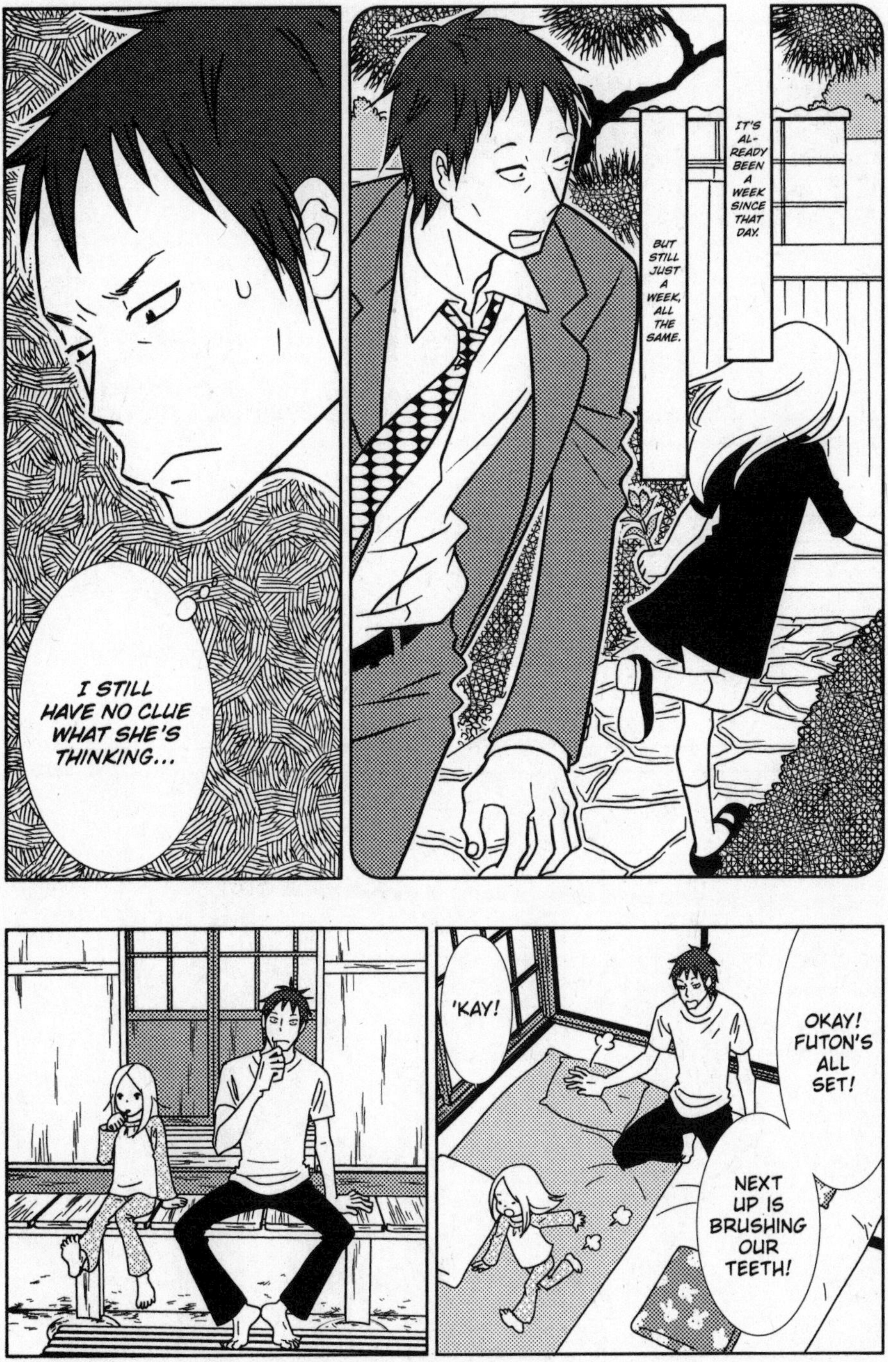
IT'S ALREADY BEEN A WEEK SINCE THAT DAY.
BUT STILL JUST A WEEK, ALL THE SAME.
I STILL HAVE NO CLUE WHAT SHE'S THINKING...
OKAY! FUTON'S ALL SET!
NEXT UP IS BRUSHING OUR TEETH!
'KAY!

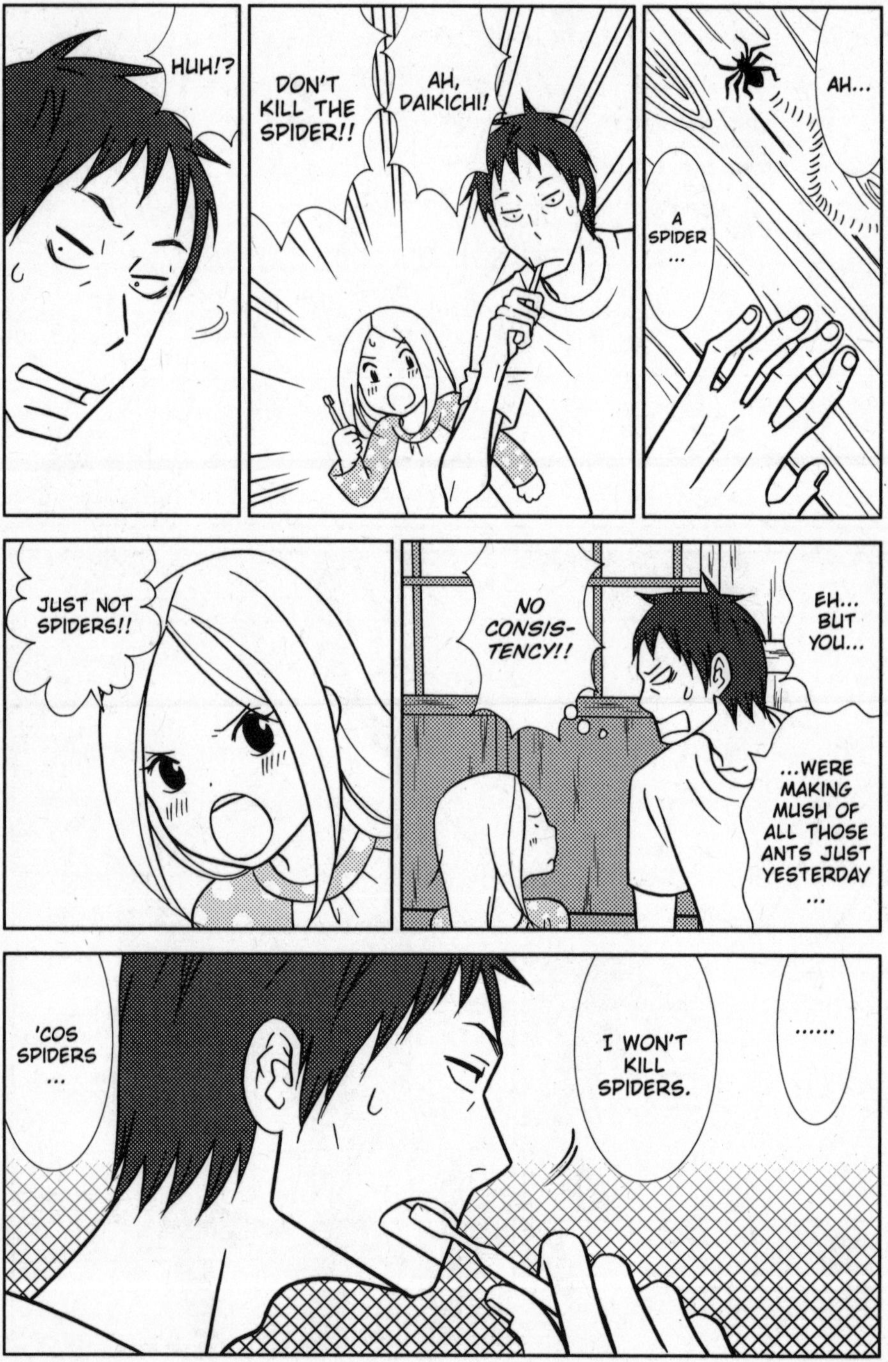
AH...
A SPIDER ...
AH, DAIKICHI!
DON'T KILL THE SPIDER!!
HUH!?
EH... BUT YOU...
...WERE MAKING MUSH OF ALL THOSE ANTS JUST YESTERDAY ...
NO CONSIS-TENCY!!
JUST NOT SPIDERS!!
......
I WON'T KILL SPIDERS.
'COS SPIDERS ...

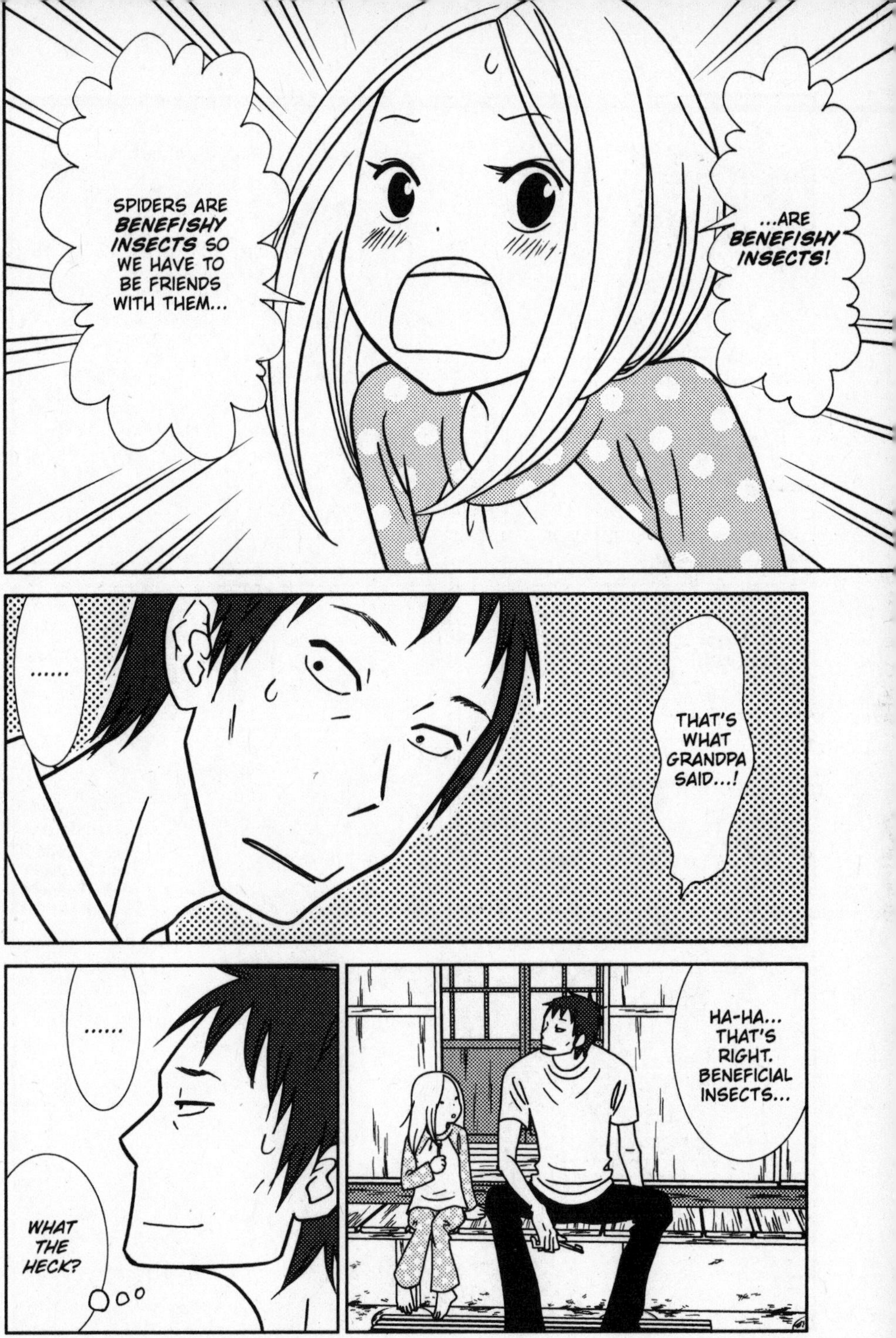
SPIDERS ARE *BENEFISHY INSECTS* SO WE HAVE TO BE FRIENDS WITH THEM...
...ARE *BENEFISHY INSECTS!*
THAT'S WHAT GRANDPA SAID...!
......
HA-HA... THAT'S RIGHT. BENEFICIAL INSECTS...
......
WHAT THE HECK?

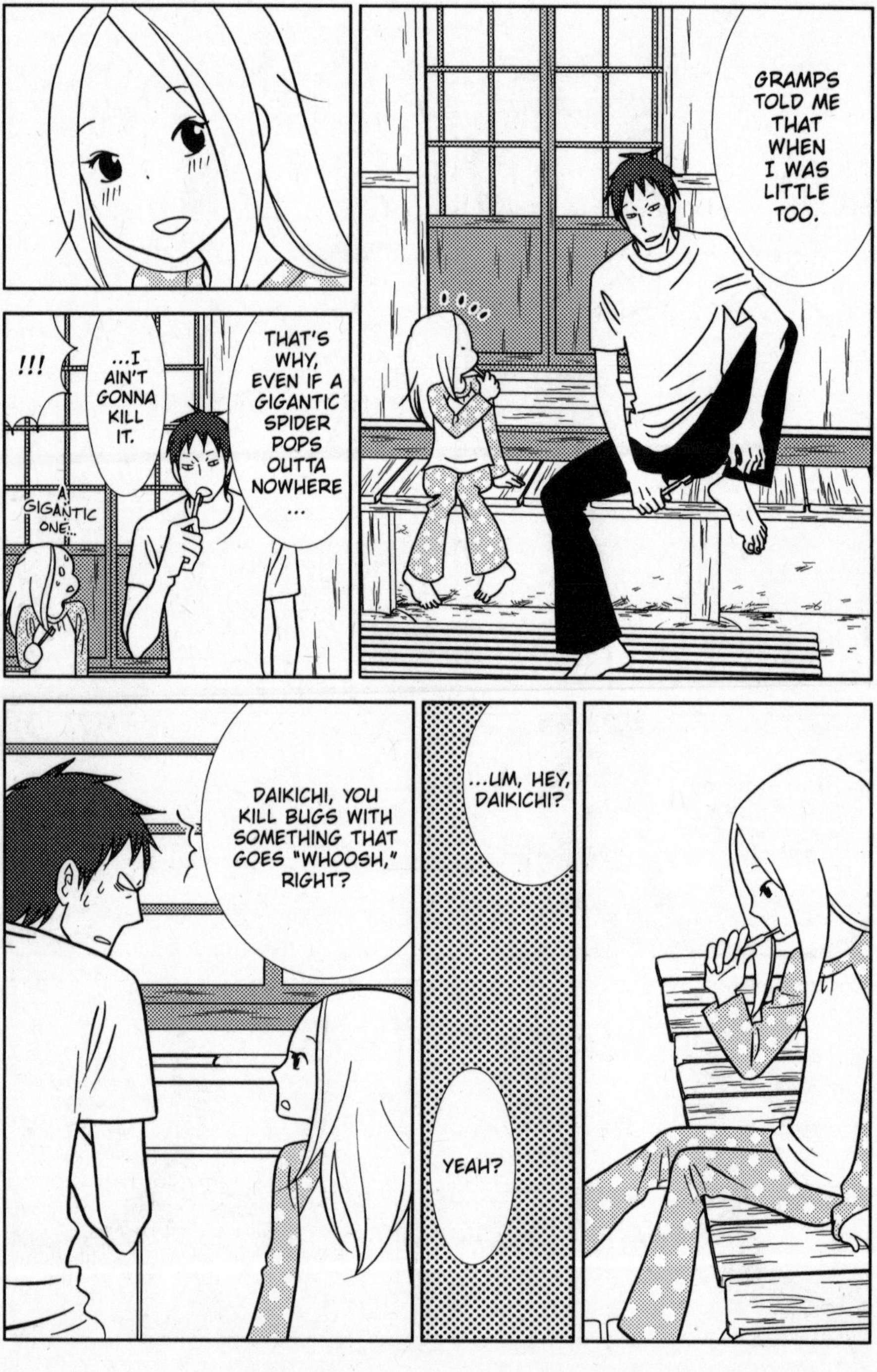
GRAMPS TOLD ME THAT WHEN I WAS LITTLE TOO.
THAT'S WHY, EVEN IF A GIGANTIC SPIDER POPS OUTTA NOWHERE...
...I AIN'T GONNA KILL IT.
!!!
A GIGANTIC ONE...
...UM, HEY, DAIKICHI?
YEAH?
DAIKICHI, YOU KILL BUGS WITH SOMETHING THAT GOES "WHOOSH," RIGHT?

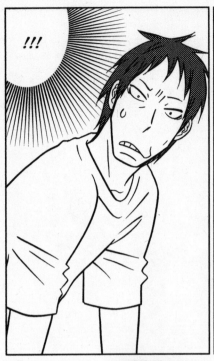

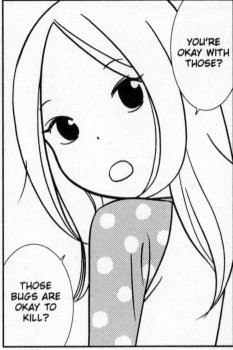

YOU'RE OKAY WITH THOSE?
THOSE BUGS ARE OKAY TO KILL?
!!!
BUGS OKAY TO KILL...
BUGS NOT OKAY TO KILL...
I'D...NEVER REALLY GIVEN IT MUCH THOUGHT BEFORE...
THAT'S A SERIOUSLY HARD QUESTION, ISN'T IT!?
LIST OF BUGS OKAY TO KILL
FLY
COCKROACH
MILLIPEDE
CENTIPEDE
LIST OF BUGS NOT OKAY TO KILL
ANT
BUTTERFLY
GRASSHOPPER
RHINOCEROS BEETLE
W-WOULD IT GO SOMETHING LIKE THIS!?

*IN JAPAN, BEETLES ARE POPULAR AS COLLECTIBLES, PETS, AND THE SUBJECT OF MANY AN ELEMENTARY AND MIDDLE SCHOOL SUMMER HOMEWORK ASSIGNMENT. MOST POPULAR ARE THE RHINOCEROS AND STAG BEETLES.

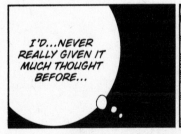

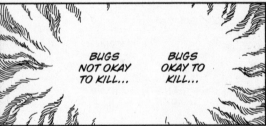

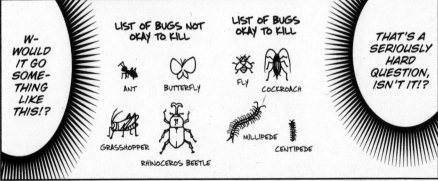

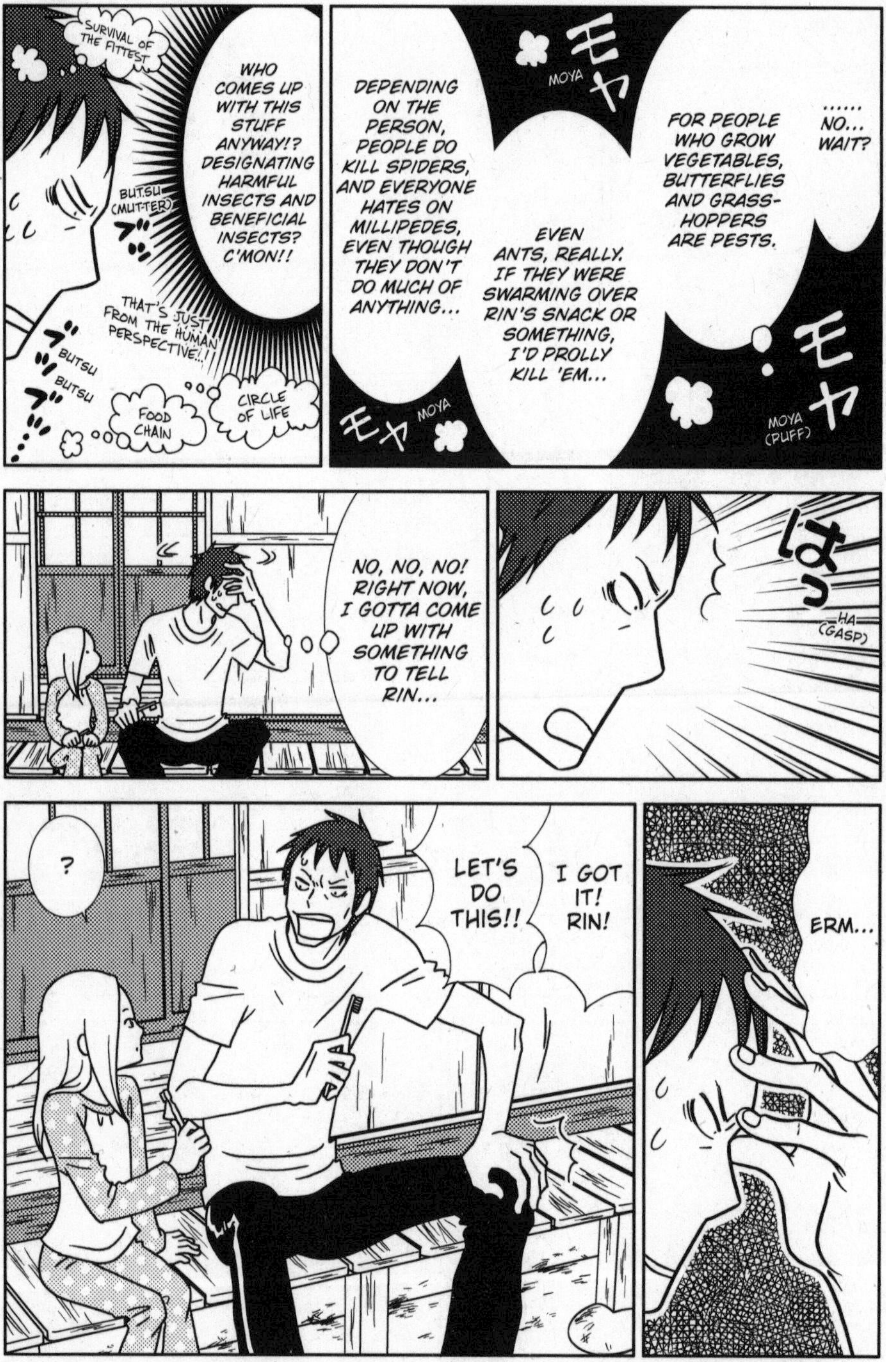

...... NO... WAIT?
FOR PEOPLE WHO GROW VEGETABLES, BUTTERFLIES AND GRASS-HOPPERS ARE PESTS.
モヤ
MOYA (PUFF)
モヤ
MOYA
EVEN ANTS, REALLY. IF THEY WERE SWARMING OVER RIN'S SNACK OR SOMETHING, I'D PROLLY KILL 'EM...
DEPENDING ON THE PERSON, PEOPLE DO KILL SPIDERS, AND EVERYONE HATES ON MILLIPEDES, EVEN THOUGH THEY DON'T DO MUCH OF ANYTHING...
モヤ
MOYA
WHO COMES UP WITH THIS STUFF ANYWAY!? DESIGNATING HARMFUL INSECTS AND BENEFICIAL INSECTS? C'MON!!
SURVIVAL OF THE FITTEST
BUTSU (MUTTER)
THAT'S JUST FROM THE HUMAN PERSPECTIVE..!
CIRCLE OF LIFE
FOOD CHAIN
BUTSU
BUTSU
はっ
HA (GASP)
NO, NO, NO! RIGHT NOW, I GOTTA COME UP WITH SOMETHING TO TELL RIN...
ERM...
I GOT IT! RIN!
LET'S DO THIS!!
?

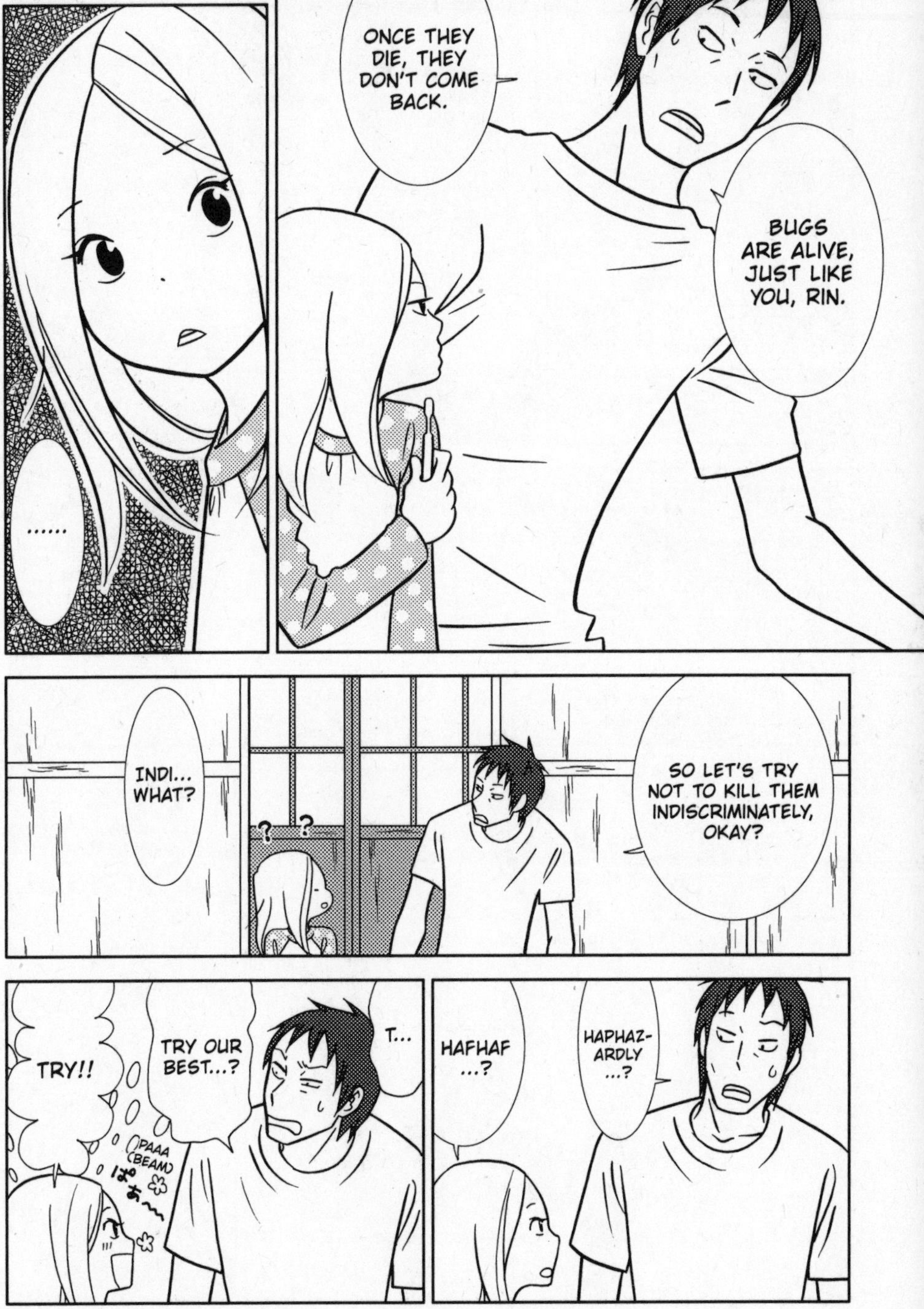
BUGS ARE ALIVE, JUST LIKE YOU, RIN.
ONCE THEY DIE, THEY DON'T COME BACK.
......
SO LET'S TRY NOT TO KILL THEM INDISCRIMINATELY, OKAY?
INDI... WHAT?
HAPHAZ-ARDLY ...?
HAFHAF ...?
T...
TRY OUR BEST...?
TRY!!
ぱあ〜
PAAA (BEAM)

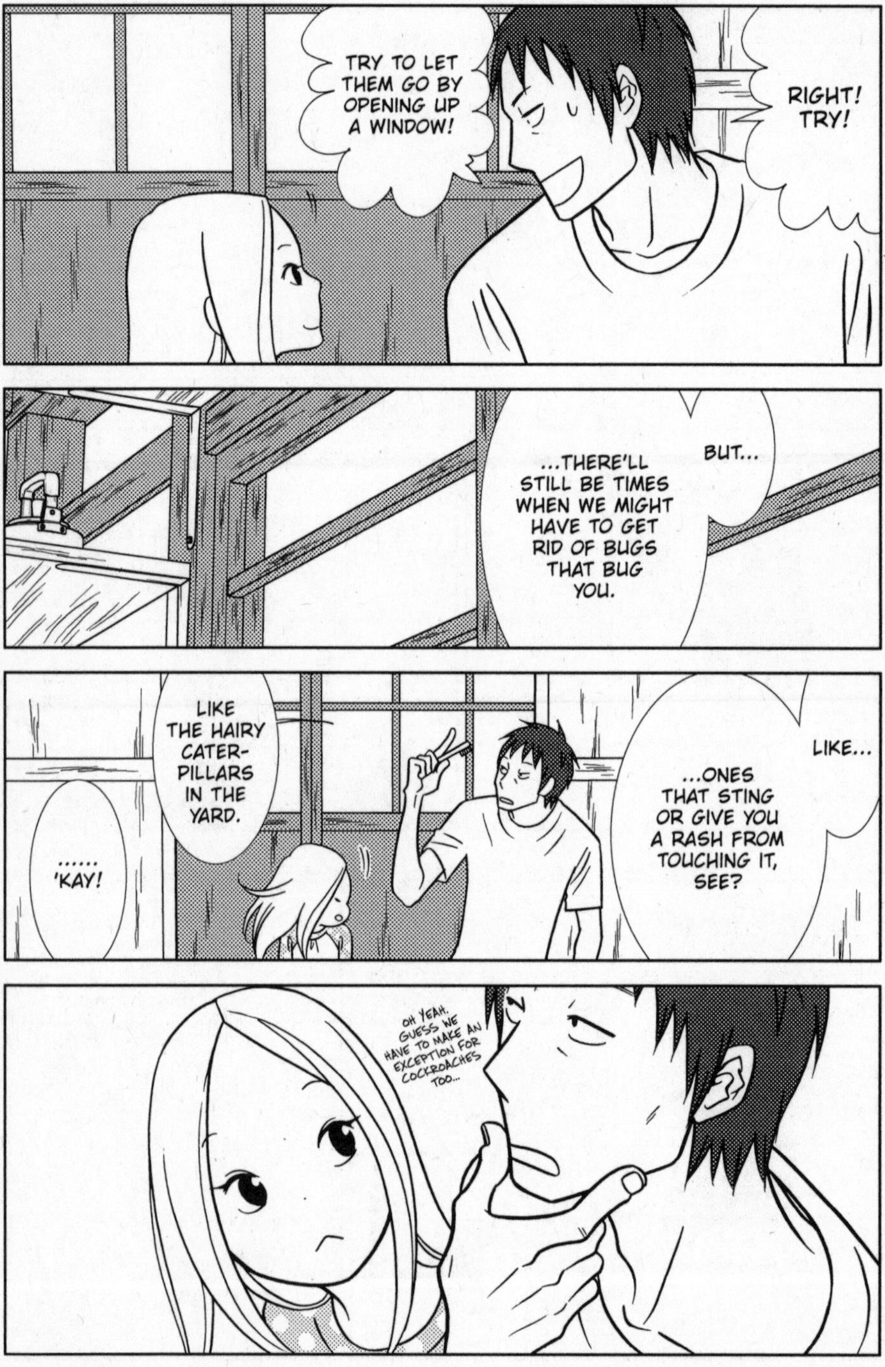
RIGHT! TRY!
TRY TO LET THEM GO BY OPENING UP A WINDOW!
BUT...
...THERE'LL STILL BE TIMES WHEN WE MIGHT HAVE TO GET RID OF BUGS THAT BUG YOU.
LIKE...
...ONES THAT STING OR GIVE YOU A RASH FROM TOUCHING IT, SEE?
LIKE THE HAIRY CATER-PILLARS IN THE YARD.
...... 'KAY!
OH YEAH. GUESS WE HAVE TO MAKE AN EXCEPTION FOR COCKROACHES TOO...

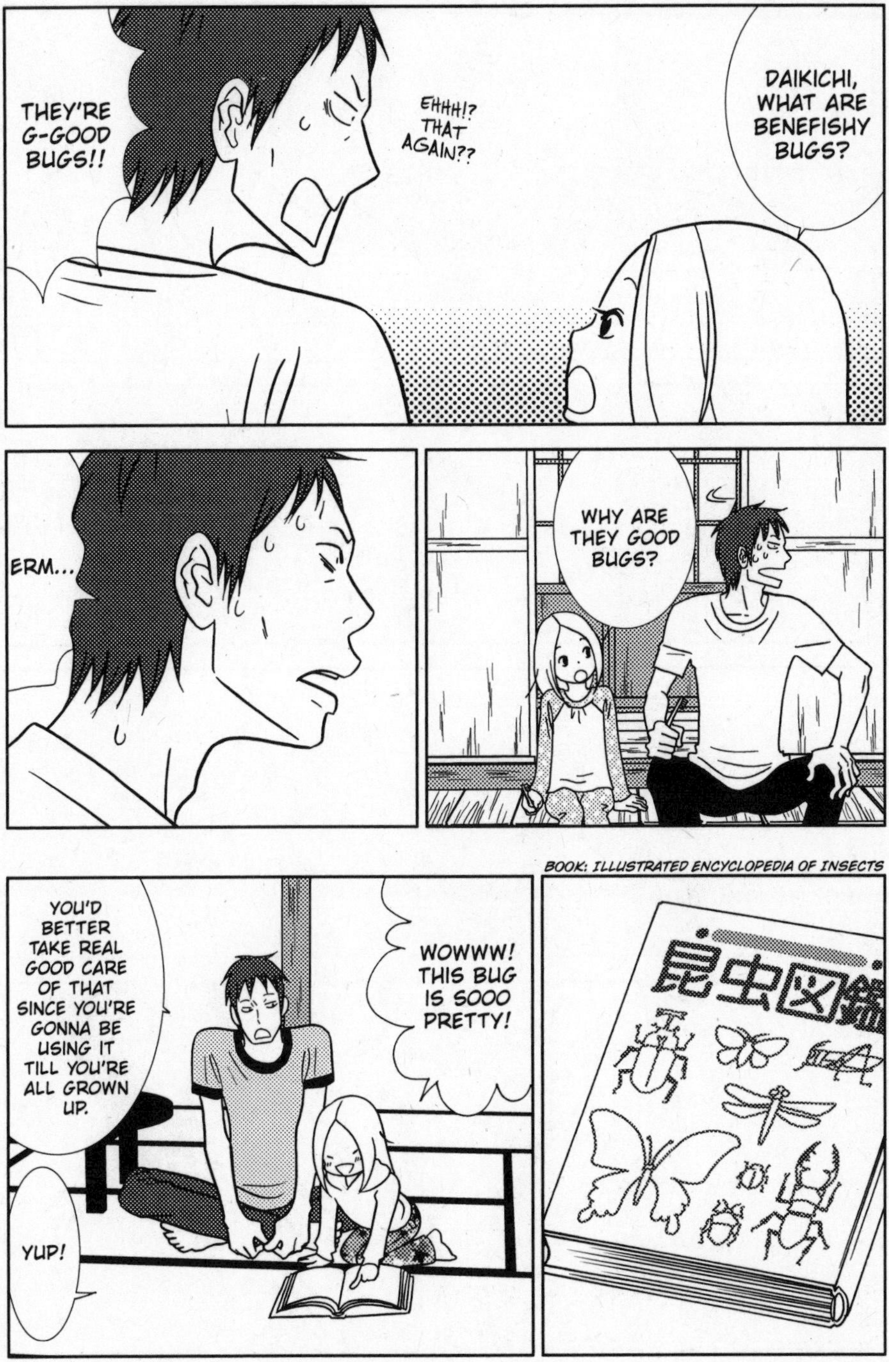
DAIKICHI, WHAT ARE BENEFISHY BUGS?
EHHH!? THAT AGAIN??
THEY'RE G-GOOD BUGS!!
WHY ARE THEY GOOD BUGS?
ERM...
BOOK: ILLUSTRATED ENCYCLOPEDIA OF INSECTS
昆虫図鑑
WOWWW! THIS BUG IS SOOO PRETTY!
YOU'D BETTER TAKE REAL GOOD CARE OF THAT SINCE YOU'RE GONNA BE USING IT TILL YOU'RE ALL GROWN UP.
YUP!

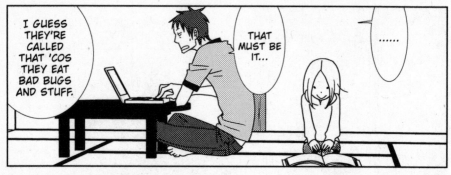

......
THAT MUST BE IT...
I GUESS THEY'RE CALLED THAT 'COS THEY EAT BAD BUGS AND STUFF.
SPIDERS DON'T EAT GOOD BUGS?
......
THEY DO ...!!
THEY'RE JUST NOT PICKY ABOUT WHAT THEY EAT...
BUT THEY'RE STILL BENEFISHY?
ER... LET'S JUST TAKE IT GRADUALLY ...
GRAD-UALLY?
ERMM...

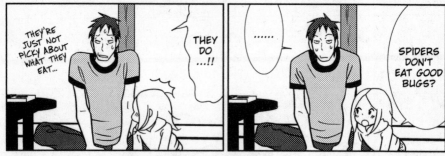

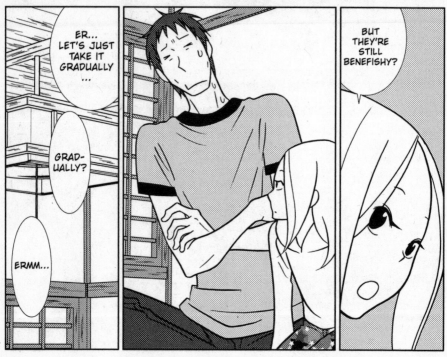

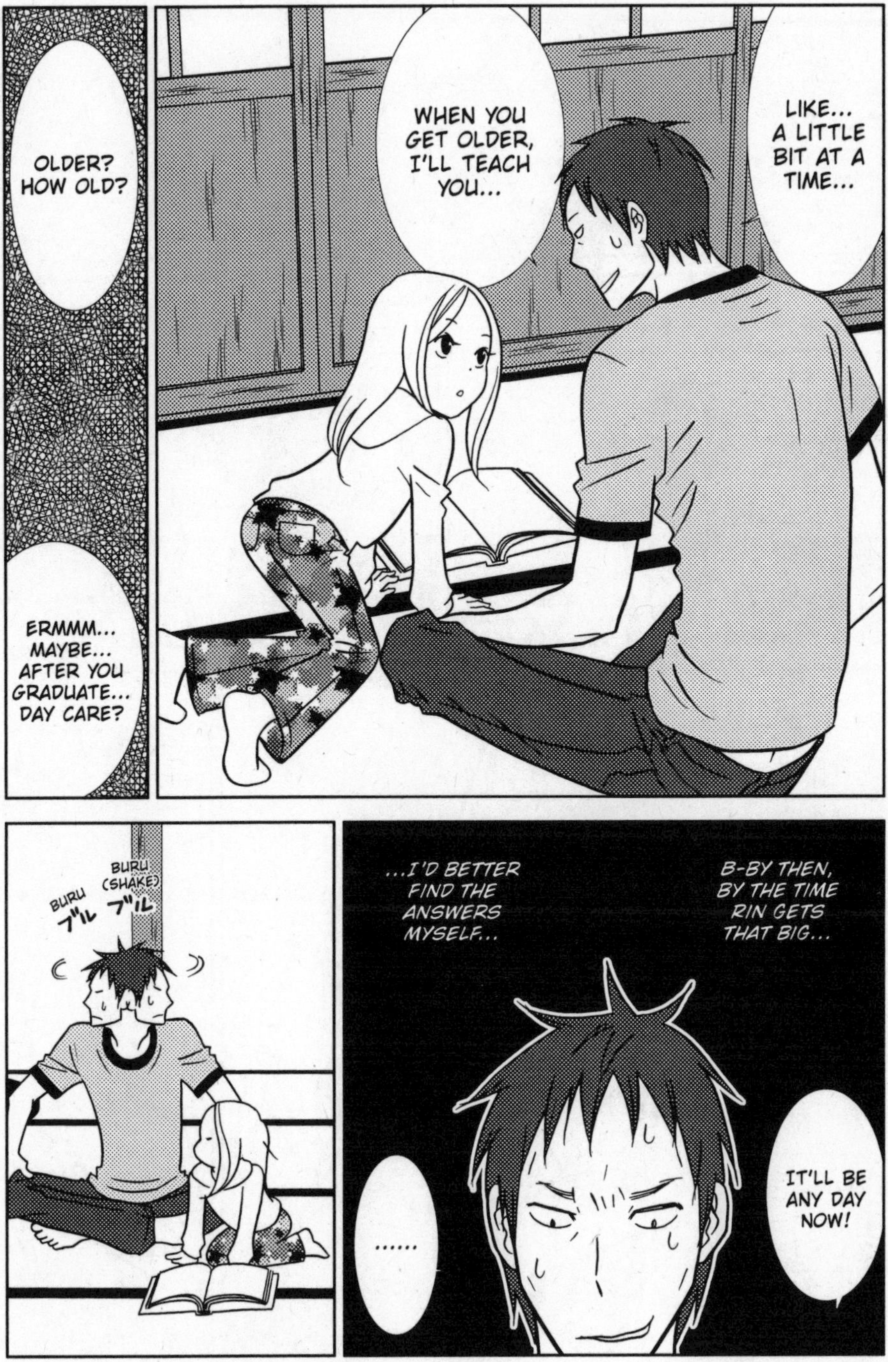
LIKE... A LITTLE BIT AT A TIME...
WHEN YOU GET OLDER, I'LL TEACH YOU...
OLDER? HOW OLD?
ERMMM... MAYBE... AFTER YOU GRADUATE... DAY CARE?
B-BY THEN, BY THE TIME RIN GETS THAT BIG...
...I'D BETTER FIND THE ANSWERS MYSELF...
IT'LL BE ANY DAY NOW!
......
BURU (SHAKE) ブル
BURU ブル

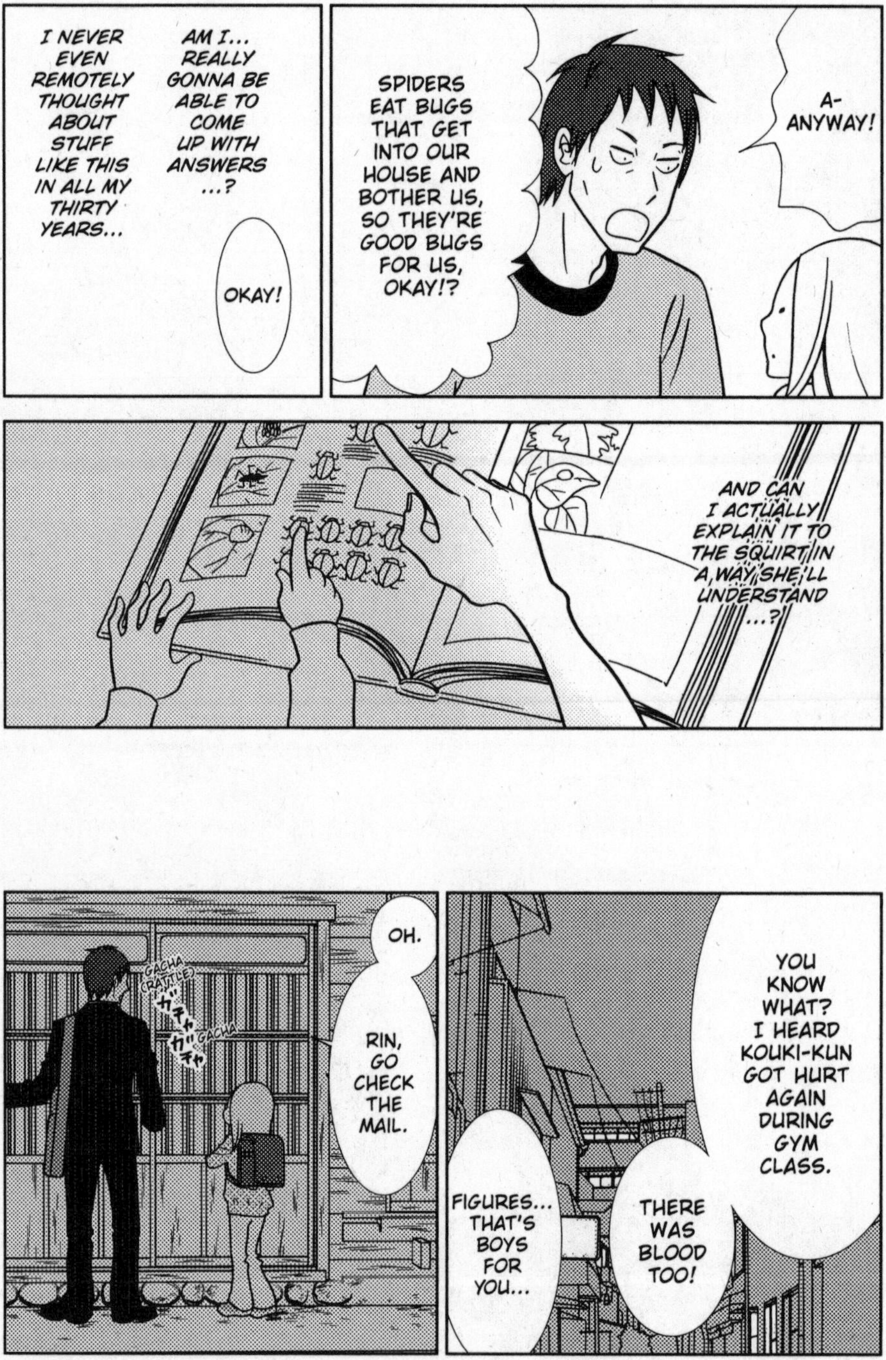
A-ANYWAY!
SPIDERS EAT BUGS THAT GET INTO OUR HOUSE AND BOTHER US, SO THEY'RE GOOD BUGS FOR US, OKAY!?
OKAY!
AM I... REALLY GONNA BE ABLE TO COME UP WITH ANSWERS ...?
I NEVER EVEN REMOTELY THOUGHT ABOUT STUFF LIKE THIS IN ALL MY THIRTY YEARS...
AND CAN I ACTUALLY EXPLAIN IT TO THE SQUIRT IN A WAY SHE'LL UNDERSTAND ...?
YOU KNOW WHAT? I HEARD KOUKI-KUN GOT HURT AGAIN DURING GYM CLASS.
THERE WAS BLOOD TOO!
FIGURES... THAT'S BOYS FOR YOU...
OH.
RIN, GO CHECK THE MAIL.
GACHA (RATTLE)
ガチャ
ガチャ
GACHA

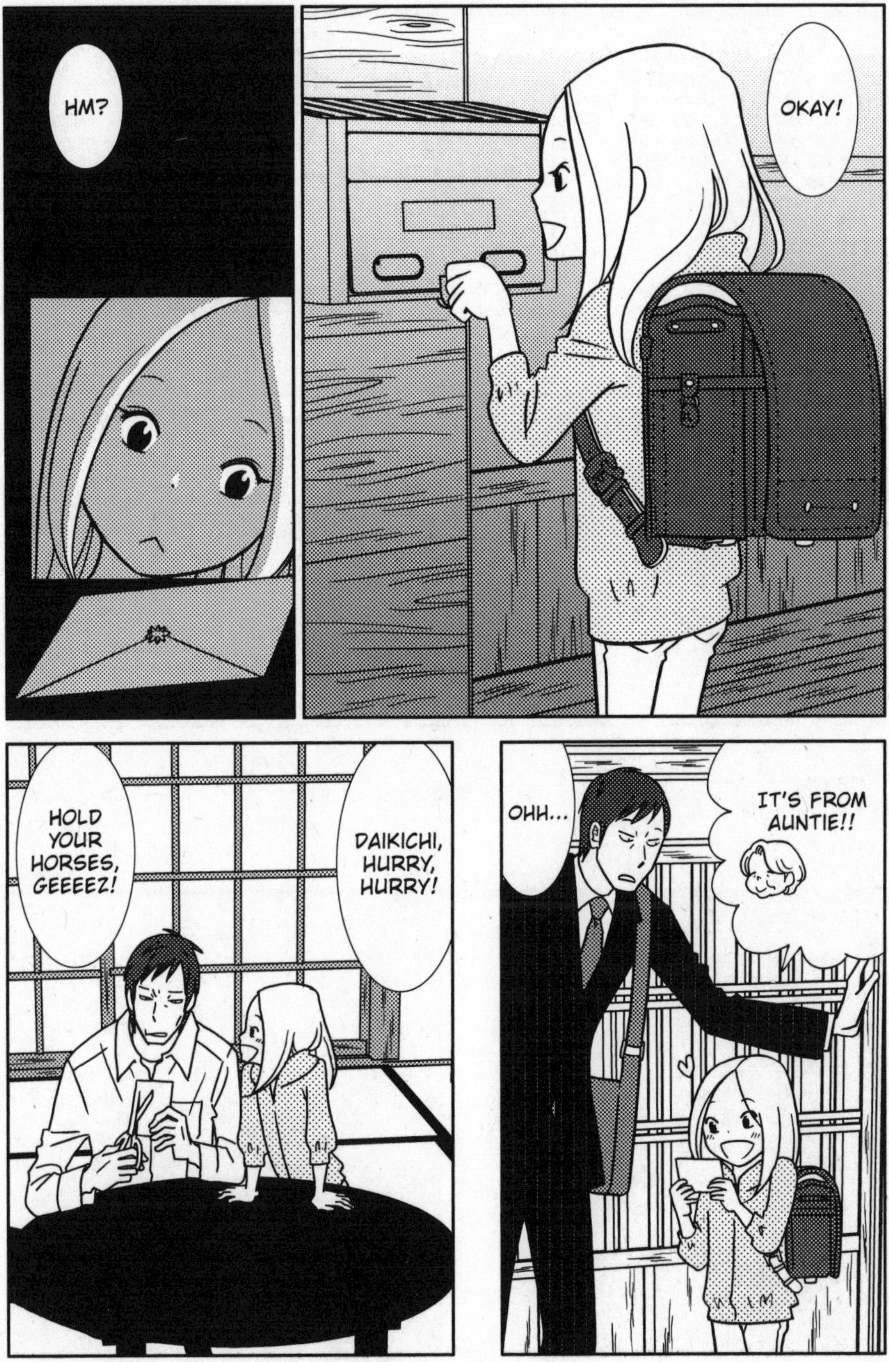
OKAY!
HM?
IT'S FROM AUNTIE!!
OHH...
DAIKICHI, HURRY, HURRY!
HOLD YOUR HORSES, GEEEEZ!

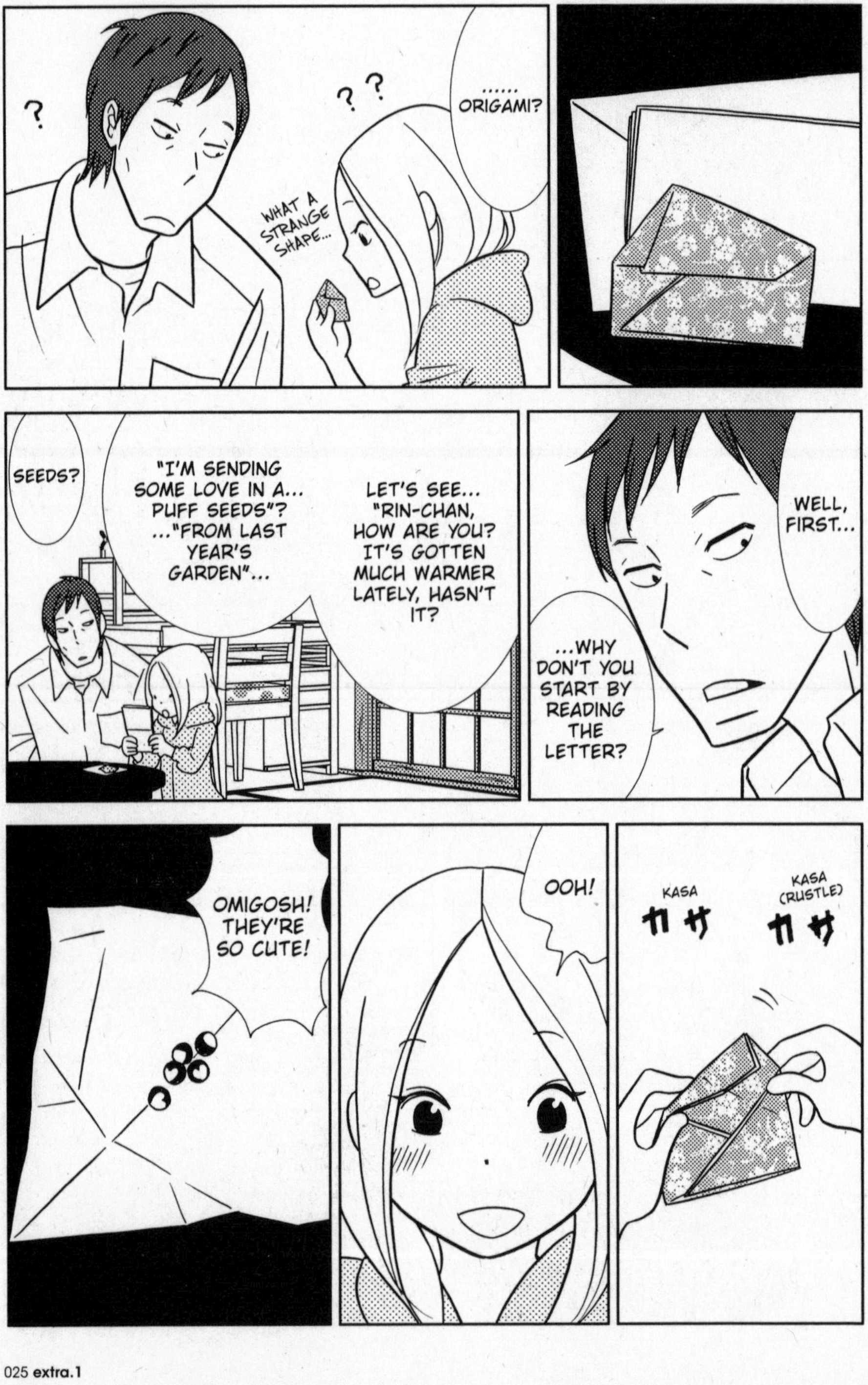

......ORIGAMI?
WHAT A STRANGE SHAPE...
WELL, FIRST...
...WHY DON'T YOU START BY READING THE LETTER?
LET'S SEE... "RIN-CHAN, HOW ARE YOU? IT'S GOTTEN MUCH WARMER LATELY, HASN'T IT?
"I'M SENDING SOME LOVE IN A... PUFF SEEDS"? ..."FROM LAST YEAR'S GARDEN"...
SEEDS?
KASA (RUSTLE)
カサ
KASA
カサ
OOH!
OMIGOSH! THEY'RE SO CUTE!

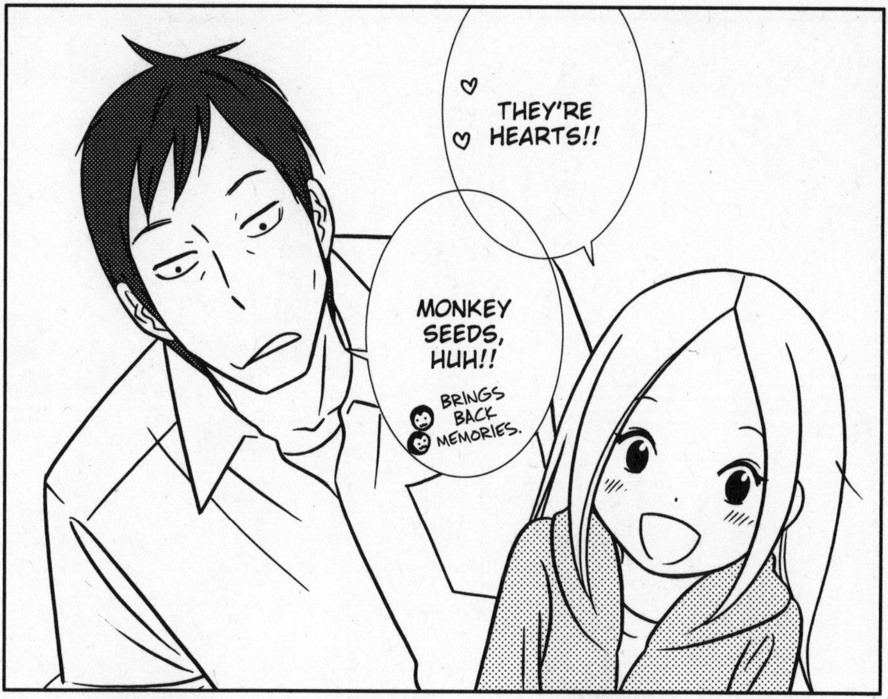
THEY'RE HEARTS!!
MONKEY SEEDS, HUH!!
BRINGS BACK MEMORIES.

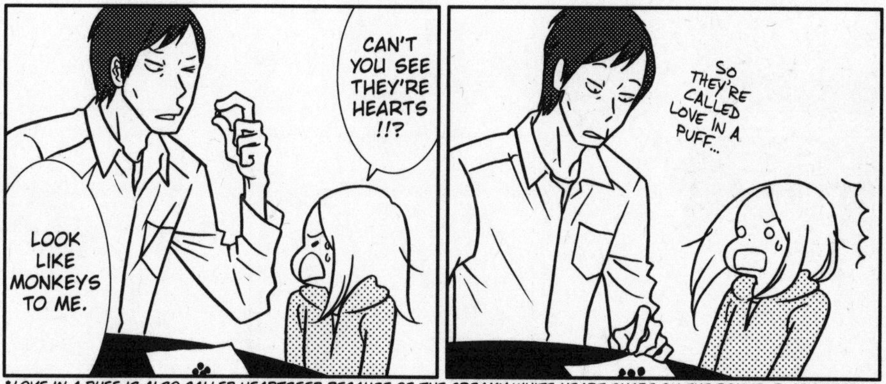
SO THEY'RE CALLED LOVE IN A PUFF...
CAN'T YOU SEE THEY'RE HEARTS!!?
LOOK LIKE MONKEYS TO ME.

*LOVE IN A PUFF IS ALSO CALLED HEARTSEED BECAUSE OF THE CREAMY WHITE HEART SHAPE ON THE ROUND, BLACK SEED. A DELICATE VINE WITH FEATHERY LEAVES, IT HAS SMALL WHITE BLOOMS THAT GIVE WAY TO BALLOON-LIKE SEED PODS.

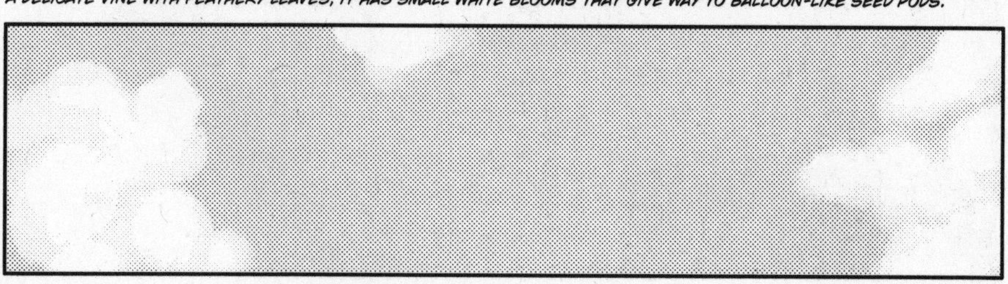

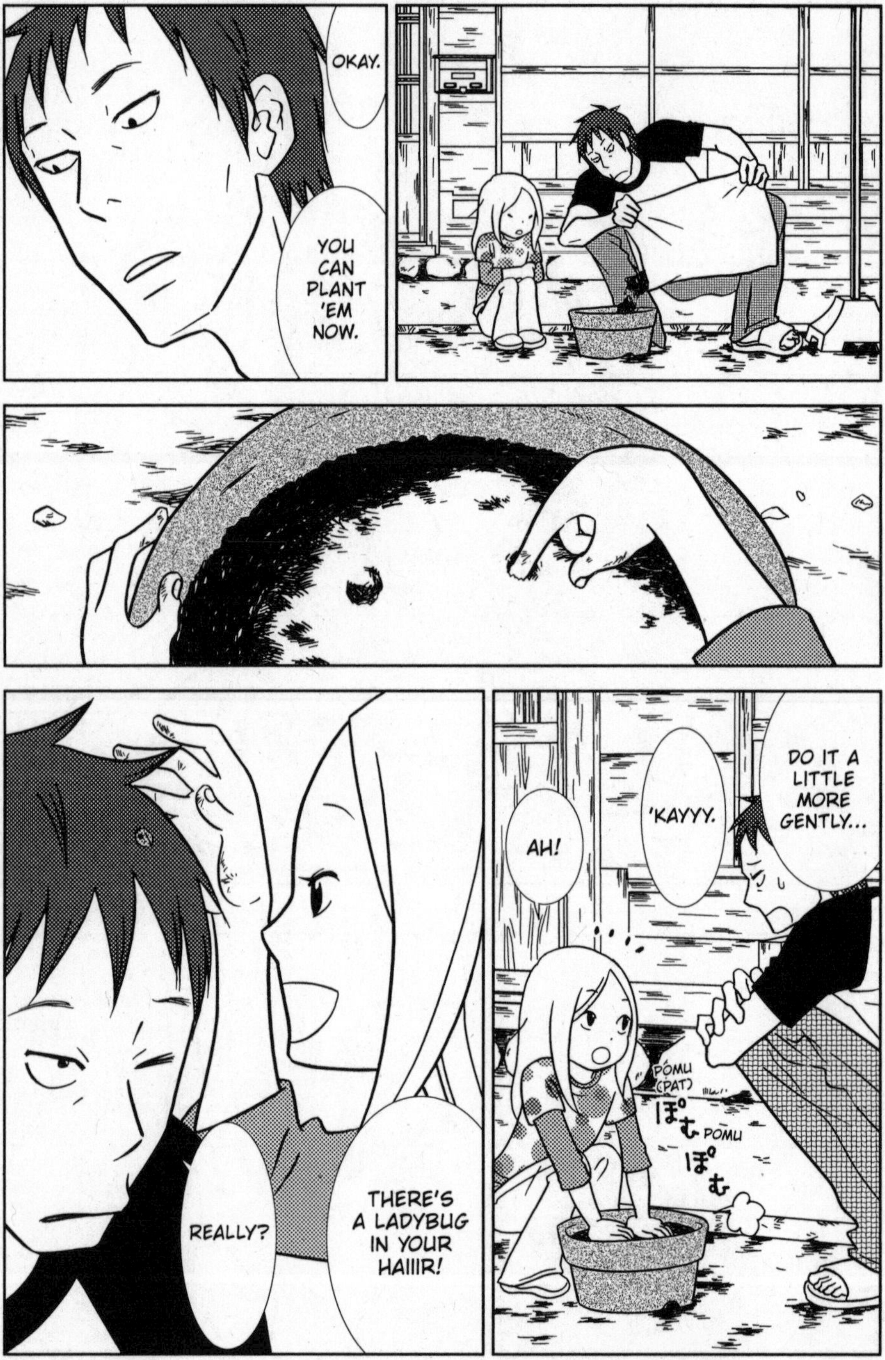
OKAY.
YOU CAN PLANT 'EM NOW.
DO IT A LITTLE MORE GENTLY...
'KAYYY.
AH!
POMU (PAT) ぽむ POMU ぽむ
THERE'S A LADYBUG IN YOUR HAIIIR!
REALLY?

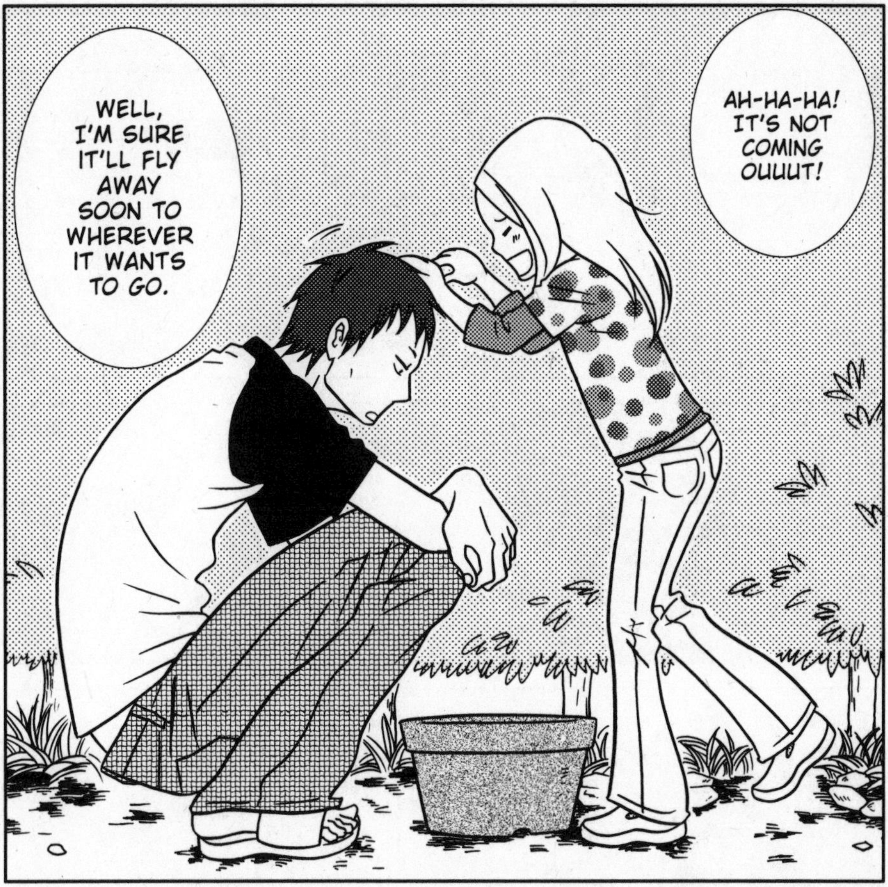
AH-HA-HA! IT'S NOT COMING OUUUT!
WELL, I'M SURE IT'LL FLY AWAY SOON TO WHEREVER IT WANTS TO GO.

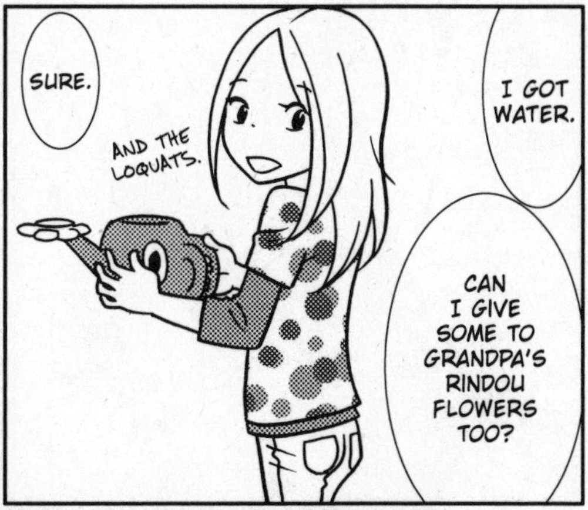
I GOT WATER.
AND THE LOQUATS.
CAN I GIVE SOME TO GRANDPA'S RINDOU FLOWERS TOO?
SURE.

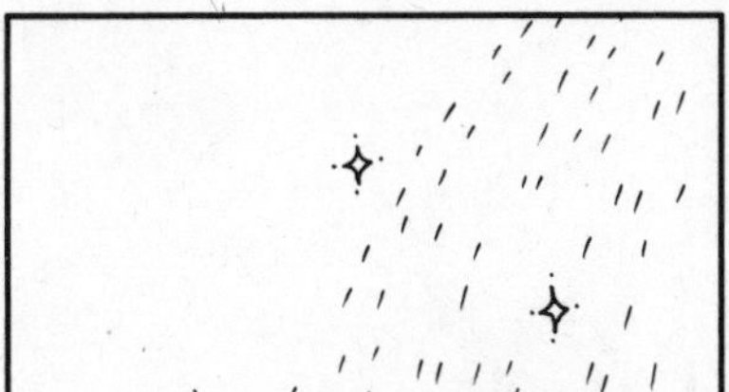

*RINDOU *IS THE JAPANESE WORD FOR "BELLFLOWER," A FLOWERING PLANT WITH A TRUMPET-SHAPED BLOOM BELONGING TO THE GENTIAN FAMILY.*

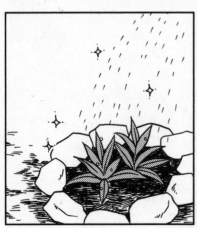

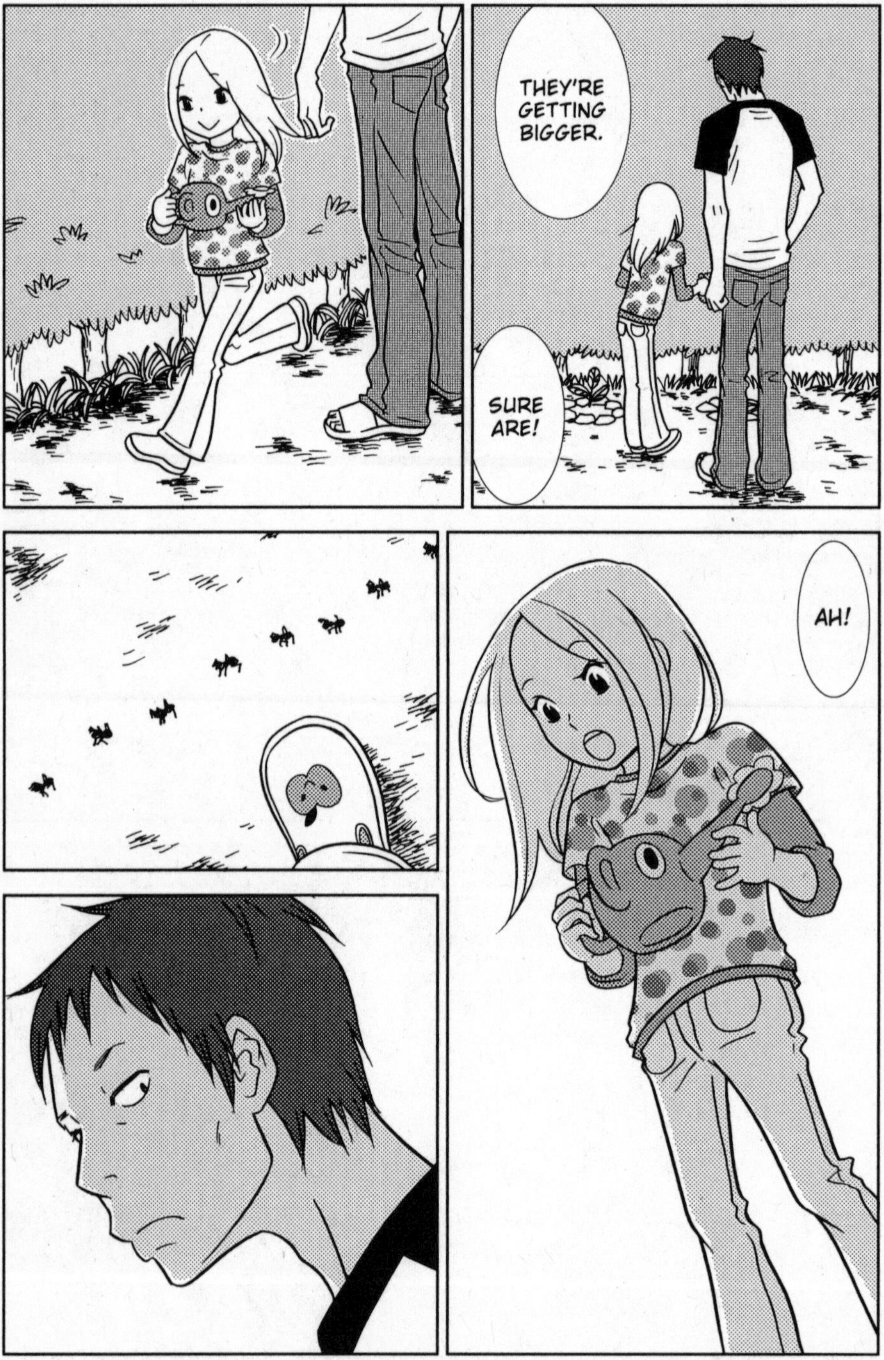
THEY'RE GETTING BIGGER.
SURE ARE!
AH!

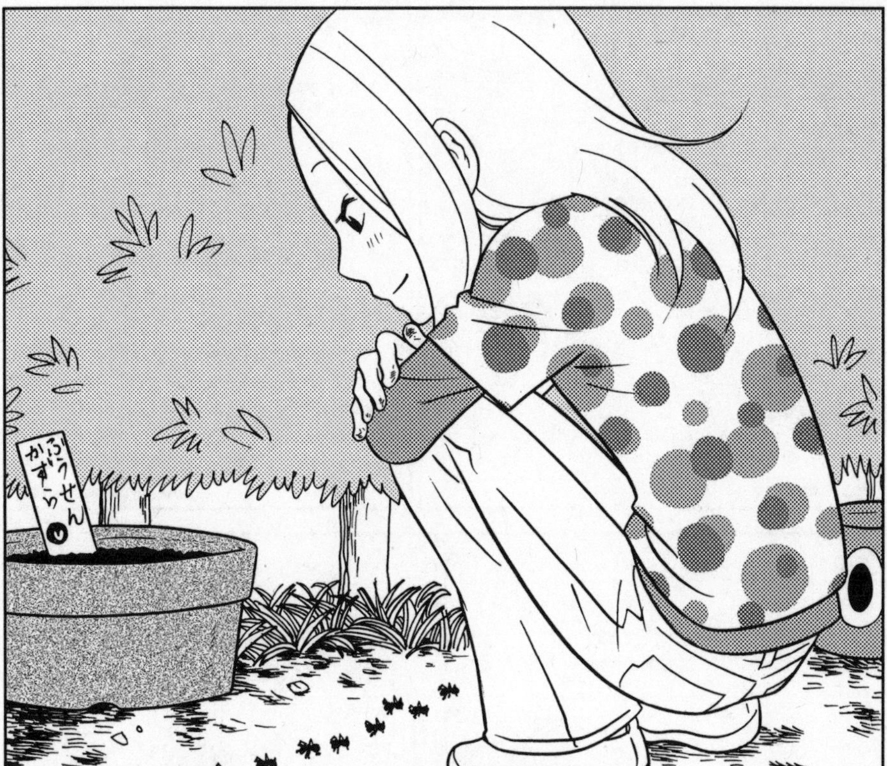
ふうせん
かずら

LABEL: LOVE IN A PUFF

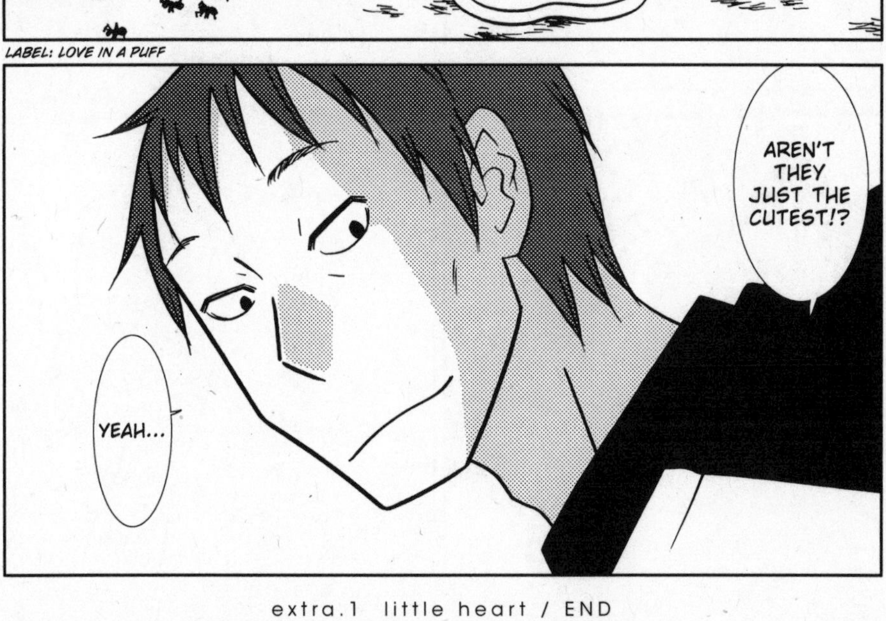
AREN'T THEY JUST THE CUTEST!?
YEAH...

extra.1 little heart / END

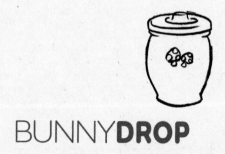

BUNNY**DROP**

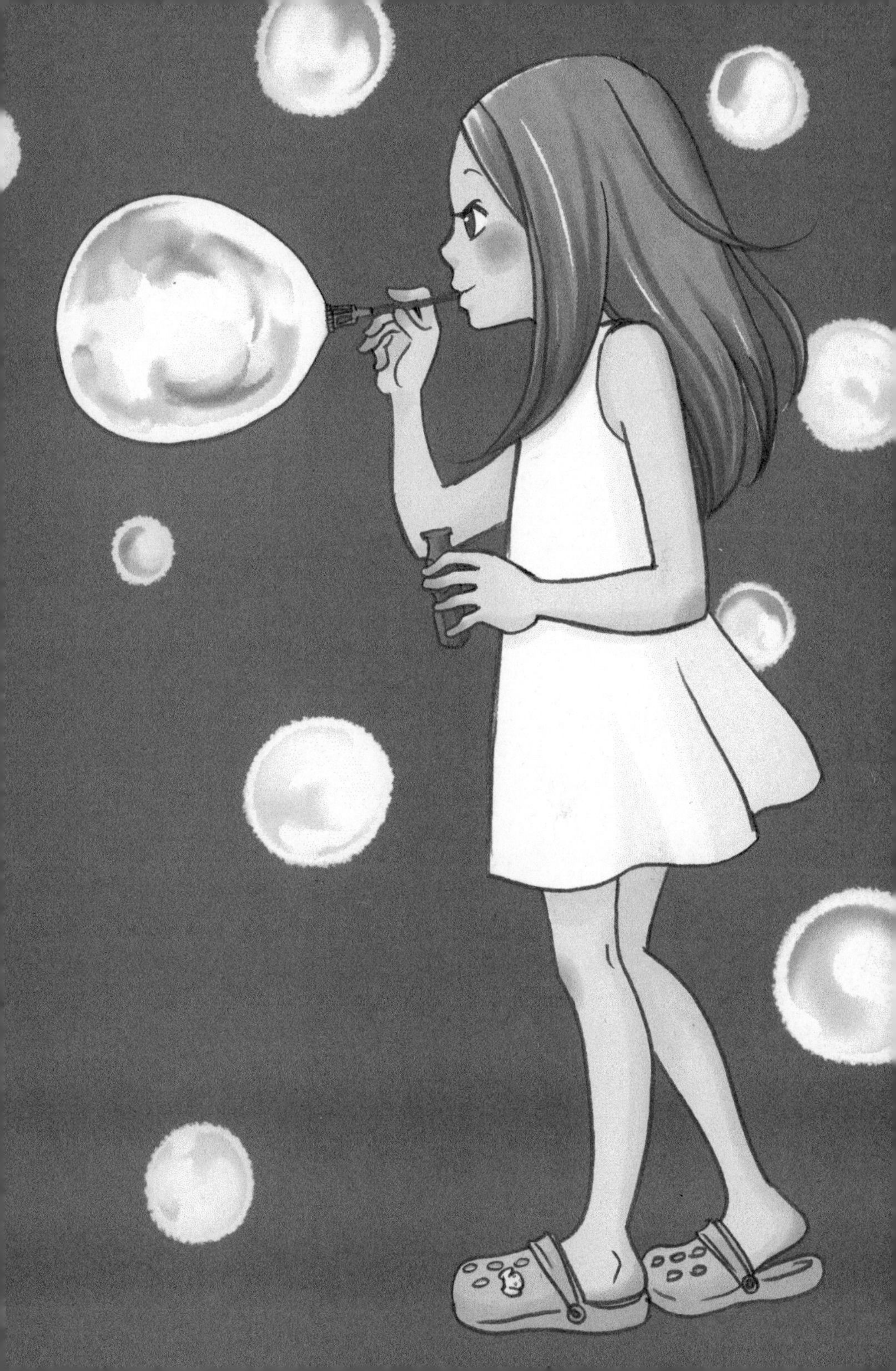

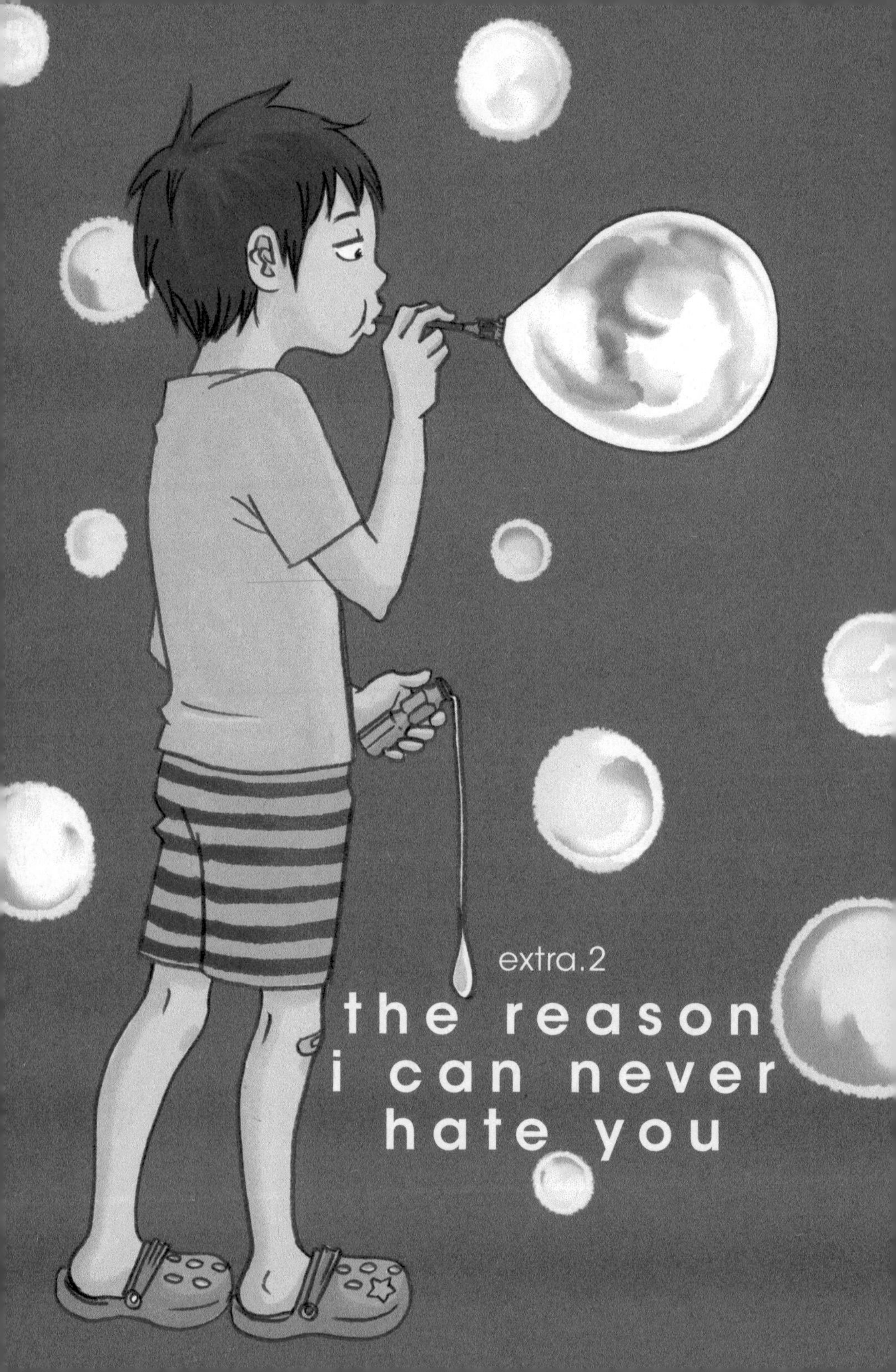
extra.2
the reason
i can never
hate you

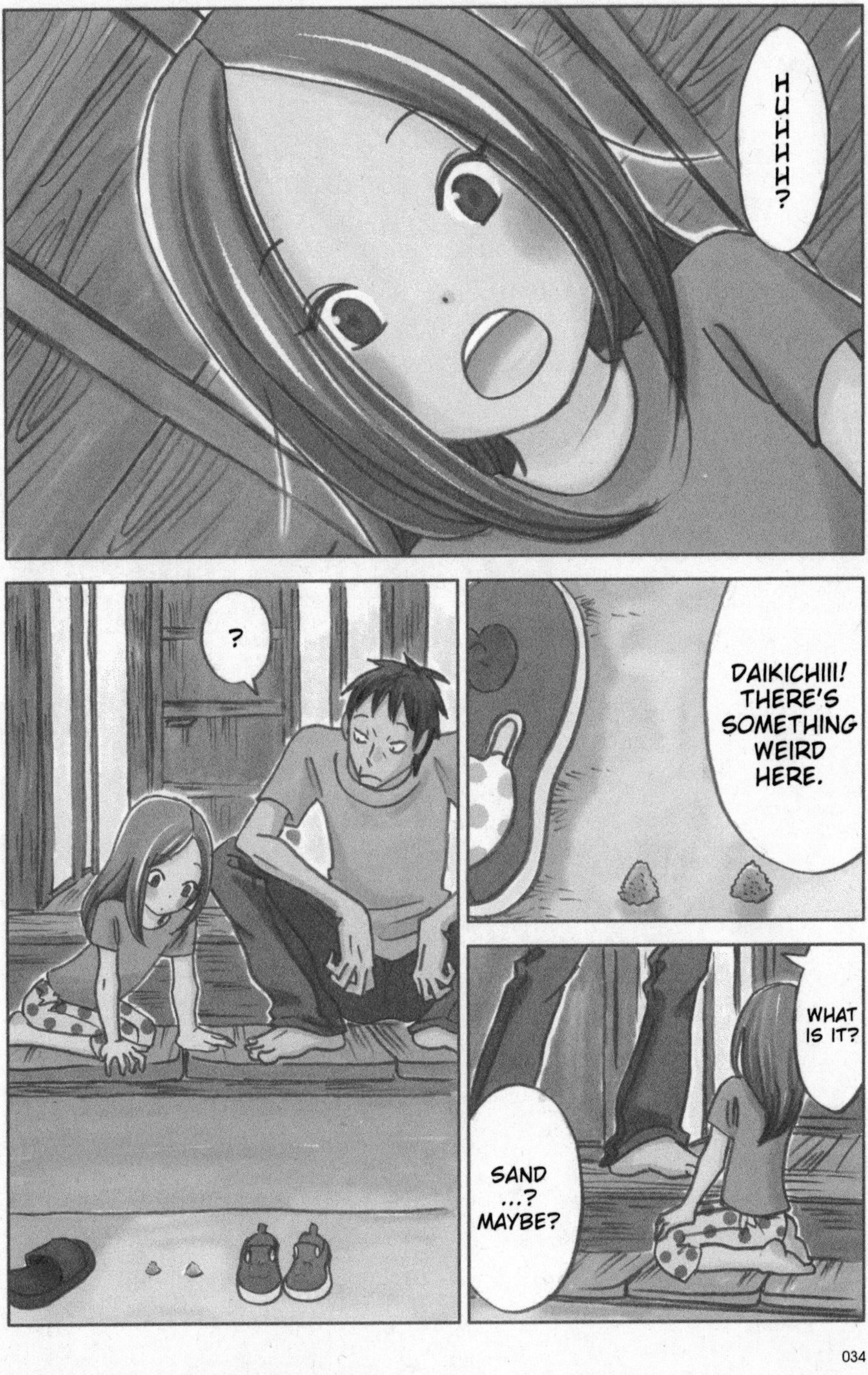
HUHHH?
DAIKICHIII! THERE'S SOMETHING WEIRD HERE.
WHAT IS IT?
SAND ...? MAYBE?
?

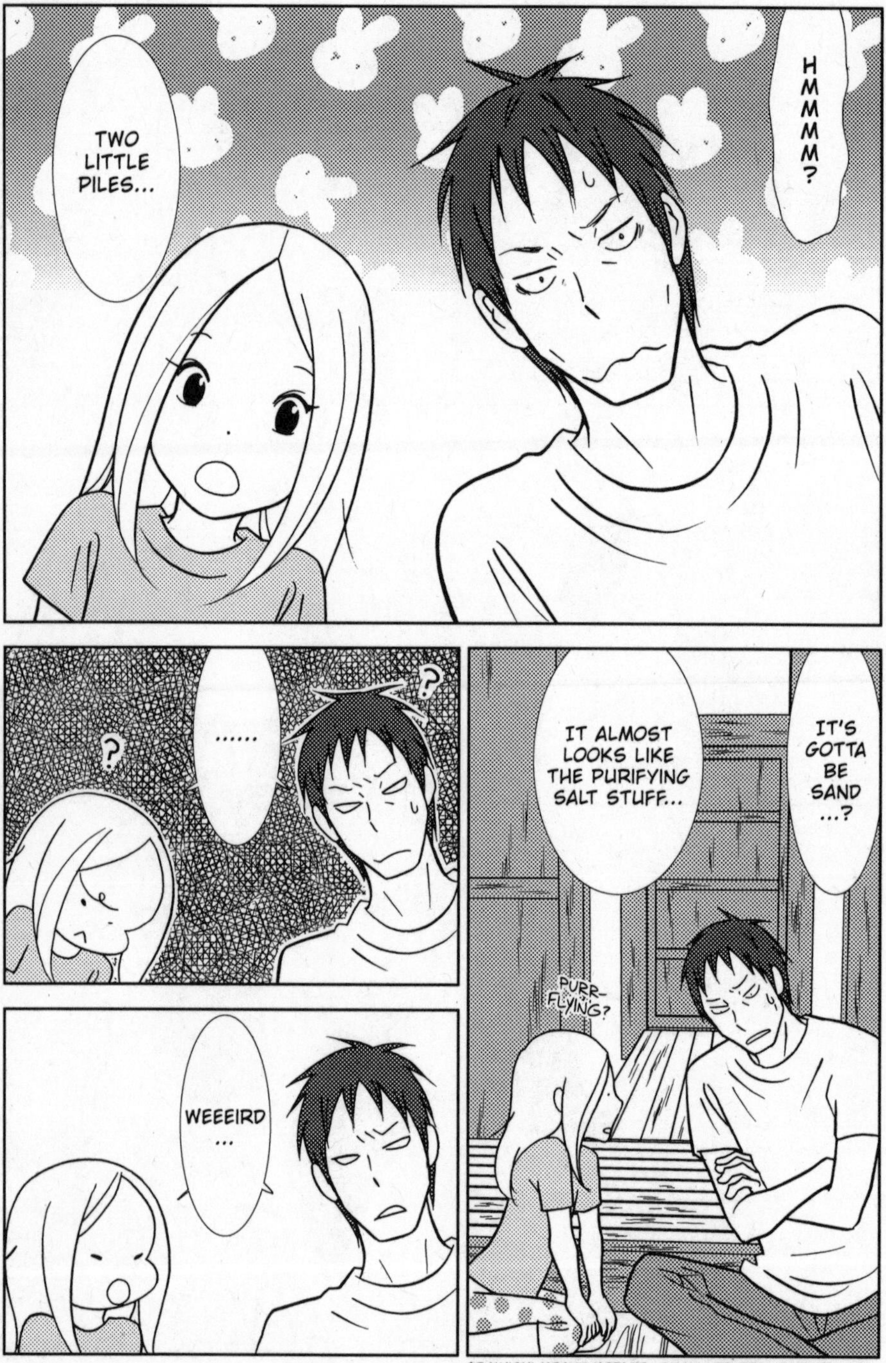
HMMMM?
TWO LITTLE PILES...
IT'S GOTTA BE SAND ...?
IT ALMOST LOOKS LIKE THE PURIFYING SALT STUFF...
PURR-FLYING?
......
WEEEIRD ...

***DAIKICHI MEANS MORIJIO, SMALL, CONICAL SALT MOUNDS ON LITTLE PLATES PLACED BY THE ENTRANCES OF HOMES AND BUSINESSES THAT ARE THOUGHT TO BRING GOOD LUCK, WARD OFF EVIL SPIRITS, AND PURIFY THE AREA.**

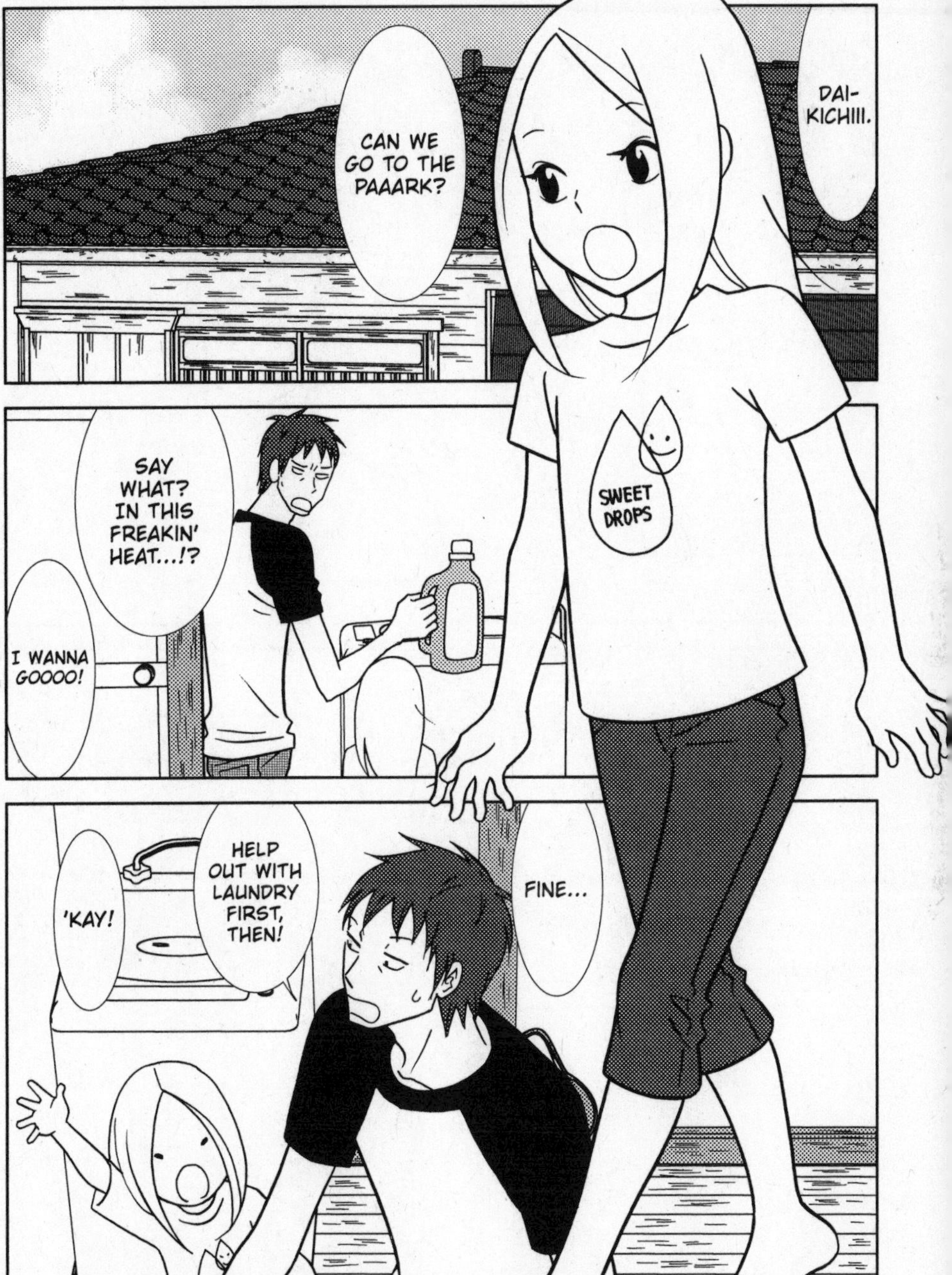
DAI-KICHIII.
CAN WE GO TO THE PAAARK?
SAY WHAT? IN THIS FREAKIN' HEAT...!?
I WANNA GOOOO!
SWEET DROPS
FINE...
HELP OUT WITH LAUNDRY FIRST, THEN!
'KAY!

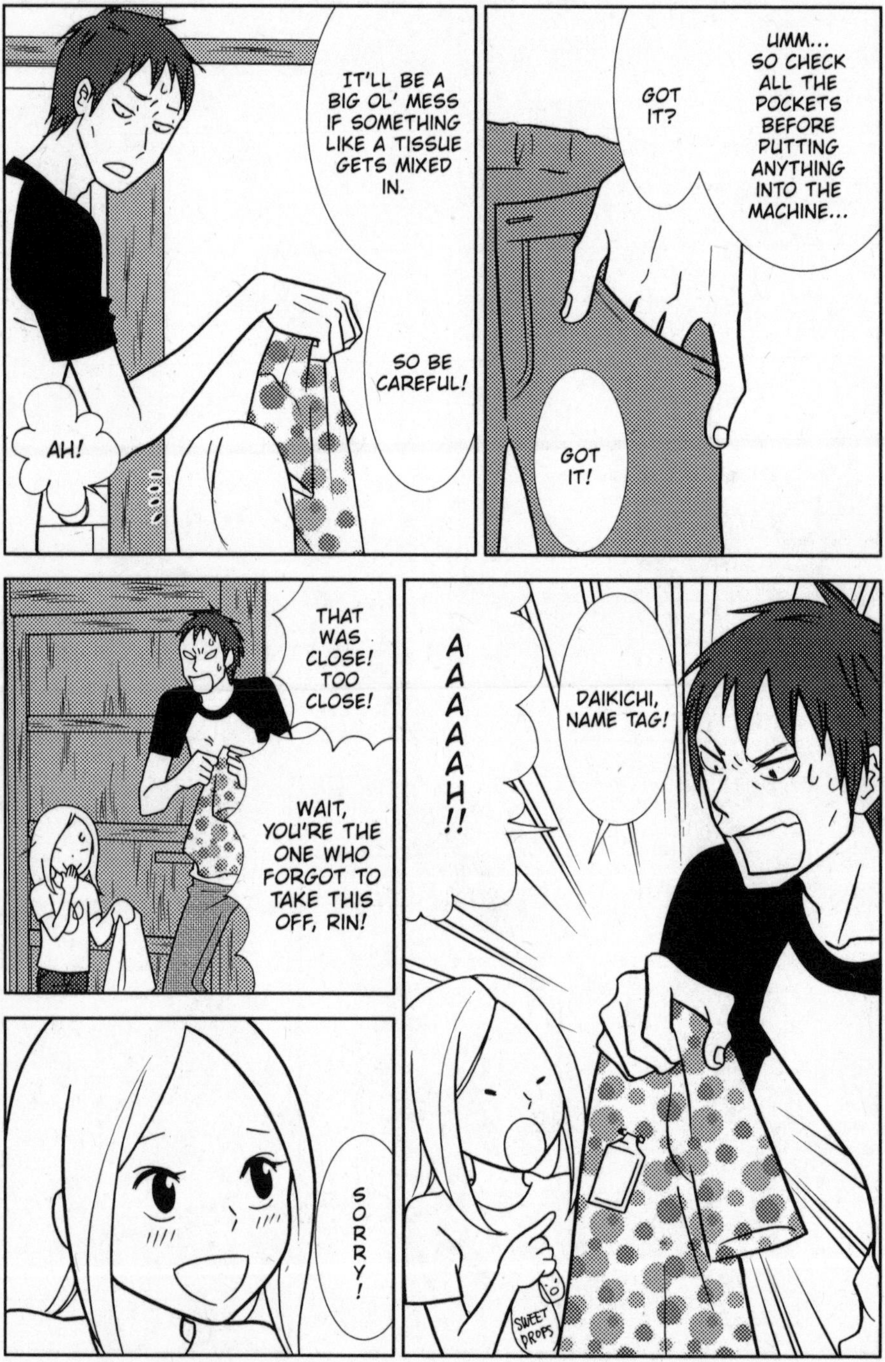
UMM... SO CHECK ALL THE POCKETS BEFORE PUTTING ANYTHING INTO THE MACHINE...
GOT IT?
GOT IT!
IT'LL BE A BIG OL' MESS IF SOMETHING LIKE A TISSUE GETS MIXED IN.
SO BE CAREFUL!
AH!
DAIKICHI, NAME TAG!
AAAAAH!!
SWEET DROPS
THAT WAS CLOSE! TOO CLOSE!
WAIT, YOU'RE THE ONE WHO FORGOT TO TAKE THIS OFF, RIN!
SORRY!

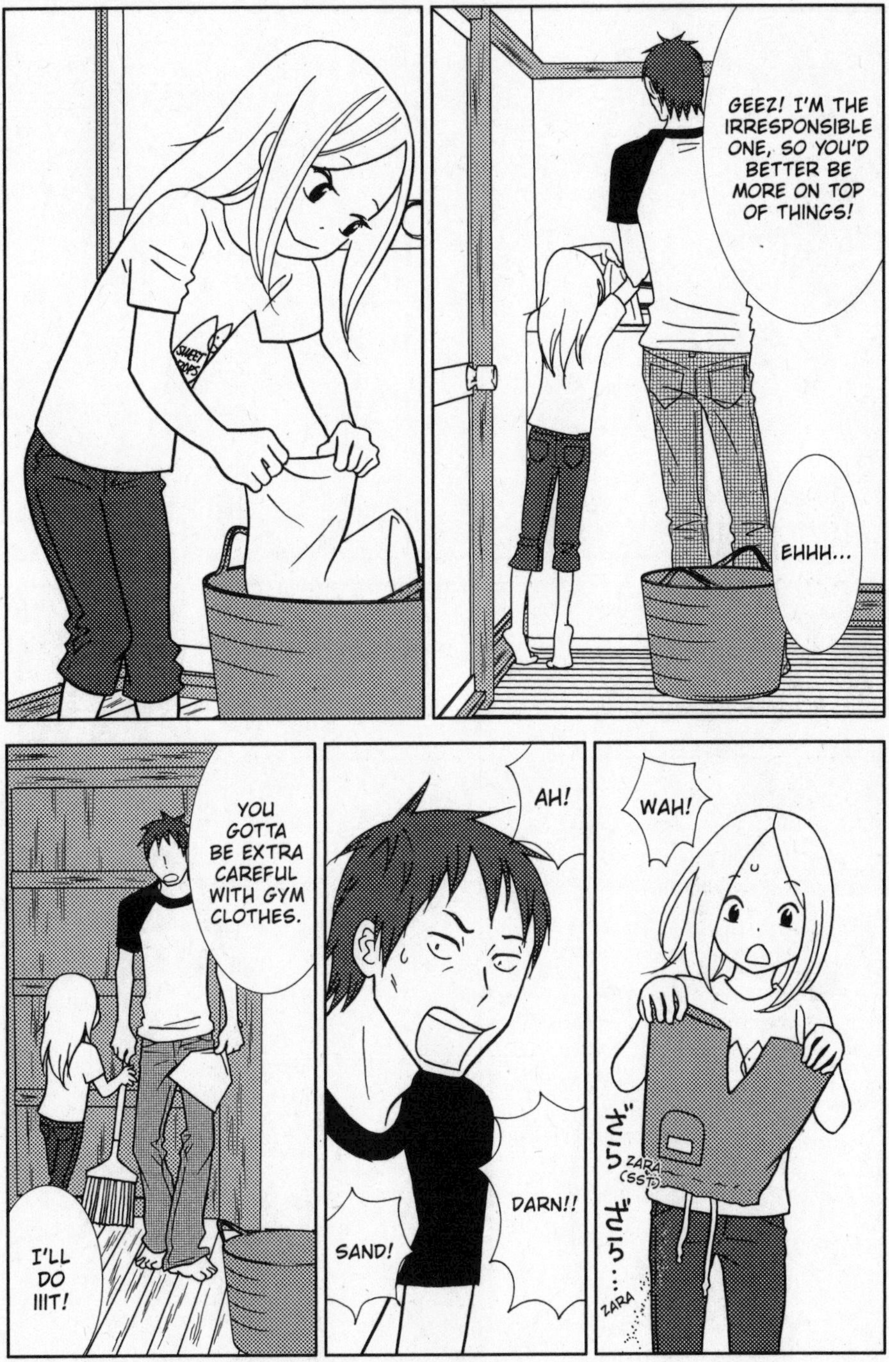
GEEZ! I'M THE IRRESPONSIBLE ONE, SO YOU'D BETTER BE MORE ON TOP OF THINGS!
EHHH...
SWEET DROPS
WAH!
ざら
ZARA (SST)
ざら...
ZARA
AH!
DARN!!
SAND!
YOU GOTTA BE EXTRA CAREFUL WITH GYM CLOTHES.
I'LL DO IIIT!

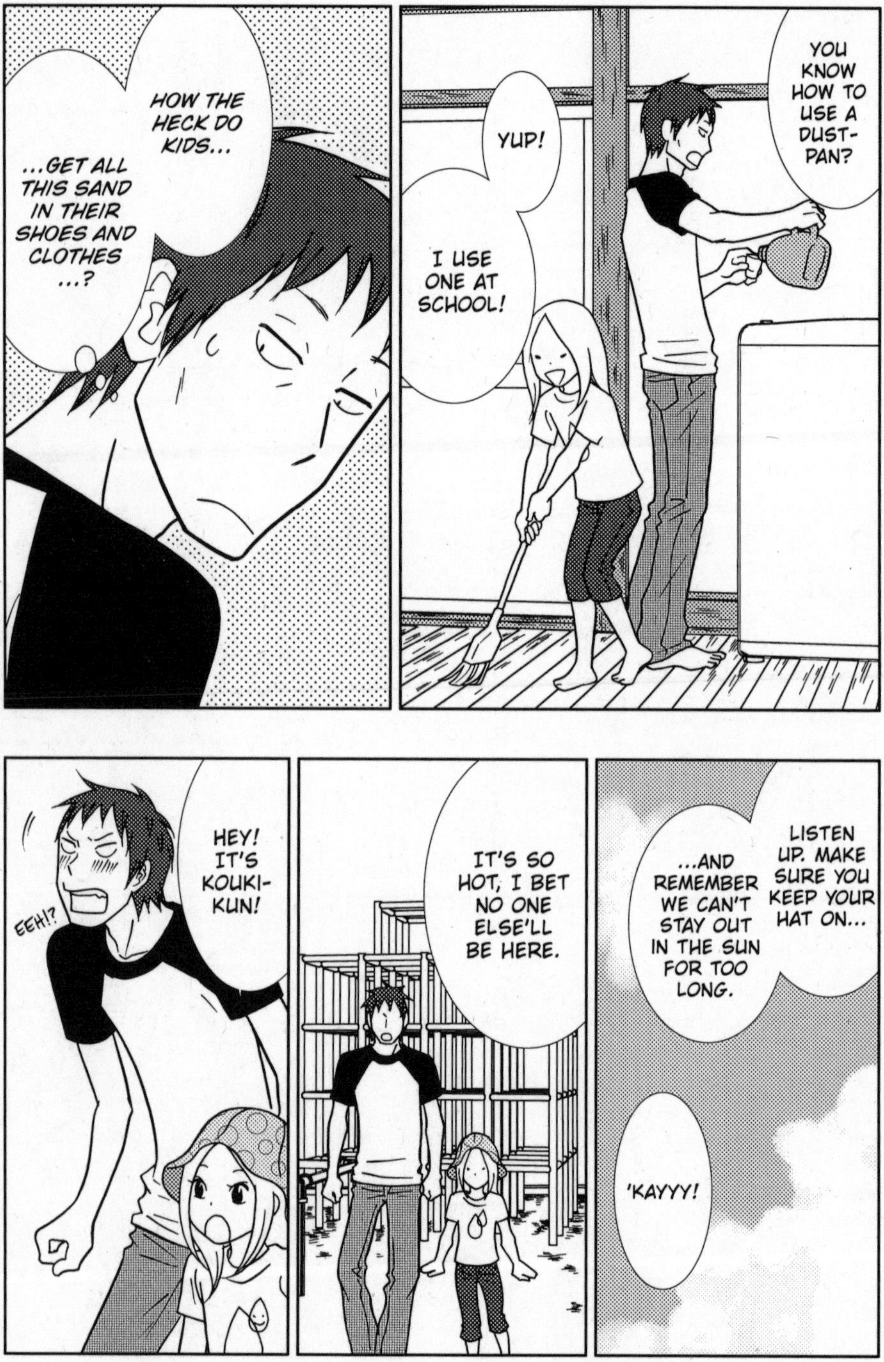
YOU KNOW HOW TO USE A DUST-PAN?
YUP!
I USE ONE AT SCHOOL!
HOW THE HECK DO KIDS...
...GET ALL THIS SAND IN THEIR SHOES AND CLOTHES ...?
LISTEN UP. MAKE SURE YOU KEEP YOUR HAT ON...
...AND REMEMBER WE CAN'T STAY OUT IN THE SUN FOR TOO LONG.
'KAYYY!
IT'S SO HOT, I BET NO ONE ELSE'LL BE HERE.
HEY! IT'S KOUKI-KUN!
EEH!?

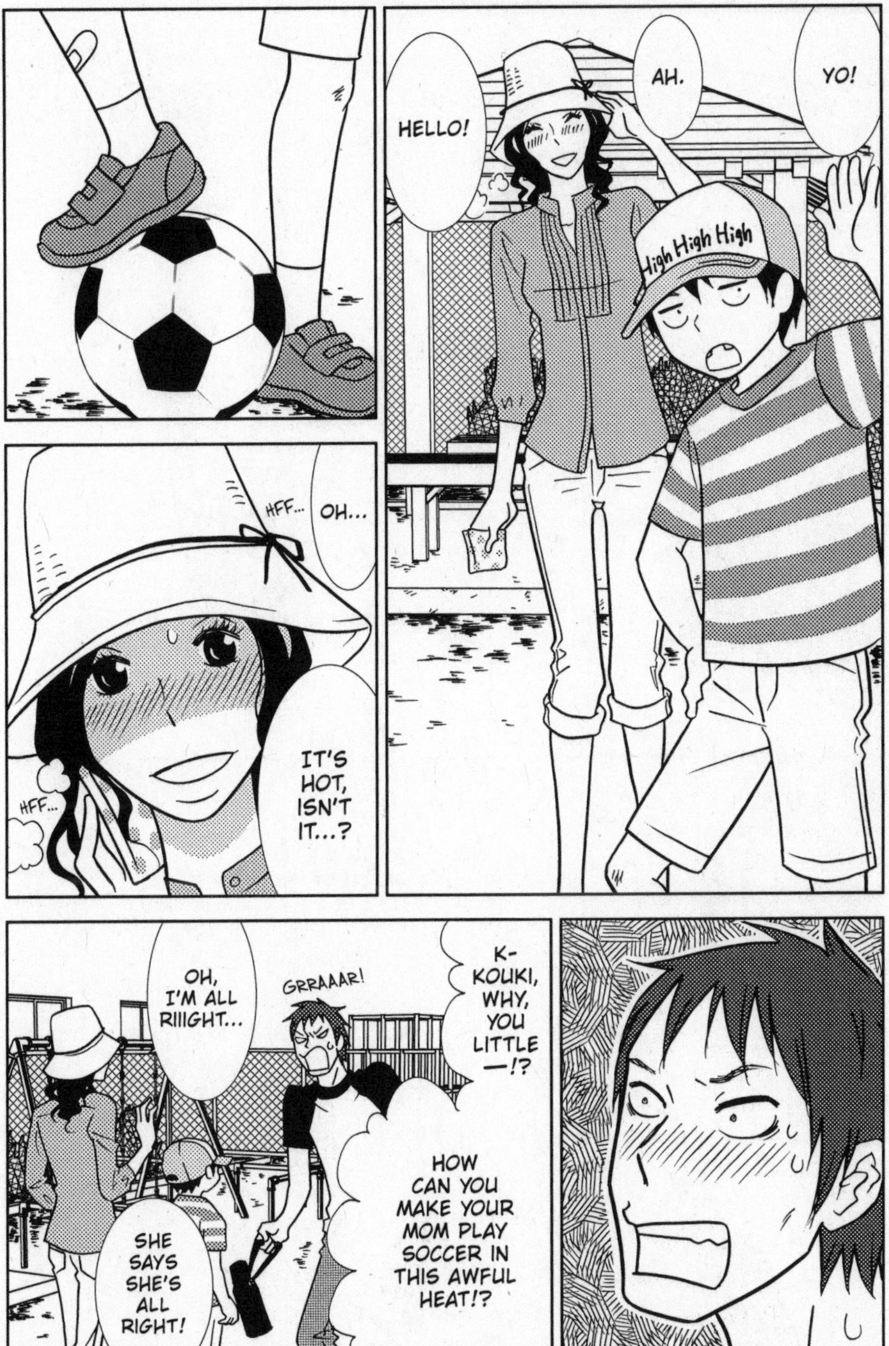
YO!
AH.
HELLO!
High High High
OH...
HFF...
IT'S HOT, ISN'T IT...?
HFF...
K-KOUKI, WHY, YOU LITTLE—!?
GRRAAAR!
OH, I'M ALL RIIIGHT...
HOW CAN YOU MAKE YOUR MOM PLAY SOCCER IN THIS AWFUL HEAT!?
SHE SAYS SHE'S ALL RIGHT!

*THE SLOGAN ON KOUKI'S HAT IS THE TITLE OF THE ENDING THEME SONG BY THE BAND KASARINCHU TO THE ANIME ADAPTATION OF BUNNY DROP.

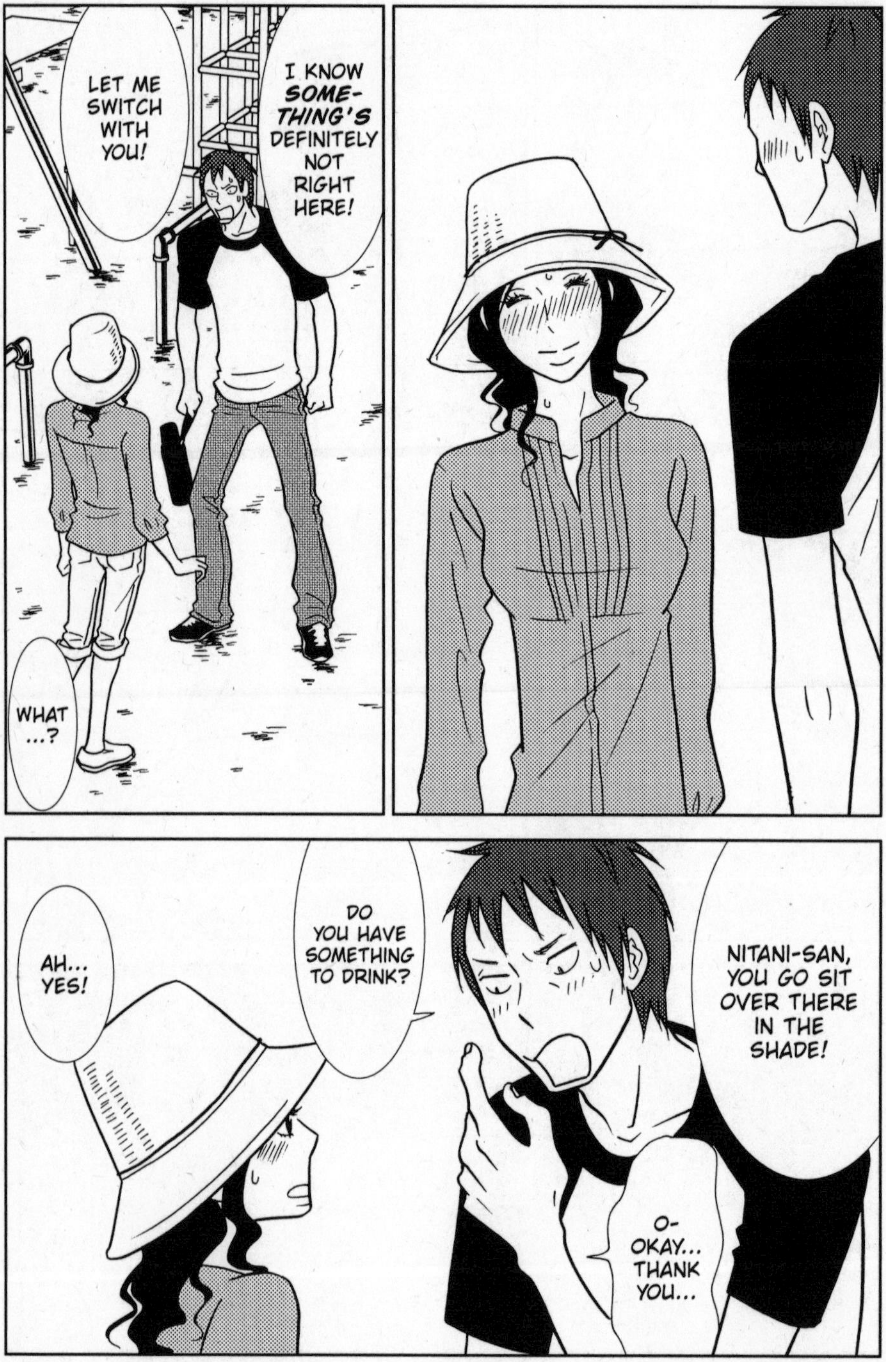
I KNOW SOMETHING'S DEFINITELY NOT RIGHT HERE!
LET ME SWITCH WITH YOU!
WHAT ...?
NITANI-SAN, YOU GO SIT OVER THERE IN THE SHADE!
O-OKAY... THANK YOU...
DO YOU HAVE SOMETHING TO DRINK?
AH... YES!

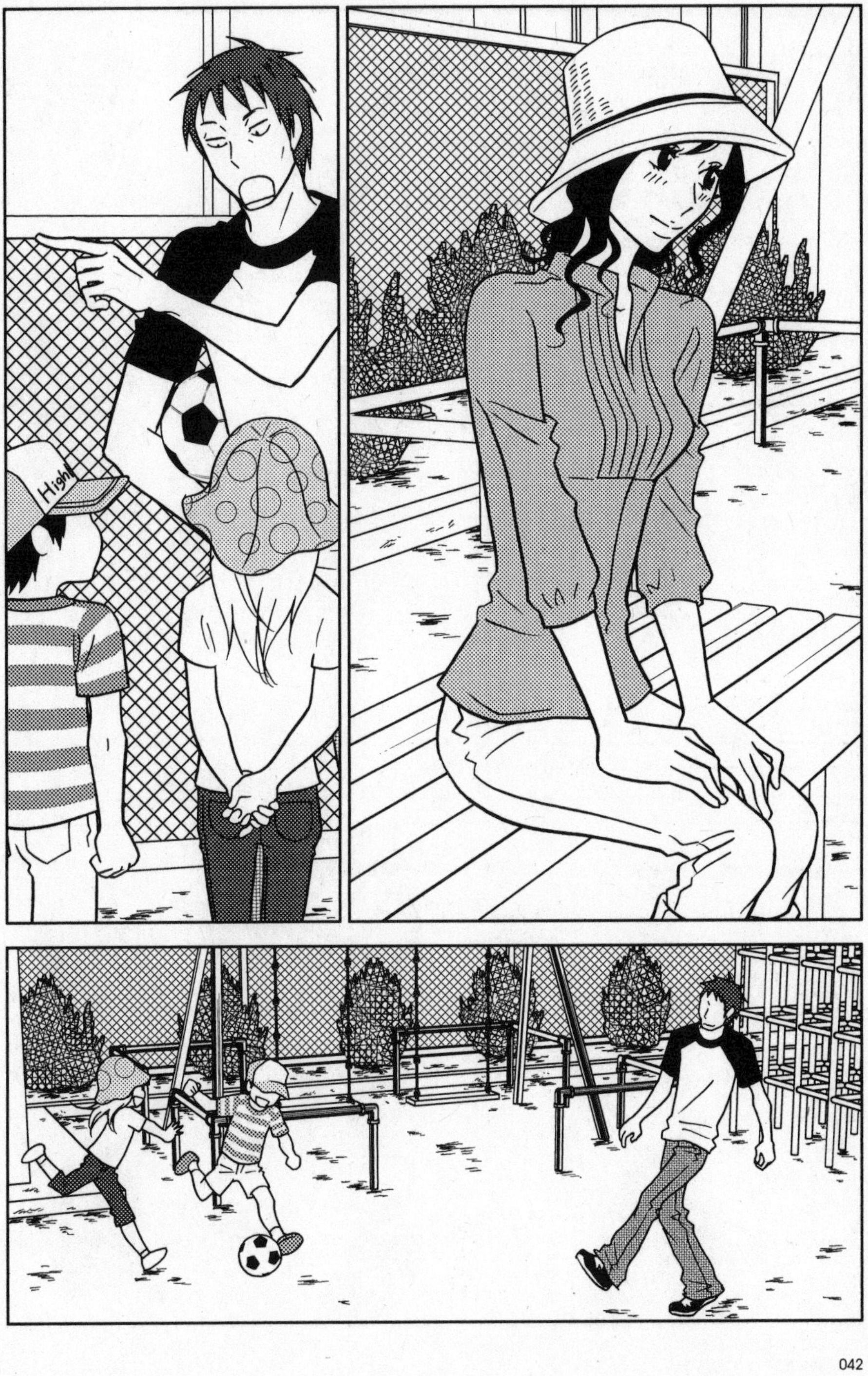
High

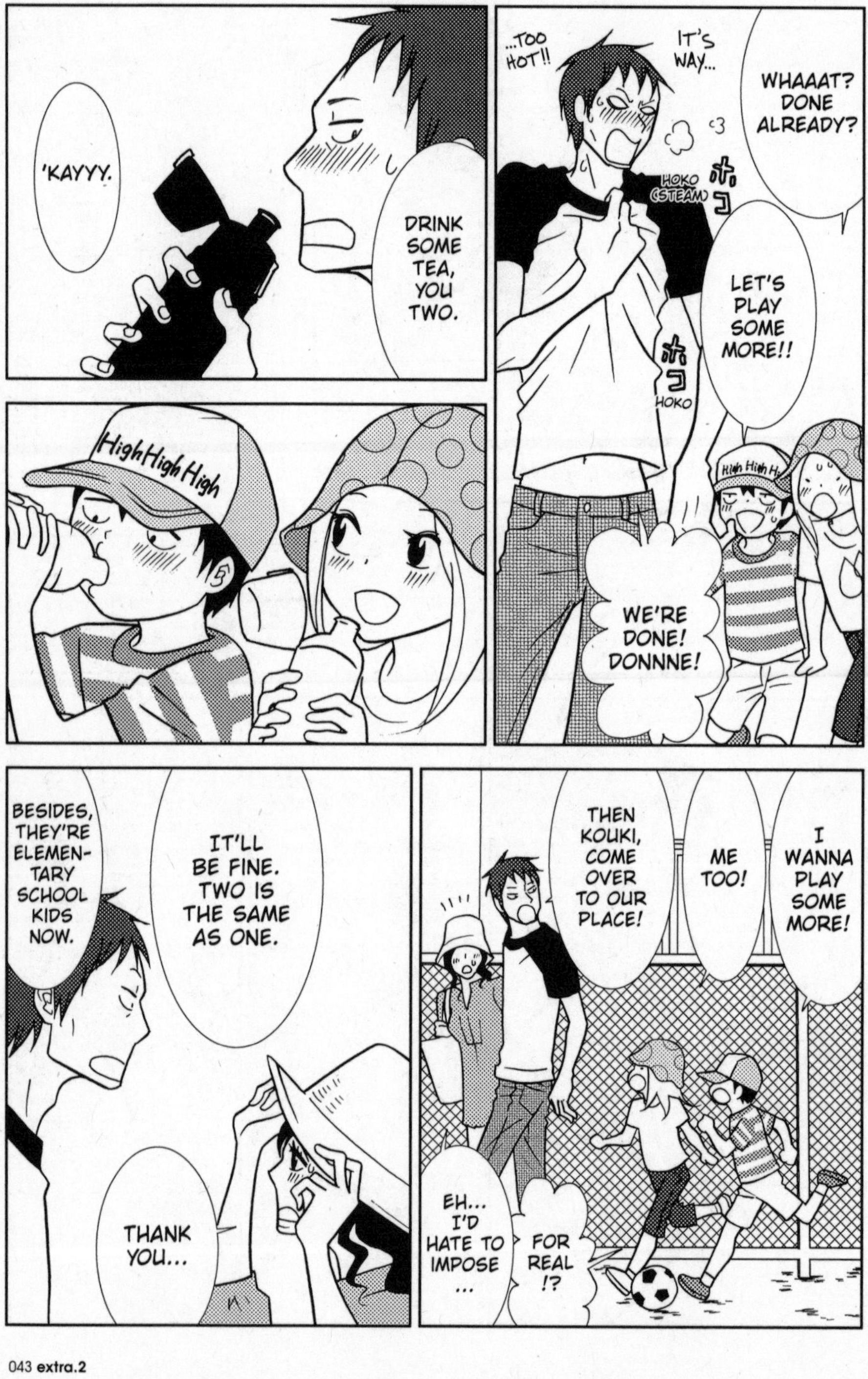
WHAAAT? DONE ALREADY?
IT'S WAY...
...TOO HOT!!
HOKO (STEAM)
LET'S PLAY SOME MORE!!
HOKO
WE'RE DONE! DONNNE!
DRINK SOME TEA, YOU TWO.
'KAYYY.
High High High
I WANNA PLAY SOME MORE!
ME TOO!
THEN KOUKI, COME OVER TO OUR PLACE!
FOR REAL!?
EH... I'D HATE TO IMPOSE...
IT'LL BE FINE. TWO IS THE SAME AS ONE.
BESIDES, THEY'RE ELEMENTARY SCHOOL KIDS NOW.
THANK YOU...

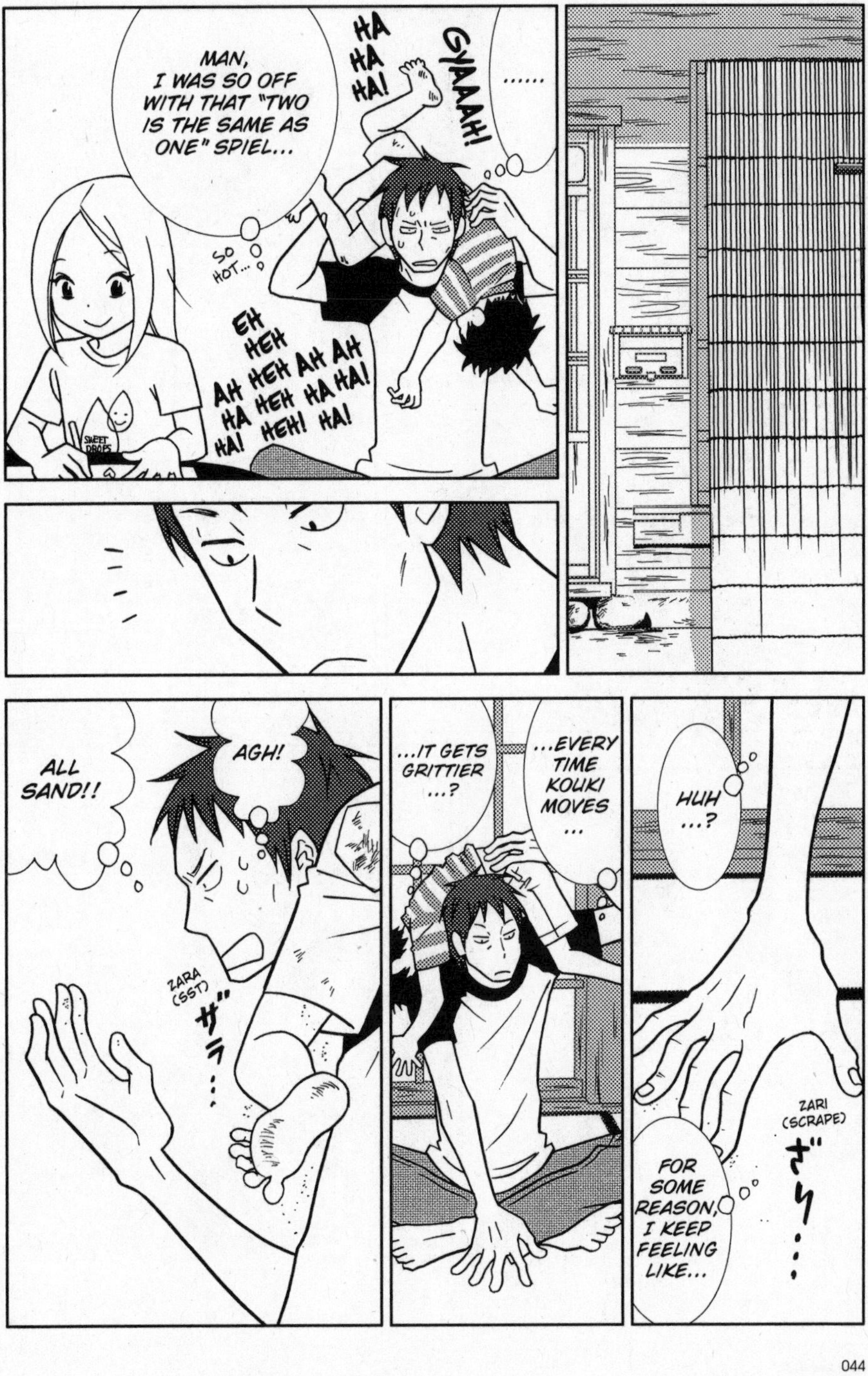
......
GYAAAH!
HA HA HA!
MAN, I WAS SO OFF WITH THAT "TWO IS THE SAME AS ONE" SPIEL...
SO HOT...
EH HEH AH HEH AH AH HA HEH HA HA! HA! HEH! HA!
HUH ...?
ZARI (SCRAPE)
ざり…
FOR SOME REASON, I KEEP FEELING LIKE...
...EVERY TIME KOUKI MOVES ...
...IT GETS GRITTIER ...?
AGH!
ALL SAND!!
ZARA (SST)
ザラ…

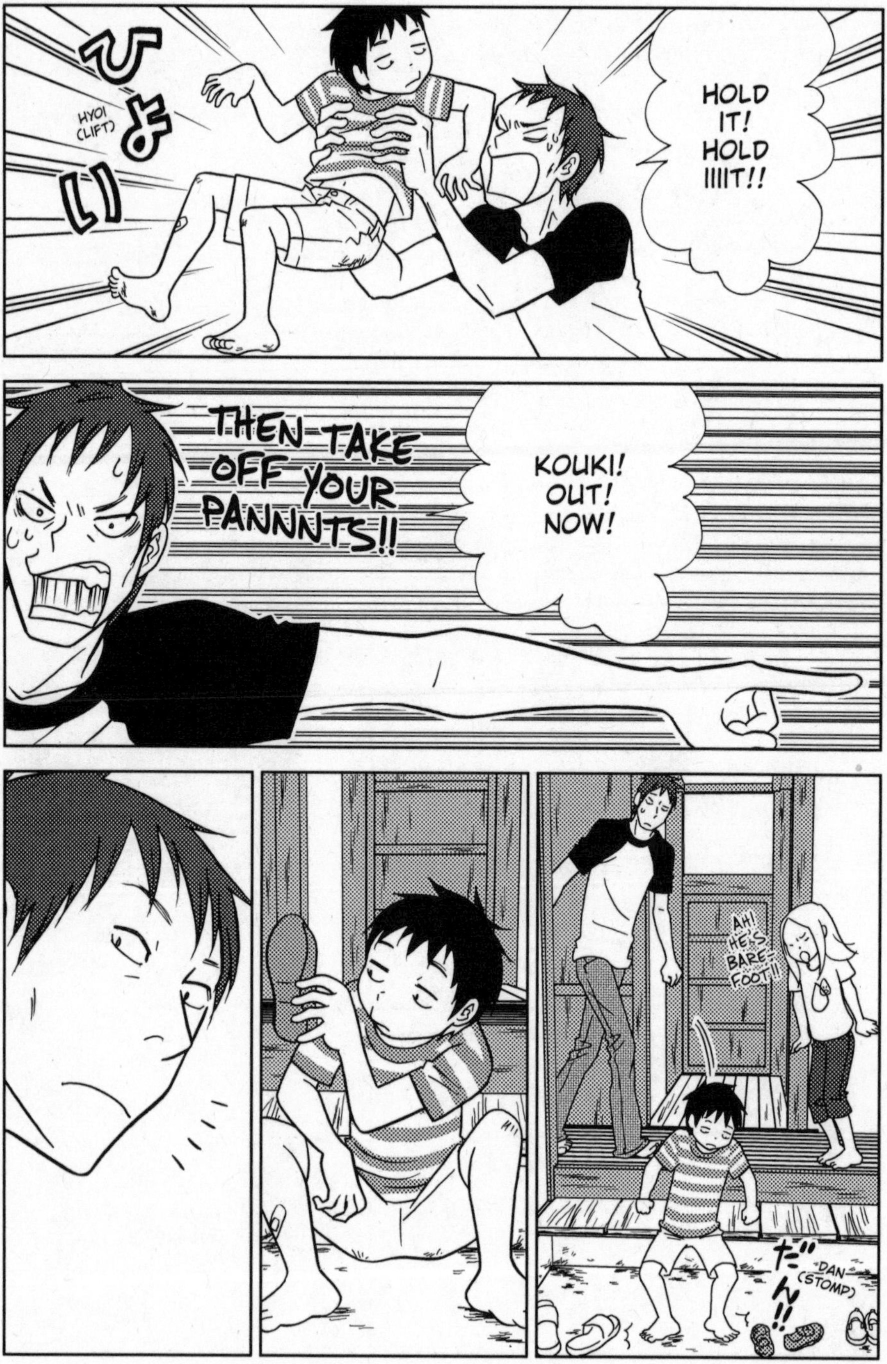
HOLD IT! HOLD IIIIT!!
ひょい
HYOI (LIFT)
KOUKI! OUT! NOW!
THEN TAKE OFF YOUR PANNNTS!!
AH! HE'S BAREFOOT!!
だん!!
DAN (STOMP)

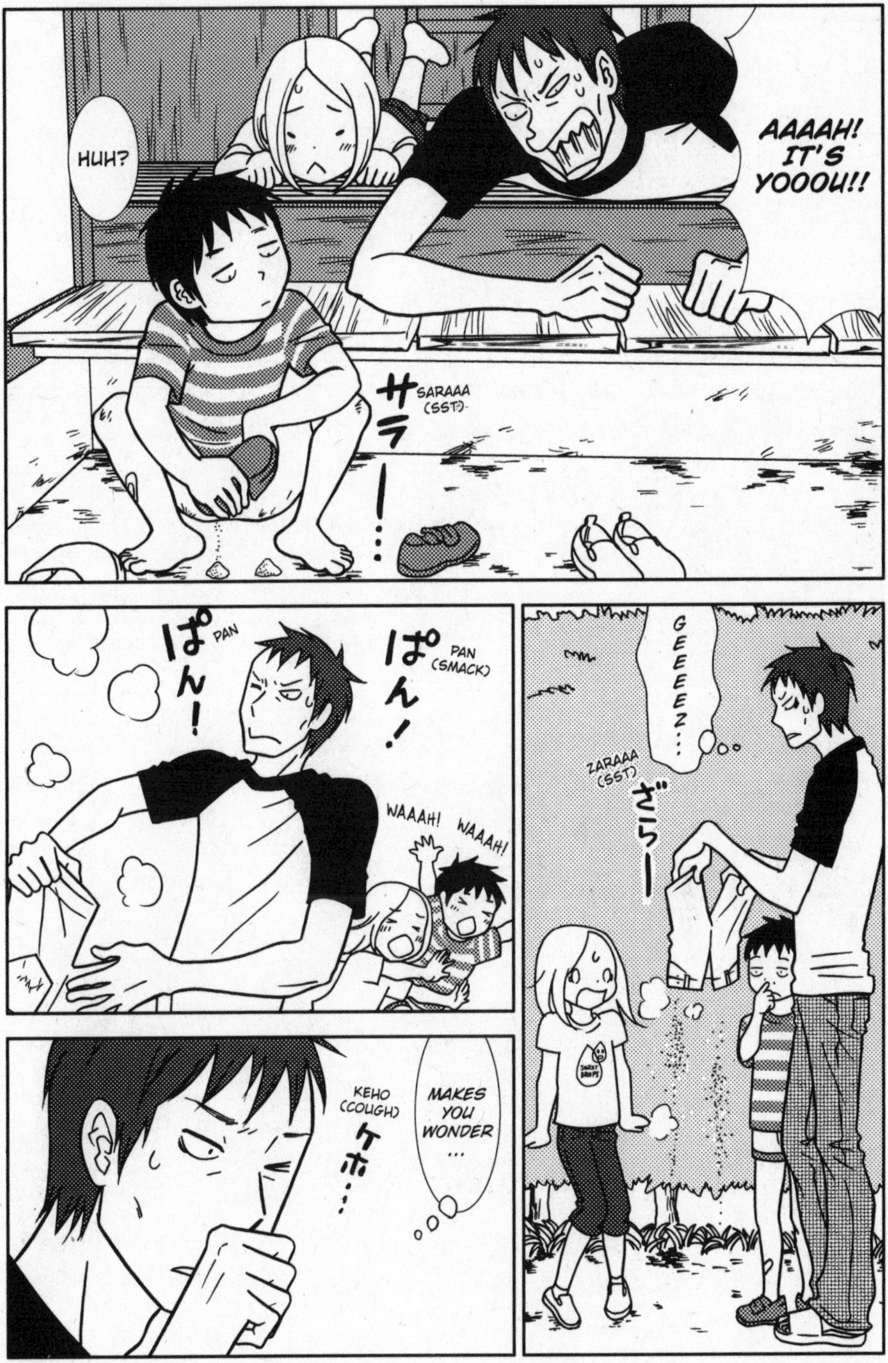
AAAAH! IT'S YOOOU!!
HUH?
サラー…
SARAAA (SST)
GEEEEZ...
ざらー
ZARAAA (SST)
ぱん!
PAN (SMACK)
ぱん!
PAN
WAAAH!
WAAAH!
MAKES YOU WONDER ...
ケホ…
KEHO (COUGH)

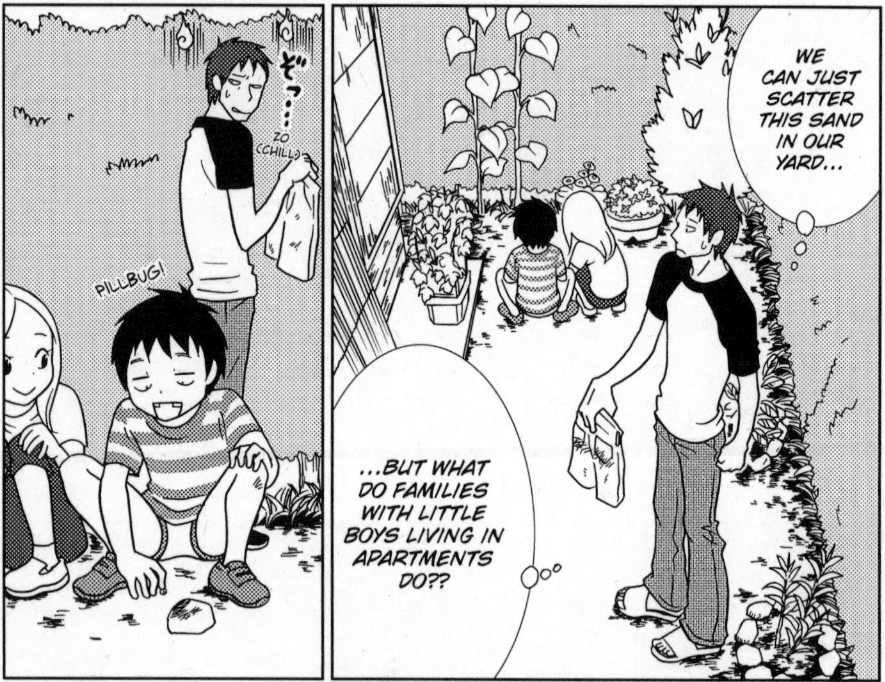
WE CAN JUST SCATTER THIS SAND IN OUR YARD...
...BUT WHAT DO FAMILIES WITH LITTLE BOYS LIVING IN APARTMENTS DO??
ぞっ...
ZO (CHILL)
PILLBUG!

*IN A COUNTRY WHERE GARBAGE SOMETIMES NEEDS TO BE SORTED TWELVE WAYS AND WATER IS SPRINKLED ON SIDEWALKS TO KEEP THEM CLEAN AND MINIMIZE DUST, DUMPING SAND IN AN APARTMENT HALLWAY OR OFF THE SIDE OF A RAILING WOULD BE GREATLY FROWNED UPON.

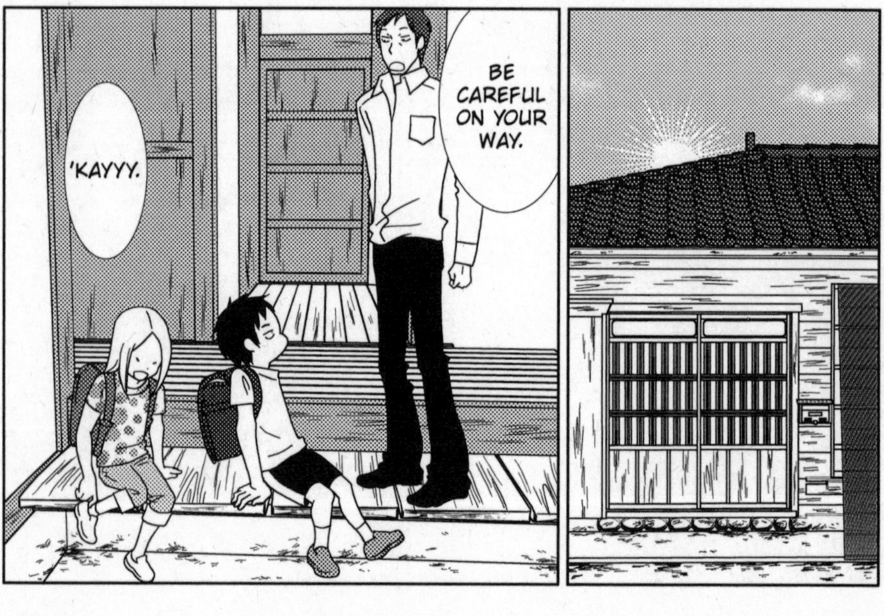
BE CAREFUL ON YOUR WAY.
'KAYYY.

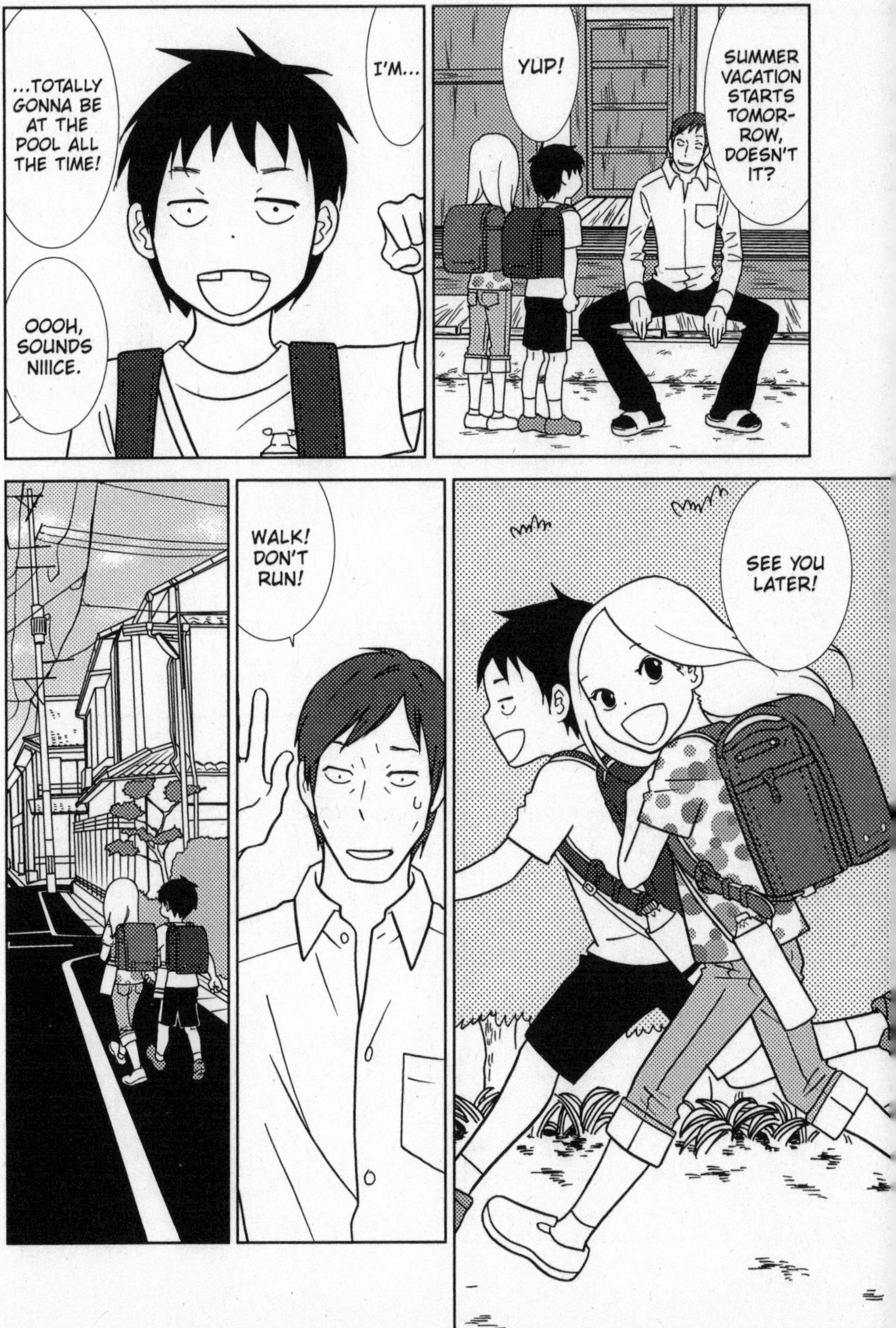
SUMMER VACATION STARTS TOMOR-ROW, DOESN'T IT?
YUP!
I'M...
...TOTALLY GONNA BE AT THE POOL ALL THE TIME!
OOOH, SOUNDS NIIICE.
SEE YOU LATER!
WALK! DON'T RUN!

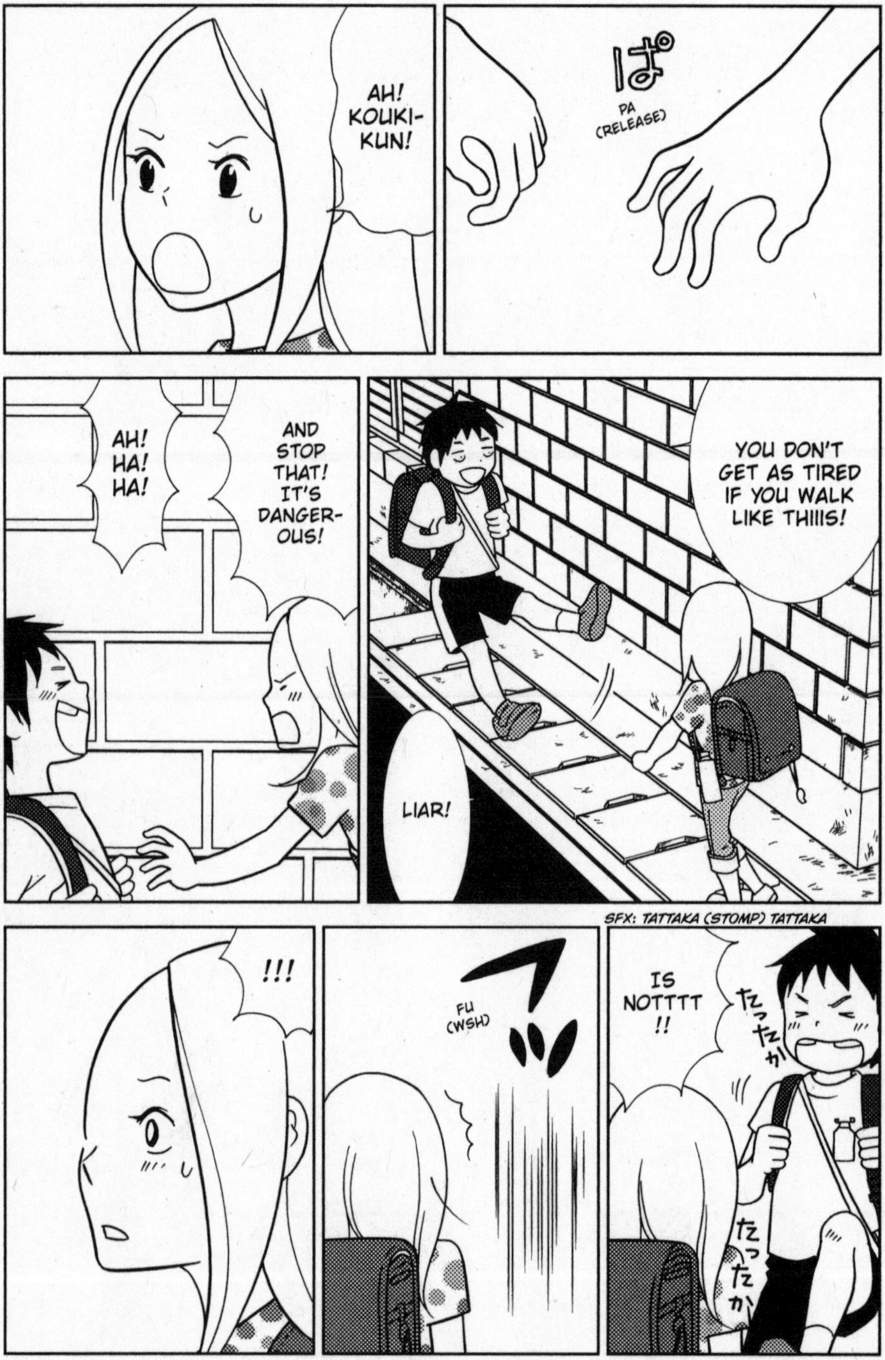
ぱ
PA (RELEASE)
AH! KOUKI-KUN!
YOU DON'T GET AS TIRED IF YOU WALK LIKE THIIIS!
LIAR!
SFX: TATTAKA (STOMP) TATTAKA
AND STOP THAT! IT'S DANGER-OUS!
AH! HA! HA!
IS NOTTTT !!
たったか
たったか
FU (WSH)
!!!

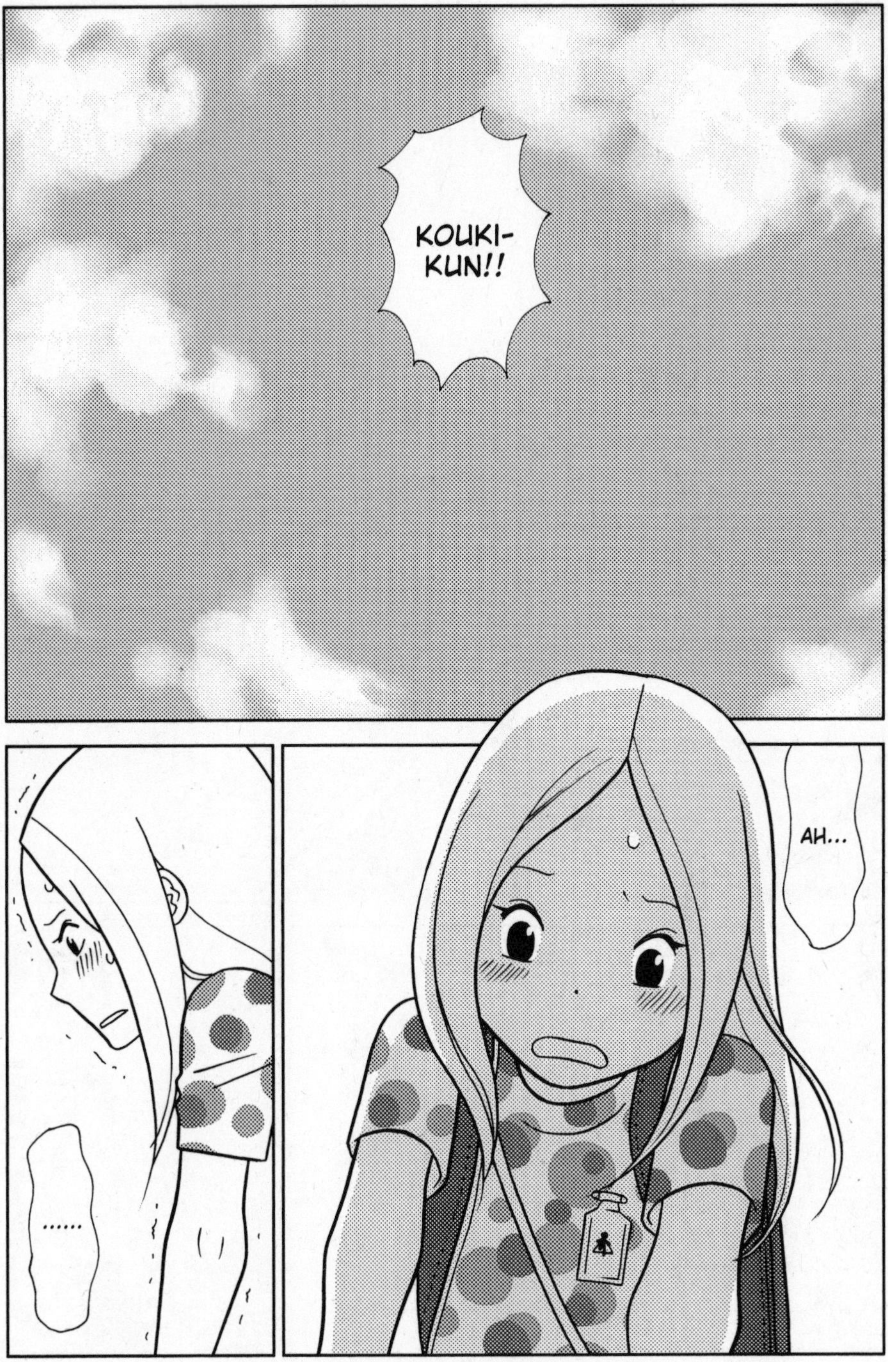
KOUKI-
KUN!!
AH...
......

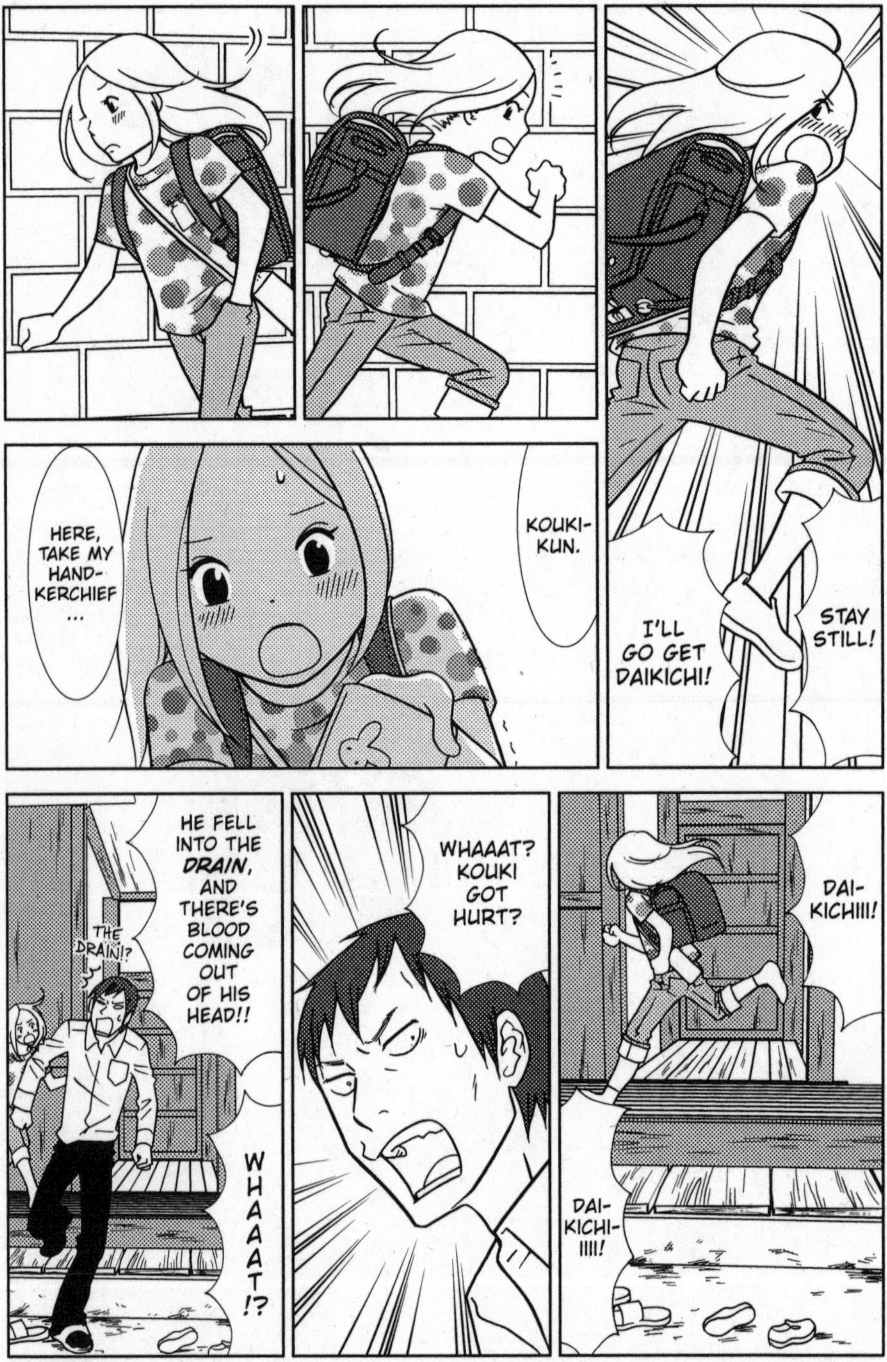
STAY STILL!
I'LL GO GET DAIKICHI!
KOUKI-KUN.
HERE, TAKE MY HAND-KERCHIEF ...
DAI-KICHIIII!
DAI-KICHI-IIII!
WHAAAT? KOUKI GOT HURT?
HE FELL INTO THE *DRAIN*, AND THERE'S BLOOD COMING OUT OF HIS HEAD!!
THE DRAIN!?
WHAAAAT!?

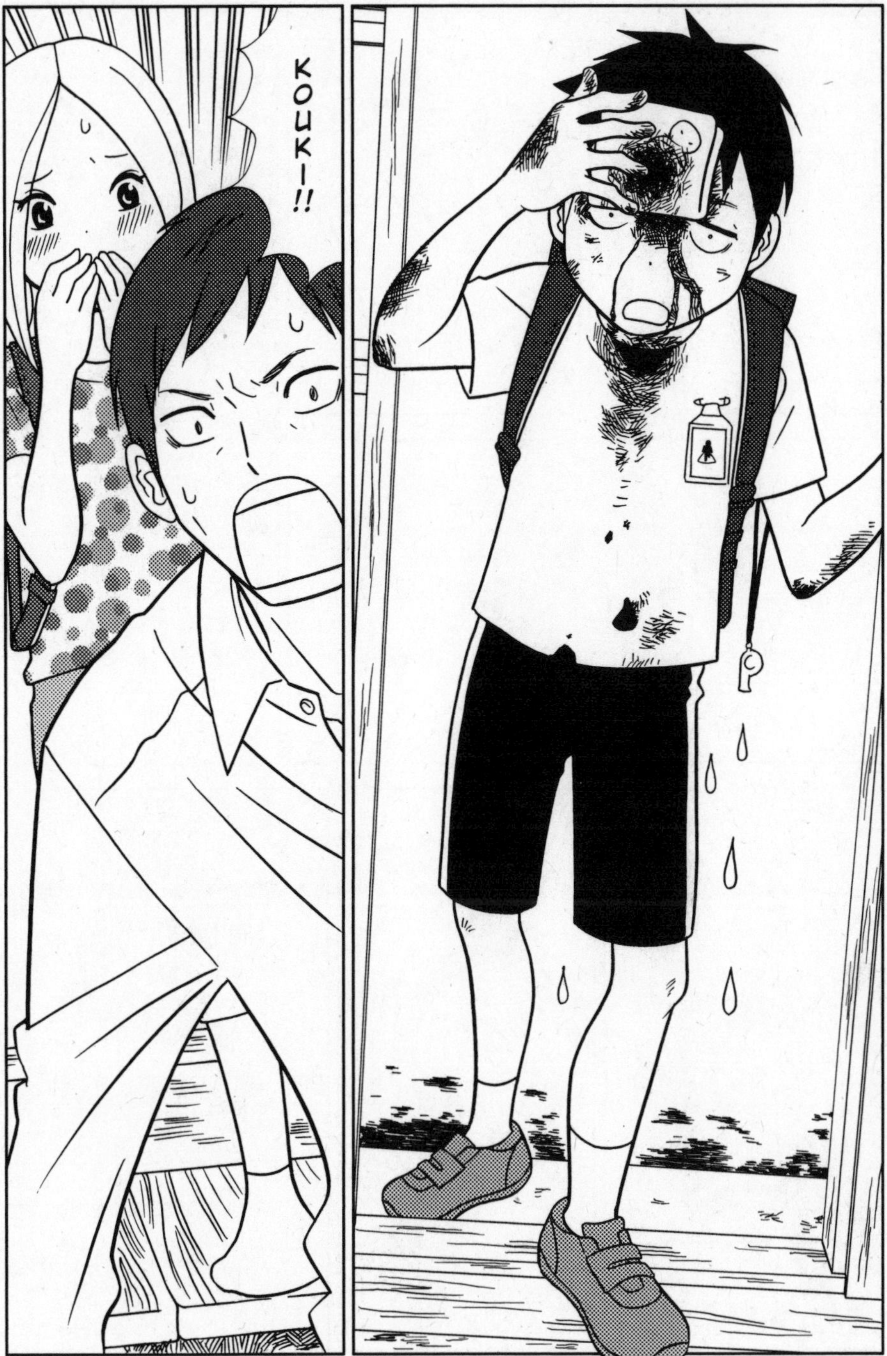
KOUKI!!

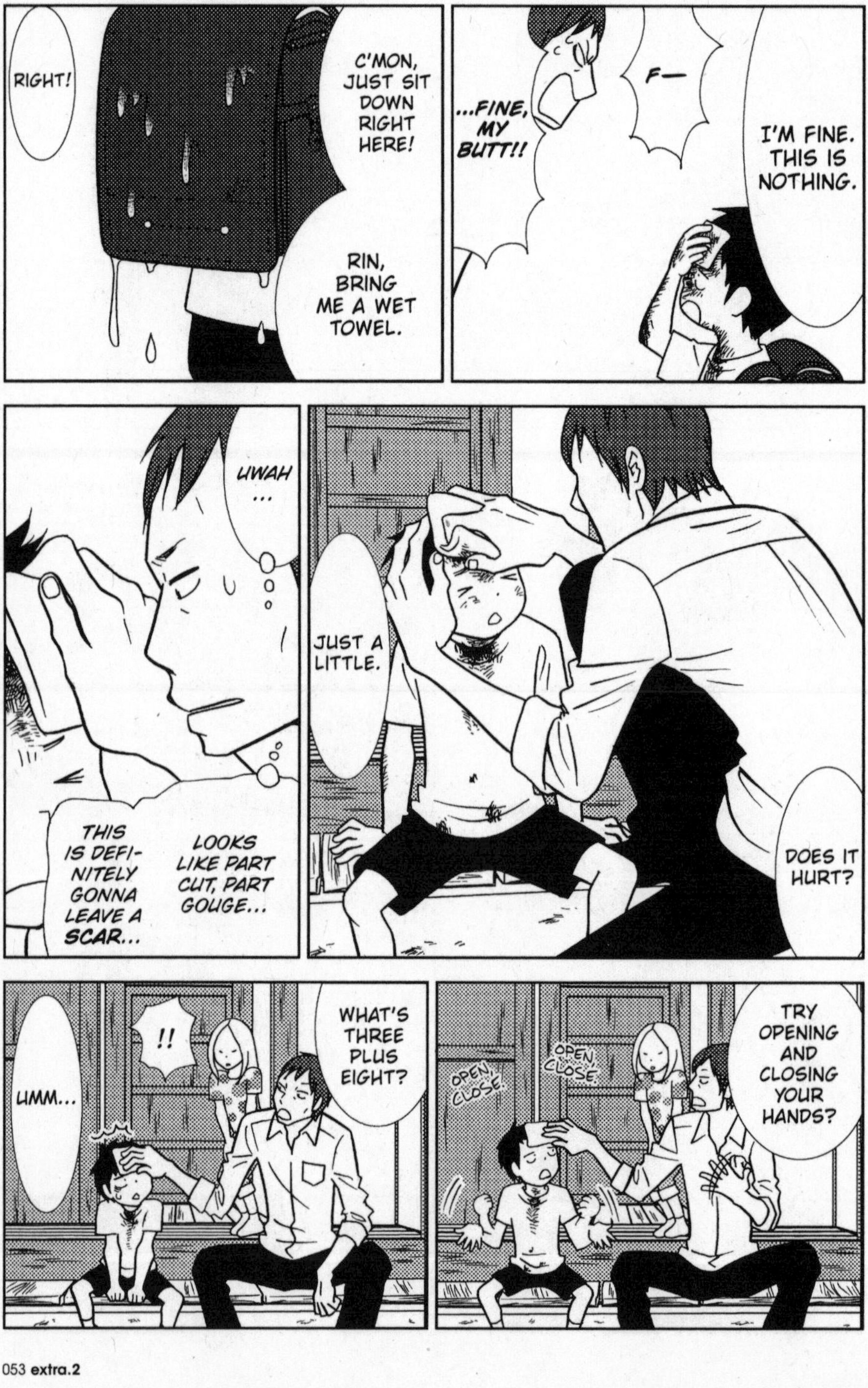
I'M FINE. THIS IS NOTHING.
F—
...FINE, MY BUTT!!
C'MON, JUST SIT DOWN RIGHT HERE!
RIN, BRING ME A WET TOWEL.
RIGHT!
DOES IT HURT?
JUST A LITTLE.
UWAH ...
LOOKS LIKE PART CUT, PART GOUGE...
THIS IS DEFI-NITELY GONNA LEAVE A SCAR...
TRY OPENING AND CLOSING YOUR HANDS?
OPEN, CLOSE.
OPEN, CLOSE.
WHAT'S THREE PLUS EIGHT?
!!
UMM...

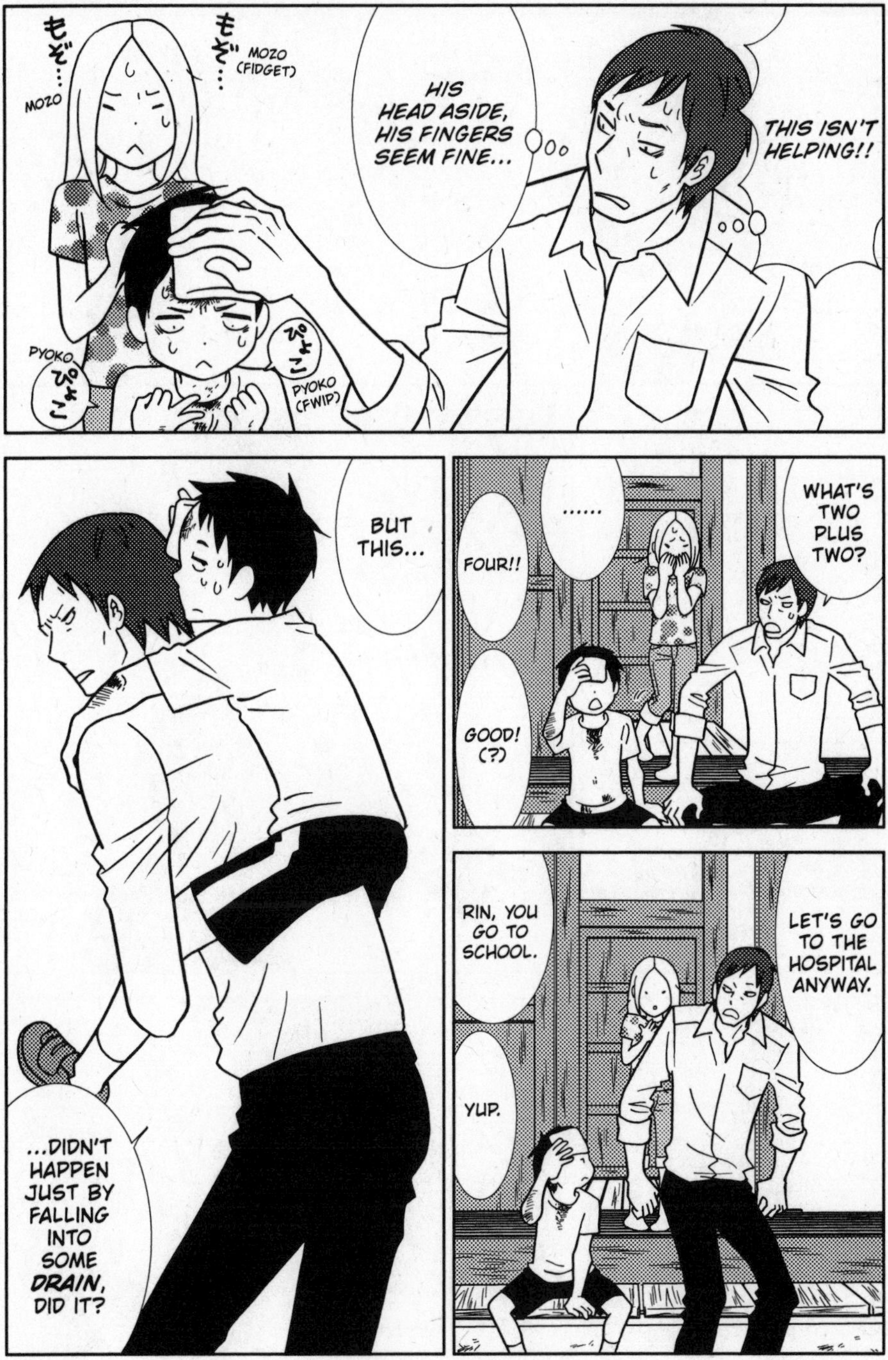
THIS ISN'T HELPING!!
HIS HEAD ASIDE, HIS FINGERS SEEM FINE...
もぞ…
MOZO (FIDGET)
もぞ…
MOZO
ぴょこ
PYOKO (FWIP)
PYOKO
ぴょこ
WHAT'S TWO PLUS TWO?
......
FOUR!!
GOOD! (?)
LET'S GO TO THE HOSPITAL ANYWAY.
RIN, YOU GO TO SCHOOL.
YUP.
BUT THIS...
...DIDN'T HAPPEN JUST BY FALLING INTO SOME ***DRAIN***, DID IT?

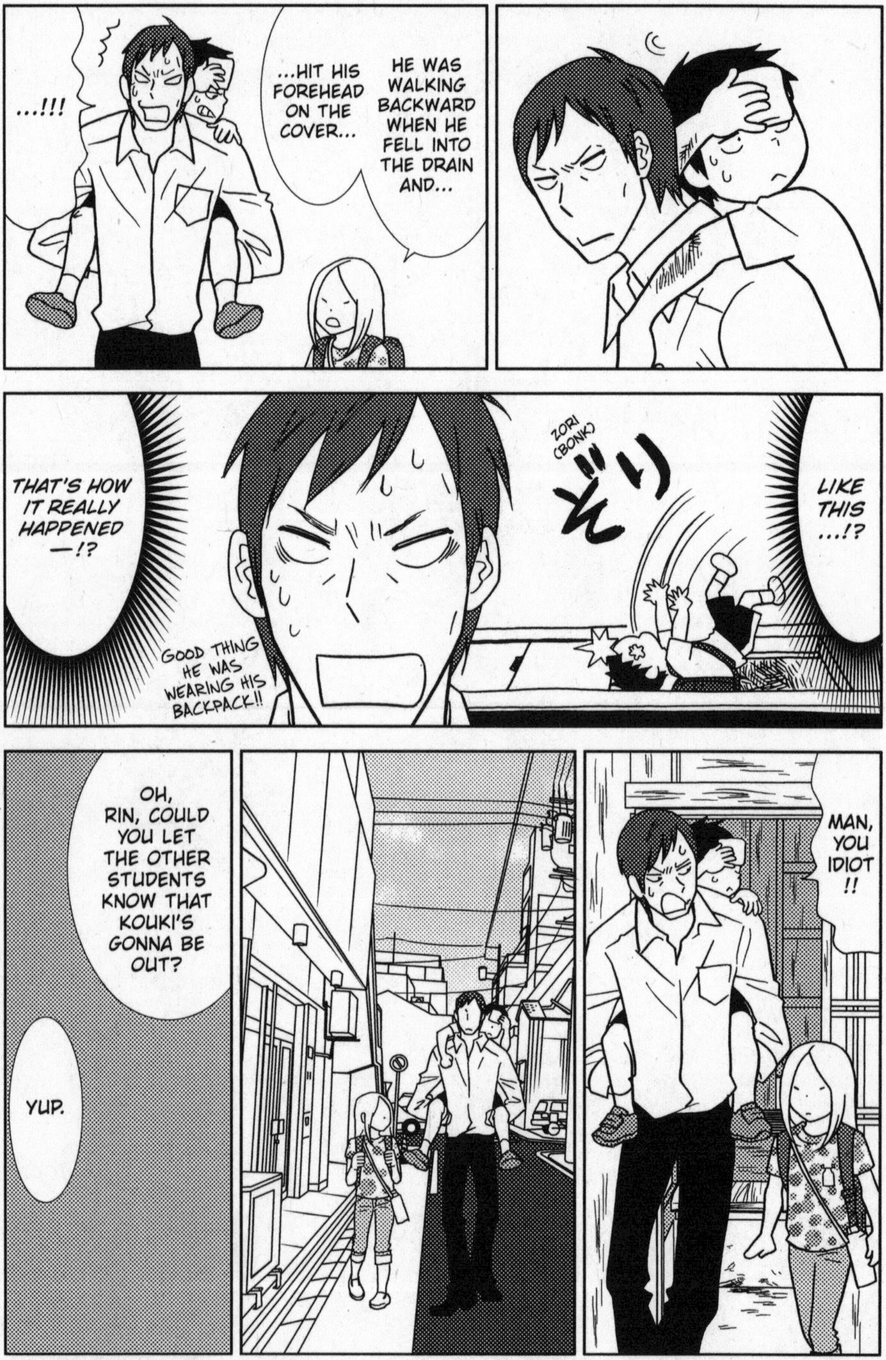
HE WAS WALKING BACKWARD WHEN HE FELL INTO THE DRAIN AND...
...HIT HIS FOREHEAD ON THE COVER...
...!!!
LIKE THIS ...!?
ZORI (BONK)
THAT'S HOW IT REALLY HAPPENED—!?
GOOD THING HE WAS WEARING HIS BACKPACK!!
MAN, YOU IDIOT!!
OH, RIN, COULD YOU LET THE OTHER STUDENTS KNOW THAT KOUKI'S GONNA BE OUT?
YUP.

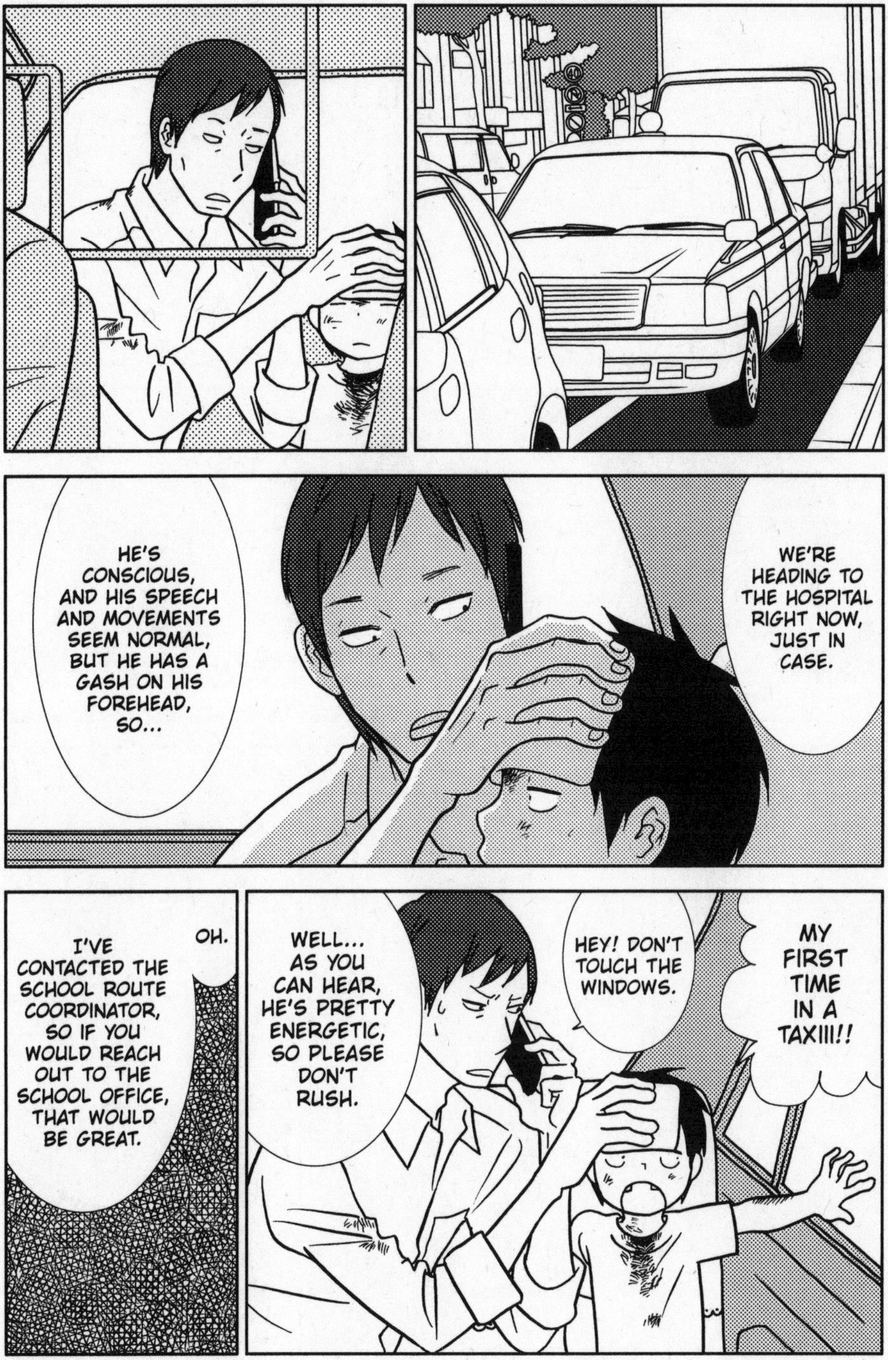

WE'RE HEADING TO THE HOSPITAL RIGHT NOW, JUST IN CASE.
HE'S CONSCIOUS, AND HIS SPEECH AND MOVEMENTS SEEM NORMAL, BUT HE HAS A GASH ON HIS FOREHEAD, SO...
MY FIRST TIME IN A TAXIII!!
HEY! DON'T TOUCH THE WINDOWS.
WELL... AS YOU CAN HEAR, HE'S PRETTY ENERGETIC, SO PLEASE DON'T RUSH.
OH.
I'VE CONTACTED THE SCHOOL ROUTE COORDINATOR, SO IF YOU WOULD REACH OUT TO THE SCHOOL OFFICE, THAT WOULD BE GREAT.

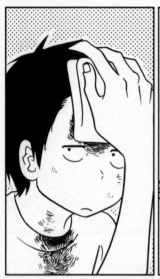

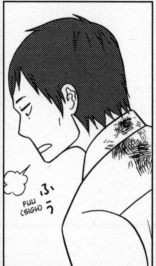

FUU
(SIGH)

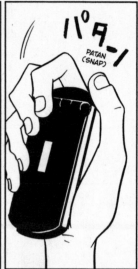

パタ―ｲ
PATAN
(SNAP)

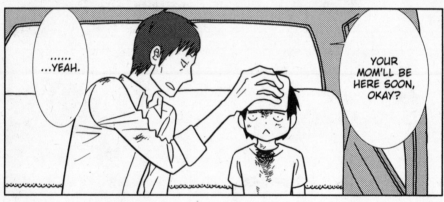

....YEAH.

YOUR MOM'LL BE HERE SOON, OKAY?

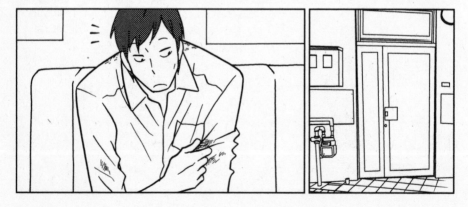

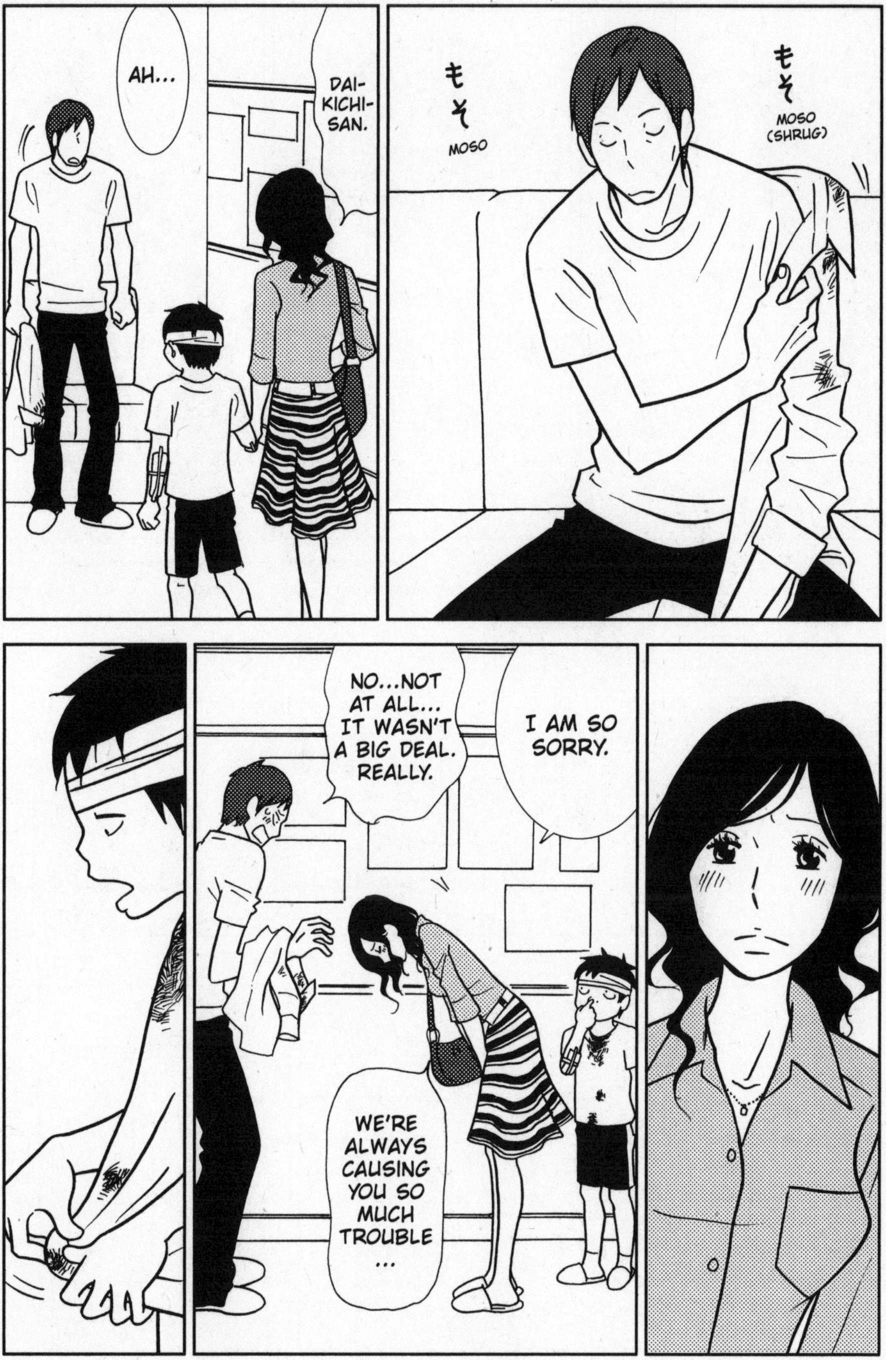
もそ
MOSO (SHRUG)
もそ
MOSO
DAI-KICHI-SAN.
AH...
I AM SO SORRY.
NO...NOT AT ALL... IT WASN'T A BIG DEAL. REALLY.
WE'RE ALWAYS CAUSING YOU SO MUCH TROUBLE ...

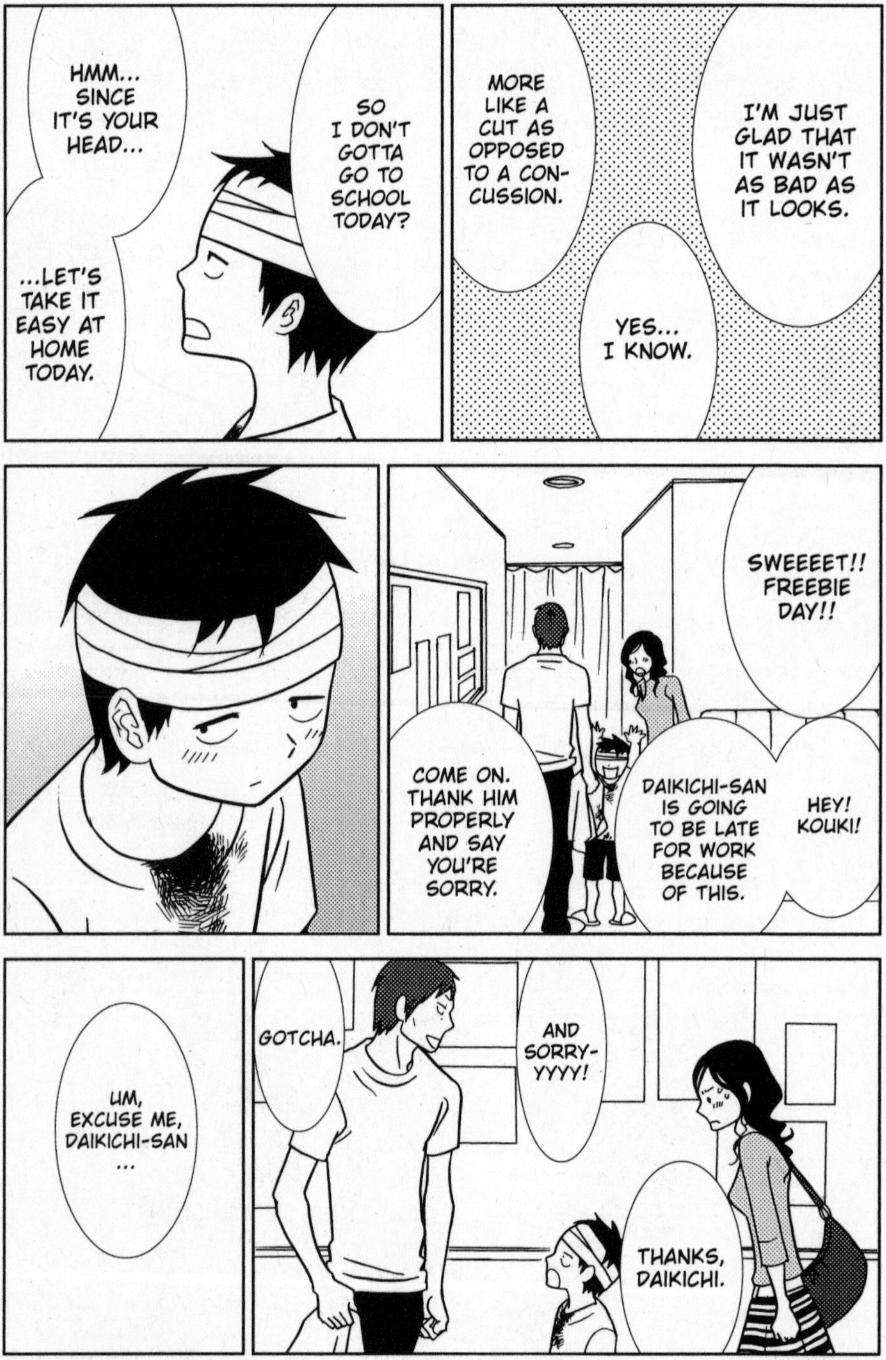
I'M JUST GLAD THAT IT WASN'T AS BAD AS IT LOOKS.
MORE LIKE A CUT AS OPPOSED TO A CON-CUSSION.
YES... I KNOW.
SO I DON'T GOTTA GO TO SCHOOL TODAY?
HMM... SINCE IT'S YOUR HEAD...
...LET'S TAKE IT EASY AT HOME TODAY.
SWEEEET!! FREEBIE DAY!!
HEY! KOUKI!
DAIKICHI-SAN IS GOING TO BE LATE FOR WORK BECAUSE OF THIS.
COME ON. THANK HIM PROPERLY AND SAY YOU'RE SORRY.
THANKS, DAIKICHI.
AND SORRY-YYYY!
GOTCHA.
UM, EXCUSE ME, DAIKICHI-SAN ...

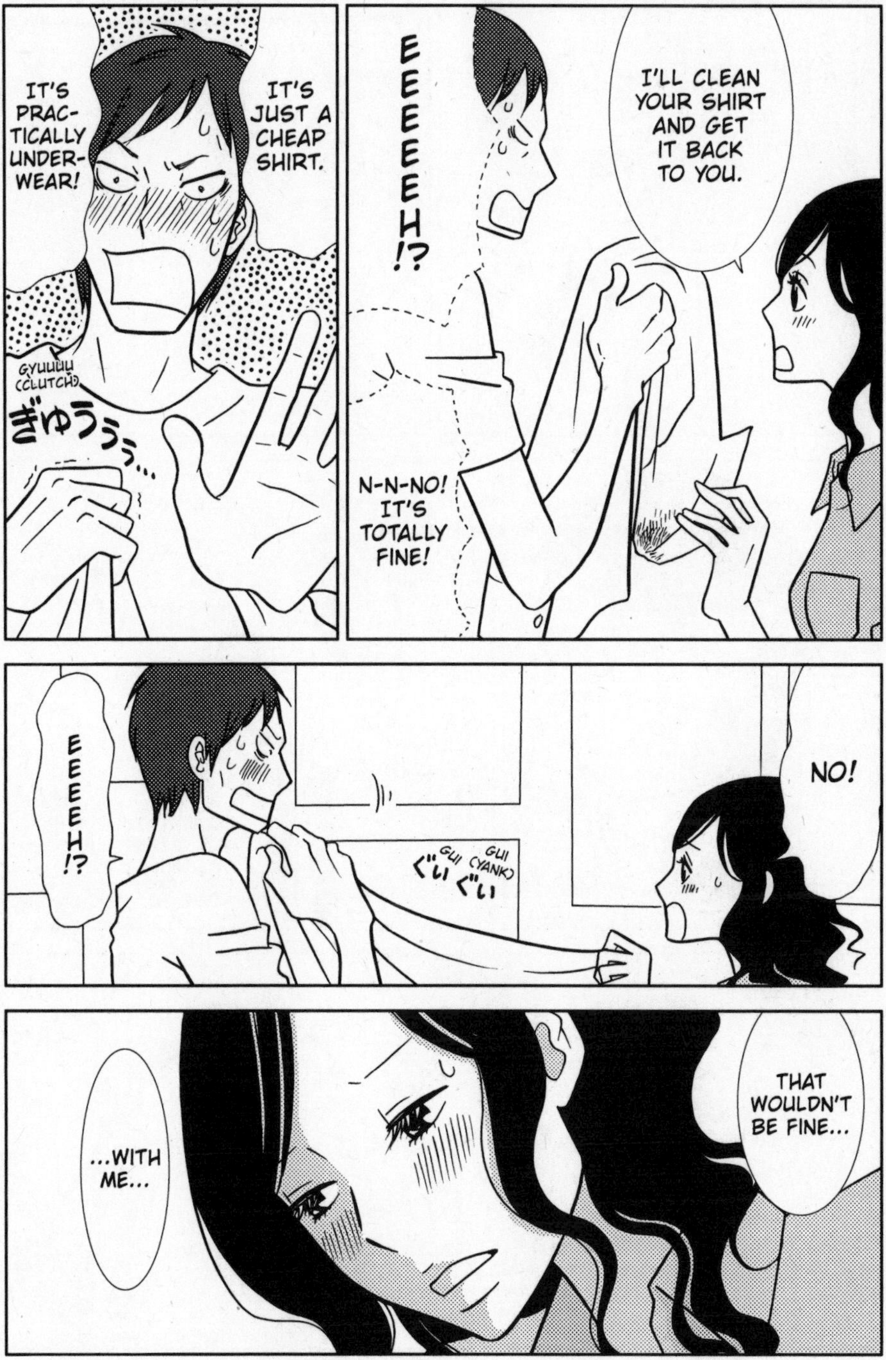
I'LL CLEAN YOUR SHIRT AND GET IT BACK TO YOU.
EEEEEH!?
N-N-NO! IT'S TOTALLY FINE!
IT'S JUST A CHEAP SHIRT.
IT'S PRAC-TICALLY UNDER-WEAR!
GYUUUU (CLUTCH)
ぎゅううう...
NO!
GUI GUI (YANK)
ぐい ぐい
EEEEEH!?
THAT WOULDN'T BE FINE...
...WITH ME...

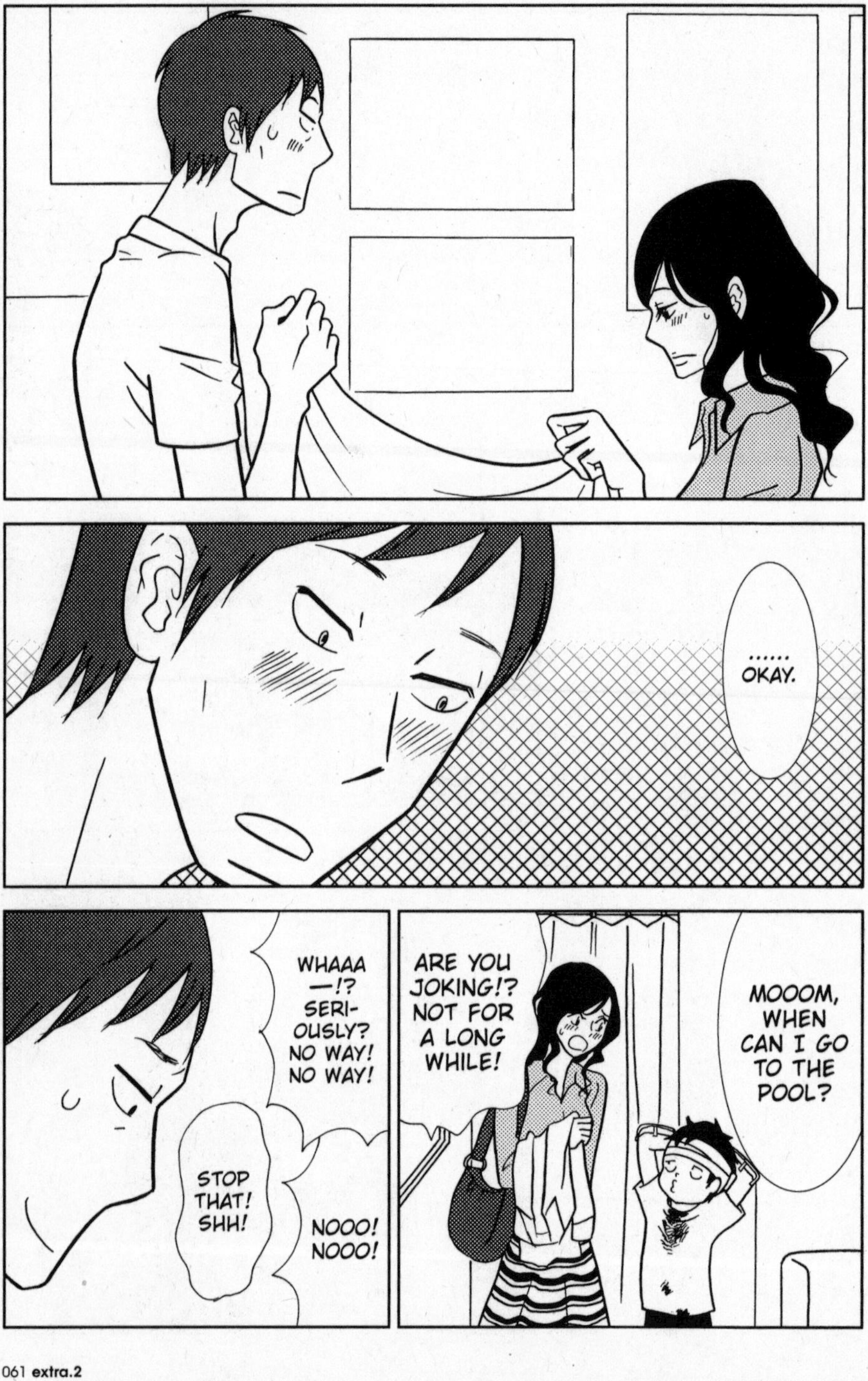
......
OKAY.
MOOOM, WHEN CAN I GO TO THE POOL?
ARE YOU JOKING!? NOT FOR A LONG WHILE!
WHAAA —!? SERI-OUSLY? NO WAY! NO WAY!
NOOO! NOOO!
STOP THAT! SHH!

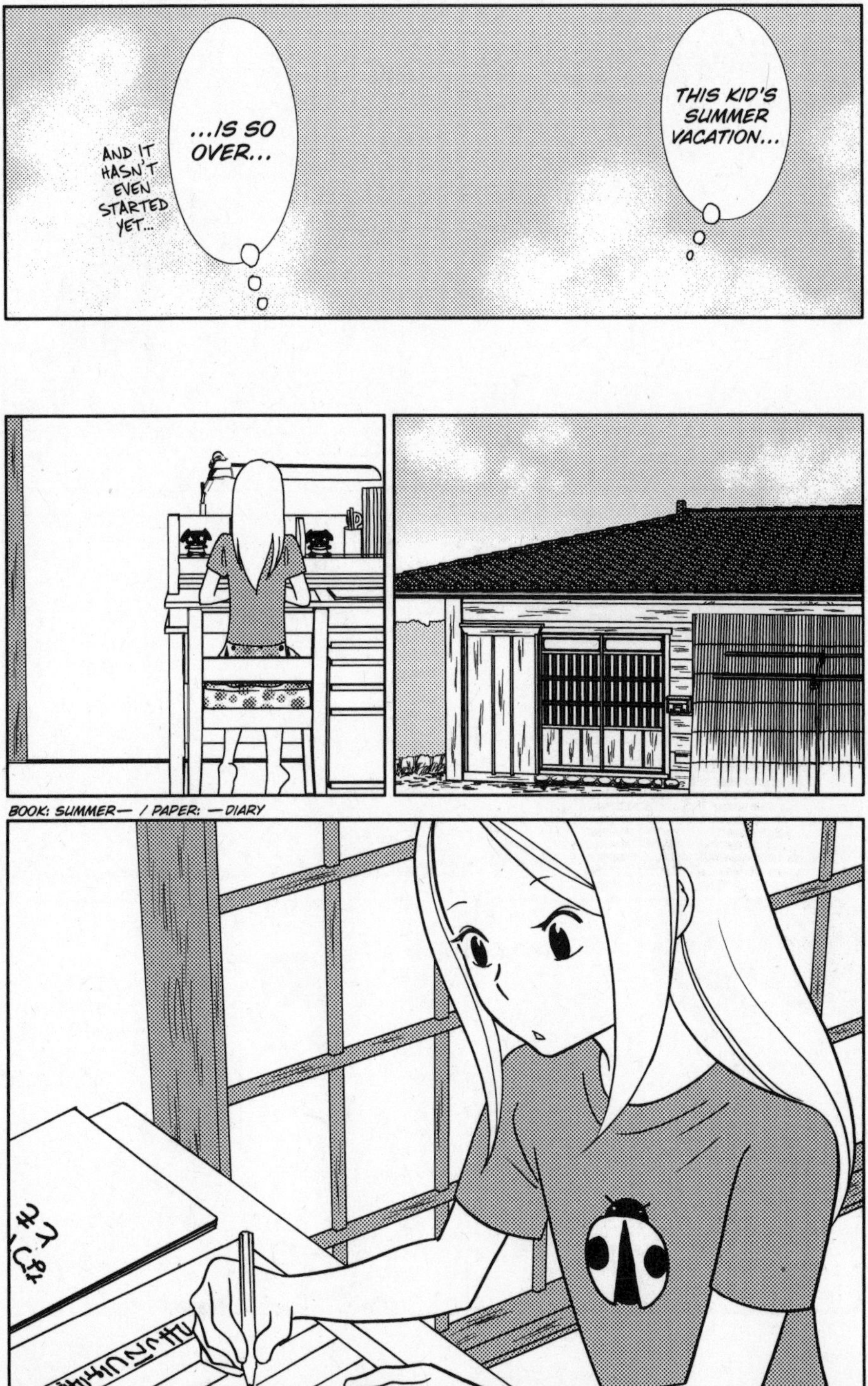
THIS KID'S SUMMER VACATION...
...IS SO OVER...
AND IT HASN'T EVEN STARTED YET...
BOOK: SUMMER— / PAPER: —DIARY

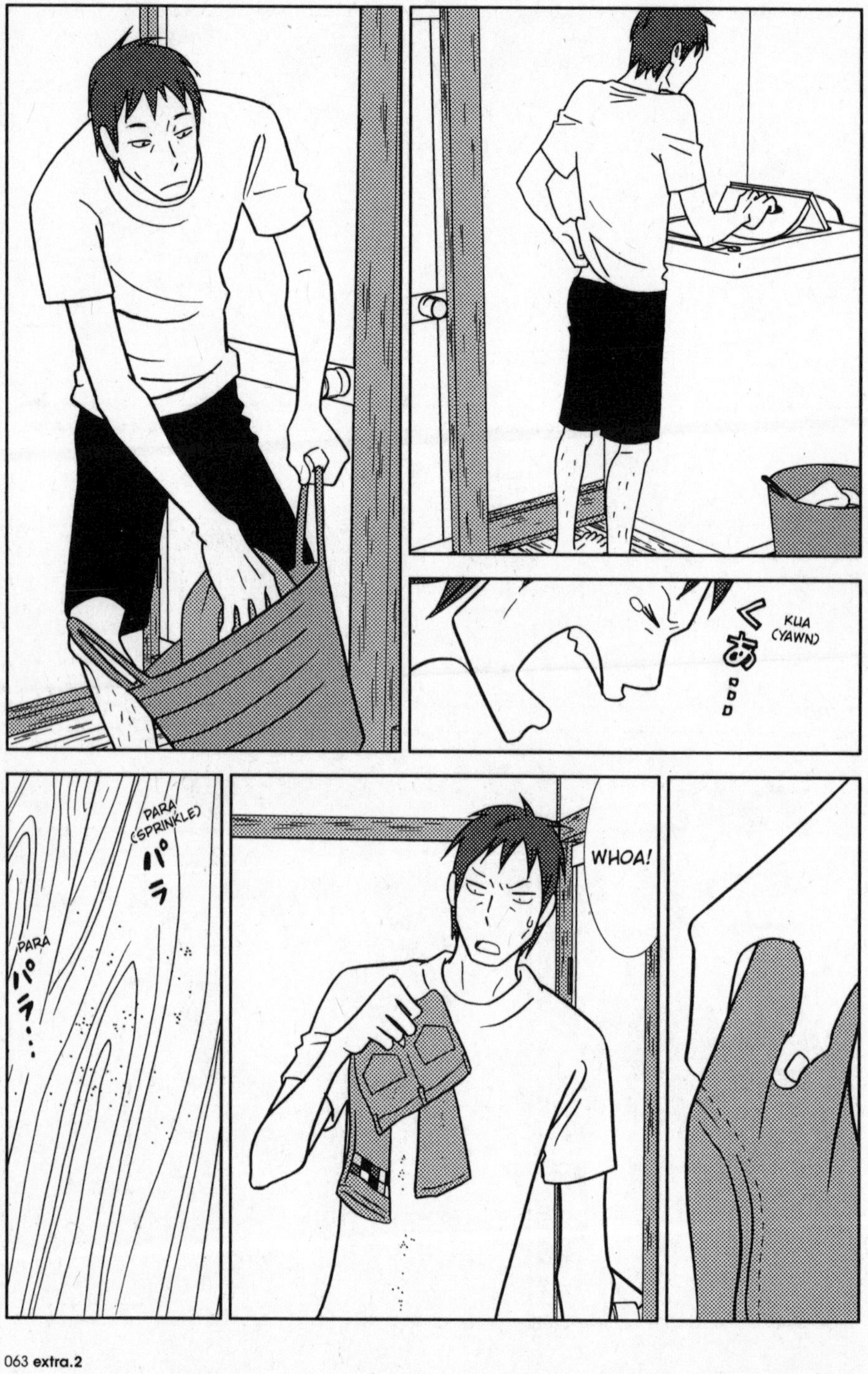
くあ
KUA (YAWN)
WHOA!
PARA (SPRINKLE)
パラ
PARA
パラ…

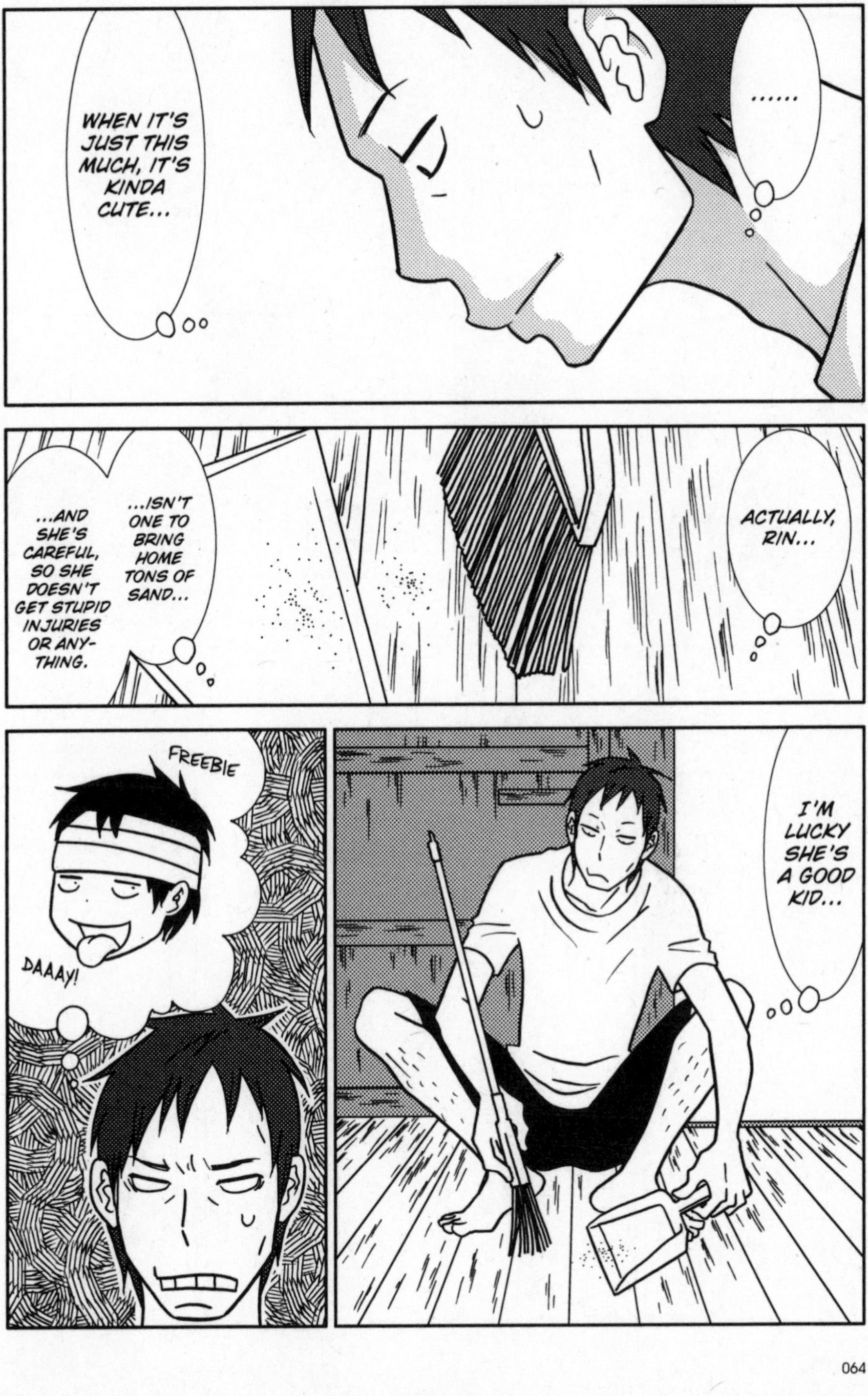
......
WHEN IT'S JUST THIS MUCH, IT'S KINDA CUTE...
ACTUALLY, RIN...
...ISN'T ONE TO BRING HOME TONS OF SAND...
...AND SHE'S CAREFUL, SO SHE DOESN'T GET STUPID INJURIES OR ANY-THING.
I'M LUCKY SHE'S A GOOD KID...
FREEBIE
DAAAY!

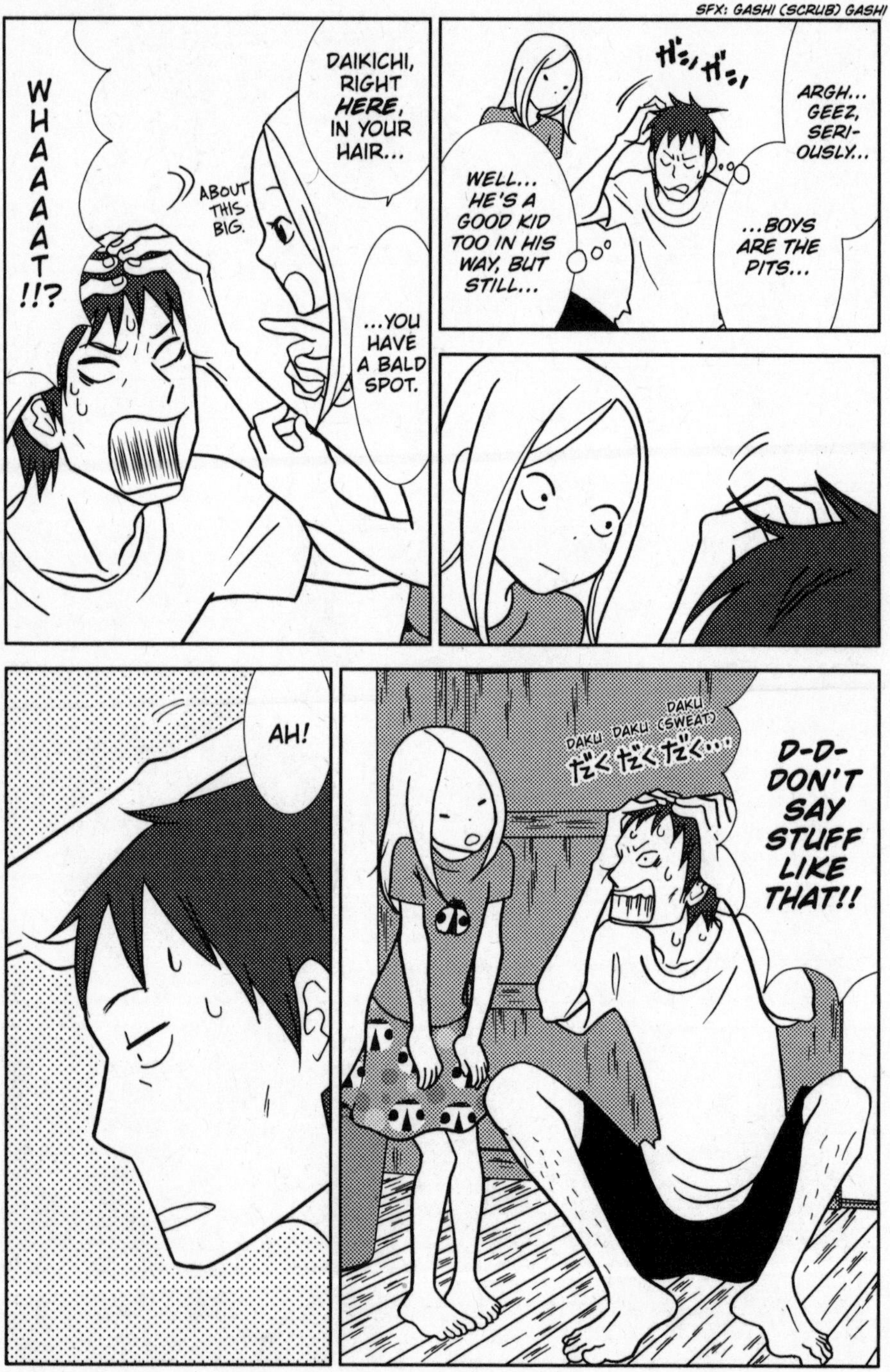
SFX: GASHI (SCRUB) GASHI
ガシッ ガシッ
ARGH... GEEZ, SERI-OUSLY...
...BOYS ARE THE PITS...
WELL... HE'S A GOOD KID TOO IN HIS WAY, BUT STILL...
DAIKICHI, RIGHT HERE, IN YOUR HAIR...
ABOUT THIS BIG.
...YOU HAVE A BALD SPOT.
WHAAAAAT!!?
D-D-DON'T SAY STUFF LIKE THAT!!
DAKU DAKU (SWEAT) DAKU
だく だく だく...
AH!

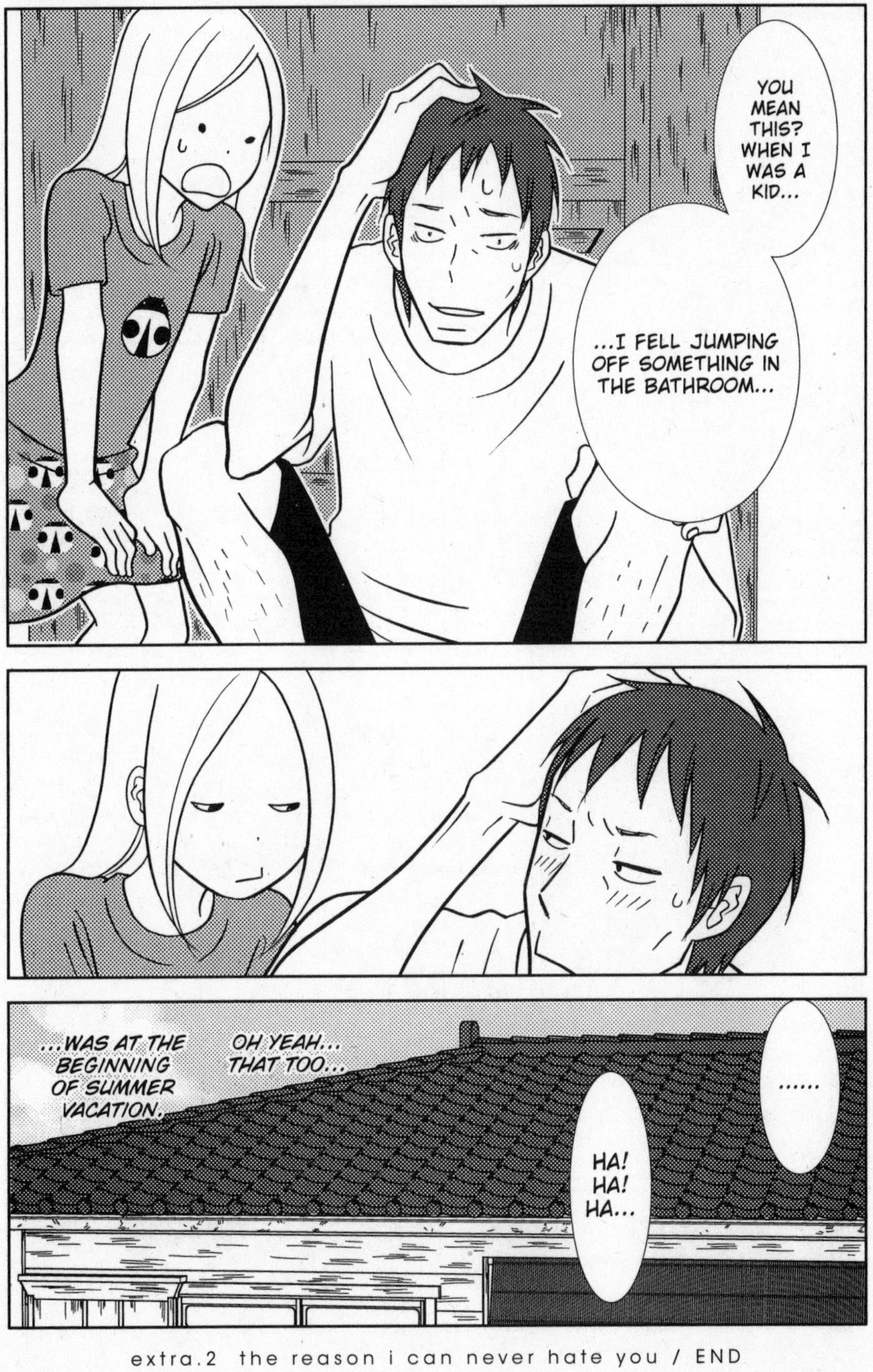
YOU MEAN THIS? WHEN I WAS A KID...
...I FELL JUMPING OFF SOMETHING IN THE BATHROOM...
......
HA! HA! HA...
OH YEAH... THAT TOO...
...WAS AT THE BEGINNING OF SUMMER VACATION.

extra.2 the reason i can never hate you / END

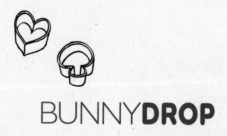

BUNNY**DROP**

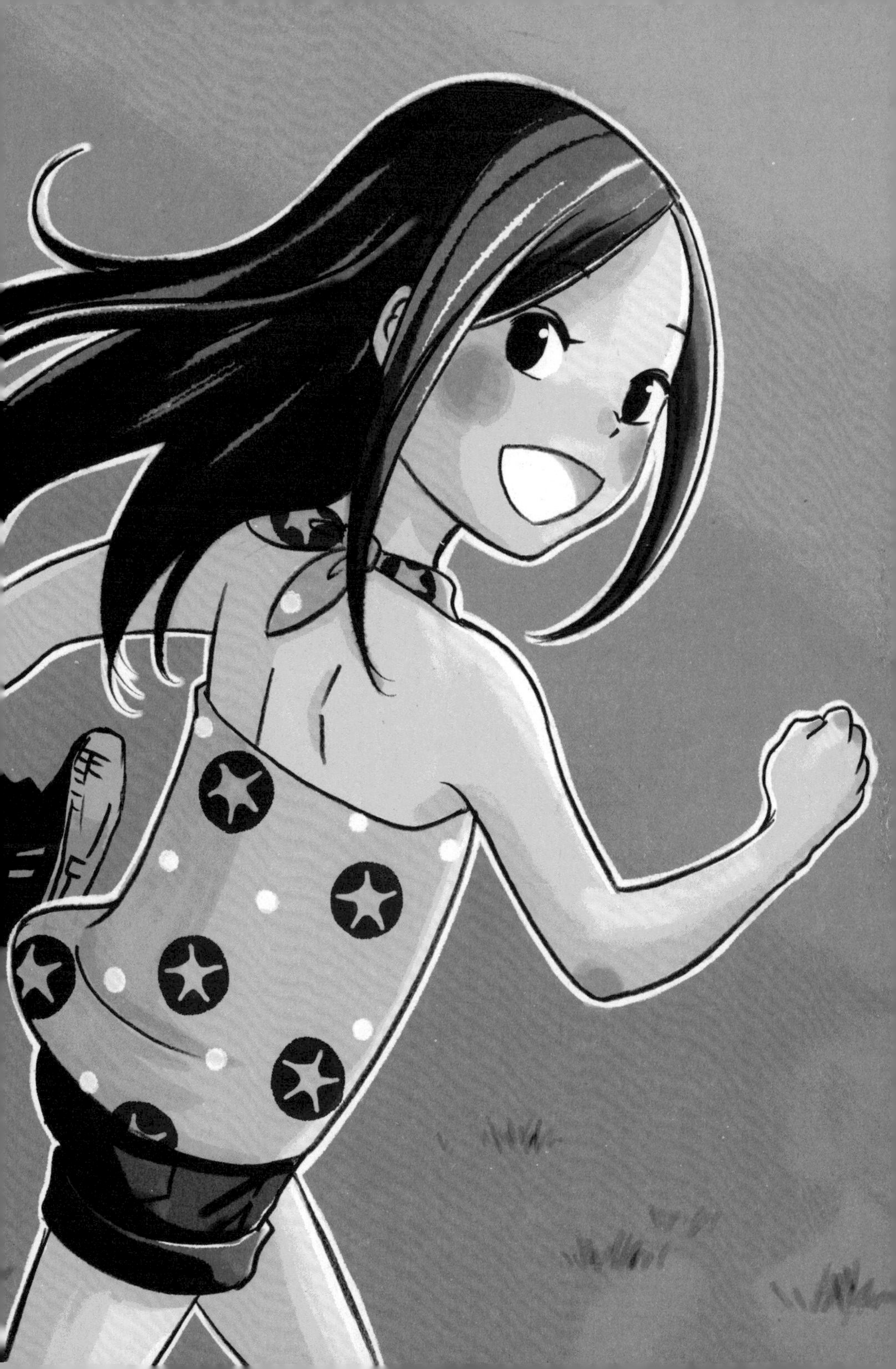

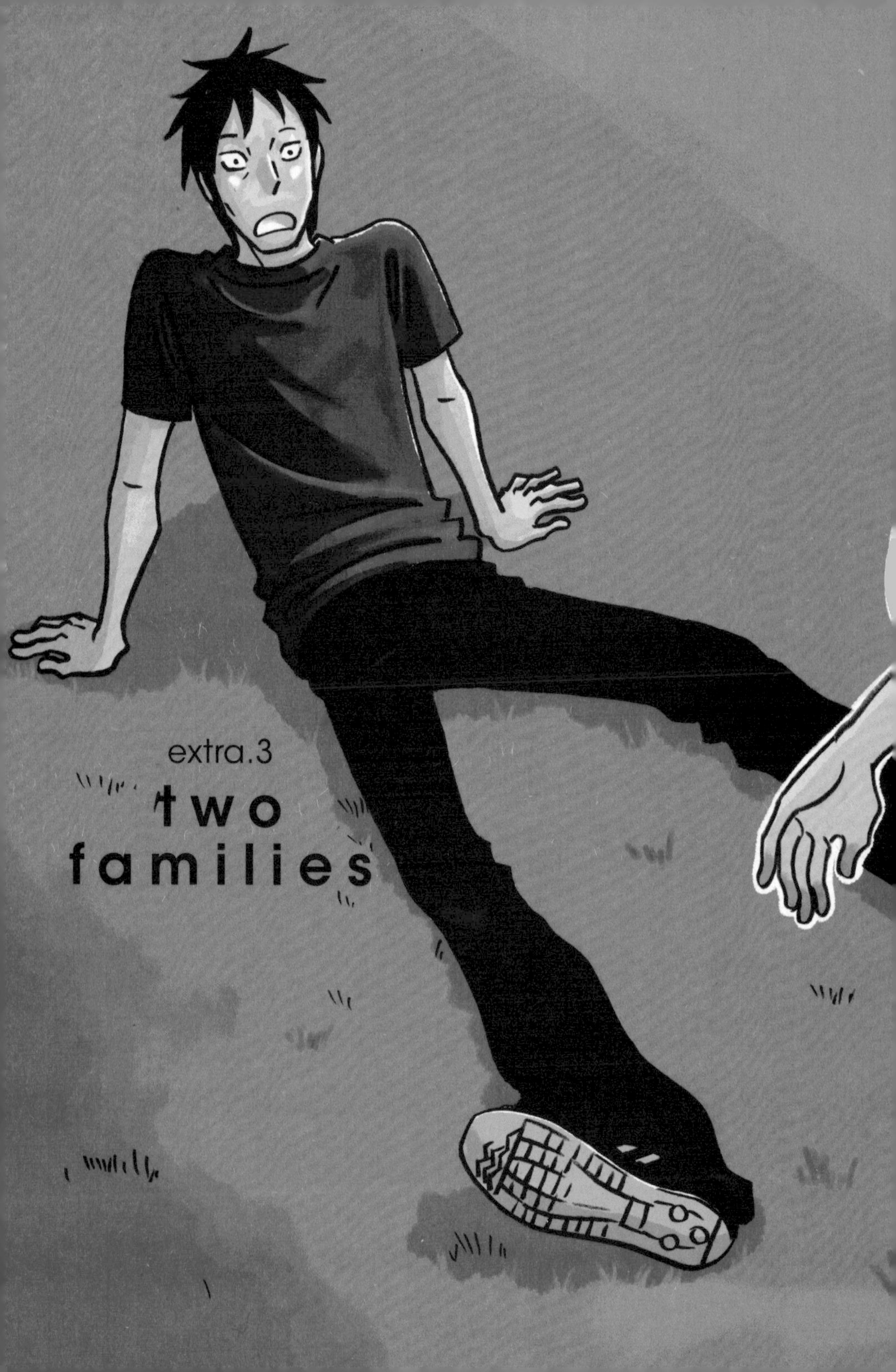
extra.3
two families

SIGN: HAPPY SMILES STUDENTS' CLUB

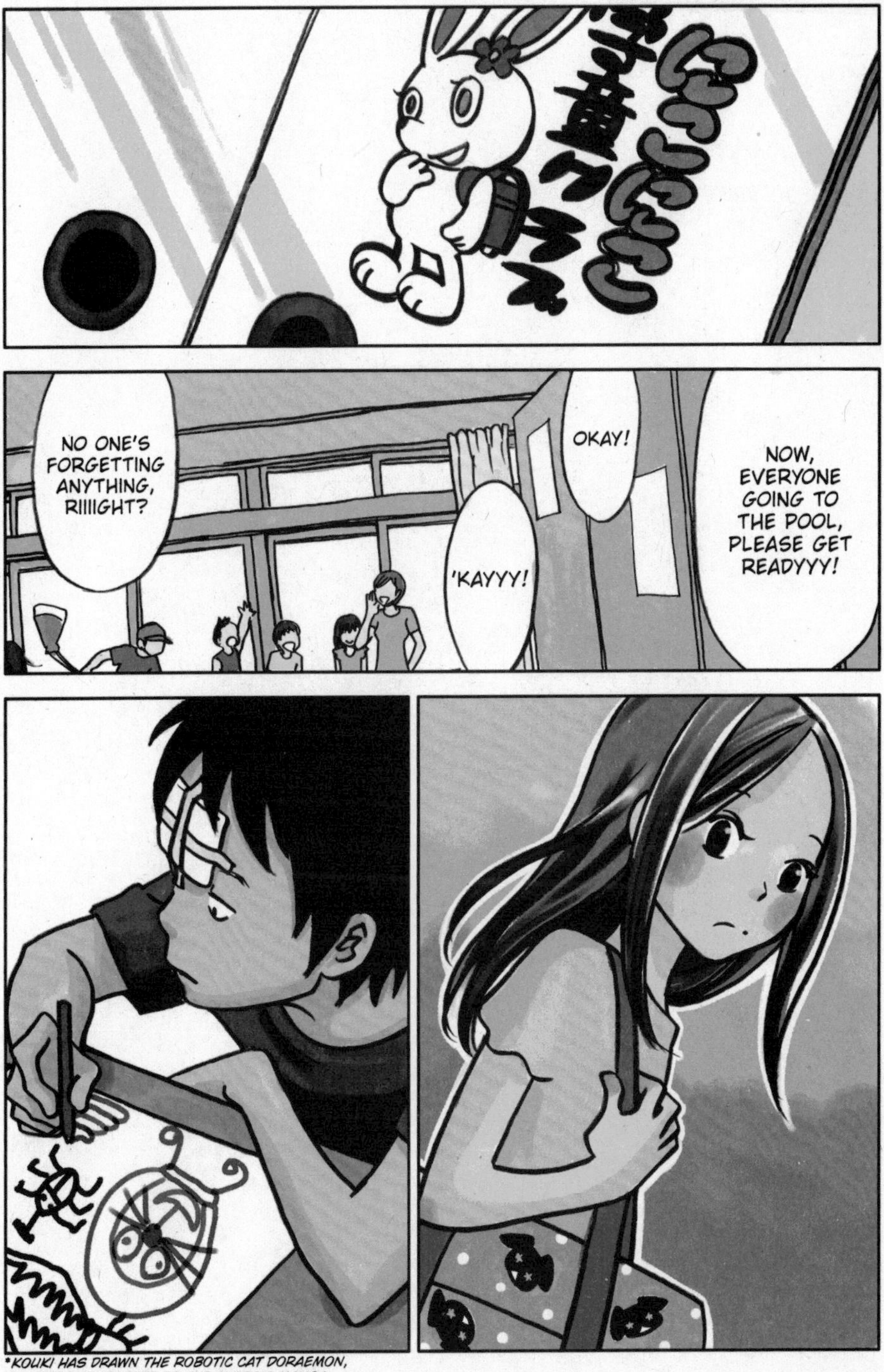
NOW, EVERYONE GOING TO THE POOL, PLEASE GET READYYY!
OKAY!
'KAYYY!
NO ONE'S FORGETTING ANYTHING, RIIIIGHT?

*KOUKI HAS DRAWN THE ROBOTIC CAT DORAEMON, THE TITLE CHARACTER OF THE CLASSIC MANGA SERIES BY THE LEGENDARY ARTIST FUJIKO FUJIO.

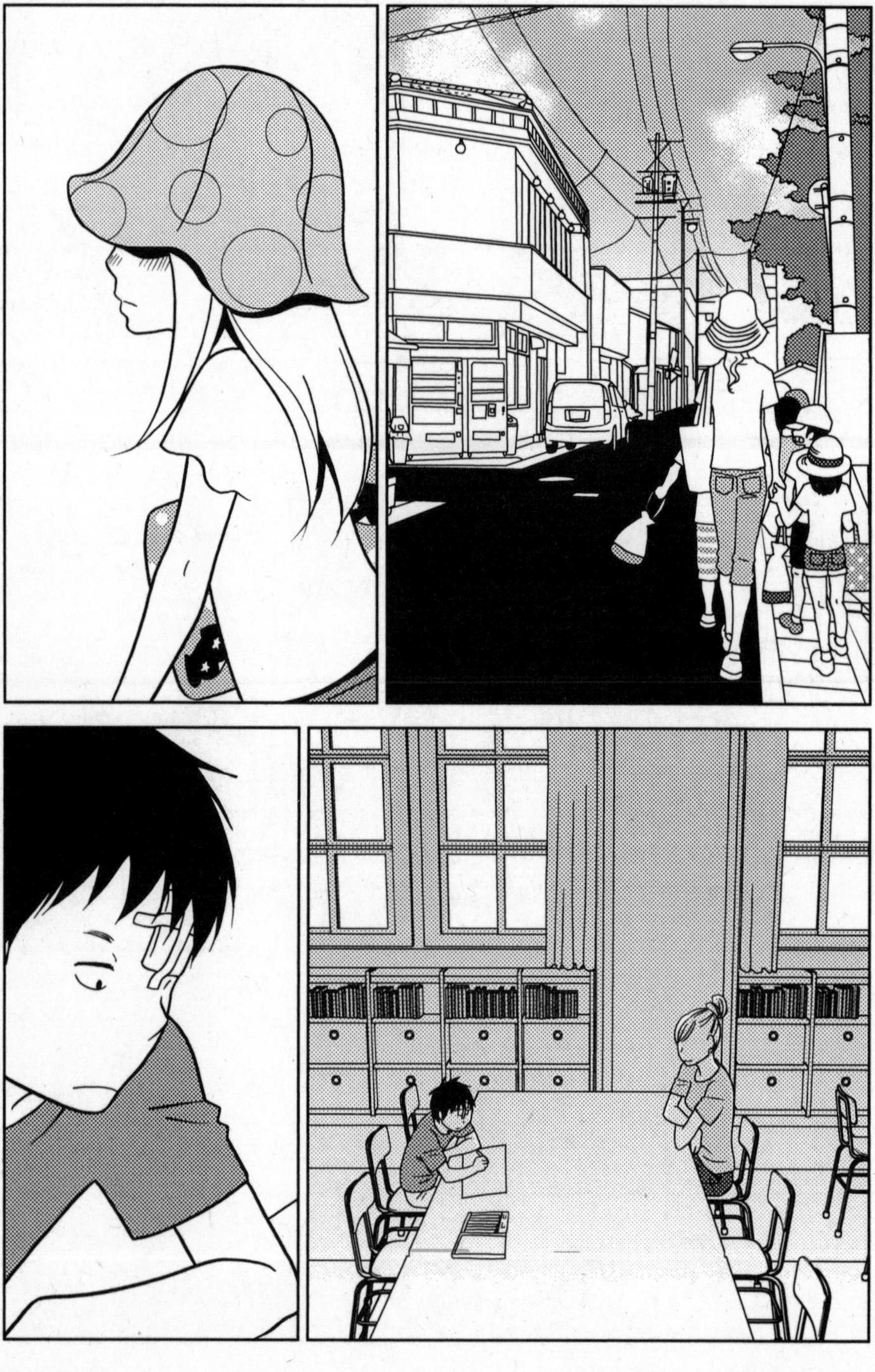

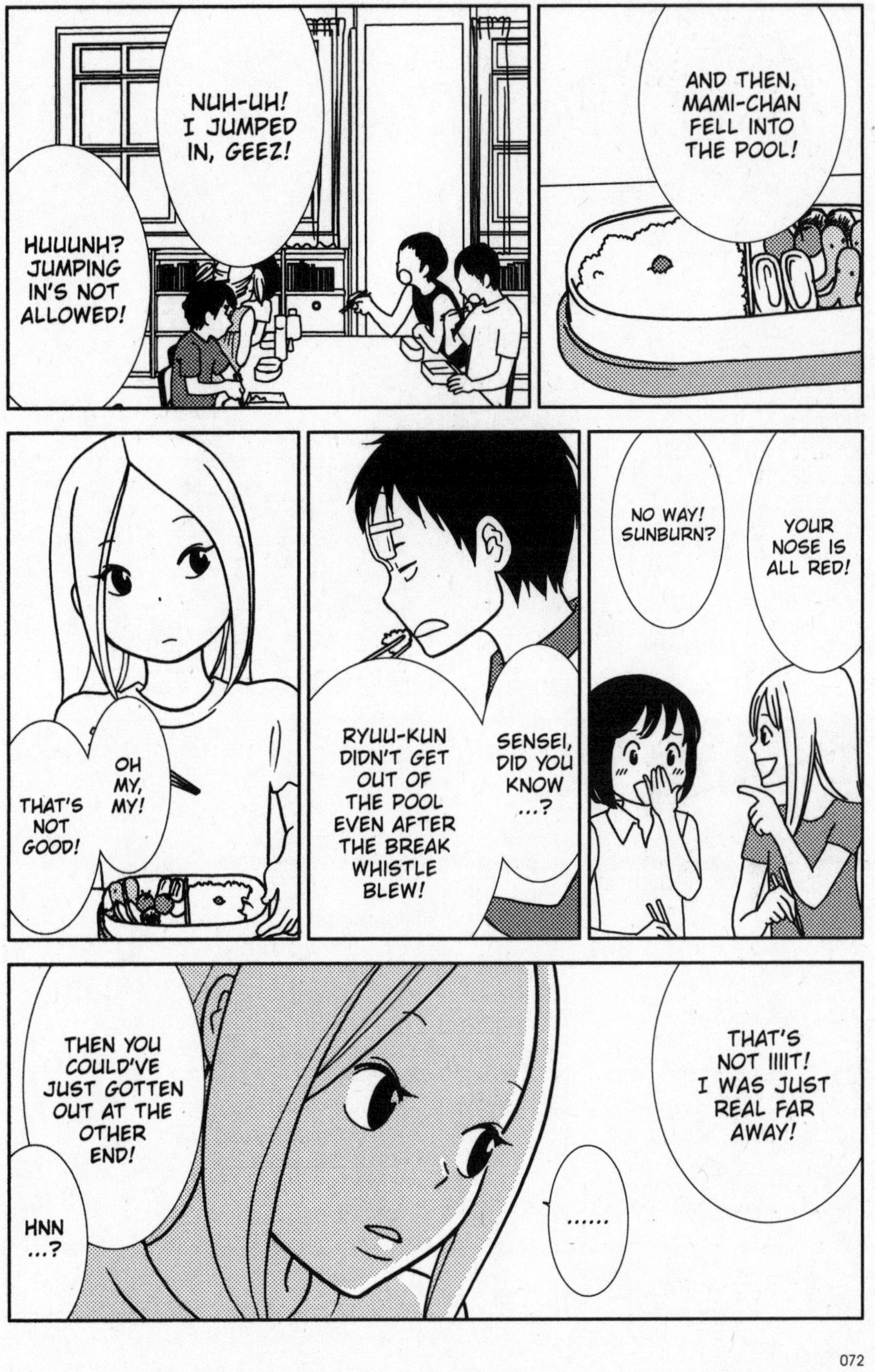
AND THEN, MAMI-CHAN FELL INTO THE POOL!
NUH-UH! I JUMPED IN, GEEZ!
HUUUNH? JUMPING IN'S NOT ALLOWED!
YOUR NOSE IS ALL RED!
NO WAY! SUNBURN?
SENSEI, DID YOU KNOW ...?
RYUU-KUN DIDN'T GET OUT OF THE POOL EVEN AFTER THE BREAK WHISTLE BLEW!
OH MY, MY!
THAT'S NOT GOOD!
THAT'S NOT IIIIT! I WAS JUST REAL FAR AWAY!
......
THEN YOU COULD'VE JUST GOTTEN OUT AT THE OTHER END!
HNN ...?

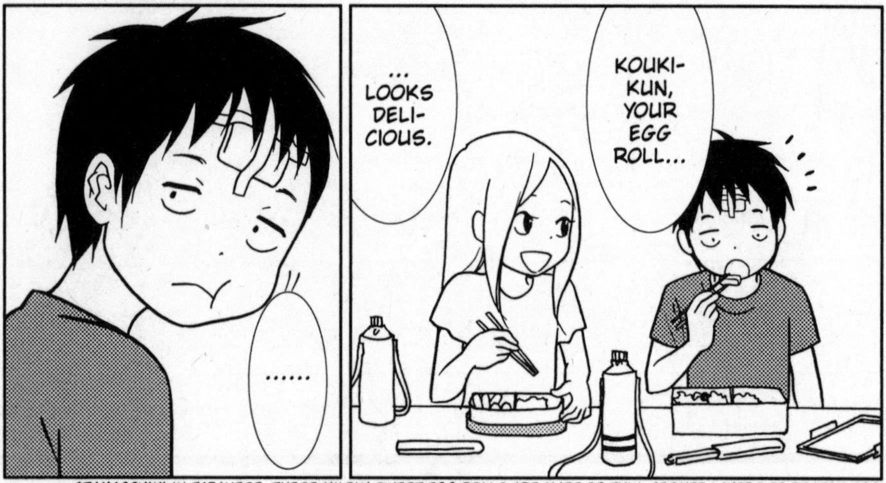
KOUKI-KUN, YOUR EGG ROLL...
...LOOKS DELI-CIOUS.
......

*TAMAGOYAKI IN JAPANESE, THESE MILDLY SWEET EGG ROLLS ARE MADE OF THIN, COOKED LAYERS OF BEATEN EGG.

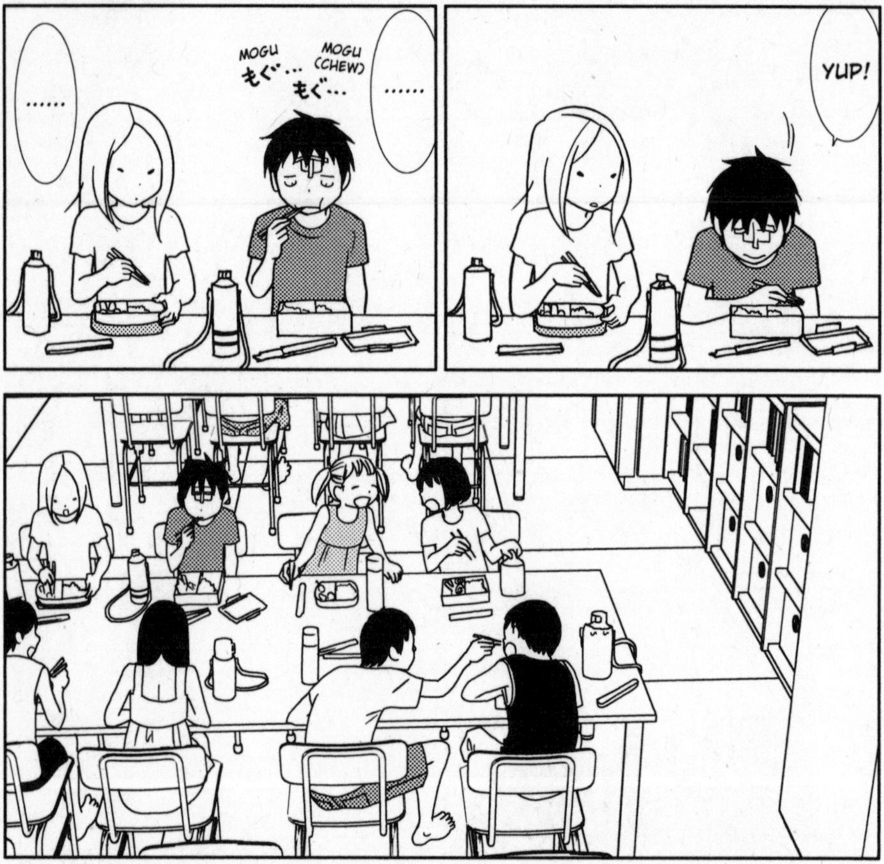
YUP!
......
MOGU (CHEW) もぐ...
MOGU もぐ...
......

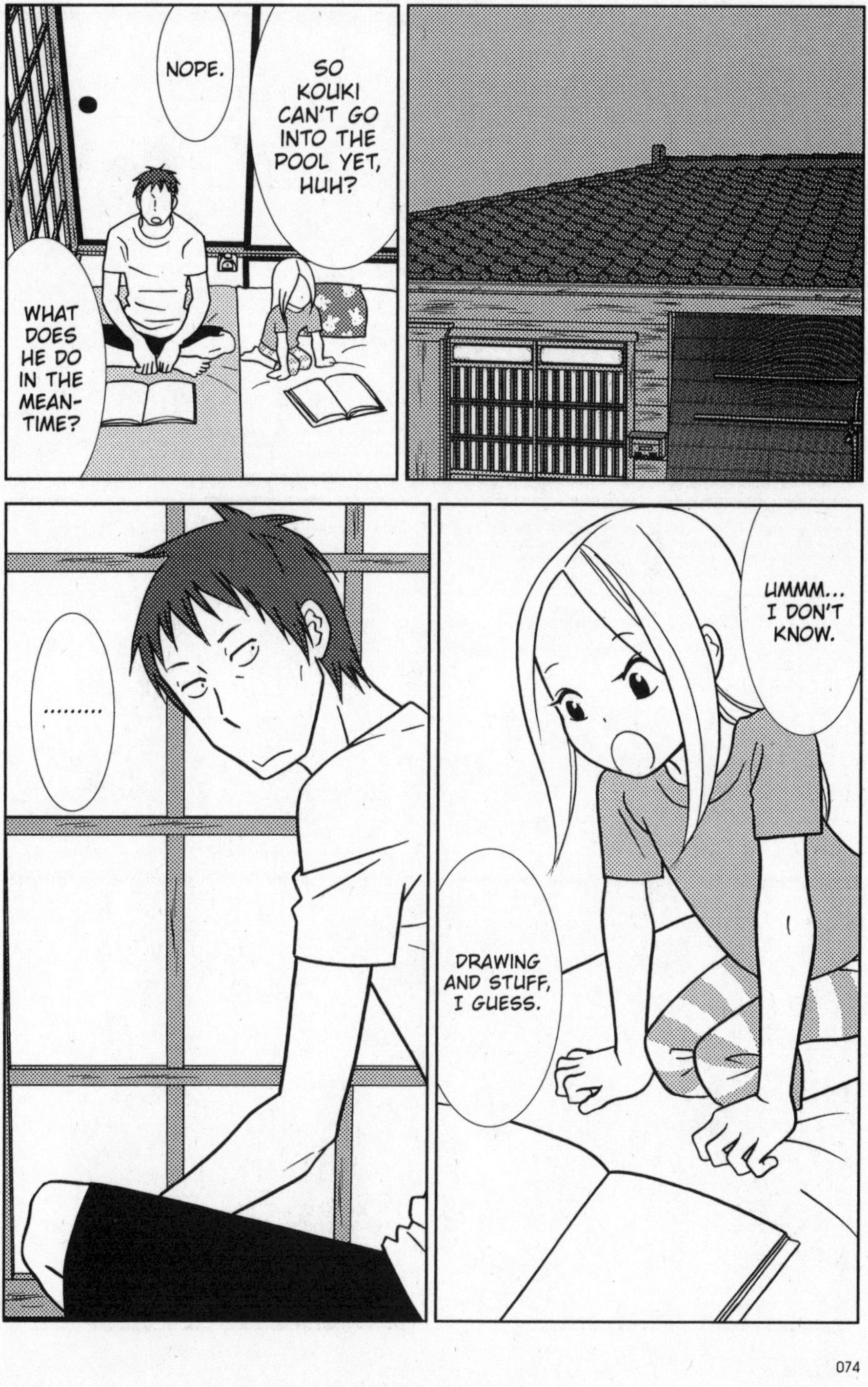
SO KOUKI CAN'T GO INTO THE POOL YET, HUH?
NOPE.
WHAT DOES HE DO IN THE MEAN-TIME?
UMMM... I DON'T KNOW.
DRAWING AND STUFF, I GUESS.
....

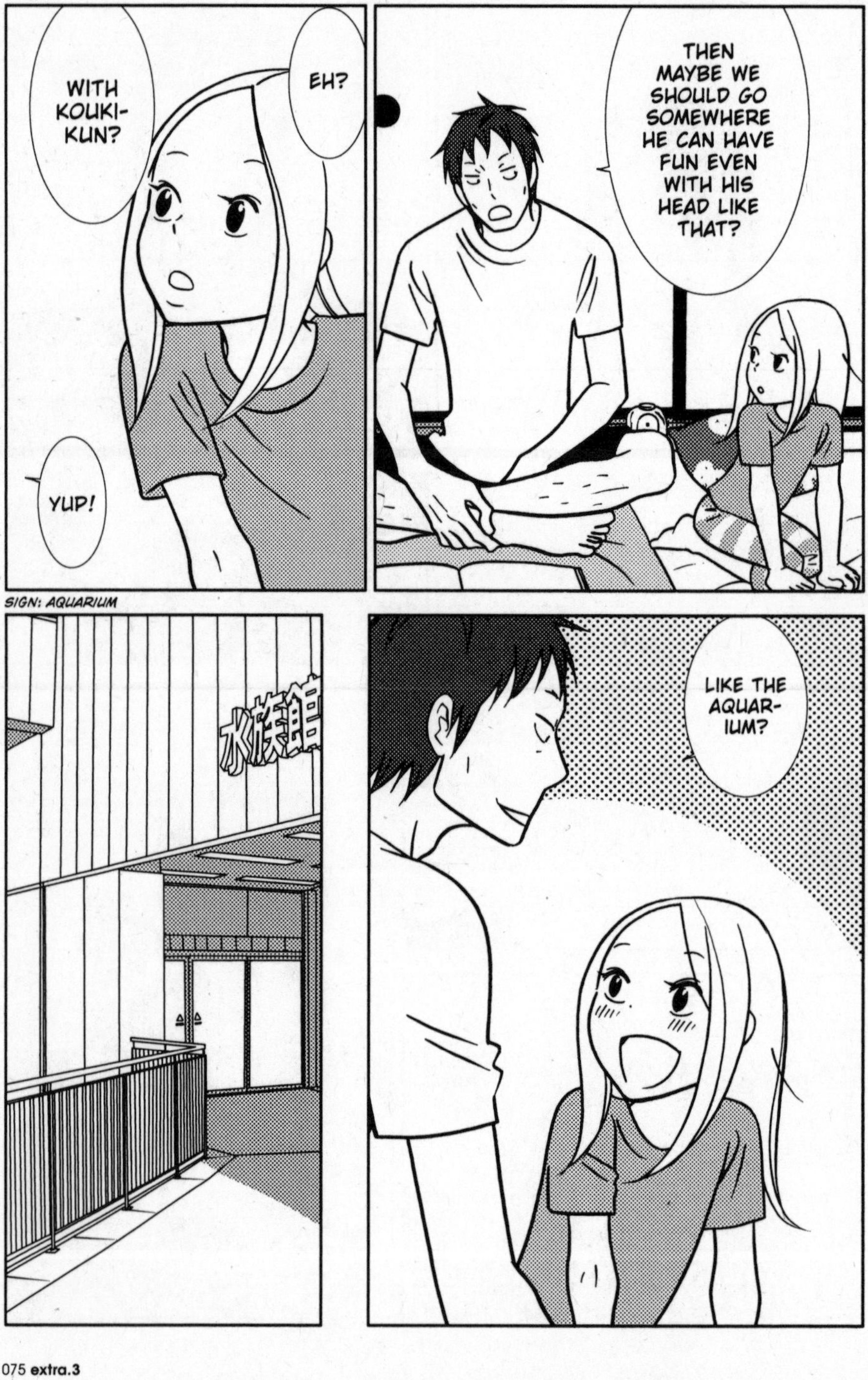
THEN MAYBE WE SHOULD GO SOMEWHERE HE CAN HAVE FUN EVEN WITH HIS HEAD LIKE THAT?
EH?
WITH KOUKI-KUN?
YUP!
LIKE THE AQUARIUM?
SIGN: AQUARIUM
水族館

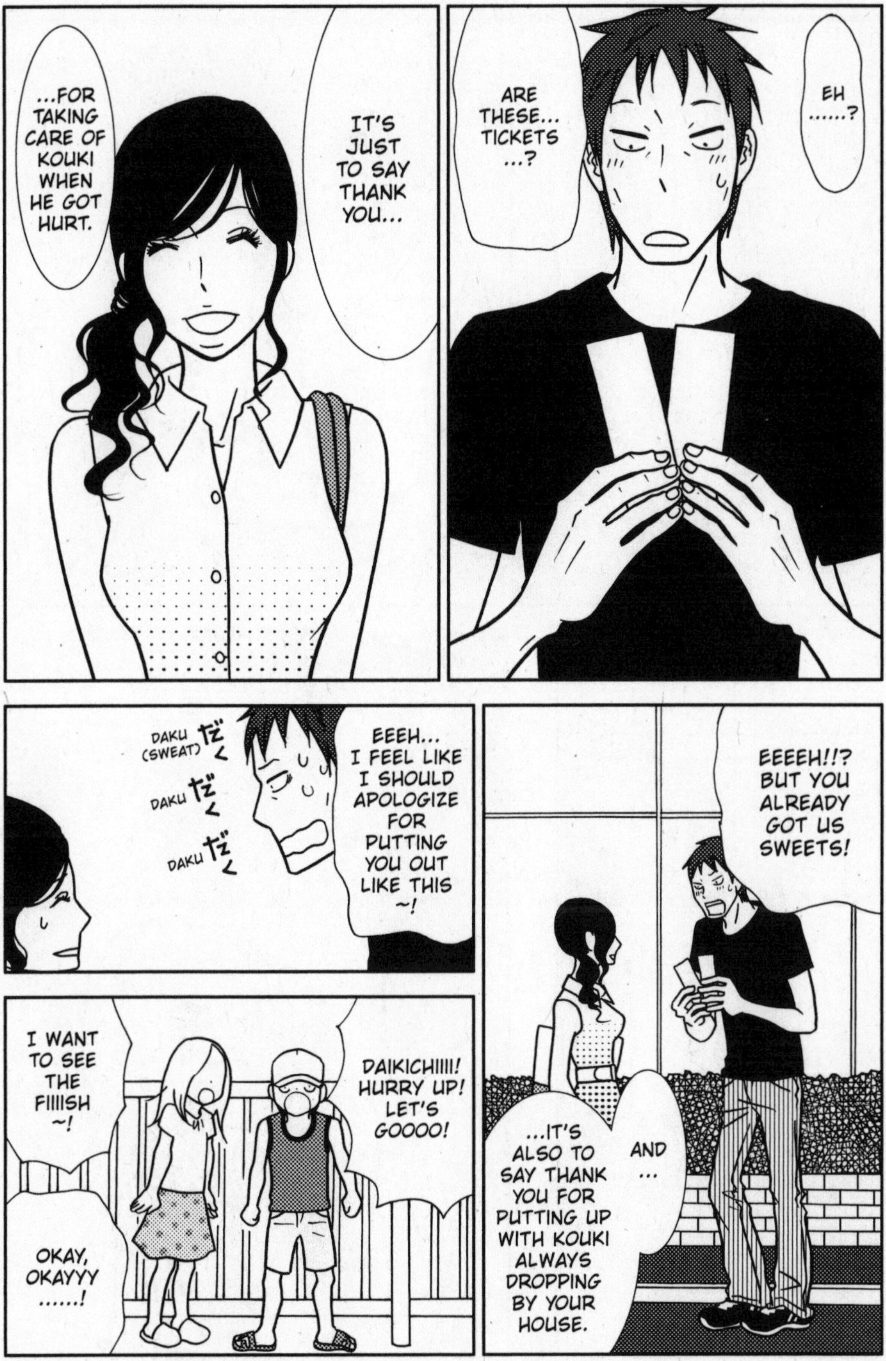

EH ......?
ARE THESE... TICKETS ...?
IT'S JUST TO SAY THANK YOU...
...FOR TAKING CARE OF KOUKI WHEN HE GOT HURT.
EEEEH!!? BUT YOU ALREADY GOT US SWEETS!
AND ...
...IT'S ALSO TO SAY THANK YOU FOR PUTTING UP WITH KOUKI ALWAYS DROPPING BY YOUR HOUSE.
EEEH... I FEEL LIKE I SHOULD APOLOGIZE FOR PUTTING YOU OUT LIKE THIS ~!
DAKU (SWEAT) だく
DAKU だく
DAKU だく
DAIKICHIIIII! HURRY UP! LET'S GOOOO!
I WANT TO SEE THE FIIIISH ~!
OKAY, OKAYYY ......!

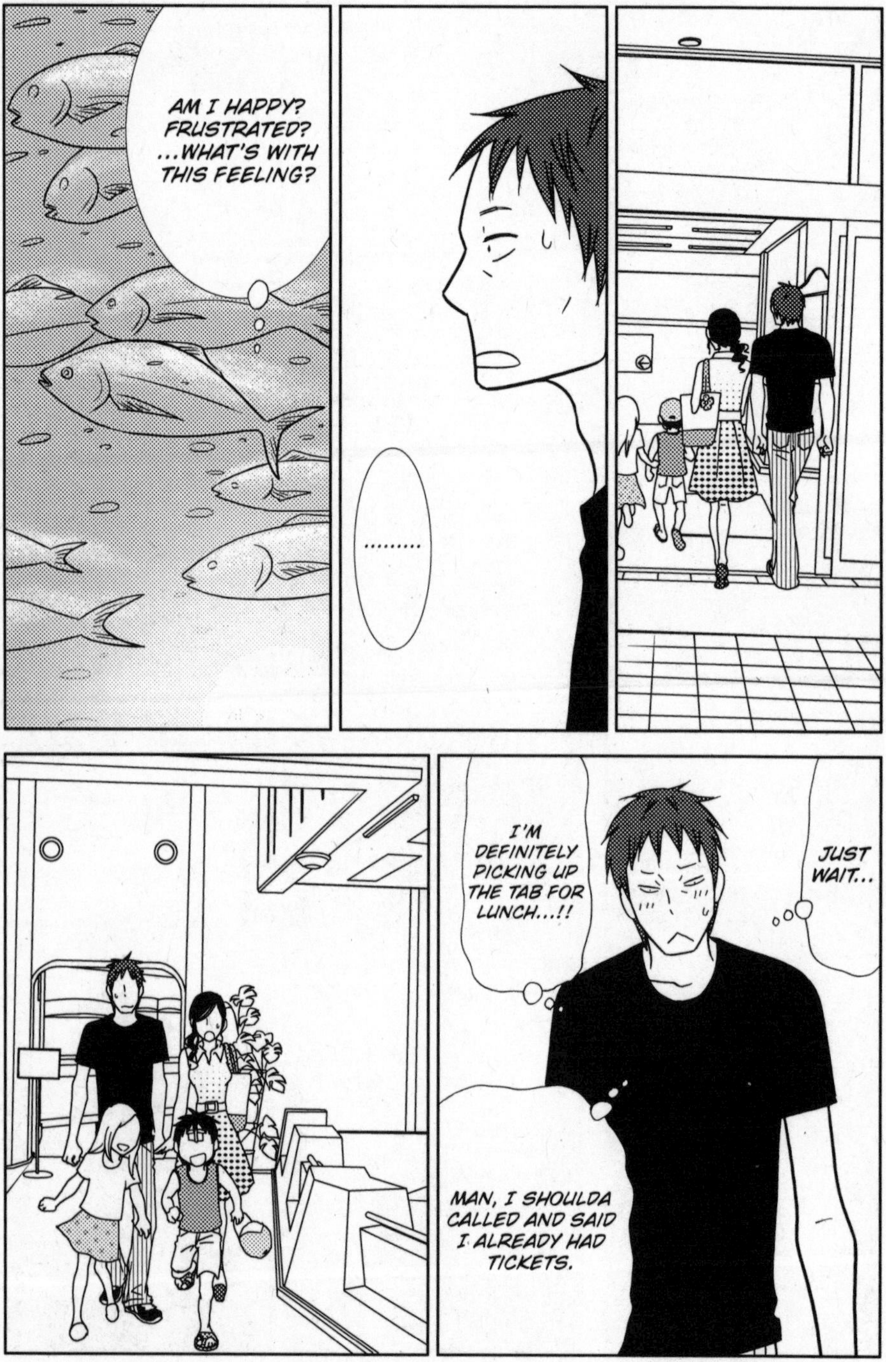
....
AM I HAPPY? FRUSTRATED? ...WHAT'S WITH THIS FEELING?
JUST WAIT...
I'M DEFINITELY PICKING UP THE TAB FOR LUNCH...!!
MAN, I SHOULDA CALLED AND SAID I ALREADY HAD TICKETS.

SIGN: AFRICAN POMPANO

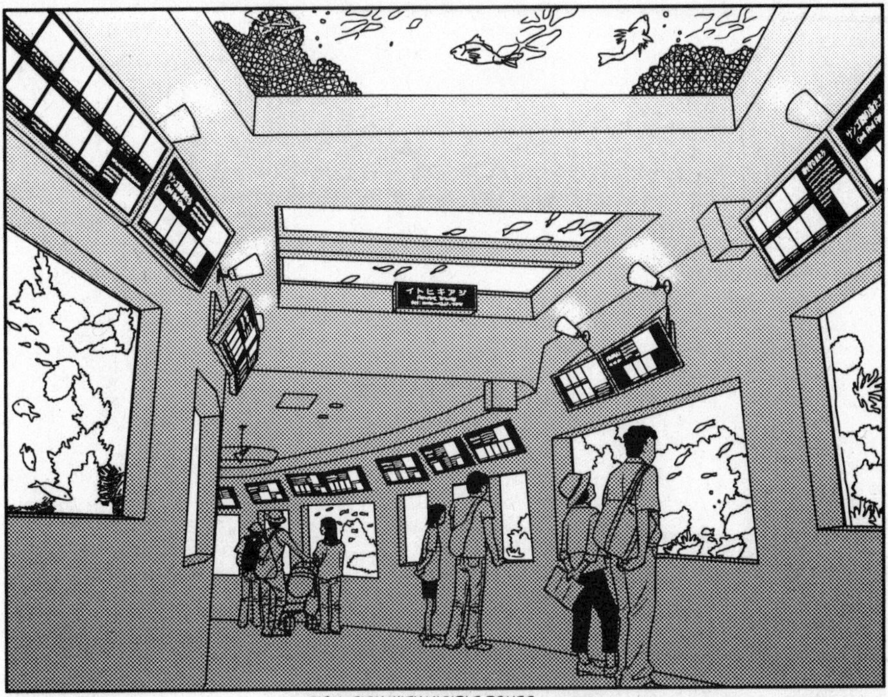

SIGN: FISH WITH VISIBLE BONES

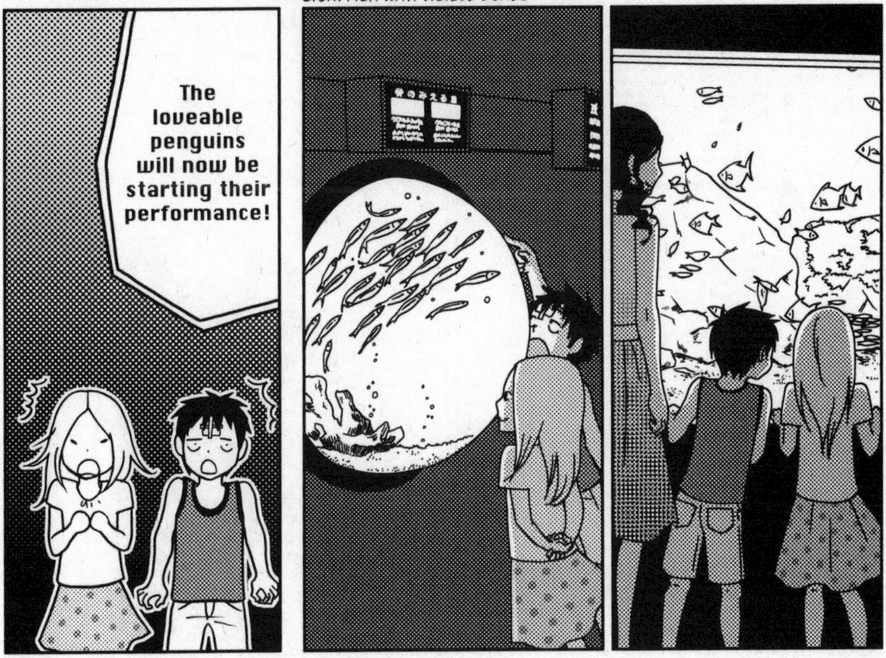
The loveable penguins will now be starting their performance!

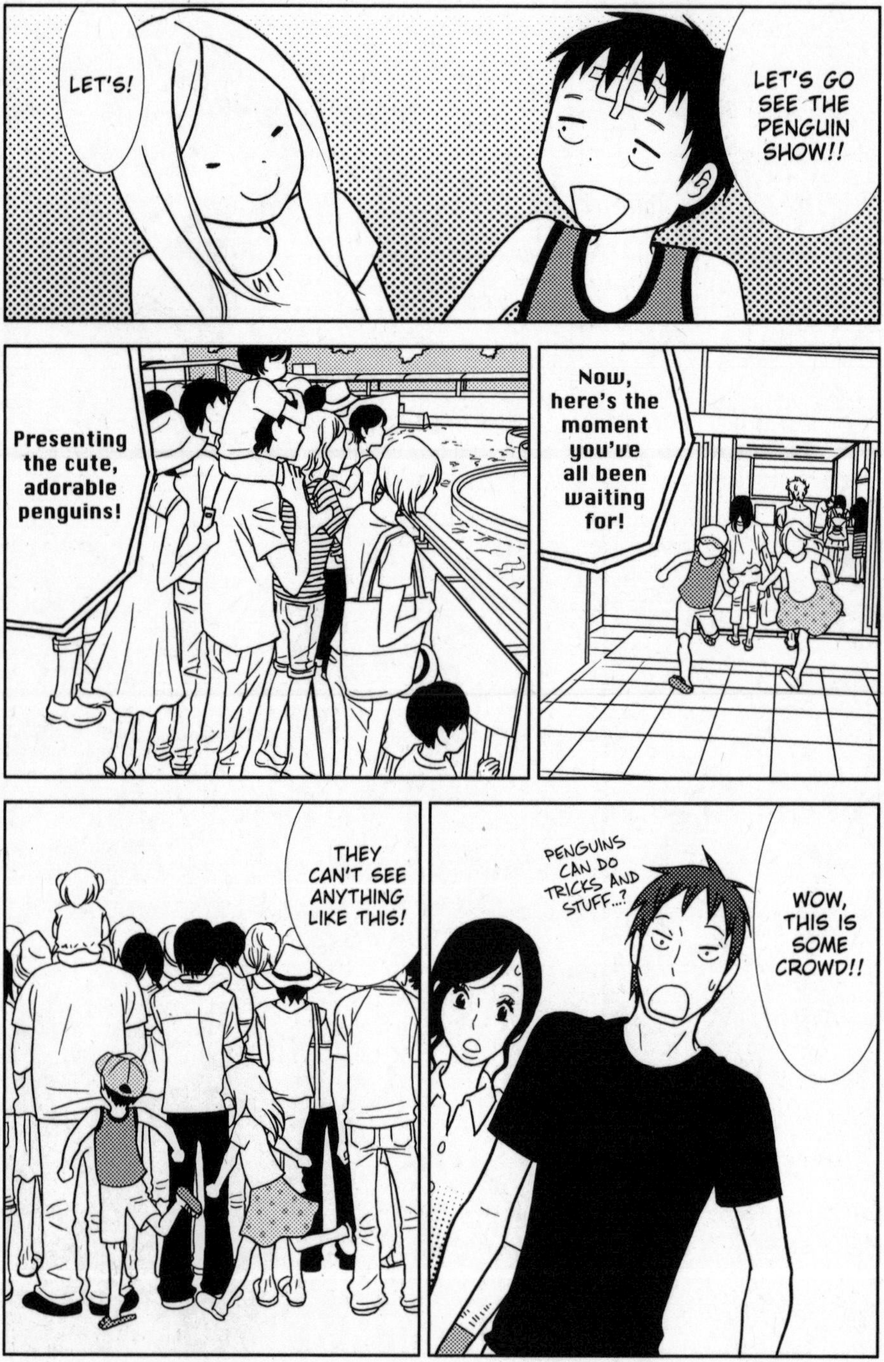
LET'S GO SEE THE PENGUIN SHOW!!
LET'S!
Now, here's the moment you've all been waiting for!
Presenting the cute, adorable penguins!
WOW, THIS IS SOME CROWD!!
PENGUINS CAN DO TRICKS AND STUFF...?
THEY CAN'T SEE ANYTHING LIKE THIS!

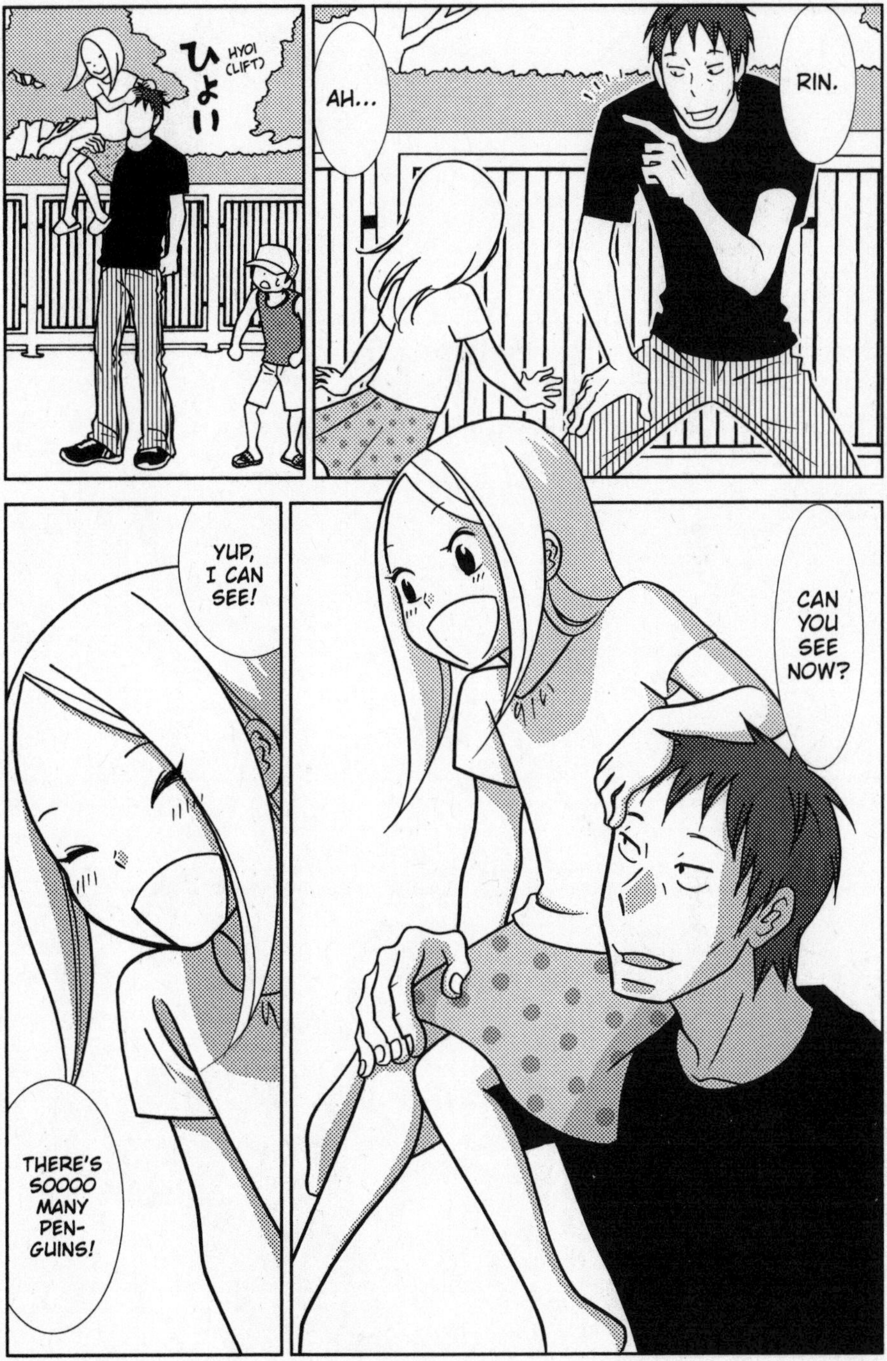
RIN.
AH...
ひょい
HYOI (LIFT)
CAN YOU SEE NOW?
YUP, I CAN SEE!
THERE'S SOOOO MANY PEN-GUINS!

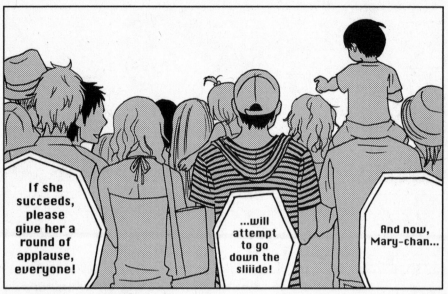

And now, Mary-chan...
...will attempt to go down the sliiide!
If she succeeds, please give her a round of applause, everyone!
LOOK AT THE LITTLE BABIES!
SO CUUUTE! ♥
HA-HA-HA. CUTE TRICKS.
High High

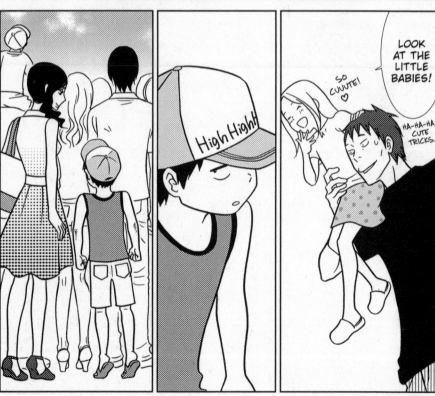

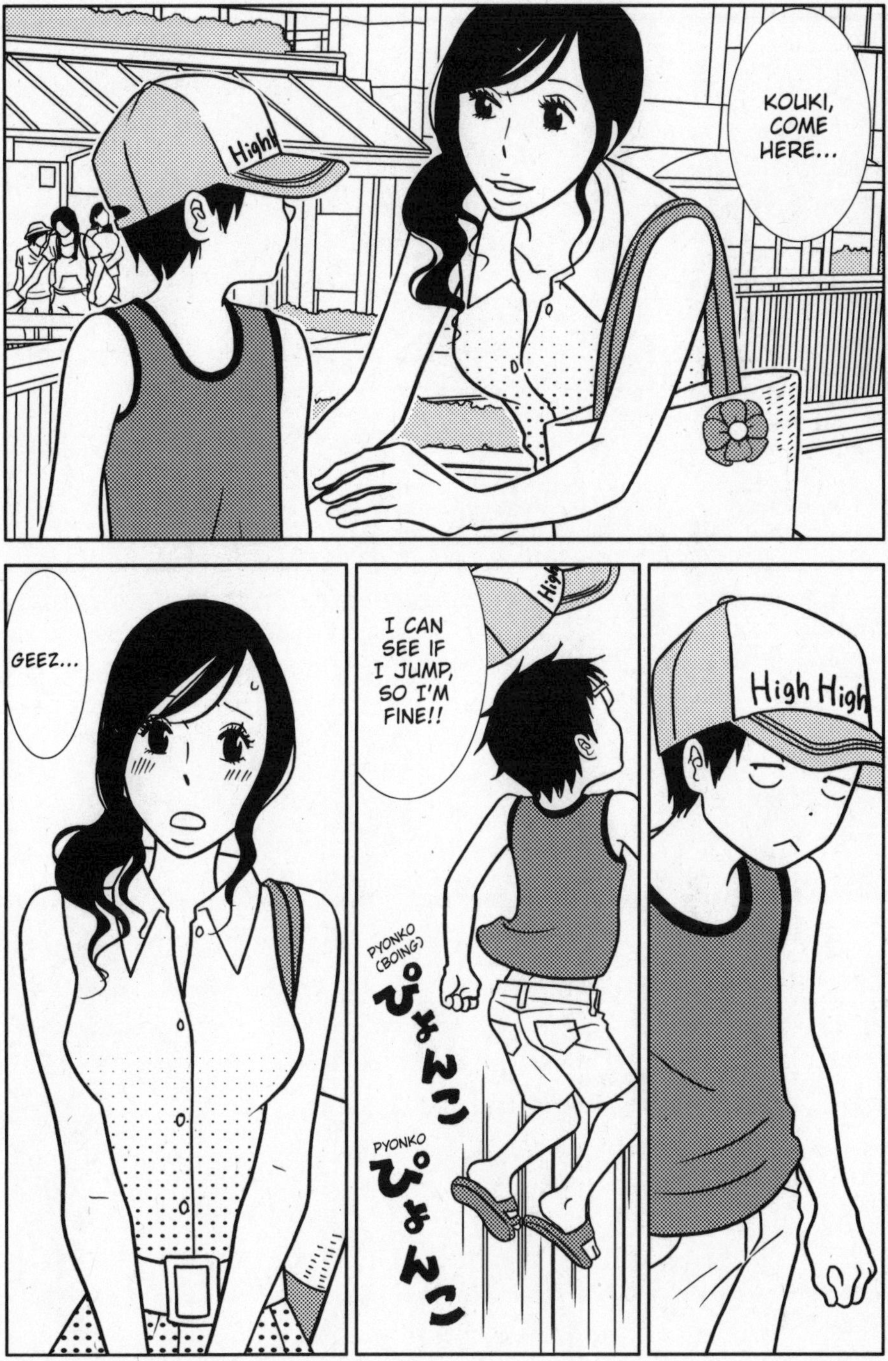
KOUKI, COME HERE...
High High
I CAN SEE IF I JUMP, SO I'M FINE!!
PYONKO (BOING)
ぴょんこ
PYONKO
ぴょんこ
GEEZ...

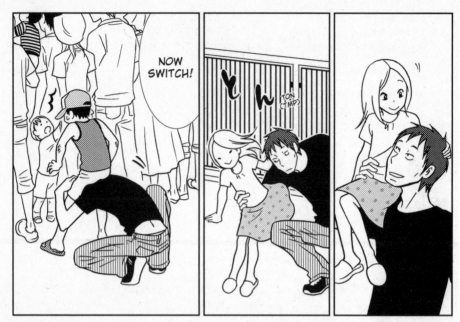

NOW
SWITCH!

ㄷ ㄴ ..
TON
(TMP)

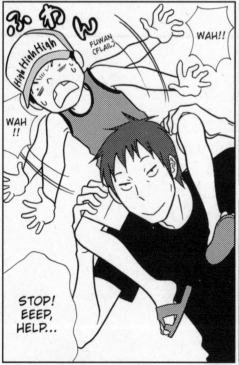

High High High
FUWAN
(FLAIL)

WAH!!

WAH
!!

STOP!
EEEP,
HELP...

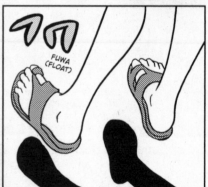

マ口
FUWA
(FLOAT)

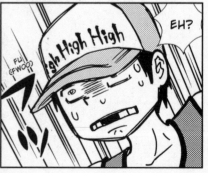

gh High High
FU
(FWOO)

EH?

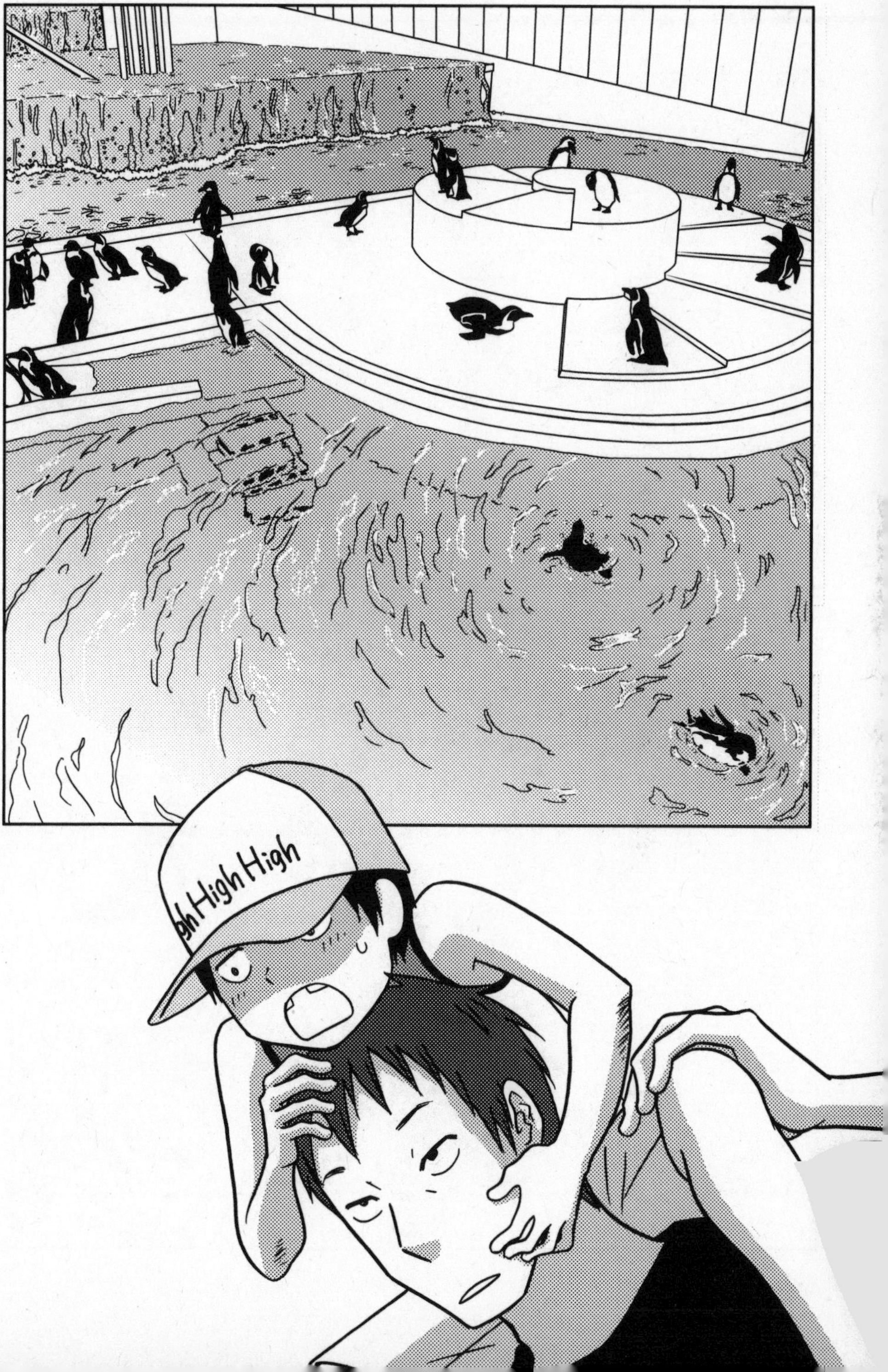
High High

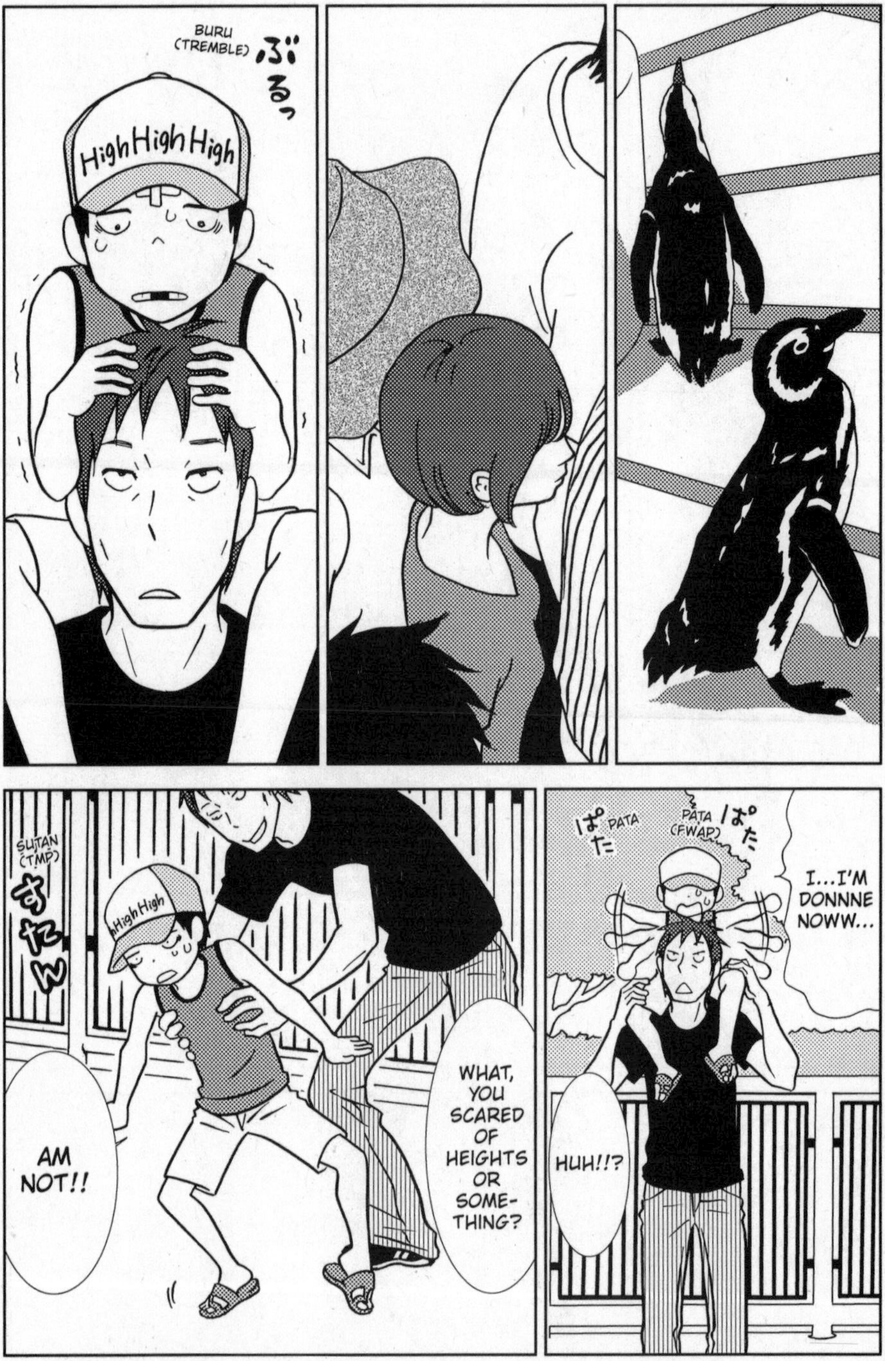
BURU (TREMBLE)
ぶるっ
PATA (FWAP)
ぱた
I...I'M DONNNE NOWW...
ぱた
PATA
HUH!!?
SUTAN (TMP)
すたん
WHAT, YOU SCARED OF HEIGHTS OR SOME-THING?
AM NOT!!

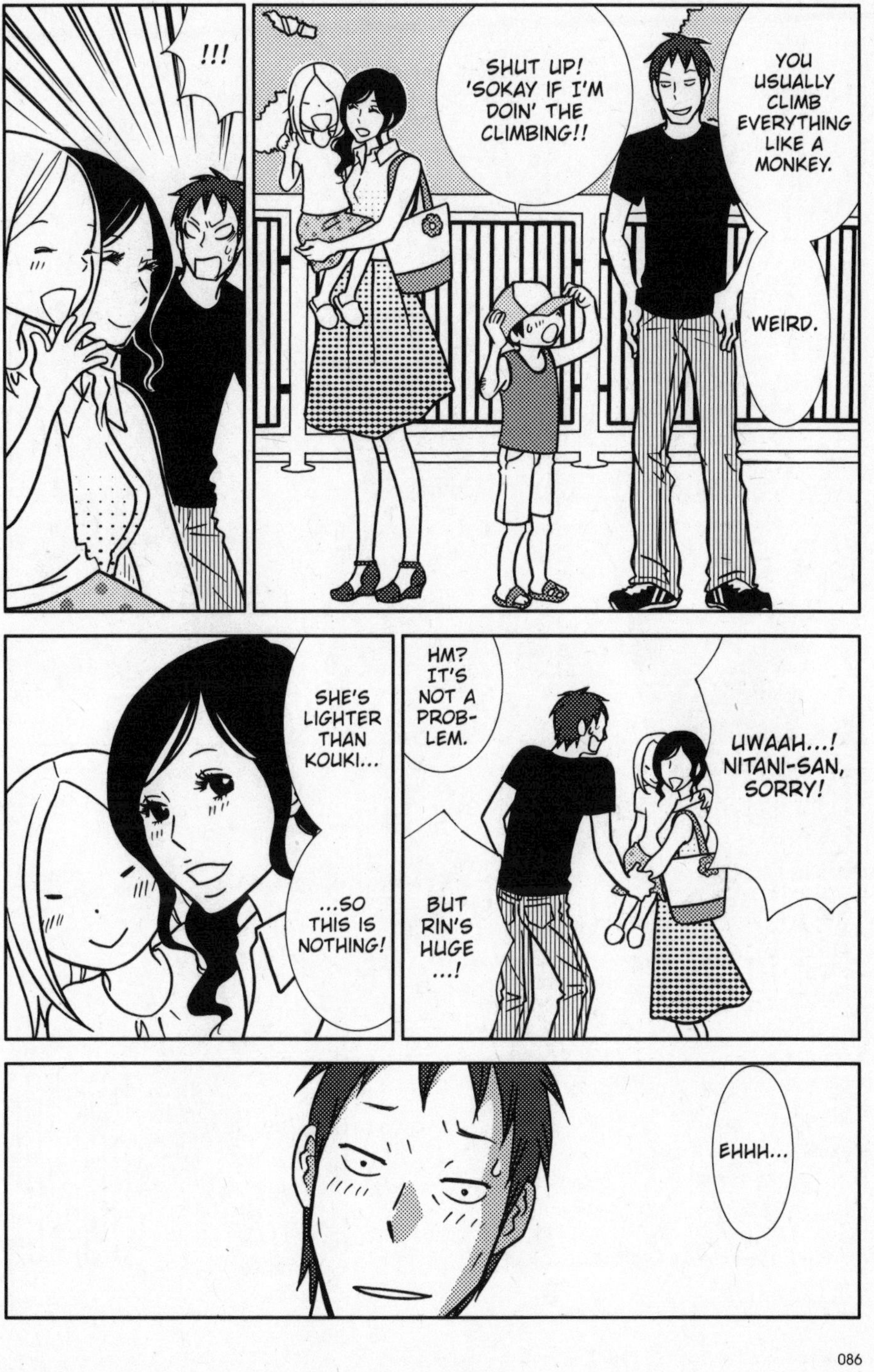
YOU USUALLY CLIMB EVERYTHING LIKE A MONKEY.
WEIRD.
SHUT UP! 'SOKAY IF I'M DOIN' THE CLIMBING!!
!!!
UWAAH...! NITANI-SAN, SORRY!
HM? IT'S NOT A PROB-LEM.
BUT RIN'S HUGE ...!
SHE'S LIGHTER THAN KOUKI...
...SO THIS IS NOTHING!
EHHH...

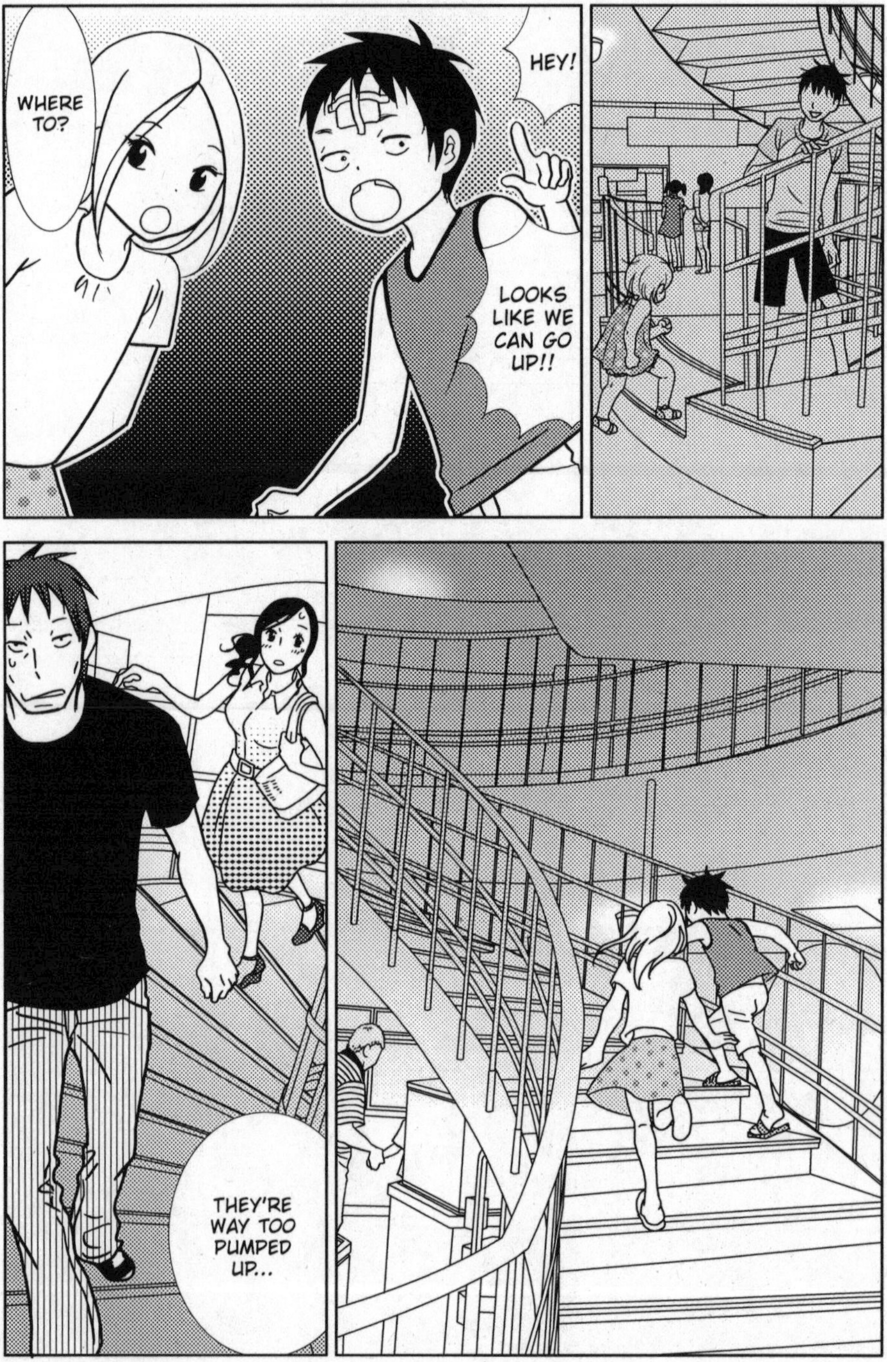
HEY!
LOOKS LIKE WE CAN GO UP!!
WHERE TO?
THEY'RE WAY TOO PUMPED UP...

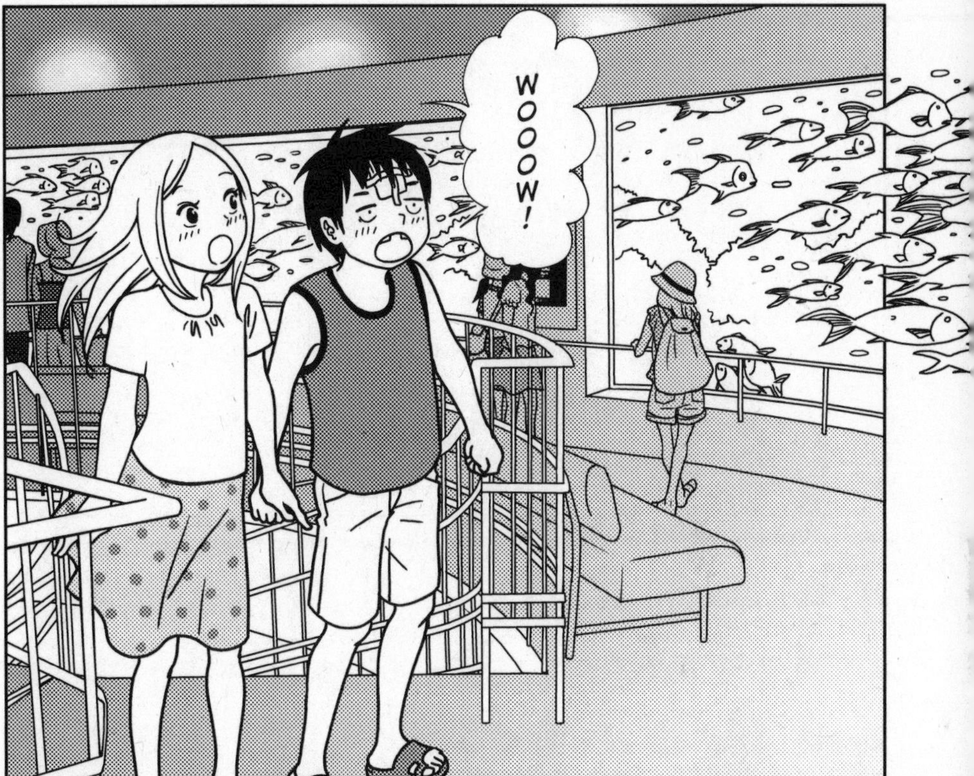
WOOOOW!
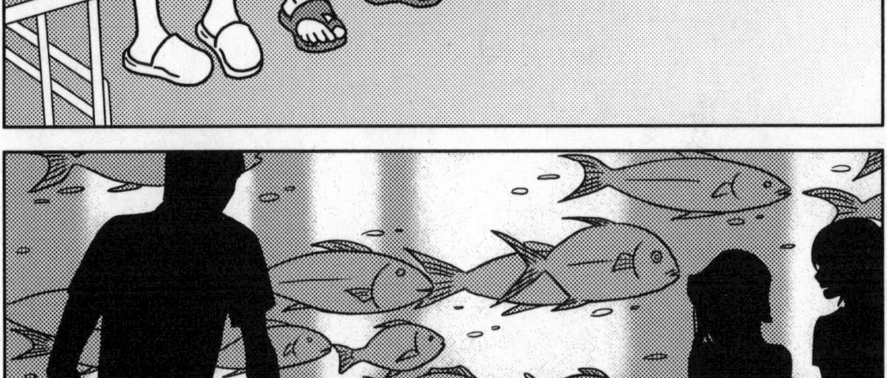

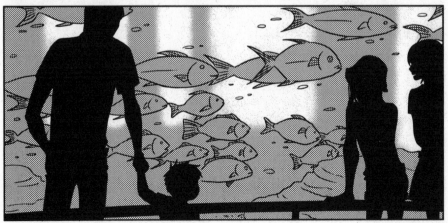

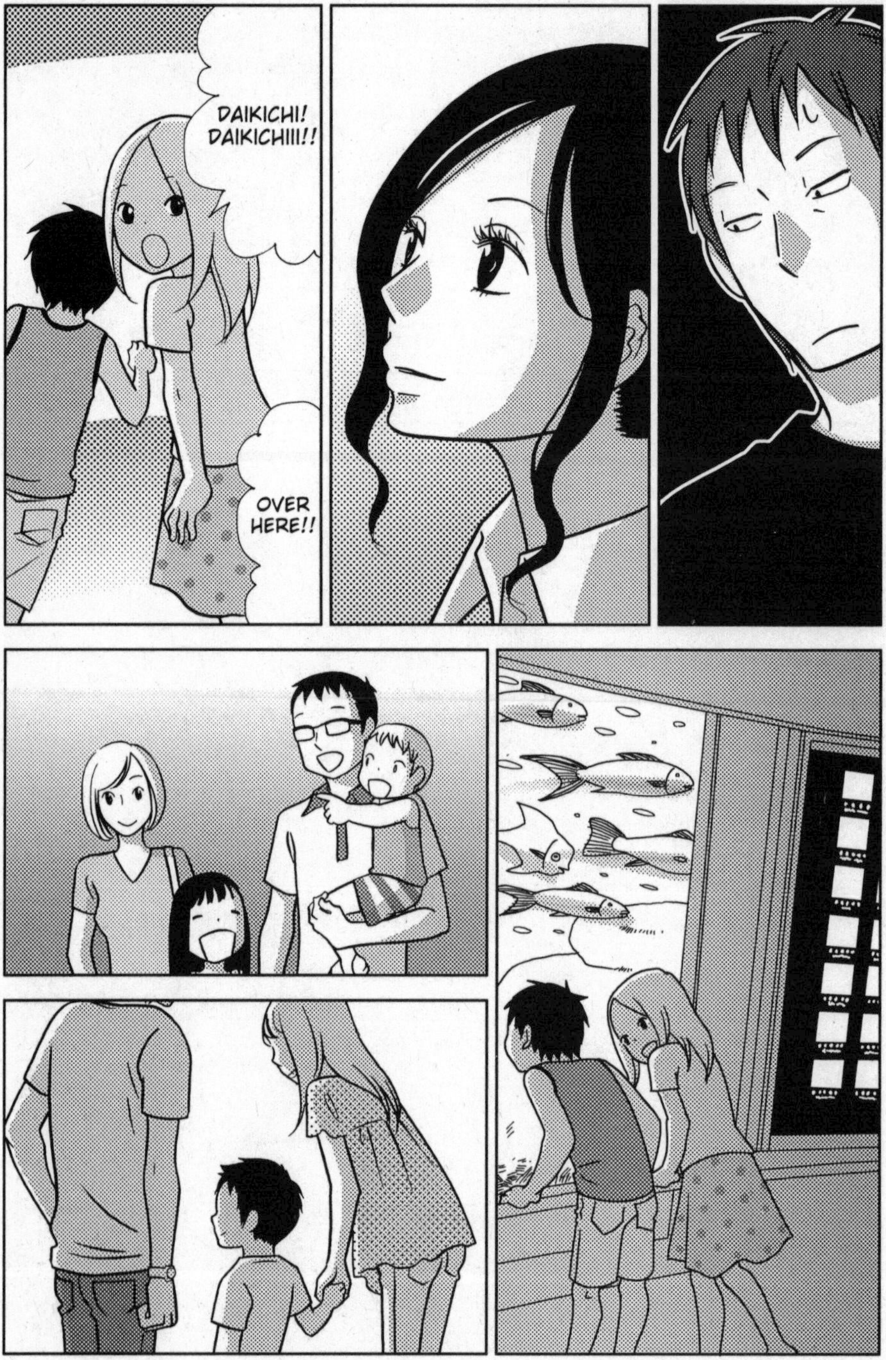
DAIKICHI! DAIKICHIII!!
OVER HERE!!

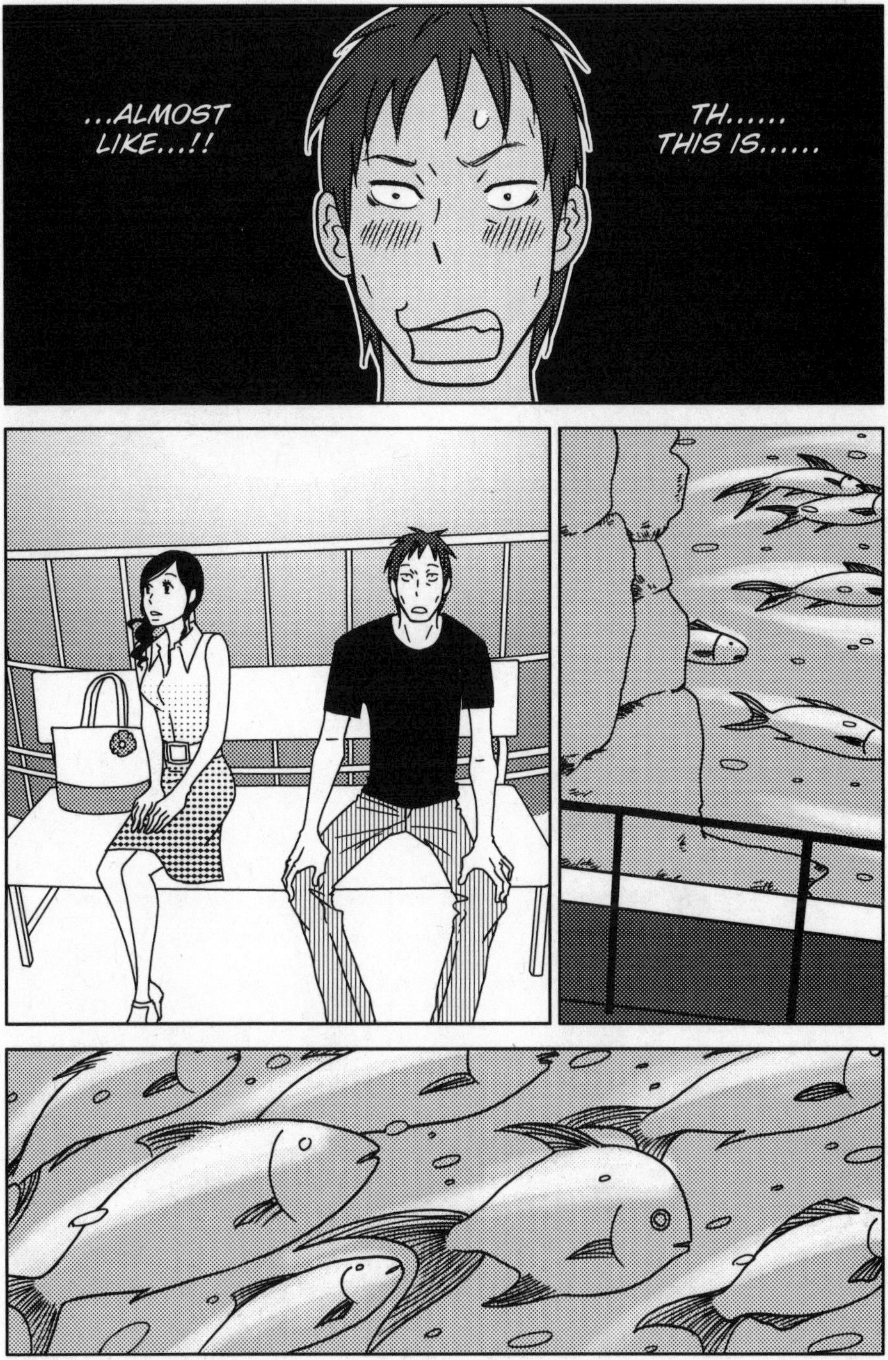
TH......
THIS IS......
...ALMOST
LIKE...!!

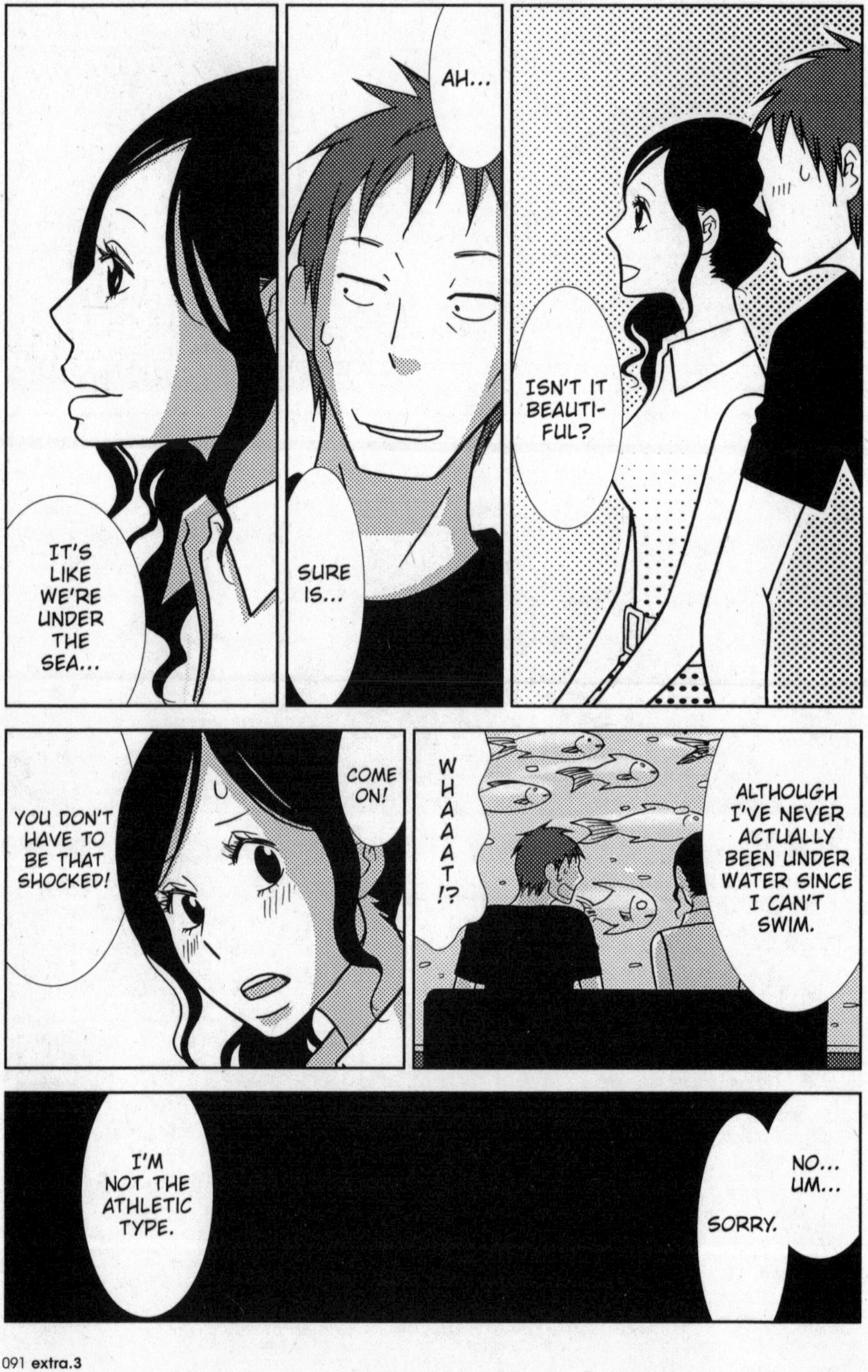
ISN'T IT BEAUTI-FUL?
AH...
SURE IS...
IT'S LIKE WE'RE UNDER THE SEA...
ALTHOUGH I'VE NEVER ACTUALLY BEEN UNDER WATER SINCE I CAN'T SWIM.
WHAAAT!?
COME ON!
YOU DON'T HAVE TO BE THAT SHOCKED!
NO... UM...
SORRY.
I'M NOT THE ATHLETIC TYPE.

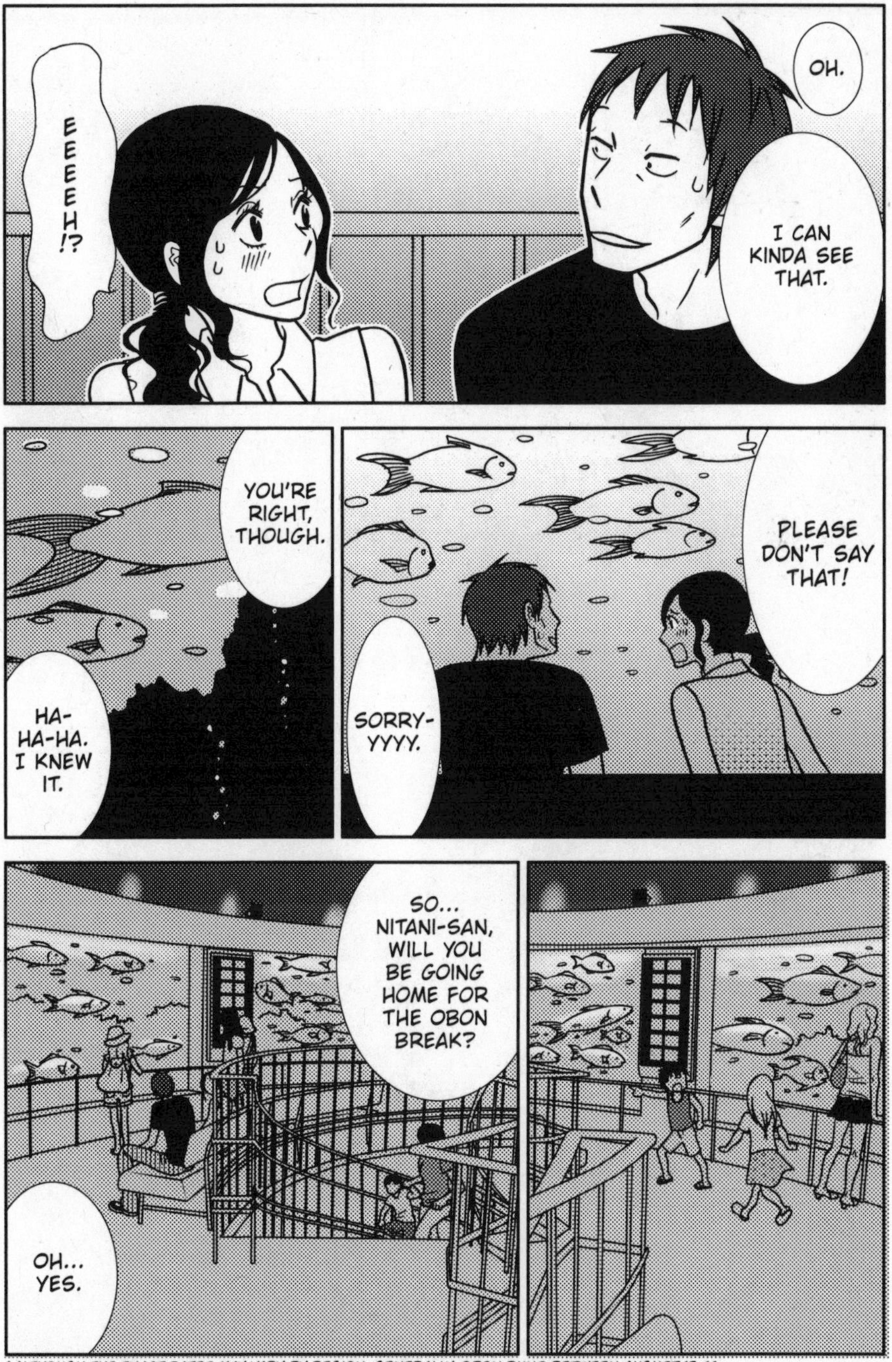
OH.
I CAN KINDA SEE THAT.
EEEEEH!?
PLEASE DON'T SAY THAT!
SORRY-YYYY.
YOU'RE RIGHT, THOUGH.
HA-HA-HA. I KNEW IT.
SO... NITANI-SAN, WILL YOU BE GOING HOME FOR THE OBON BREAK?
OH... YES.

*ALTHOUGH THE EXACT DATES MAY VARY BY REGION, GENERALLY, OBON RUNS BETWEEN AUGUST 13-16. PEOPLE TYPICALLY VISIT FAMILY AND PAY THEIR RESPECTS TO THEIR ANCESTORS AT GRAVE SITES.

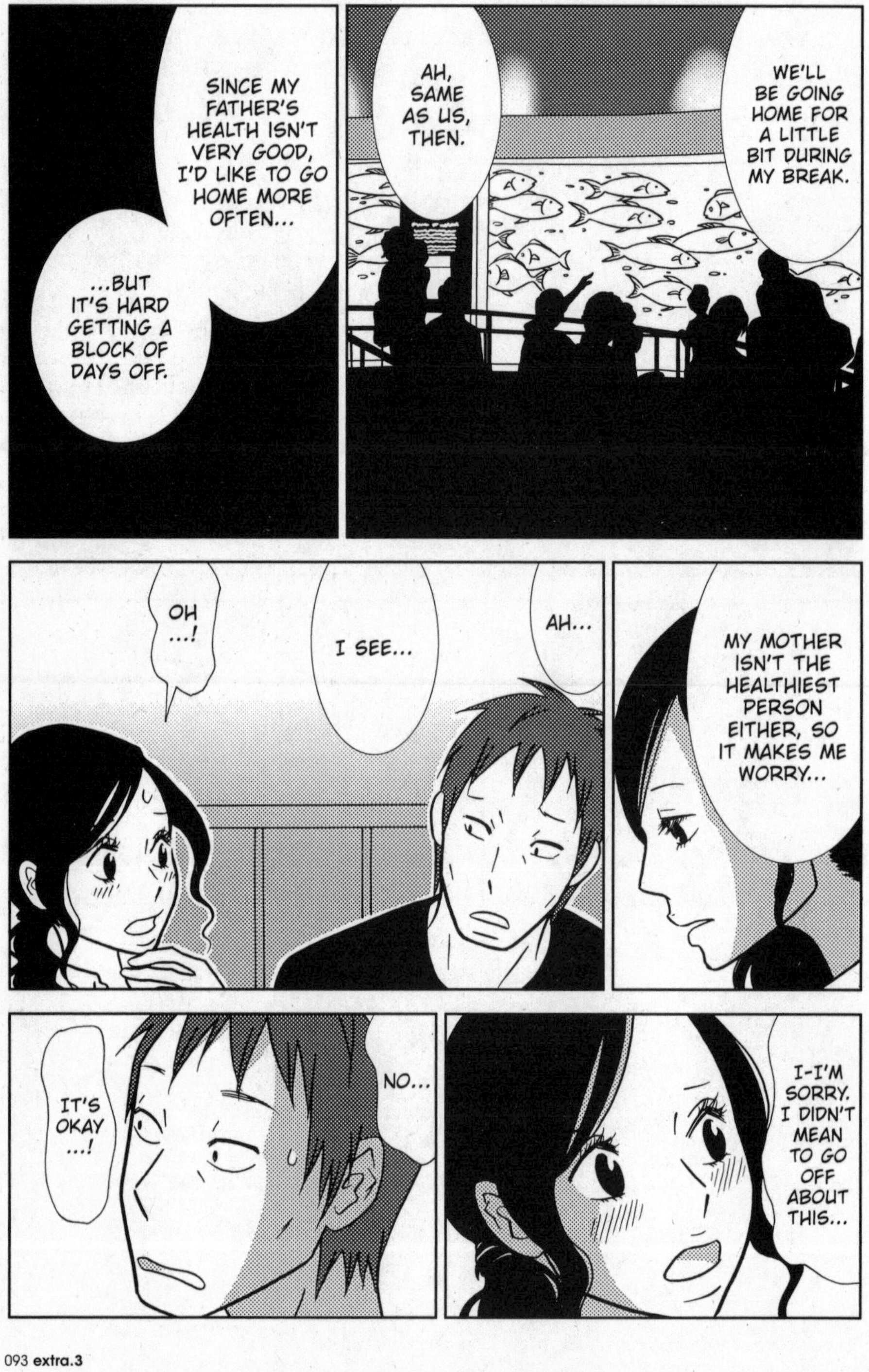
WE'LL BE GOING HOME FOR A LITTLE BIT DURING MY BREAK.
AH, SAME AS US, THEN.
SINCE MY FATHER'S HEALTH ISN'T VERY GOOD, I'D LIKE TO GO HOME MORE OFTEN...
...BUT IT'S HARD GETTING A BLOCK OF DAYS OFF.
MY MOTHER ISN'T THE HEALTHIEST PERSON EITHER, SO IT MAKES ME WORRY...
AH...
I SEE...
OH ...!
I-I'M SORRY. I DIDN'T MEAN TO GO OFF ABOUT THIS...
NO...
IT'S OKAY ...!

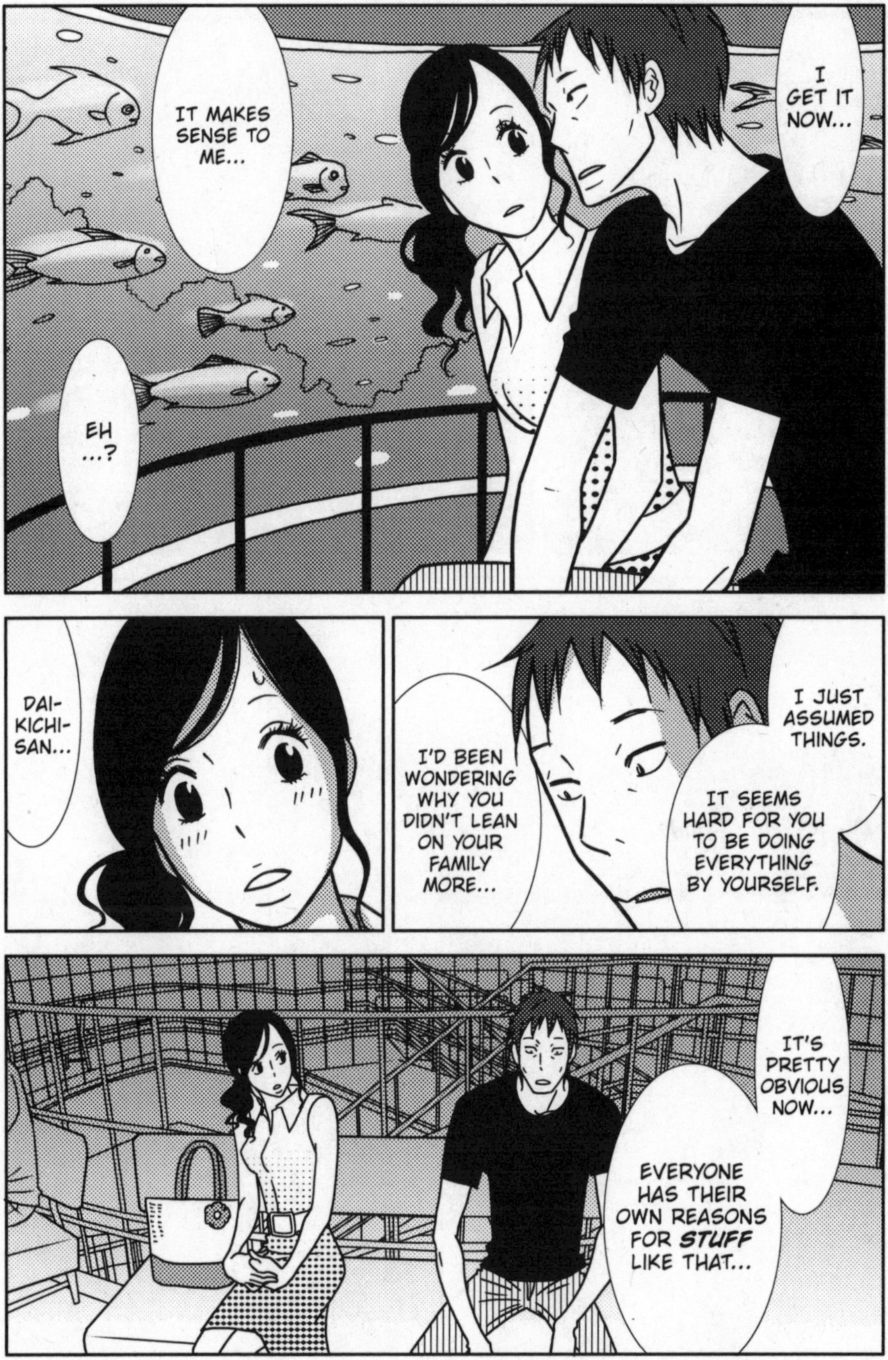
I GET IT NOW...
IT MAKES SENSE TO ME...
EH ...?
I JUST ASSUMED THINGS.
IT SEEMS HARD FOR YOU TO BE DOING EVERYTHING BY YOURSELF.
I'D BEEN WONDERING WHY YOU DIDN'T LEAN ON YOUR FAMILY MORE...
DAI-KICHI-SAN...
IT'S PRETTY OBVIOUS NOW...
EVERYONE HAS THEIR OWN REASONS FOR **STUFF** LIKE THAT...

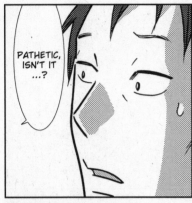

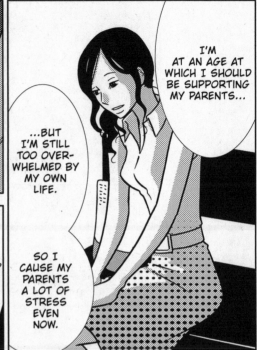

I'M AT AN AGE AT WHICH I SHOULD BE SUPPORTING MY PARENTS...
...BUT I'M STILL TOO OVER-WHELMED BY MY OWN LIFE.
SO I CAUSE MY PARENTS A LOT OF STRESS EVEN NOW.
PATHETIC, ISN'T IT ...?
EH...!? PATHETIC? NO WAY...
NITANI-SAN, YOU AREN'T THAT AT ALL!
WHOA.
MY OWN PARENTS HAVE BEEN HEALTHY, SO I HAVEN'T HAD TO GIVE MUCH THOUGHT TO STUFF LIKE THAT...
....

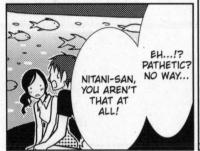

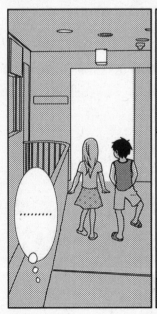

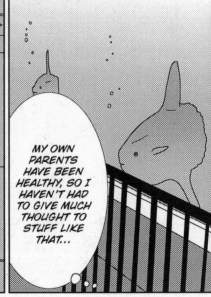

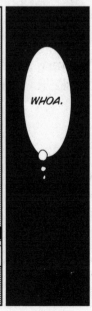

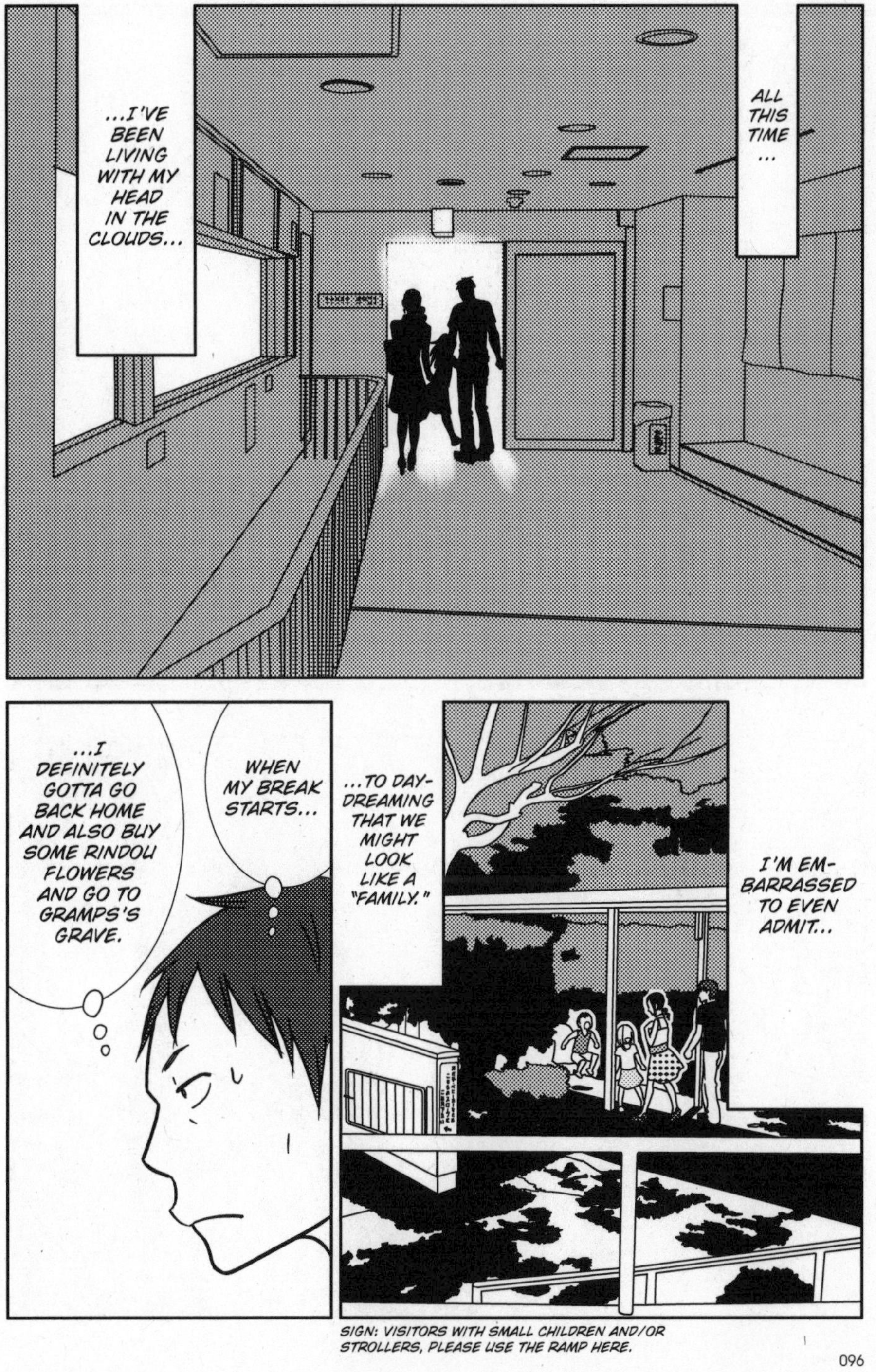
ALL THIS TIME ...
...I'VE BEEN LIVING WITH MY HEAD IN THE CLOUDS...
I'M EM-BARRASSED TO EVEN ADMIT...
...TO DAY-DREAMING THAT WE MIGHT LOOK LIKE A "FAMILY."
WHEN MY BREAK STARTS...
...I DEFINITELY GOTTA GO BACK HOME AND ALSO BUY SOME RINDOU FLOWERS AND GO TO GRAMPS'S GRAVE.

SIGN: VISITORS WITH SMALL CHILDREN AND/OR STROLLERS, PLEASE USE THE RAMP HERE.

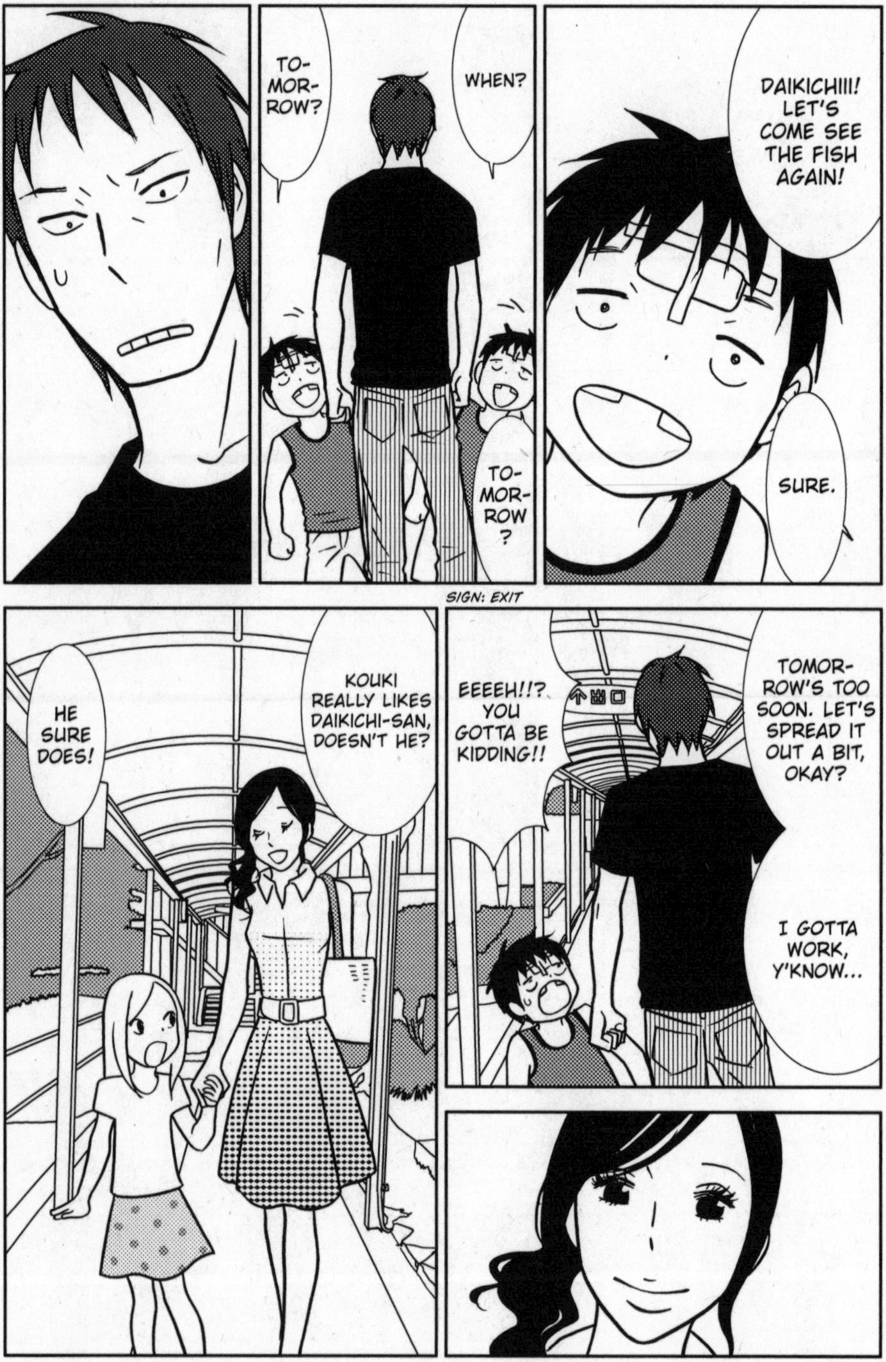
DAIKICHIII! LET'S COME SEE THE FISH AGAIN!
SURE.
WHEN?
TO-MORROW?
TO-MORROW?
SIGN: EXIT
TOMORROW'S TOO SOON. LET'S SPREAD IT OUT A BIT, OKAY?
EEEEH!!? YOU GOTTA BE KIDDING!!
I GOTTA WORK, Y'KNOW...
KOUKI REALLY LIKES DAIKICHI-SAN, DOESN'T HE?
HE SURE DOES!

AND I LIKE KOUKI-KUN'S MOM A LOT TOO!
THANK YOU.
I LIKE YOU A LOT TOO, RIN-CHAN!

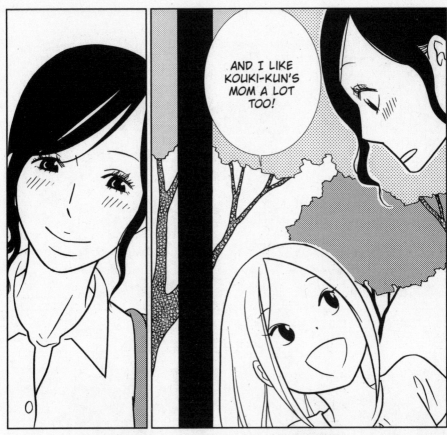

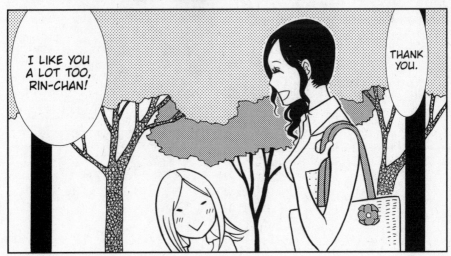

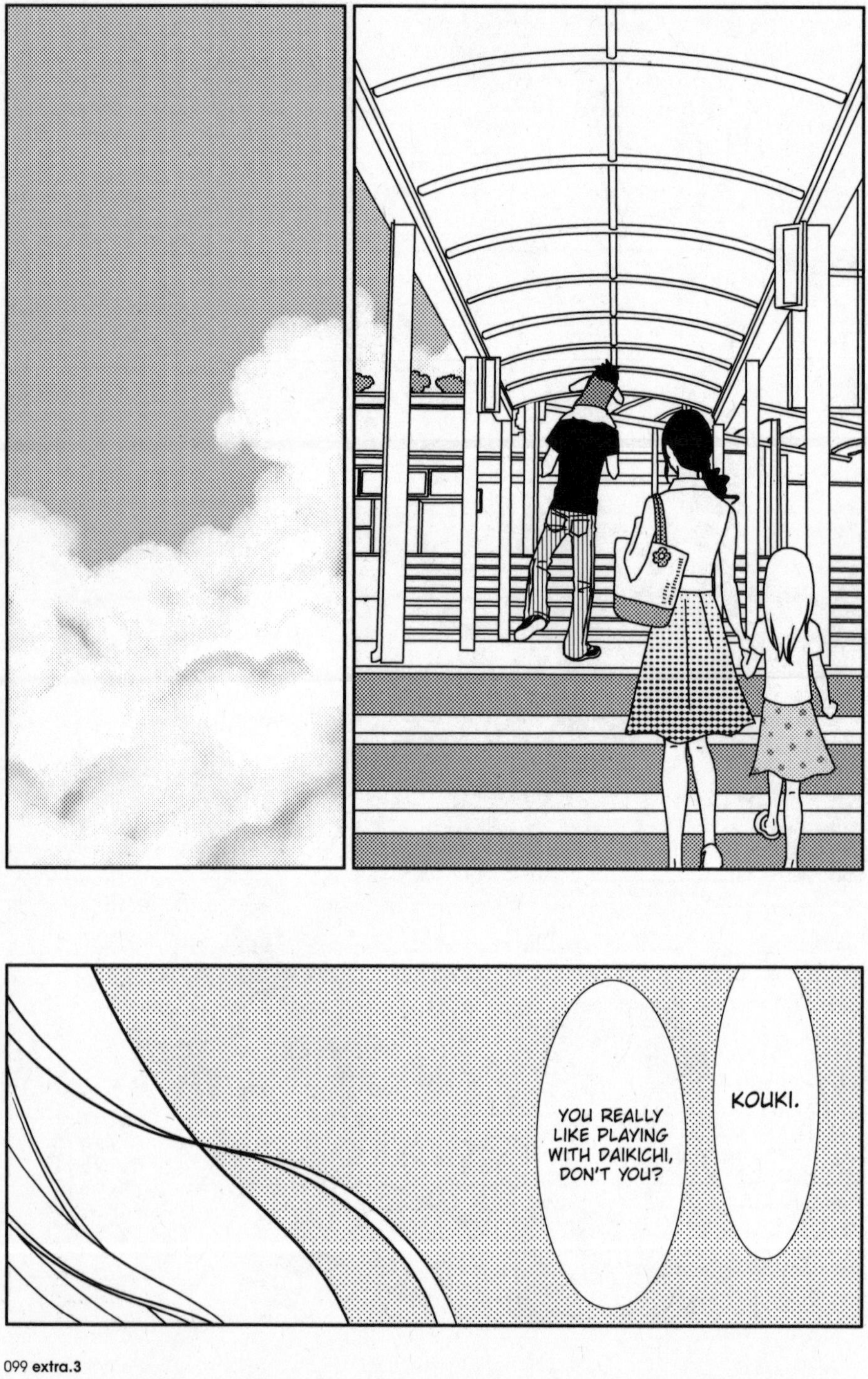
KOUKI.
YOU REALLY LIKE PLAYING WITH DAIKICHI, DON'T YOU?

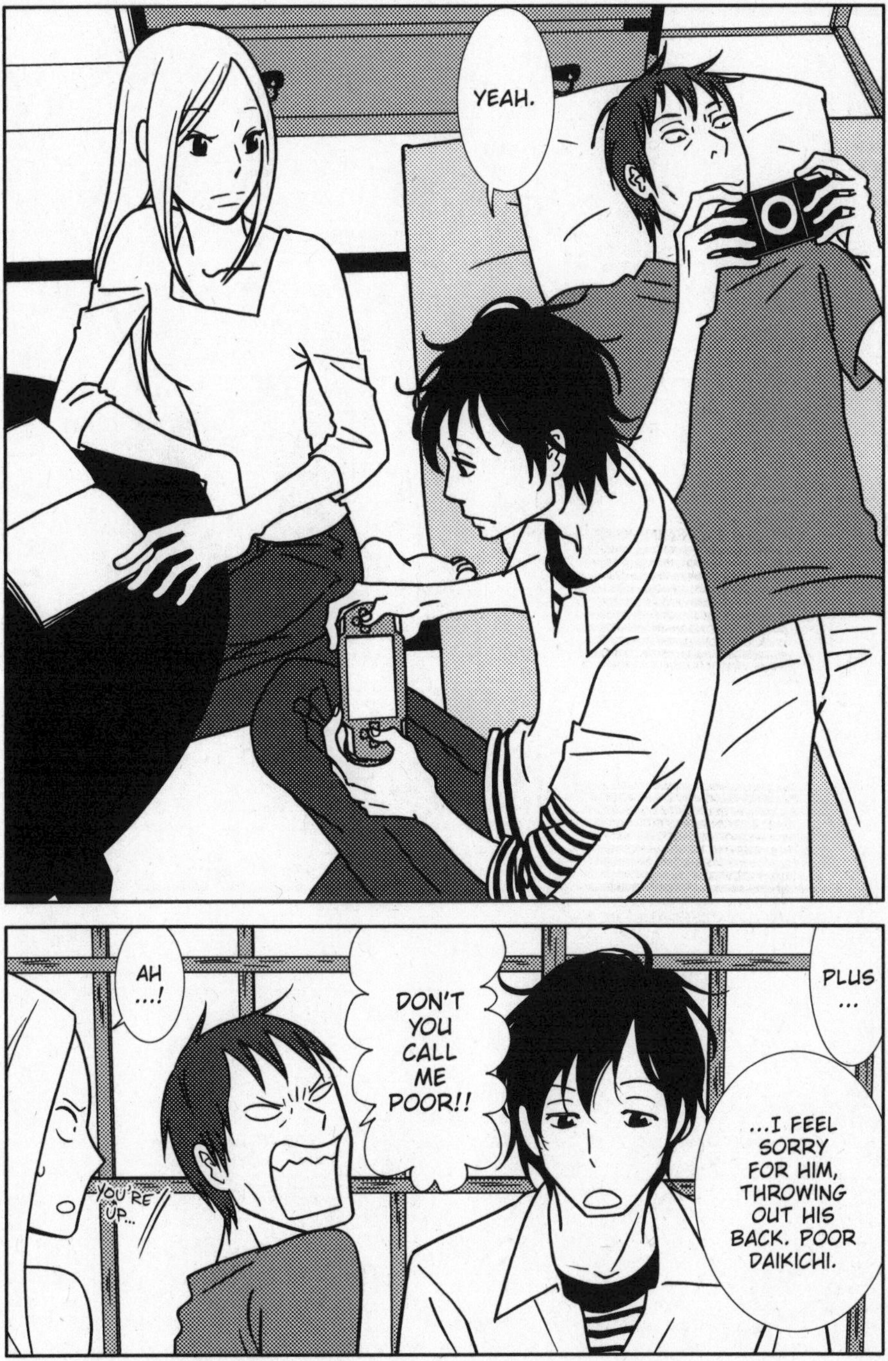
YEAH.
PLUS ...
...I FEEL SORRY FOR HIM, THROWING OUT HIS BACK. POOR DAIKICHI.
DON'T YOU CALL ME POOR!!
AH ...!
YOU'RE UP...

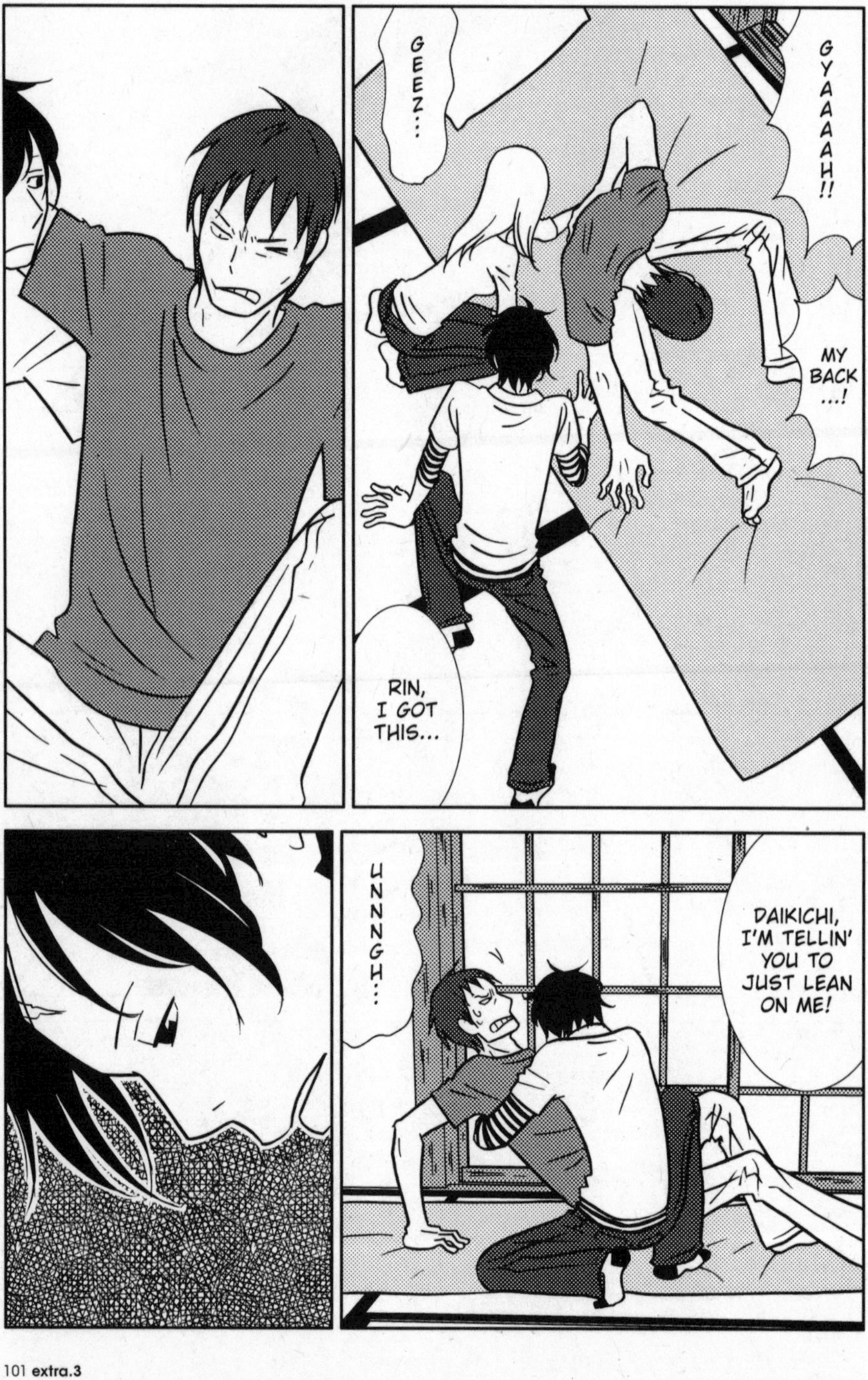
GYAAAAAH!!
GEEZ...
MY BACK ...!
RIN, I GOT THIS...
DAIKICHI, I'M TELLIN' YOU TO JUST LEAN ON ME!
UNNNGH...

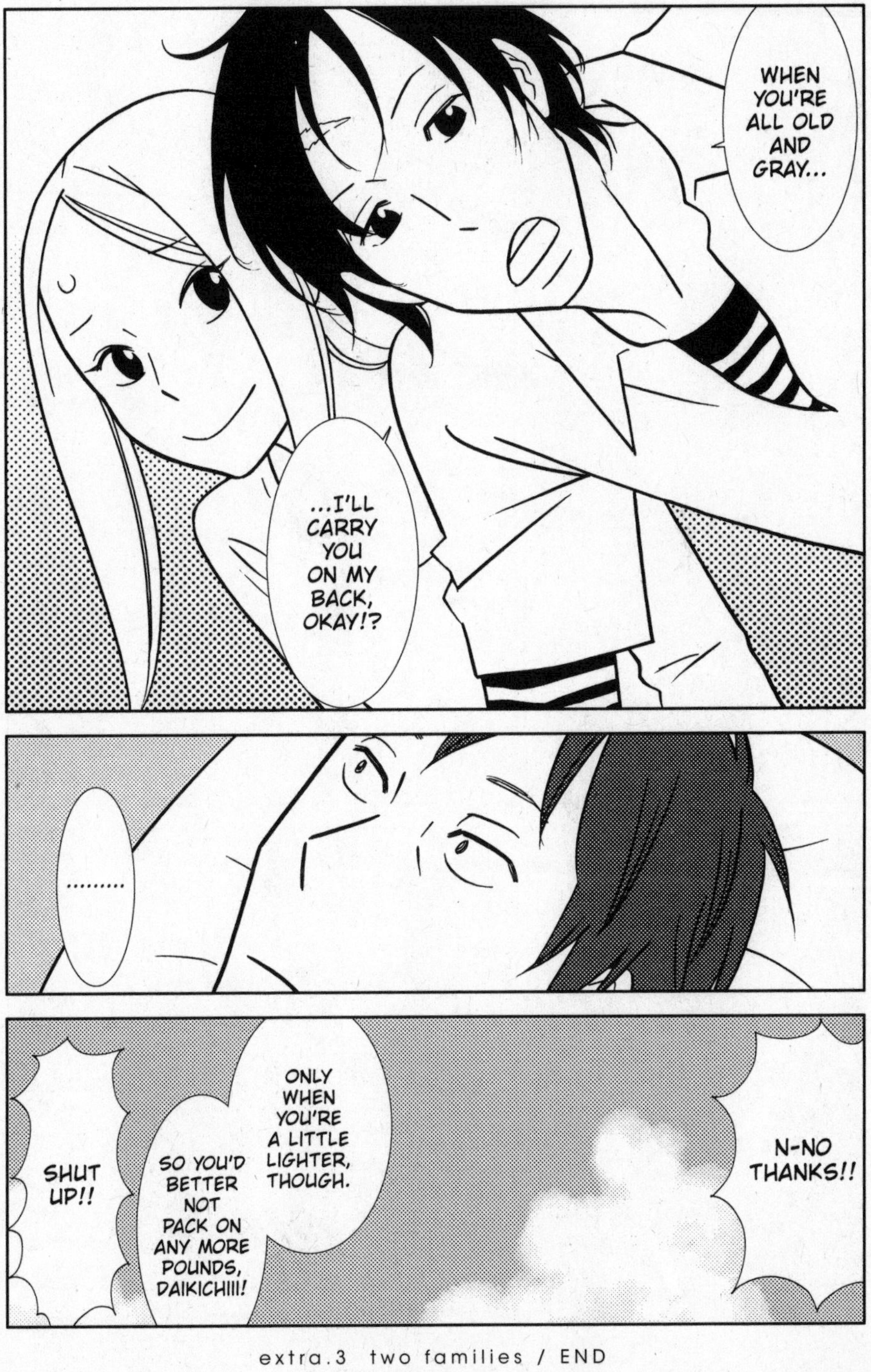
WHEN YOU'RE ALL OLD AND GRAY...
...I'LL CARRY YOU ON MY BACK, OKAY!?
....
N-NO THANKS!!
ONLY WHEN YOU'RE A LITTLE LIGHTER, THOUGH.
SO YOU'D BETTER NOT PACK ON ANY MORE POUNDS, DAIKICHIII!
SHUT UP!!

extra.3 two families / END

extra.4

eyeglass drop

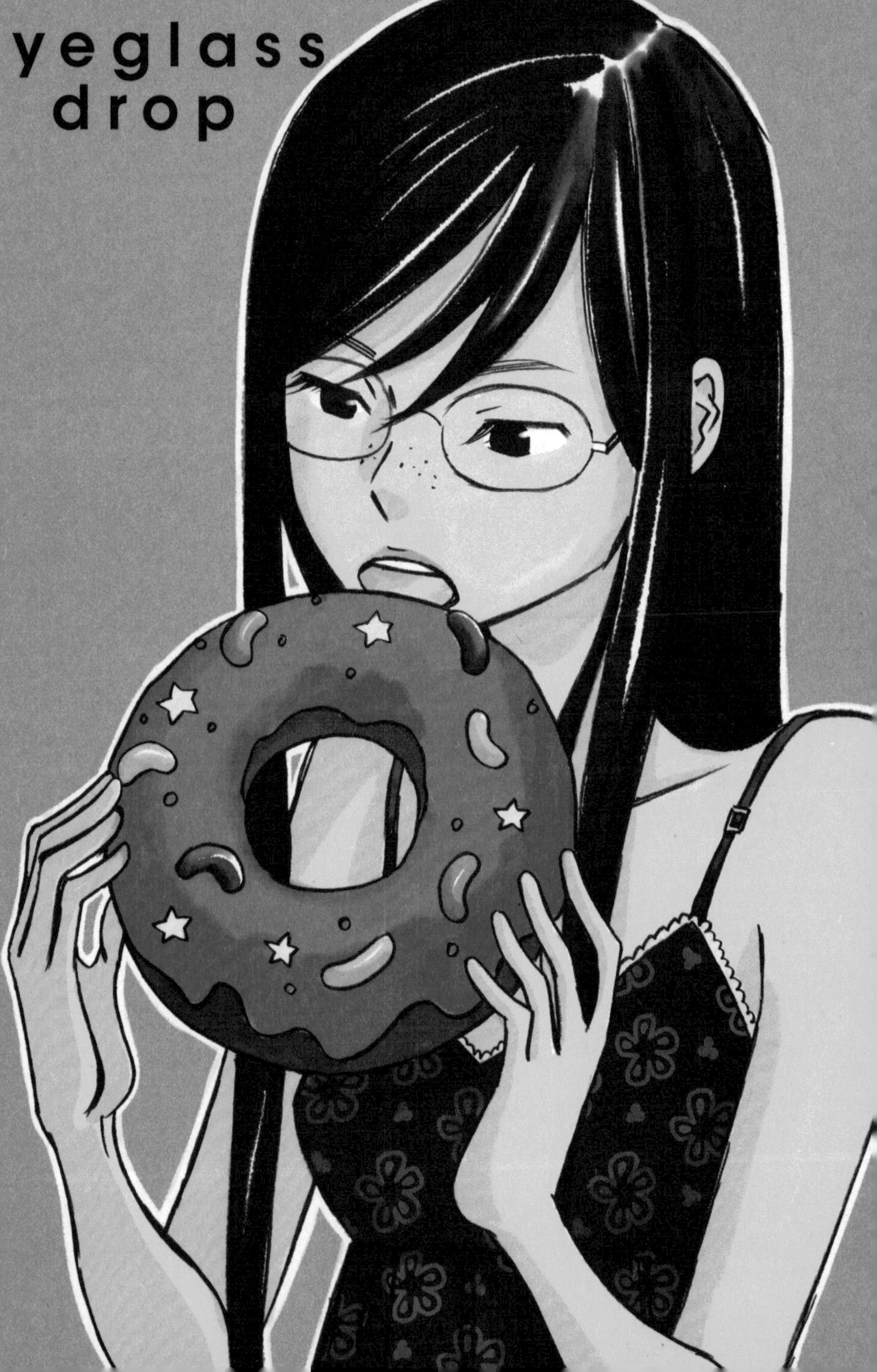

BUNNY**DROP**

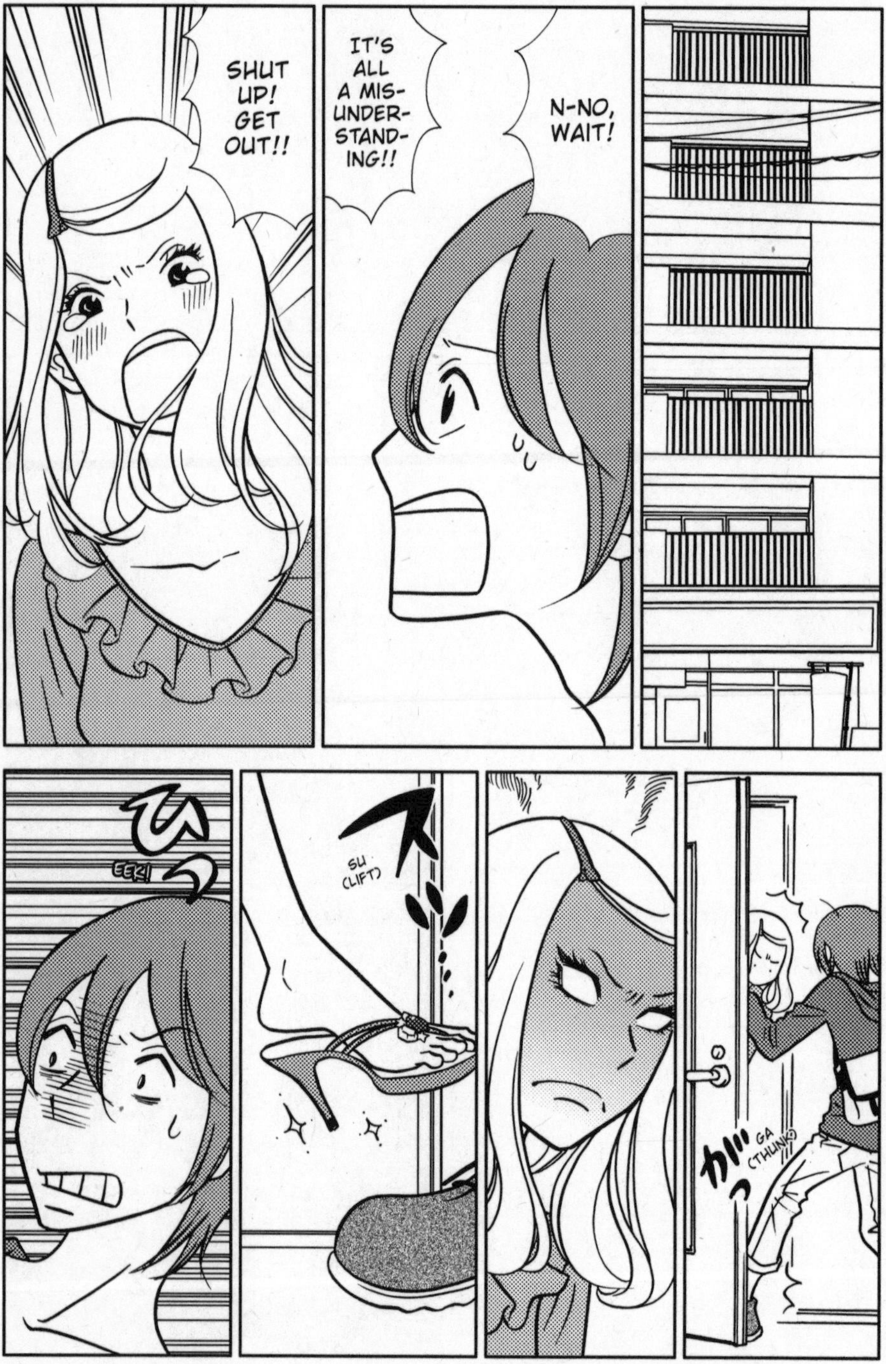
N-NO, WAIT!
IT'S ALL A MIS-UNDER-STAND-ING!!
SHUT UP! GET OUT!!
がっ
GA (THUNK)
SU (LIFT)
ひっ
EEK!

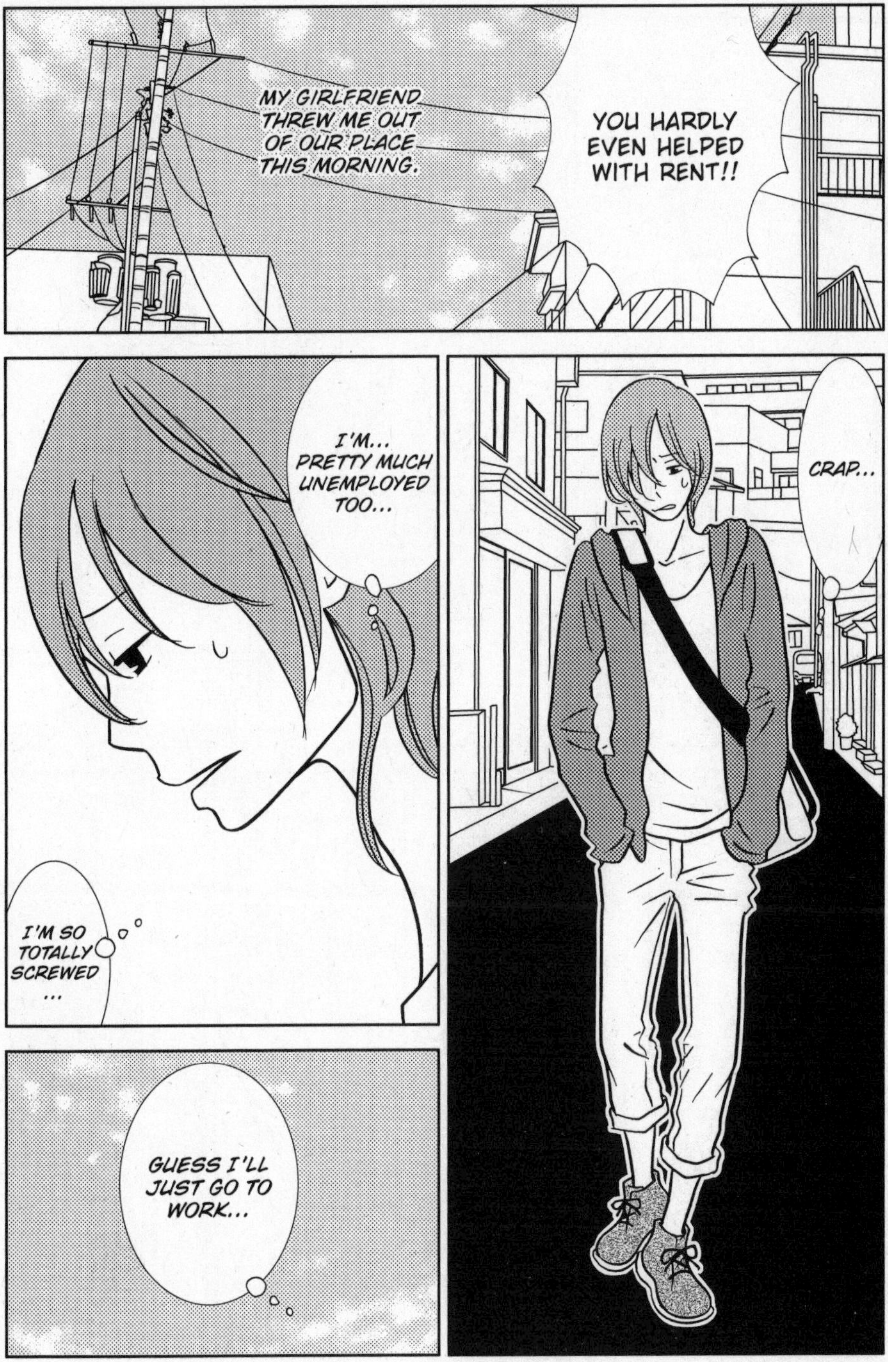
YOU HARDLY EVEN HELPED WITH RENT!!
MY GIRLFRIEND THREW ME OUT OF OUR PLACE THIS MORNING.
CRAP...
I'M... PRETTY MUCH UNEMPLOYED TOO...
I'M SO TOTALLY SCREWED ...
GUESS I'LL JUST GO TO WORK...

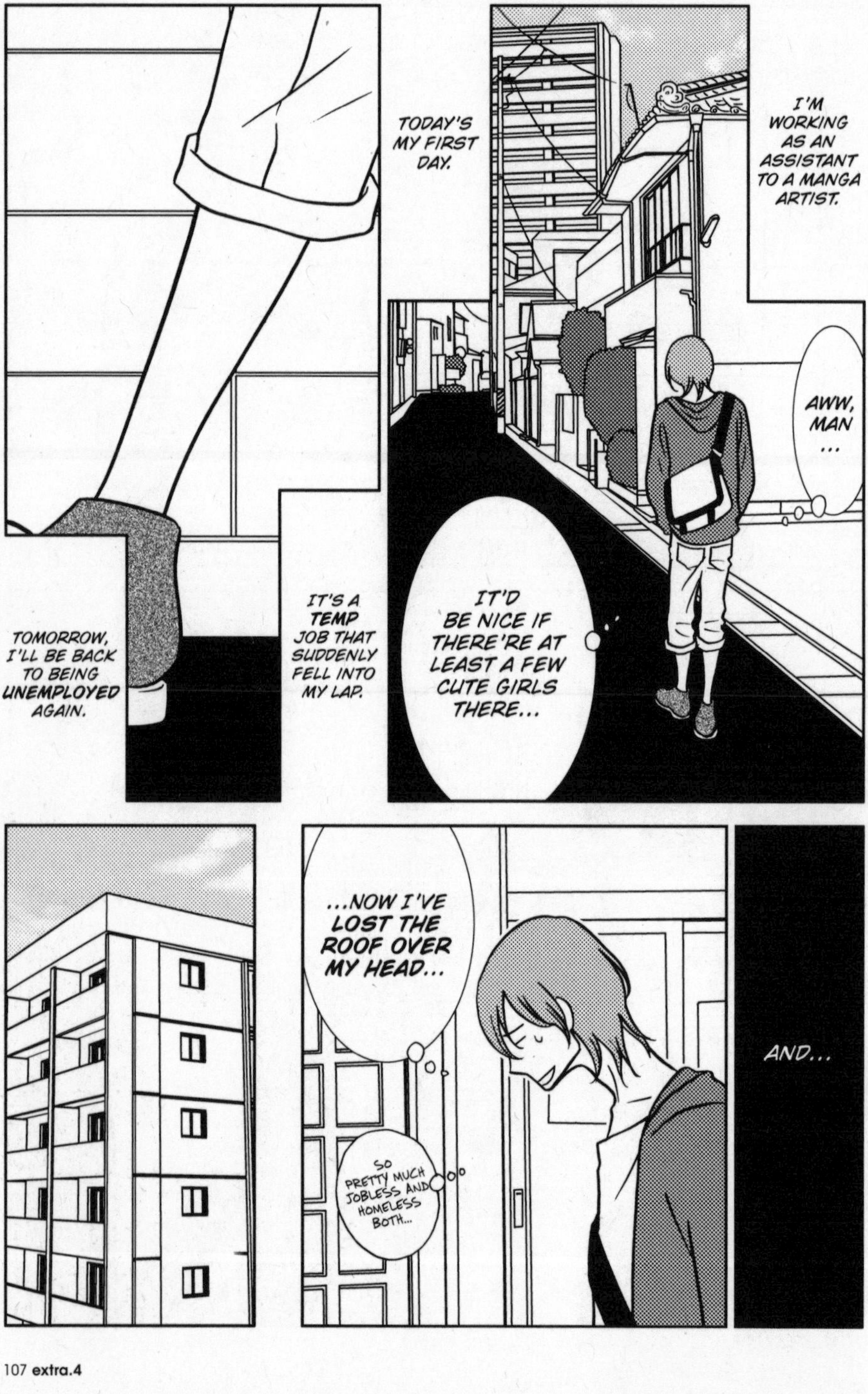
I'M WORKING AS AN ASSISTANT TO A MANGA ARTIST.
TODAY'S MY FIRST DAY.
AWW, MAN...
IT'D BE NICE IF THERE'RE AT LEAST A FEW CUTE GIRLS THERE...
IT'S A TEMP JOB THAT SUDDENLY FELL INTO MY LAP.
TOMORROW, I'LL BE BACK TO BEING UNEMPLOYED AGAIN.
AND...
...NOW I'VE LOST THE ROOF OVER MY HEAD...
SO PRETTY MUCH JOBLESS AND HOMELESS BOTH...

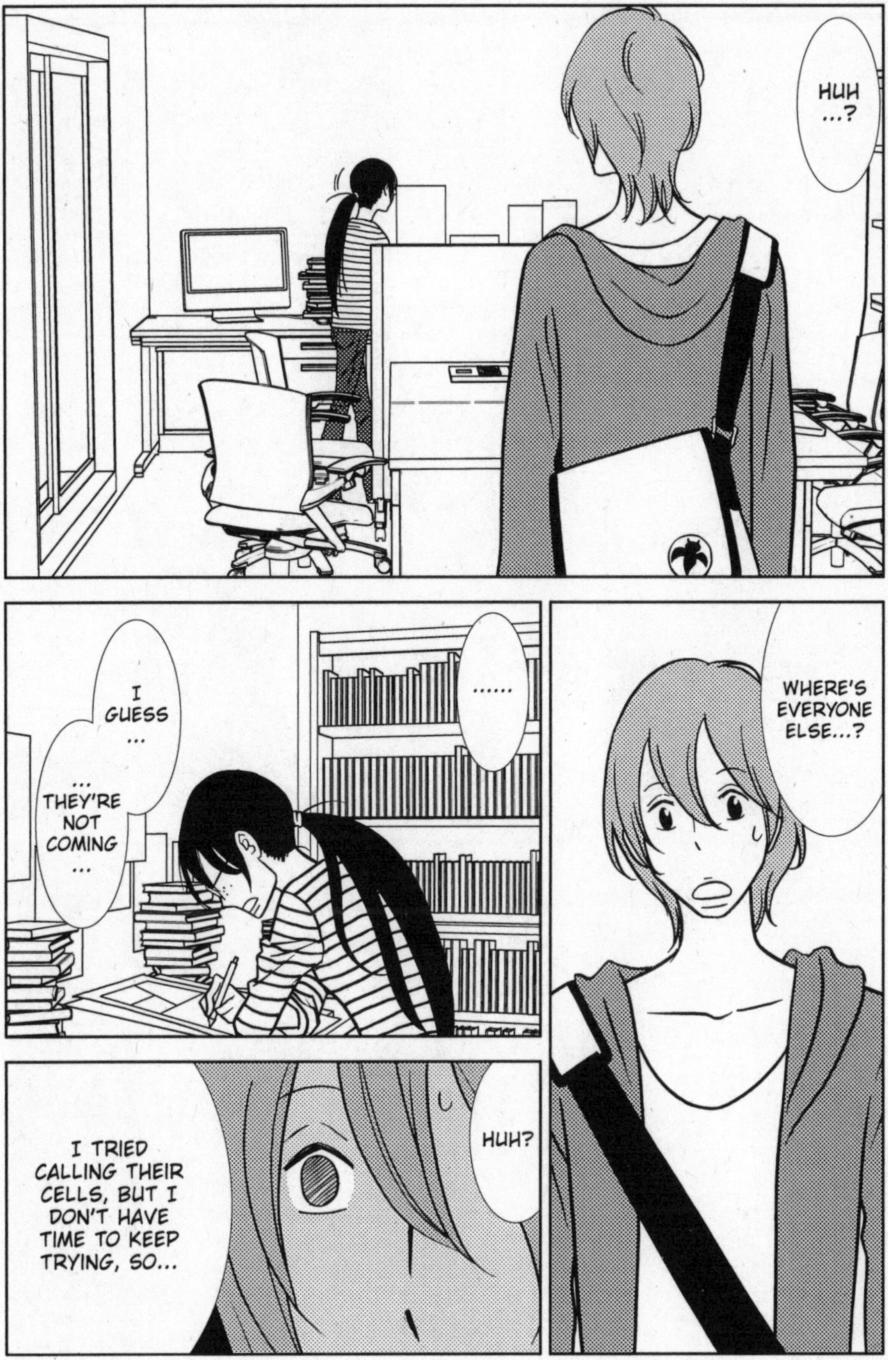
HUH ...?
WHERE'S EVERYONE ELSE...?
......
I GUESS ...
... THEY'RE NOT COMING ...
HUH?
I TRIED CALLING THEIR CELLS, BUT I DON'T HAVE TIME TO KEEP TRYING, SO...

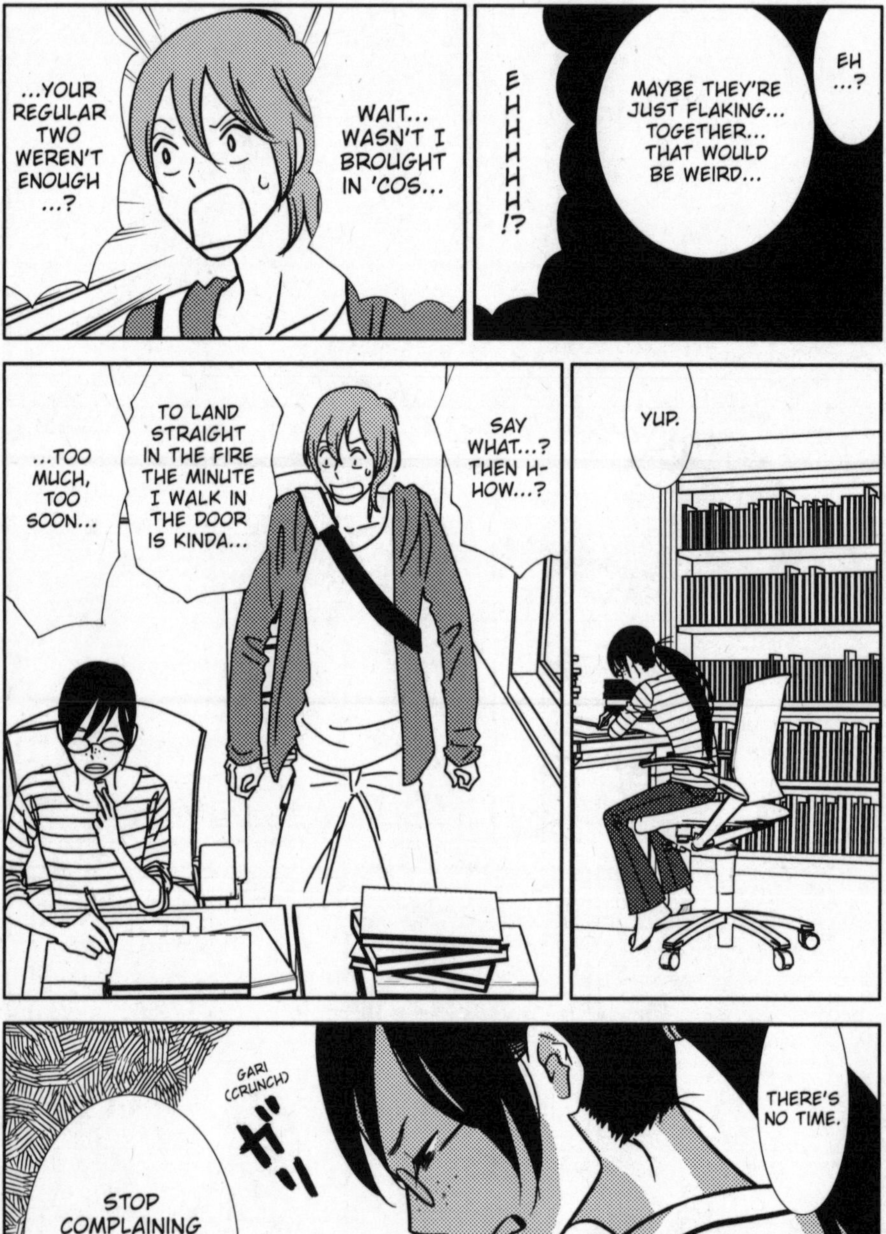
EH ...?
MAYBE THEY'RE JUST FLAKING... TOGETHER... THAT WOULD BE WEIRD...
EHHHHHH!?
WAIT... WASN'T I BROUGHT IN 'COS...
...YOUR REGULAR TWO WEREN'T ENOUGH ...?
YUP.
SAY WHAT...? THEN H-HOW...?
TO LAND STRAIGHT IN THE FIRE THE MINUTE I WALK IN THE DOOR IS KINDA...
...TOO MUCH, TOO SOON...
THERE'S NO TIME.
GARI (CRUNCH)
STOP COMPLAINING AND JUST GET TO WORK!

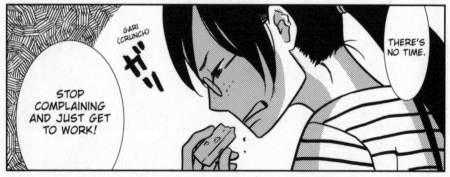

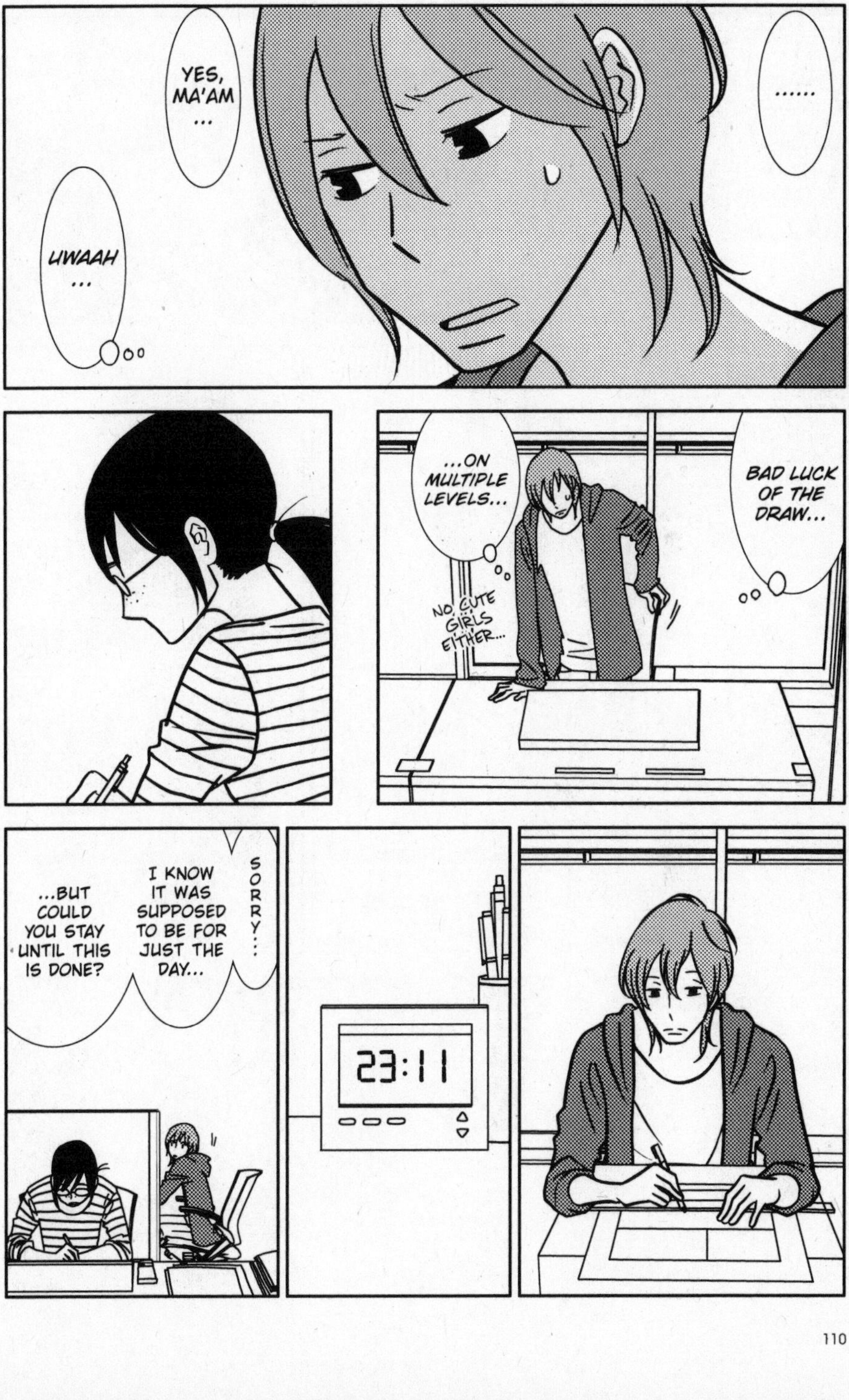
......
YES, MA'AM ...
UWAAH ...
BAD LUCK OF THE DRAW...
...ON MULTIPLE LEVELS...
NO CUTE GIRLS EITHER...
23:11
SORRY...
I KNOW IT WAS SUPPOSED TO BE FOR JUST THE DAY...
...BUT COULD YOU STAY UNTIL THIS IS DONE?

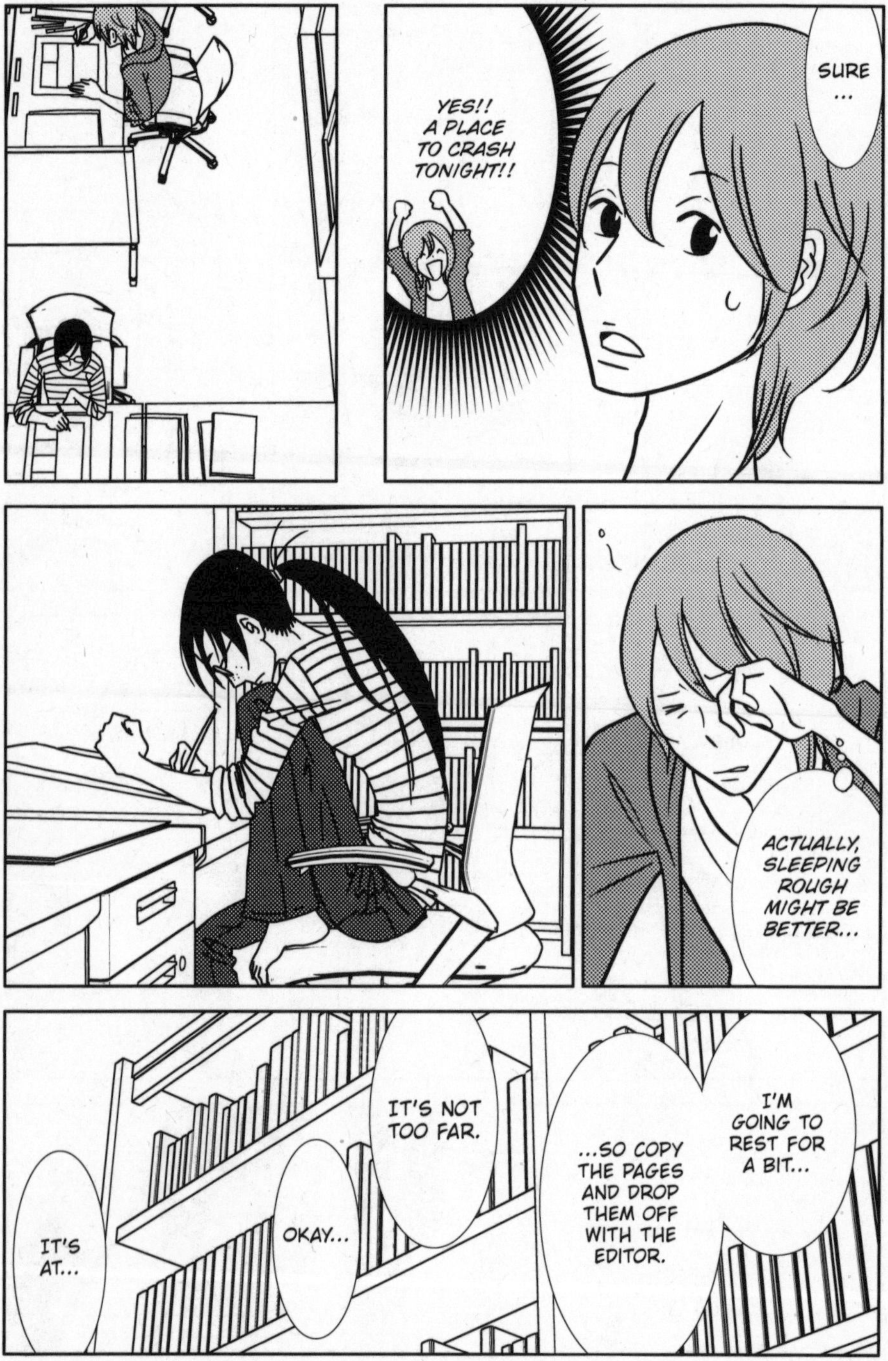
SURE ...
YES!! A PLACE TO CRASH TONIGHT!!
ACTUALLY, SLEEPING ROUGH MIGHT BE BETTER...
I'M GOING TO REST FOR A BIT...
...SO COPY THE PAGES AND DROP THEM OFF WITH THE EDITOR.
IT'S NOT TOO FAR.
OKAY...
IT'S AT...

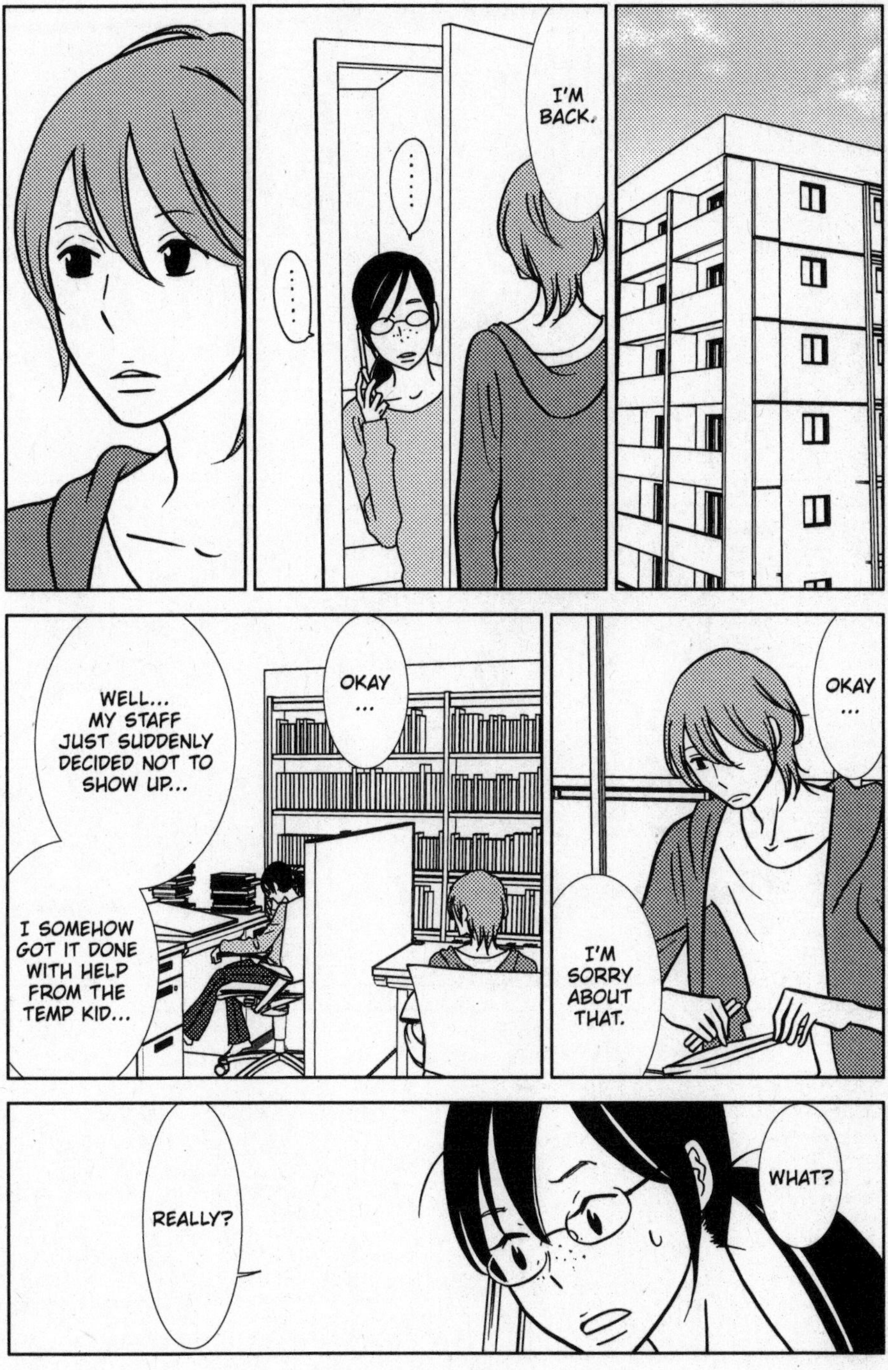
I'M BACK.
......
......
OKAY ...
I'M SORRY ABOUT THAT.
OKAY ...
WELL... MY STAFF JUST SUDDENLY DECIDED NOT TO SHOW UP...
I SOMEHOW GOT IT DONE WITH HELP FROM THE TEMP KID...
WHAT?
REALLY?

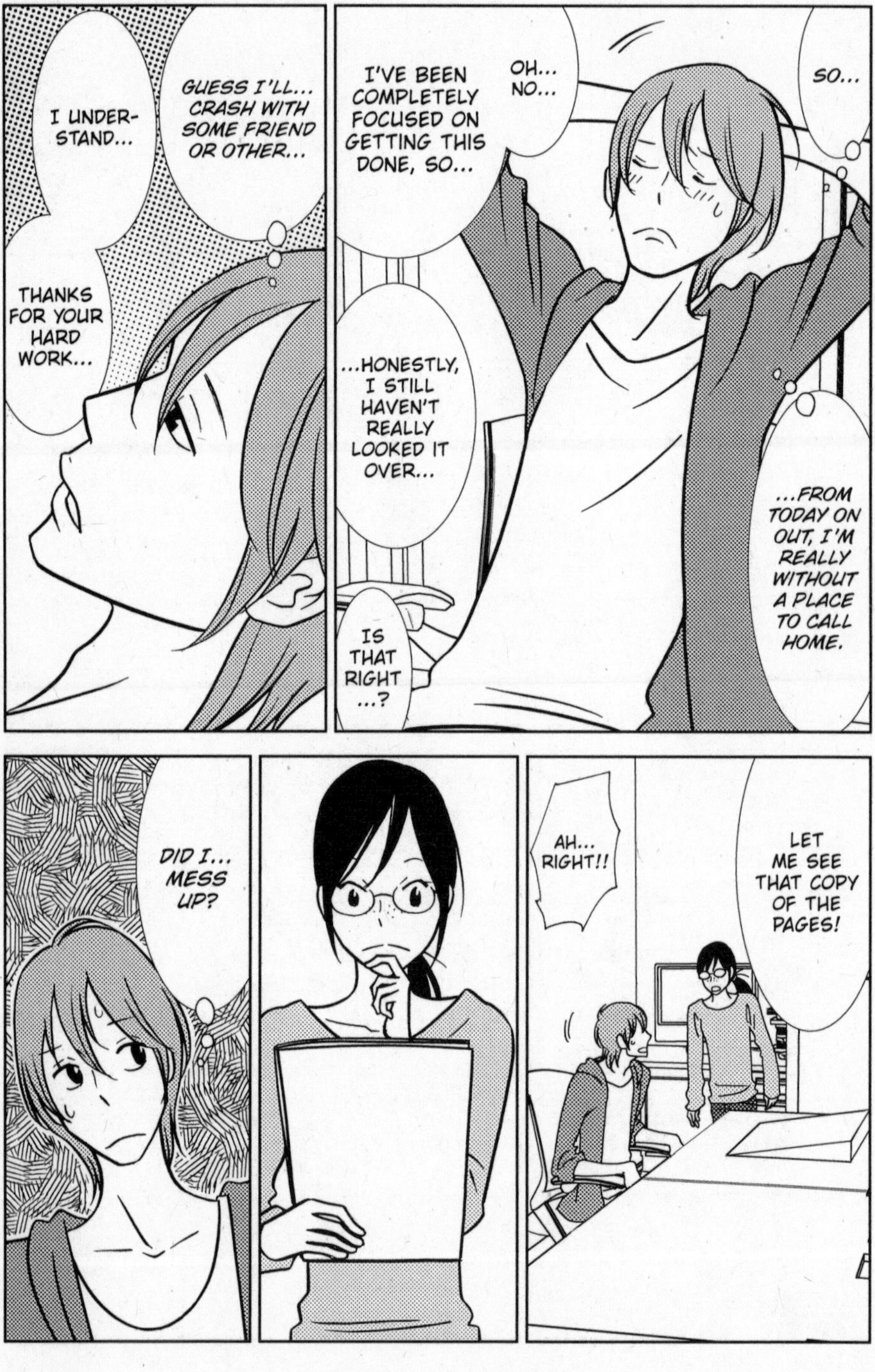
SO...
...FROM TODAY ON OUT, I'M REALLY WITHOUT A PLACE TO CALL HOME.
OH... NO...
I'VE BEEN COMPLETELY FOCUSED ON GETTING THIS DONE, SO...
...HONESTLY, I STILL HAVEN'T REALLY LOOKED IT OVER...
IS THAT RIGHT ...?
GUESS I'LL... CRASH WITH SOME FRIEND OR OTHER...
I UNDER-STAND...
THANKS FOR YOUR HARD WORK...
LET ME SEE THAT COPY OF THE PAGES!
AH... RIGHT!!
DID I... MESS UP?

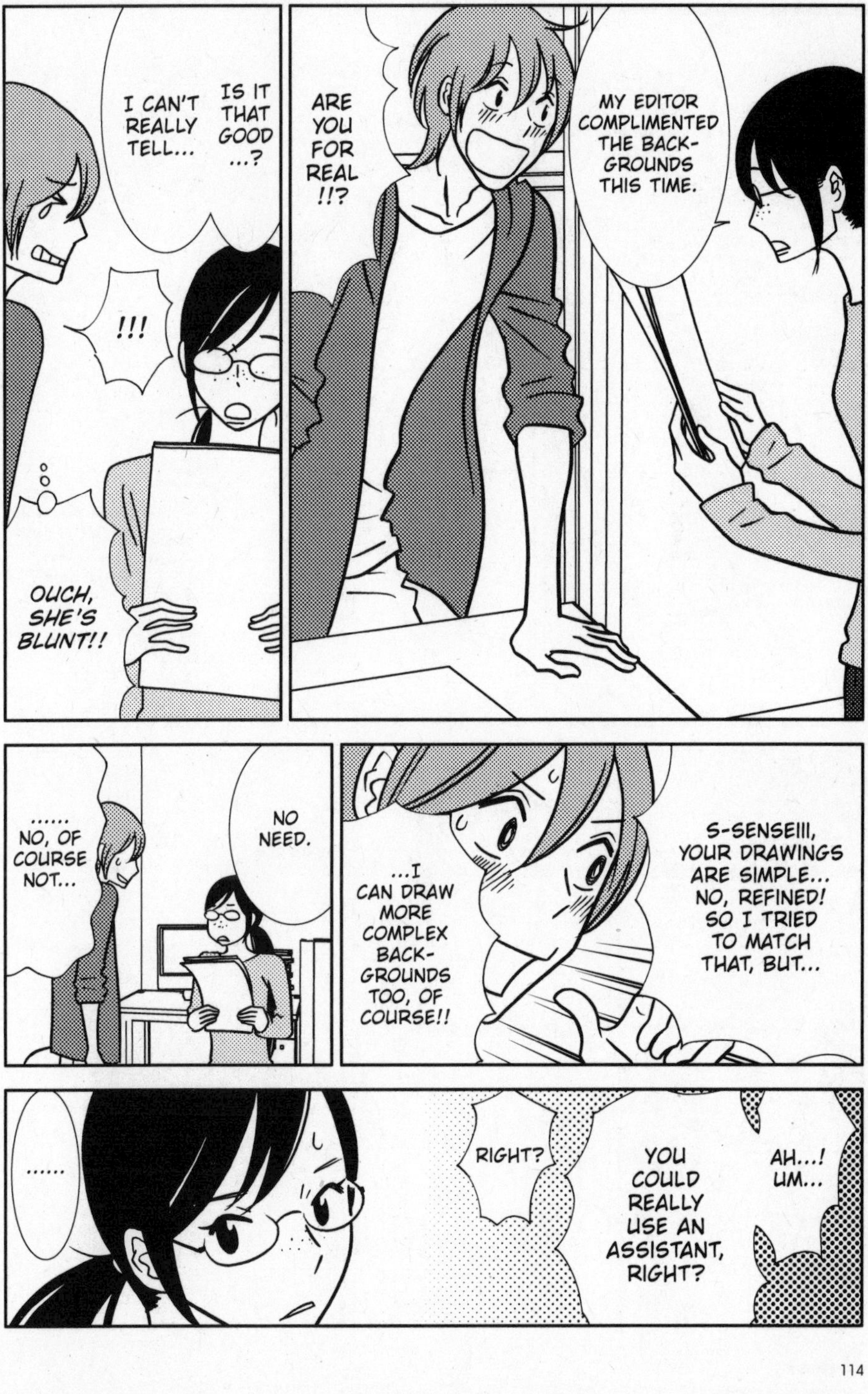
MY EDITOR COMPLIMENTED THE BACK-GROUNDS THIS TIME.
ARE YOU FOR REAL !!?
IS IT THAT GOOD ...?
I CAN'T REALLY TELL...
!!!
OUCH, SHE'S BLUNT!!
S-SENSEIII, YOUR DRAWINGS ARE SIMPLE... NO, REFINED! SO I TRIED TO MATCH THAT, BUT...
...I CAN DRAW MORE COMPLEX BACK-GROUNDS TOO, OF COURSE!!
NO NEED.
...... NO, OF COURSE NOT...
AH...! UM...
YOU COULD REALLY USE AN ASSISTANT, RIGHT?
RIGHT?
......

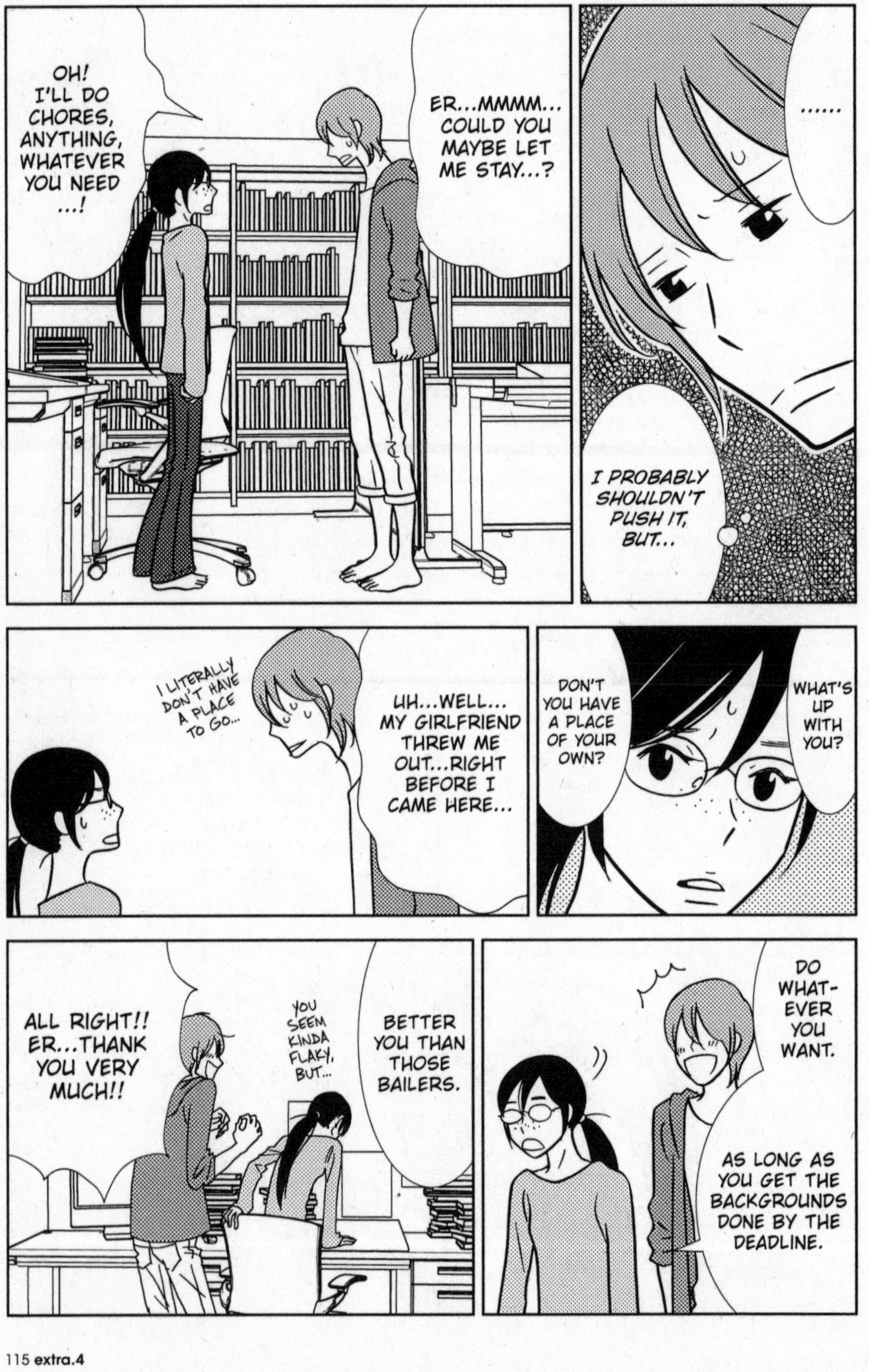
......
I PROBABLY SHOULDN'T PUSH IT, BUT...
ER...MMMM... COULD YOU MAYBE LET ME STAY...?
OH! I'LL DO CHORES, ANYTHING, WHATEVER YOU NEED ...!
WHAT'S UP WITH YOU?
DON'T YOU HAVE A PLACE OF YOUR OWN?
UH...WELL... MY GIRLFRIEND THREW ME OUT...RIGHT BEFORE I CAME HERE...
I LITERALLY DON'T HAVE A PLACE TO GO...
DO WHATEVER YOU WANT.
AS LONG AS YOU GET THE BACKGROUNDS DONE BY THE DEADLINE.
BETTER YOU THAN THOSE BAILERS.
YOU SEEM KINDA FLAKY, BUT...
ALL RIGHT!! ER...THANK YOU VERY MUCH!!

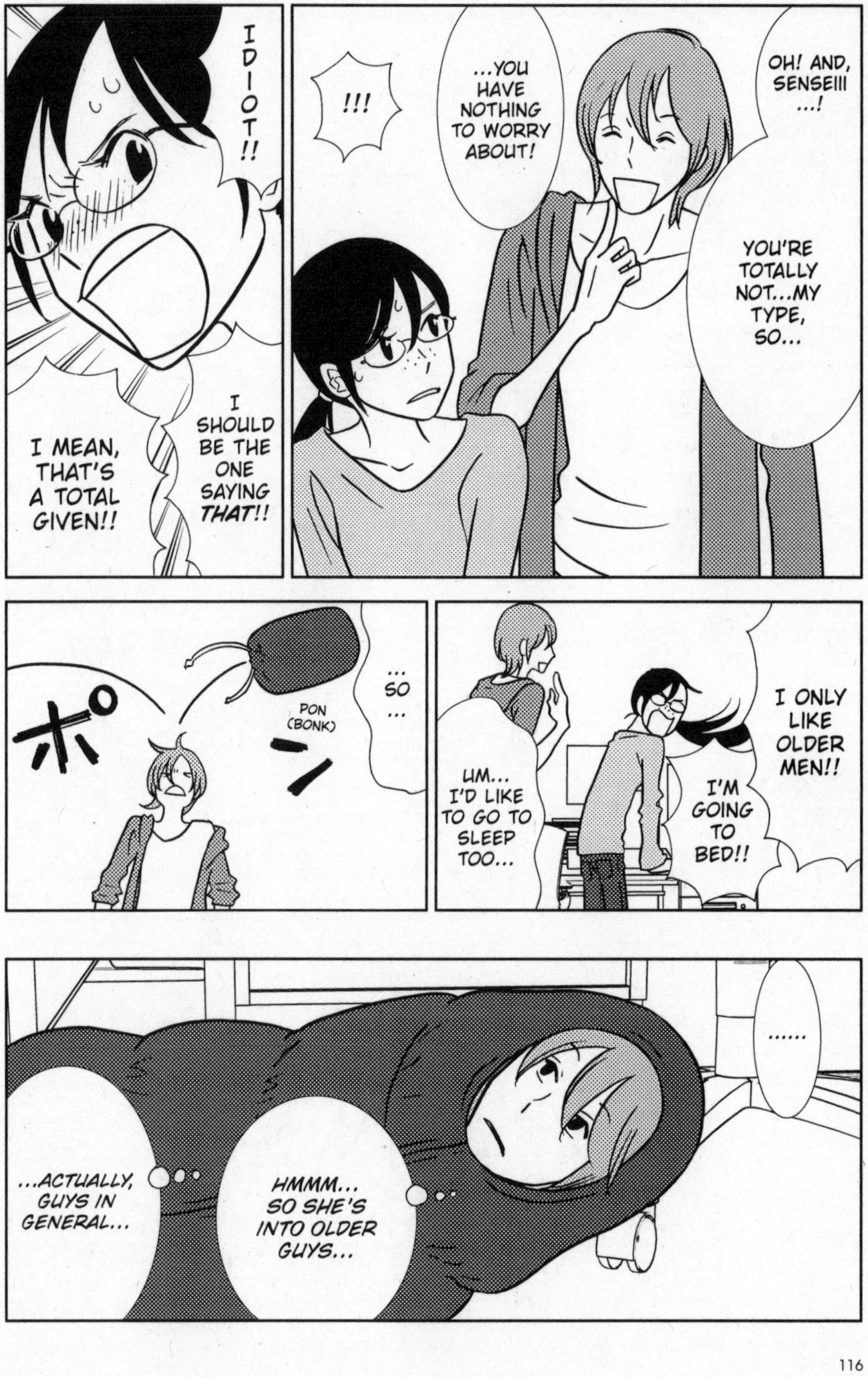
OH! AND, SENSEIII ...!
YOU'RE TOTALLY NOT...MY TYPE, SO...
...YOU HAVE NOTHING TO WORRY ABOUT!
!!!
IDIOT!!
I SHOULD BE THE ONE SAYING *THAT*!!
I MEAN, THAT'S A TOTAL GIVEN!!
I ONLY LIKE OLDER MEN!!
I'M GOING TO BED!!
UM... I'D LIKE TO GO TO SLEEP TOO...
... SO ...
PON (BONK)
......
HMMM... SO SHE'S INTO OLDER GUYS...
...ACTUALLY, GUYS IN GENERAL...

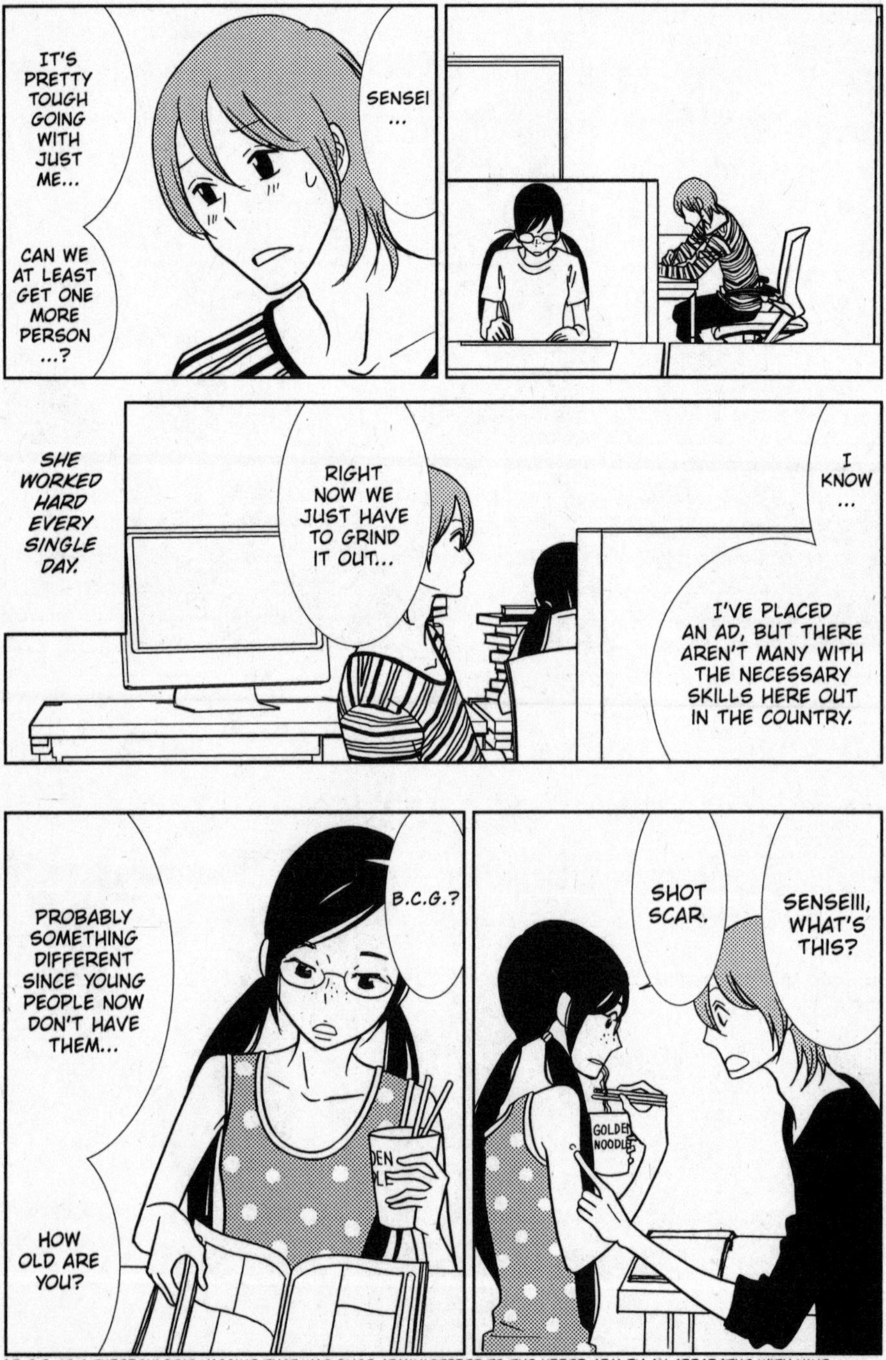
SENSEI ...
IT'S PRETTY TOUGH GOING WITH JUST ME...
CAN WE AT LEAST GET ONE MORE PERSON ...?
I KNOW ...
I'VE PLACED AN AD, BUT THERE AREN'T MANY WITH THE NECESSARY SKILLS HERE OUT IN THE COUNTRY.
RIGHT NOW WE JUST HAVE TO GRIND IT OUT...
SHE WORKED HARD EVERY SINGLE DAY.
SENSEIII, WHAT'S THIS?
SHOT SCAR.
B.C.G.?
PROBABLY SOMETHING DIFFERENT SINCE YOUNG PEOPLE NOW DON'T HAVE THEM...
HOW OLD ARE YOU?

*B.C.G. IS A TUBERCULOSIS VACCINE THAT WAS ONCE ADMINISTERED TO THE UPPER ARM BY AN APPARATUS WITH NINE SHORT NEEDLES IN A CIRCULAR PATTERN. THE RESULTING SCAR WAS READILY IDENTIFIABLE AS BEING FROM THIS VACCINE.

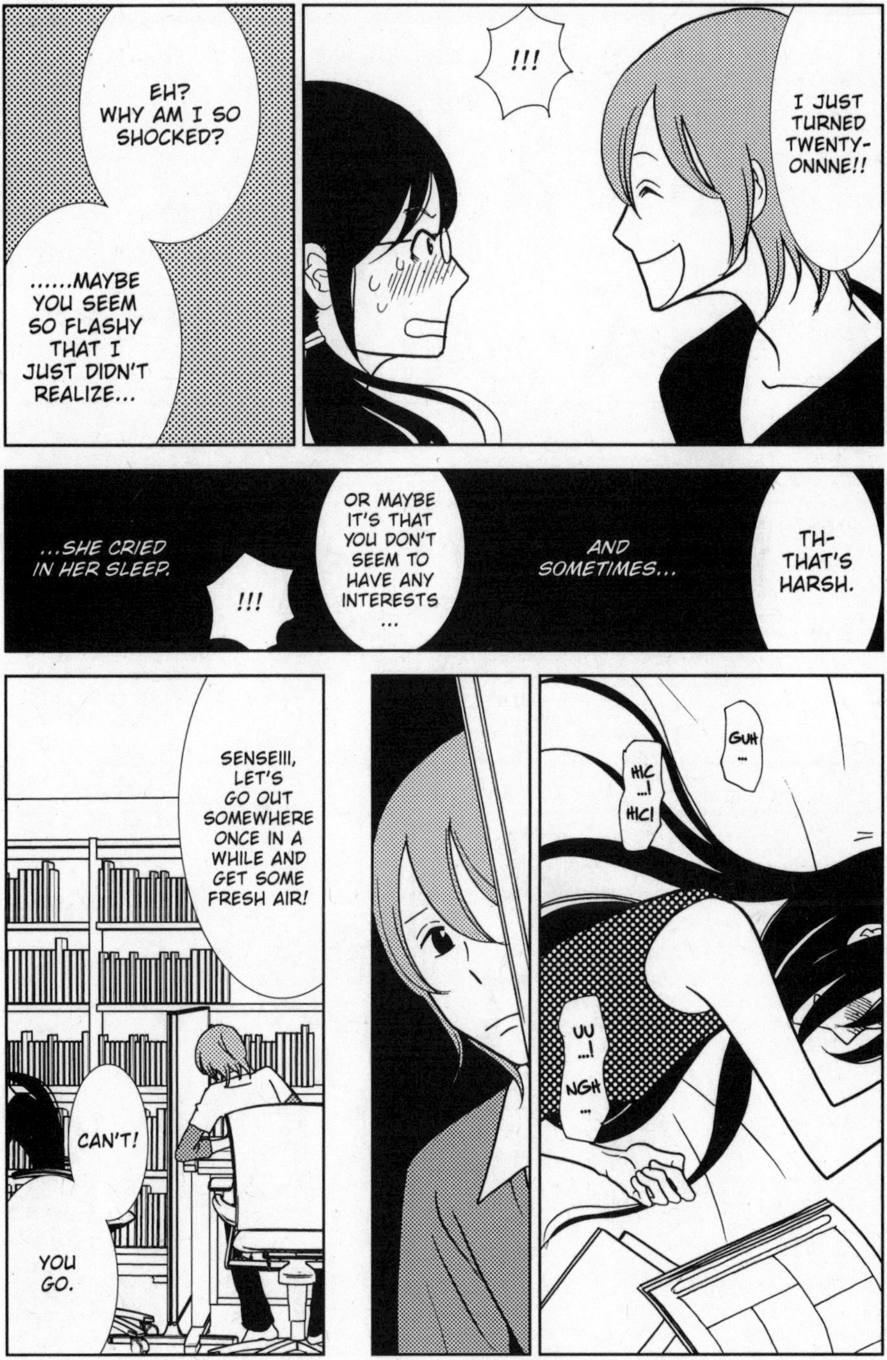

I JUST TURNED TWENTY-ONNNE!!
!!!
EH? WHY AM I SO SHOCKED?
......MAYBE YOU SEEM SO FLASHY THAT I JUST DIDN'T REALIZE...
TH- THAT'S HARSH.
AND SOMETIMES...
OR MAYBE IT'S THAT YOU DON'T SEEM TO HAVE ANY INTERESTS ...
!!!
...SHE CRIED IN HER SLEEP.
GUH ...
HIC ...! HIC!
UU ...! NGH ...
SENSEIII, LET'S GO OUT SOMEWHERE ONCE IN A WHILE AND GET SOME FRESH AIR!
CAN'T!
YOU GO.

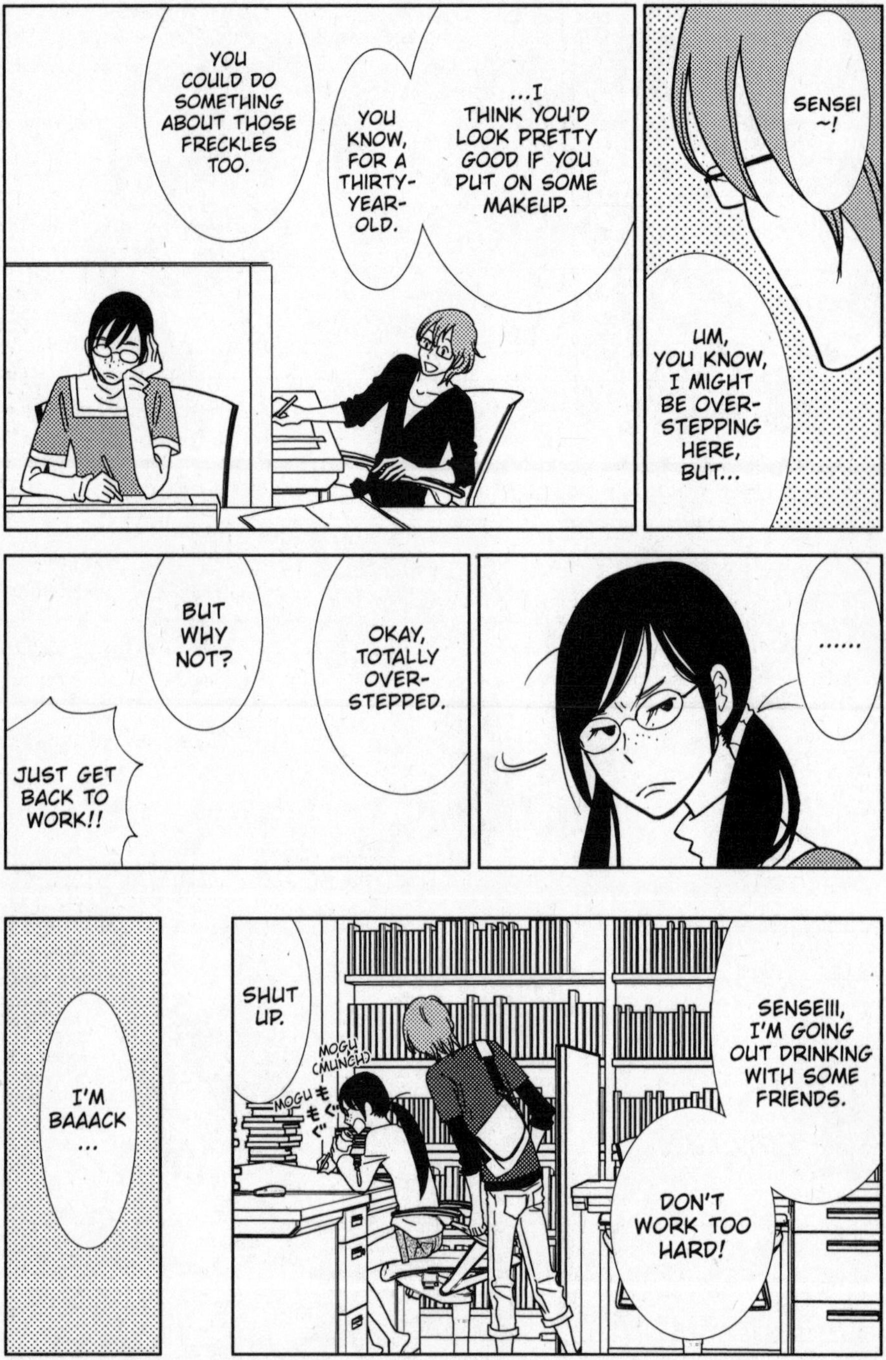
SENSEI ~!
UM, YOU KNOW, I MIGHT BE OVER-STEPPING HERE, BUT...
...I THINK YOU'D LOOK PRETTY GOOD IF YOU PUT ON SOME MAKEUP.
YOU KNOW, FOR A THIRTY-YEAR-OLD.
YOU COULD DO SOMETHING ABOUT THOSE FRECKLES TOO.
......
OKAY, TOTALLY OVER-STEPPED.
BUT WHY NOT?
JUST GET BACK TO WORK!!
SENSEIII, I'M GOING OUT DRINKING WITH SOME FRIENDS.
DON'T WORK TOO HARD!
SHUT UP.
MOGU (MUNCH)
MOGU
もぐもぐ
I'M BAAACK ...

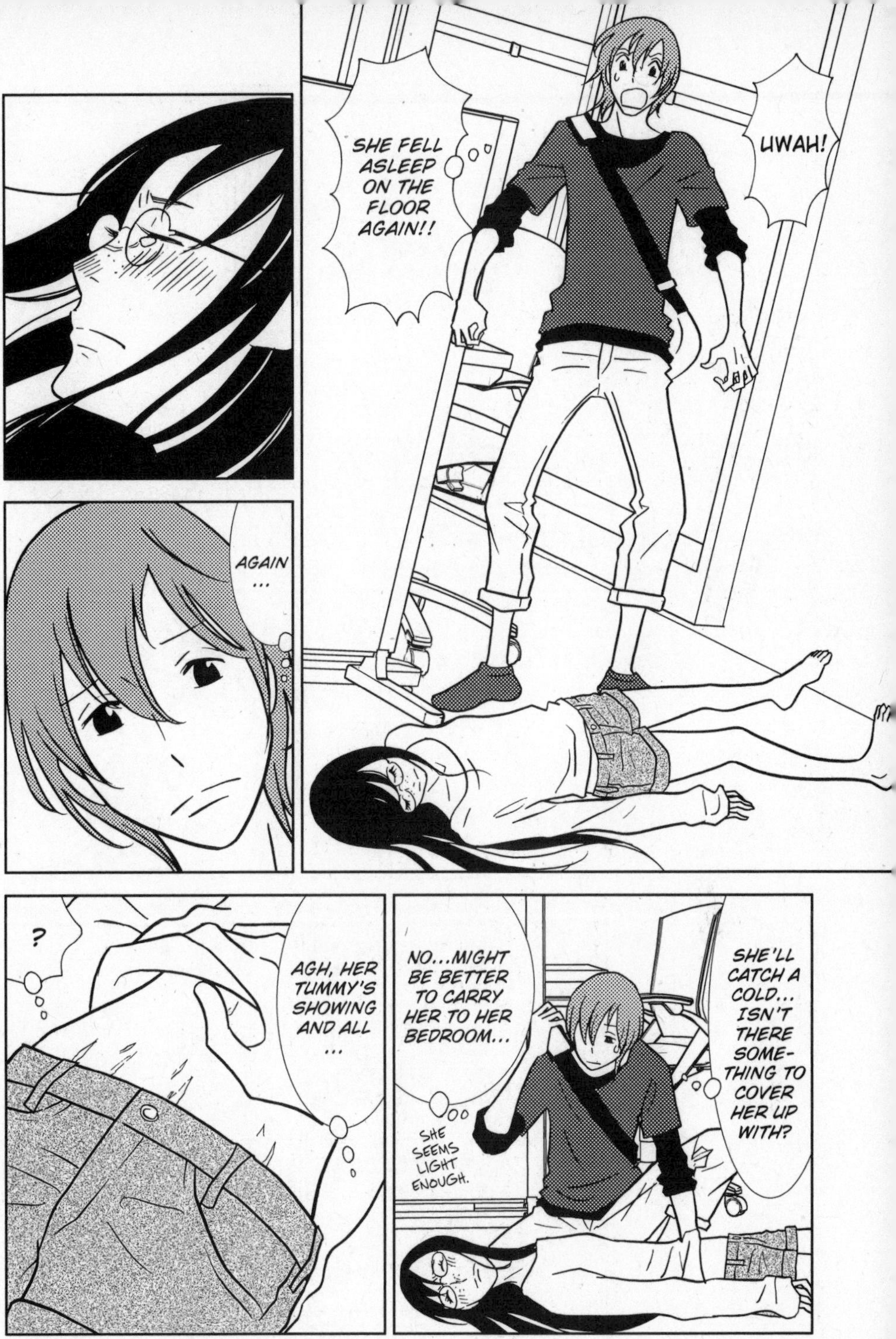
UWAH!
SHE FELL ASLEEP ON THE FLOOR AGAIN!!
AGAIN ...
SHE'LL CATCH A COLD... ISN'T THERE SOME-THING TO COVER HER UP WITH?
NO...MIGHT BE BETTER TO CARRY HER TO HER BEDROOM...
SHE SEEMS LIGHT ENOUGH.
AGH, HER TUMMY'S SHOWING AND ALL ...
?

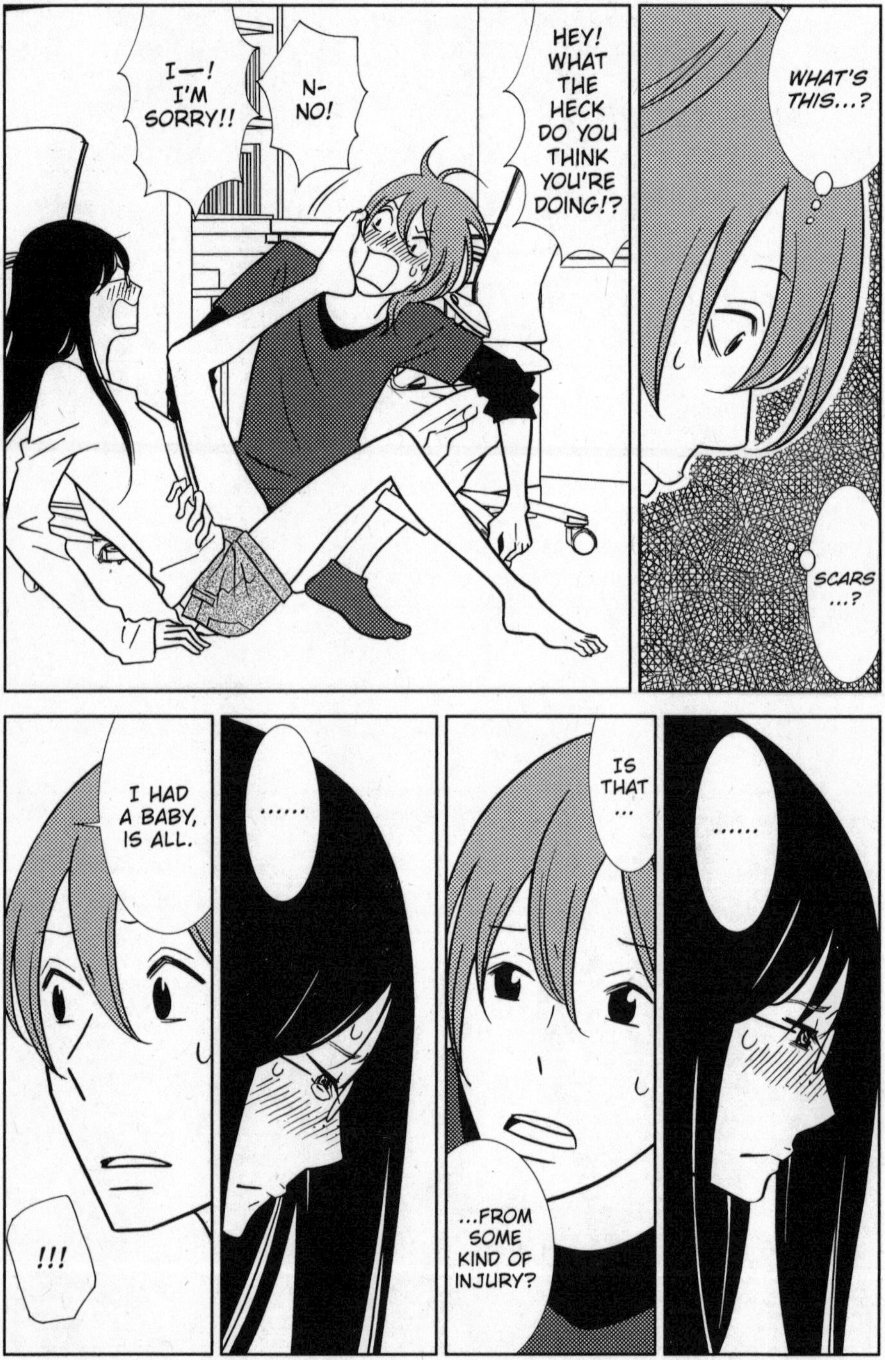
WHAT'S THIS...?
SCARS ...?
HEY! WHAT THE HECK DO YOU THINK YOU'RE DOING!?
N-NO!
I—! I'M SORRY!!
......
IS THAT ...
...FROM SOME KIND OF INJURY?
......
I HAD A BABY, IS ALL.
!!!

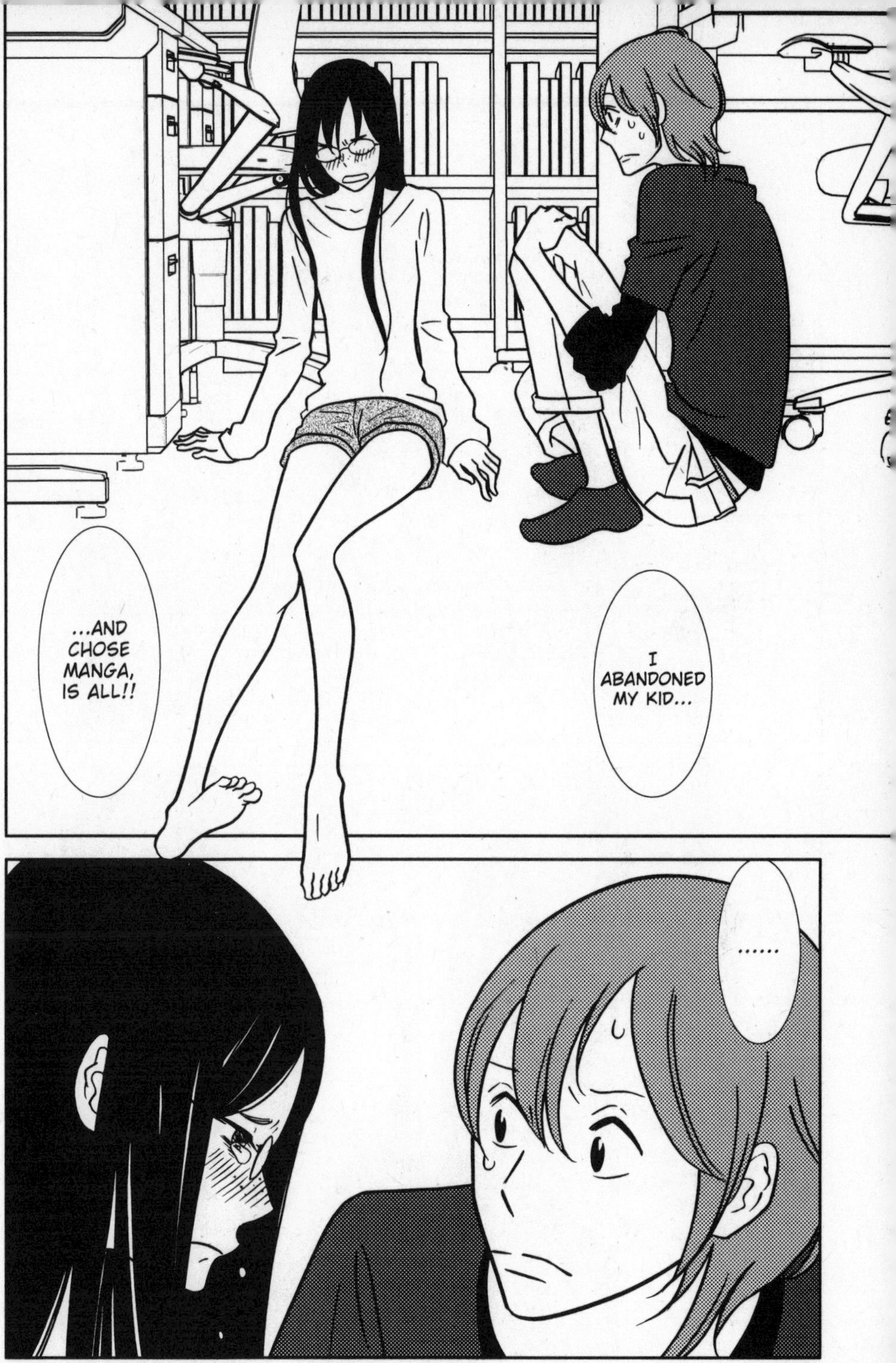
I ABANDONED MY KID...
...AND CHOSE MANGA, IS ALL!!
......

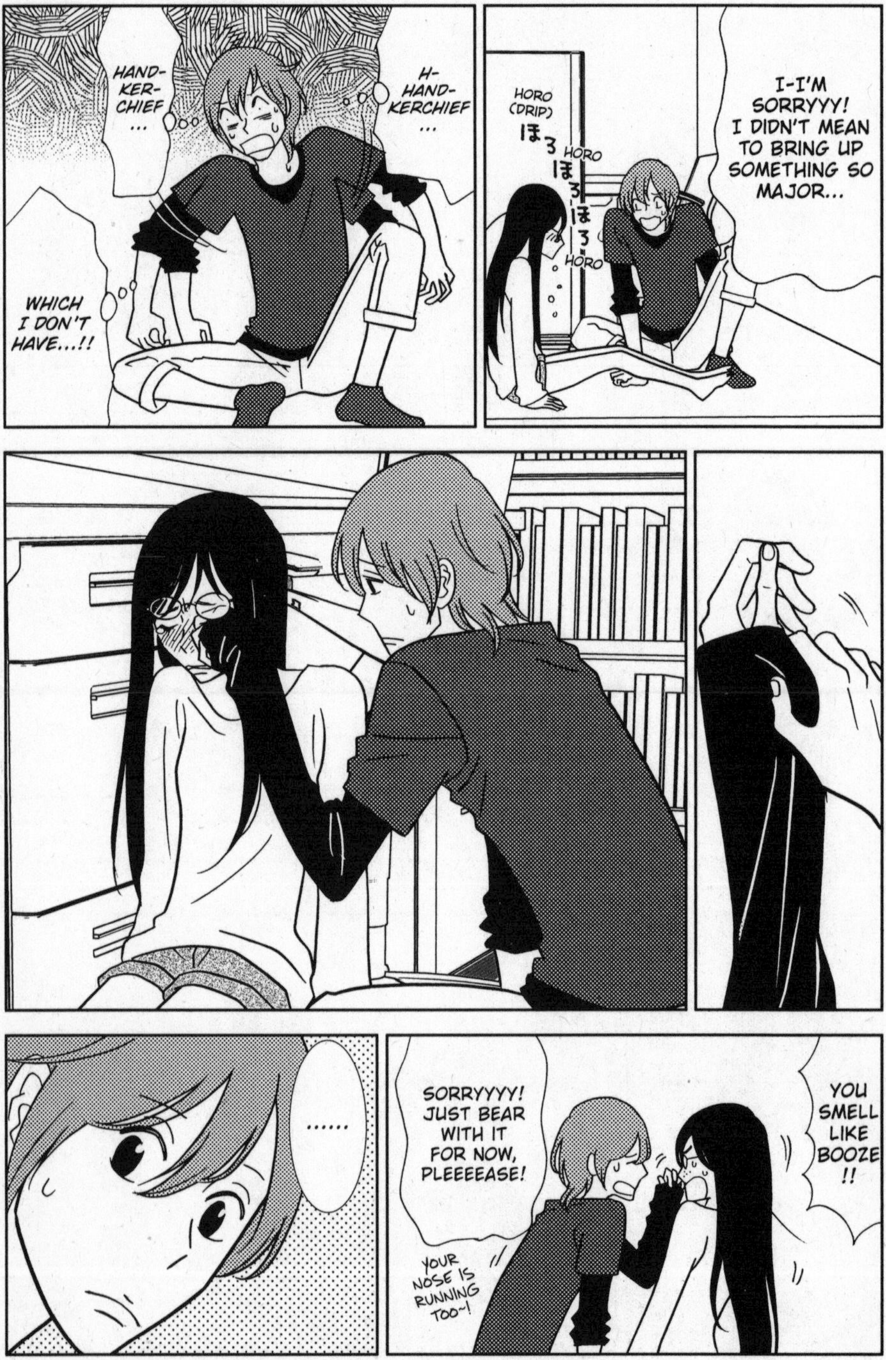
I-I'M SORRYYY! I DIDN'T MEAN TO BRING UP SOMETHING SO MAJOR...
HORO (DRIP) ほろ
HORO ほろ
ほろ
HORO
H-HANDKERCHIEF...
HANDKERCHIEF...
WHICH I DON'T HAVE...!!
YOU SMELL LIKE BOOZE!!
SORRYYYY! JUST BEAR WITH IT FOR NOW, PLEEEEASE!
YOUR NOSE IS RUNNING TOO~!
......

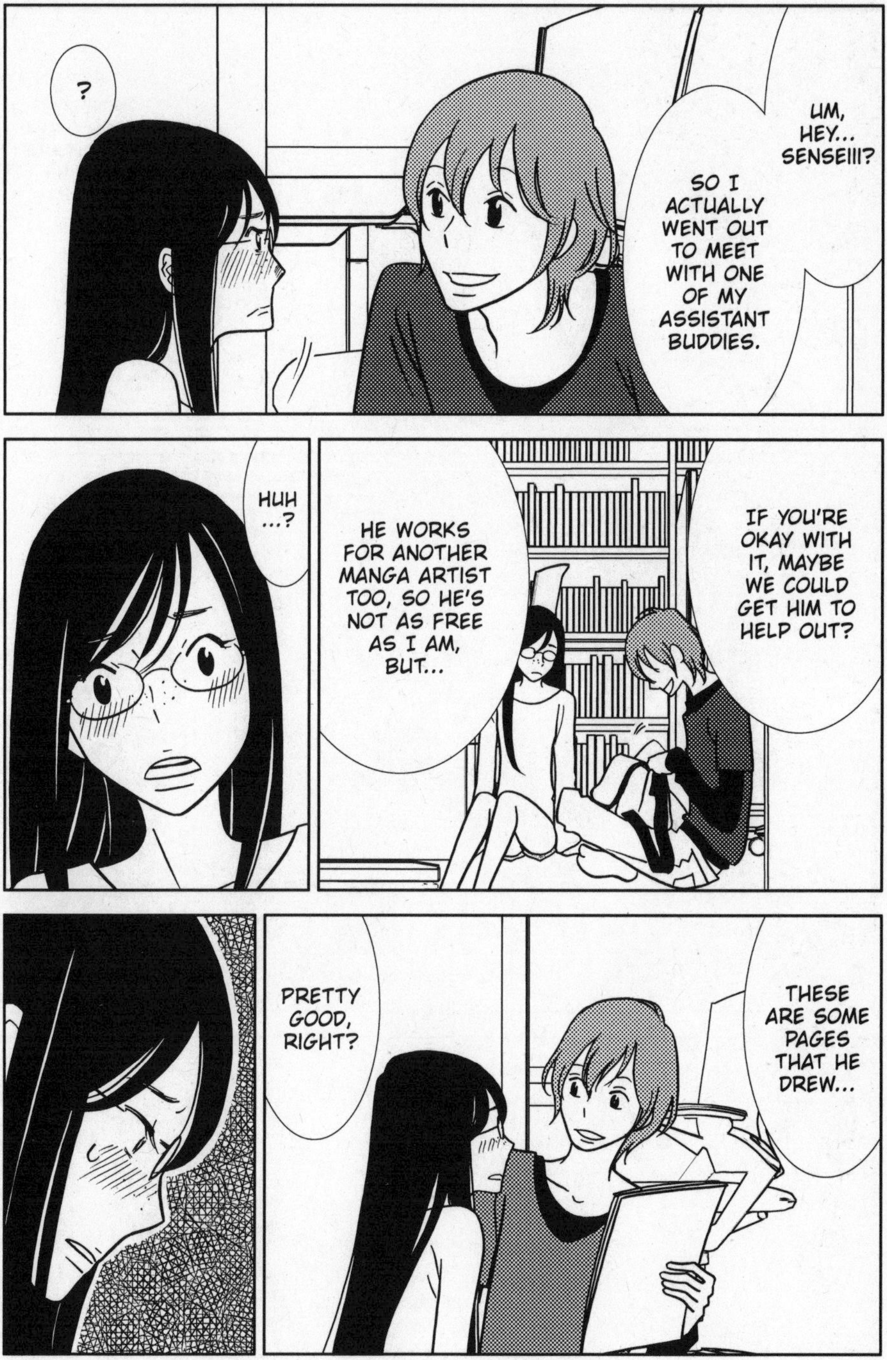
UM, HEY... SENSEIII?
SO I ACTUALLY WENT OUT TO MEET WITH ONE OF MY ASSISTANT BUDDIES.
?
IF YOU'RE OKAY WITH IT, MAYBE WE COULD GET HIM TO HELP OUT?
HE WORKS FOR ANOTHER MANGA ARTIST TOO, SO HE'S NOT AS FREE AS I AM, BUT...
HUH ...?
THESE ARE SOME PAGES THAT HE DREW...
PRETTY GOOD, RIGHT?

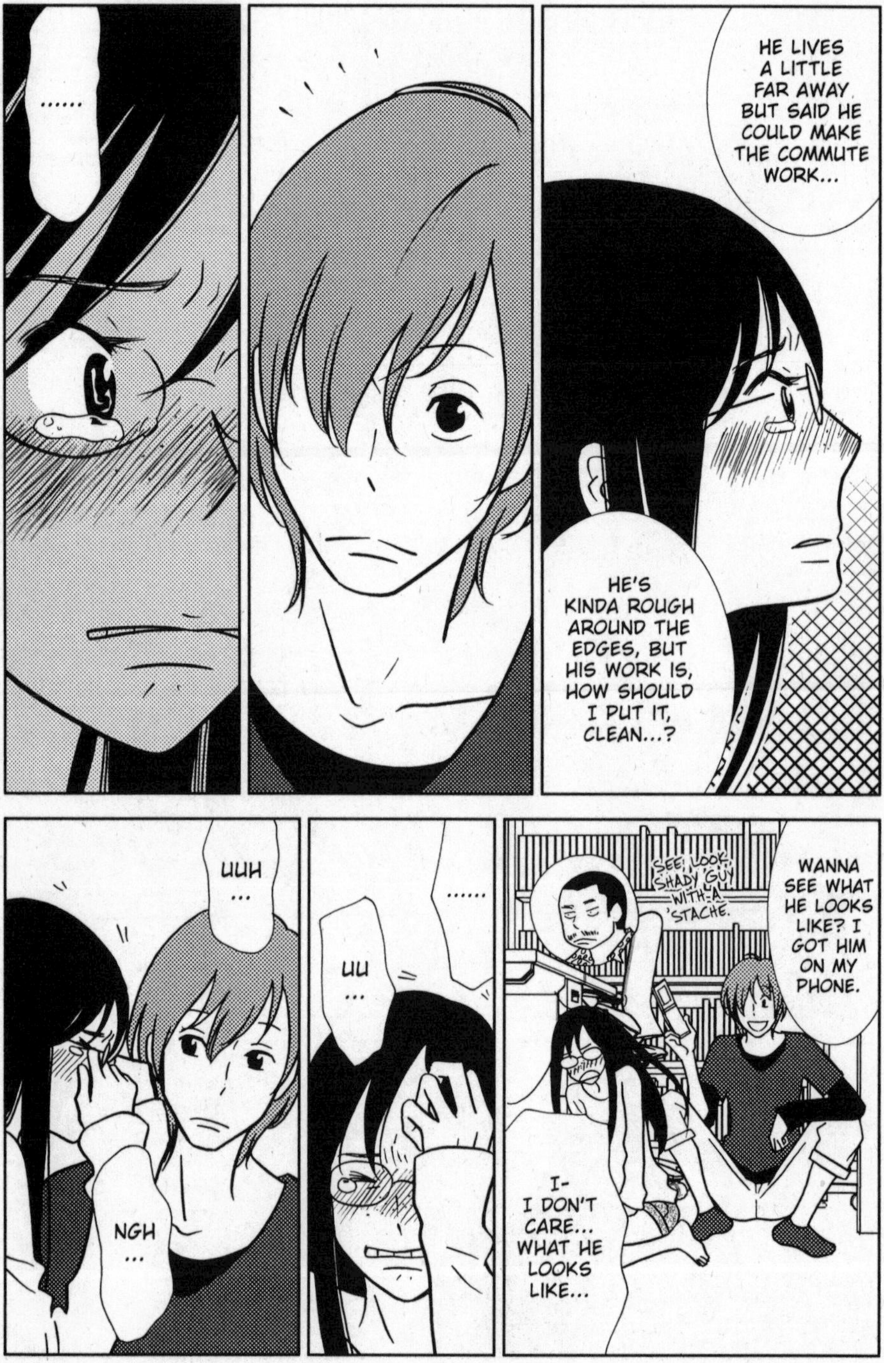
HE LIVES A LITTLE FAR AWAY BUT SAID HE COULD MAKE THE COMMUTE WORK...
HE'S KINDA ROUGH AROUND THE EDGES, BUT HIS WORK IS, HOW SHOULD I PUT IT, CLEAN...?
......
WANNA SEE WHAT HE LOOKS LIKE? I GOT HIM ON MY PHONE.
SEE, LOOK. SHADY GUY WITH A 'STACHE.
I- I DON'T CARE... WHAT HE LOOKS LIKE...
......
UU ...
UUH ...
NGH ...

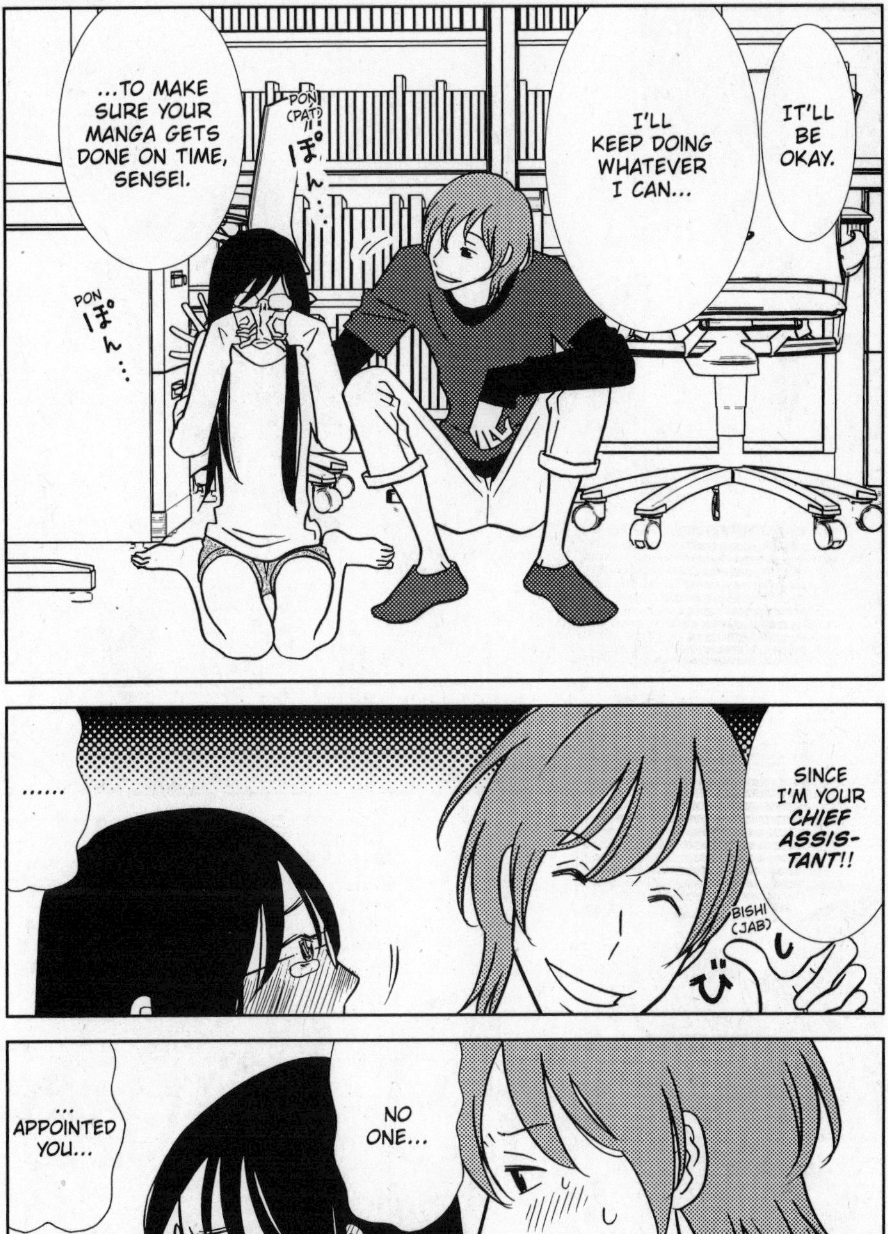
IT'LL BE OKAY.
I'LL KEEP DOING WHATEVER I CAN...
PON (PAT)
ぽん…
...TO MAKE SURE YOUR MANGA GETS DONE ON TIME, SENSEI.
PON
ぽん…
SINCE I'M YOUR CHIEF ASSISTANT!!
BISHI (JAB)
びし
......
NO ONE...
... APPOINTED YOU...
CRAPPY CHIEF.

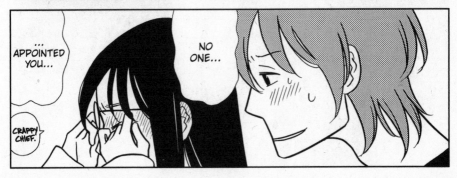

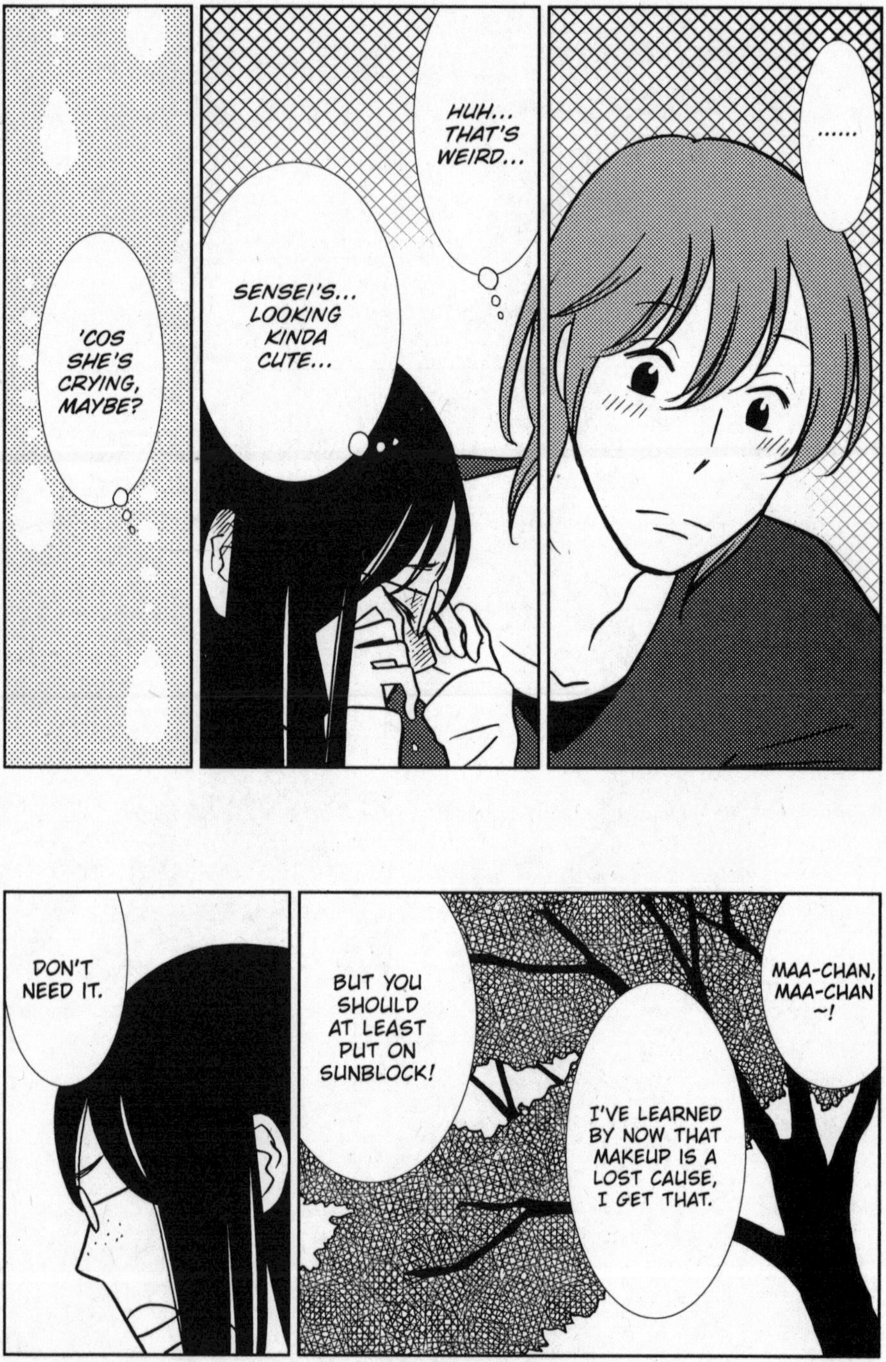
......
HUH... THAT'S WEIRD...
SENSEI'S... LOOKING KINDA CUTE...
'COS SHE'S CRYING, MAYBE?
MAA-CHAN, MAA-CHAN ~!
I'VE LEARNED BY NOW THAT MAKEUP IS A LOST CAUSE, I GET THAT.
BUT YOU SHOULD AT LEAST PUT ON SUNBLOCK!
DON'T NEED IT.

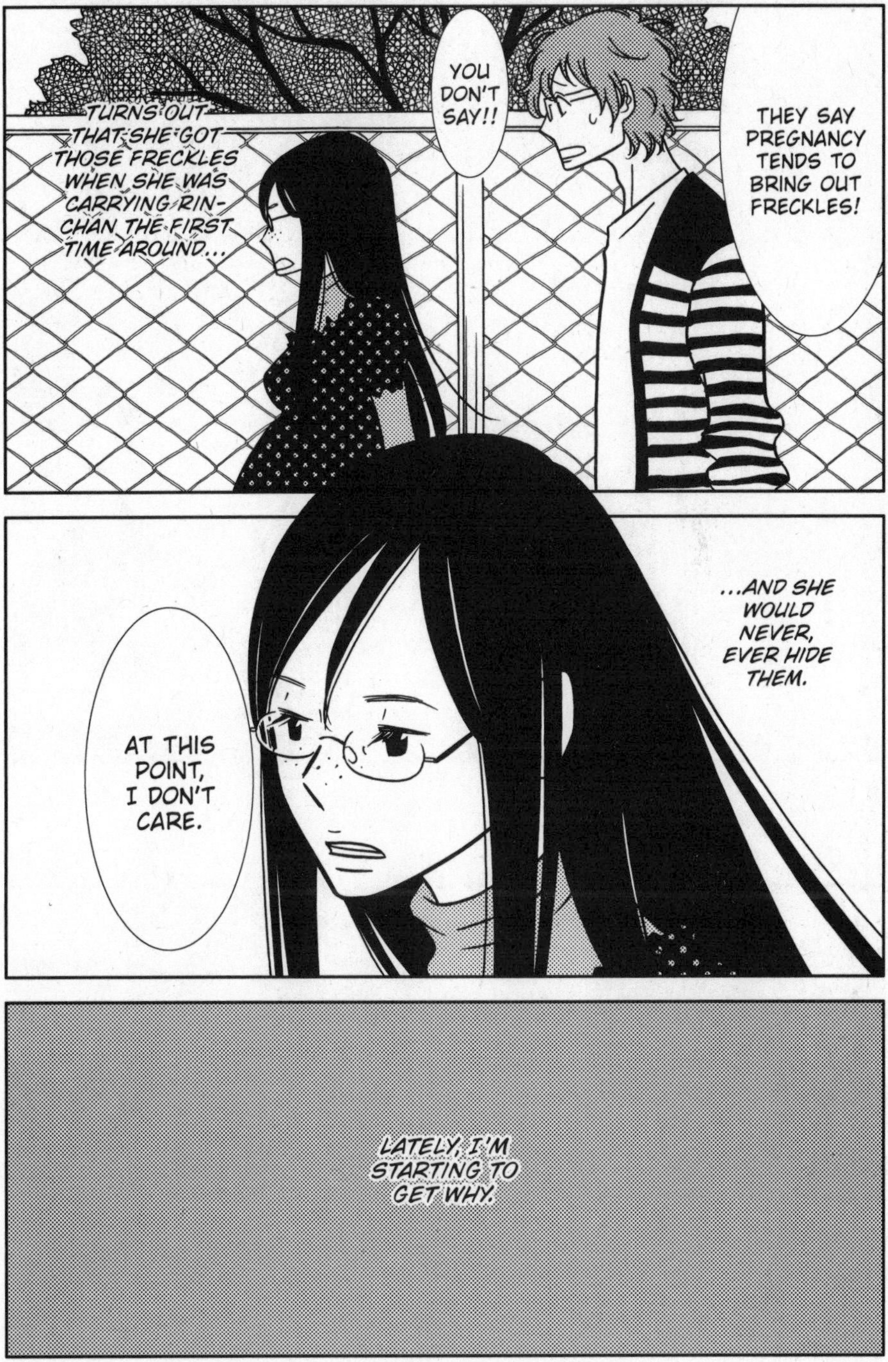
THEY SAY PREGNANCY TENDS TO BRING OUT FRECKLES!
YOU DON'T SAY!!
TURNS OUT THAT SHE GOT THOSE FRECKLES WHEN SHE WAS CARRYING RIN-CHAN THE FIRST TIME AROUND...
...AND SHE WOULD NEVER, EVER HIDE THEM.
AT THIS POINT, I DON'T CARE.
LATELY, I'M STARTING TO GET WHY.

extra.4 eyeglass drop / END

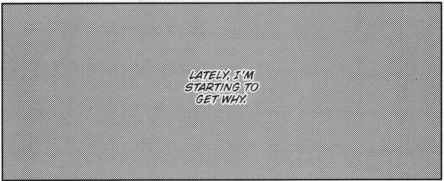

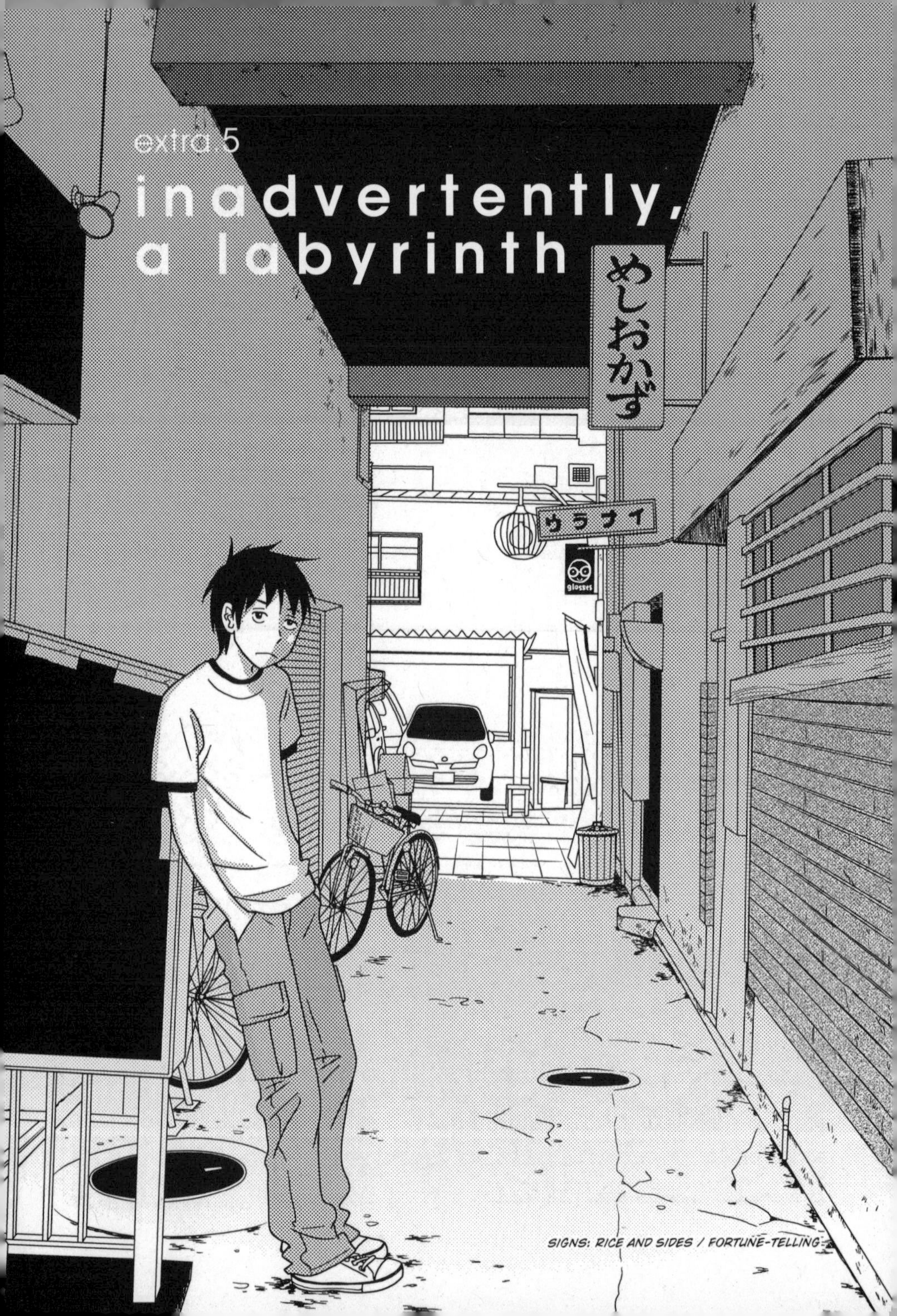
extra.5
inadvertently,
a labyrinth
めしおかず
ウラナイ
glasses
SIGNS: RICE AND SIDES / FORTUNE-TELLING

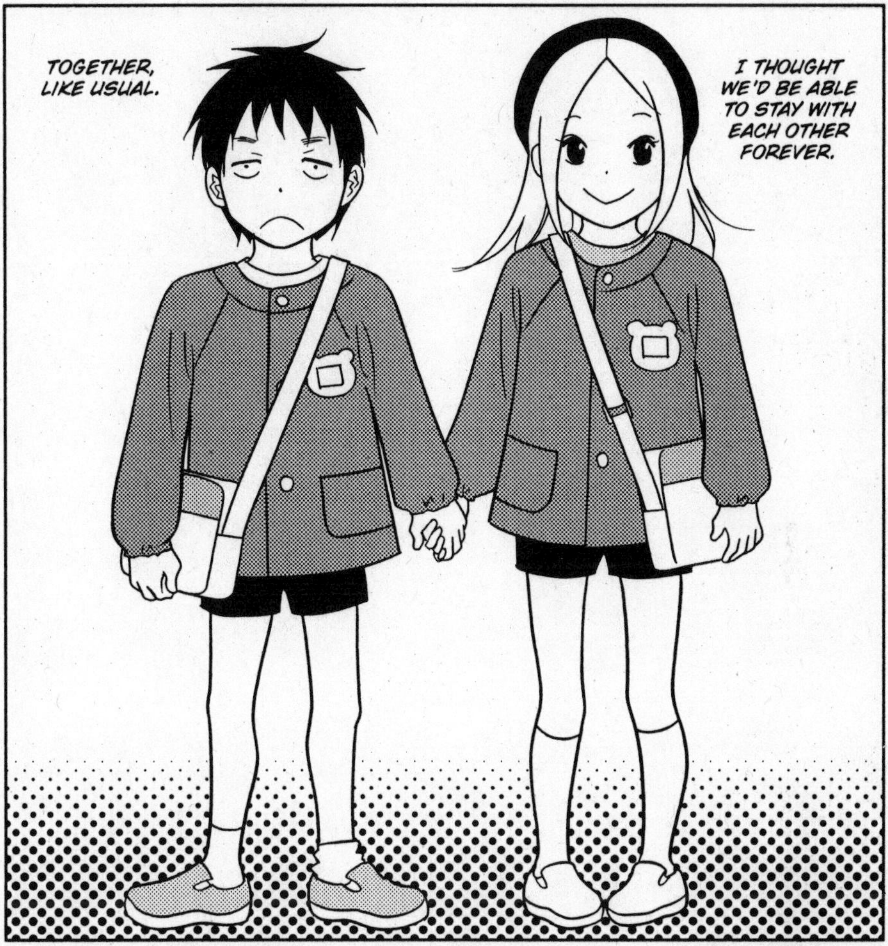
I THOUGHT WE'D BE ABLE TO STAY WITH EACH OTHER FOREVER.
TOGETHER, LIKE USUAL.

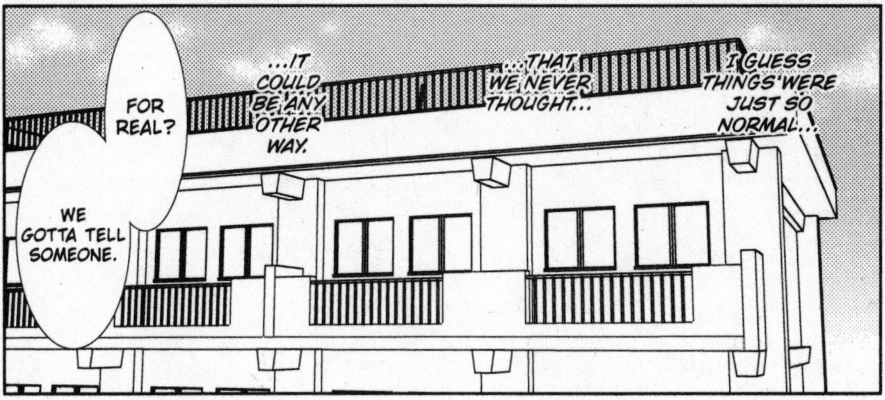
I GUESS THINGS WERE JUST SO NORMAL...
...THAT WE NEVER THOUGHT...
...IT COULD BE ANY OTHER WAY.
FOR REAL?
WE GOTTA TELL SOMEONE.

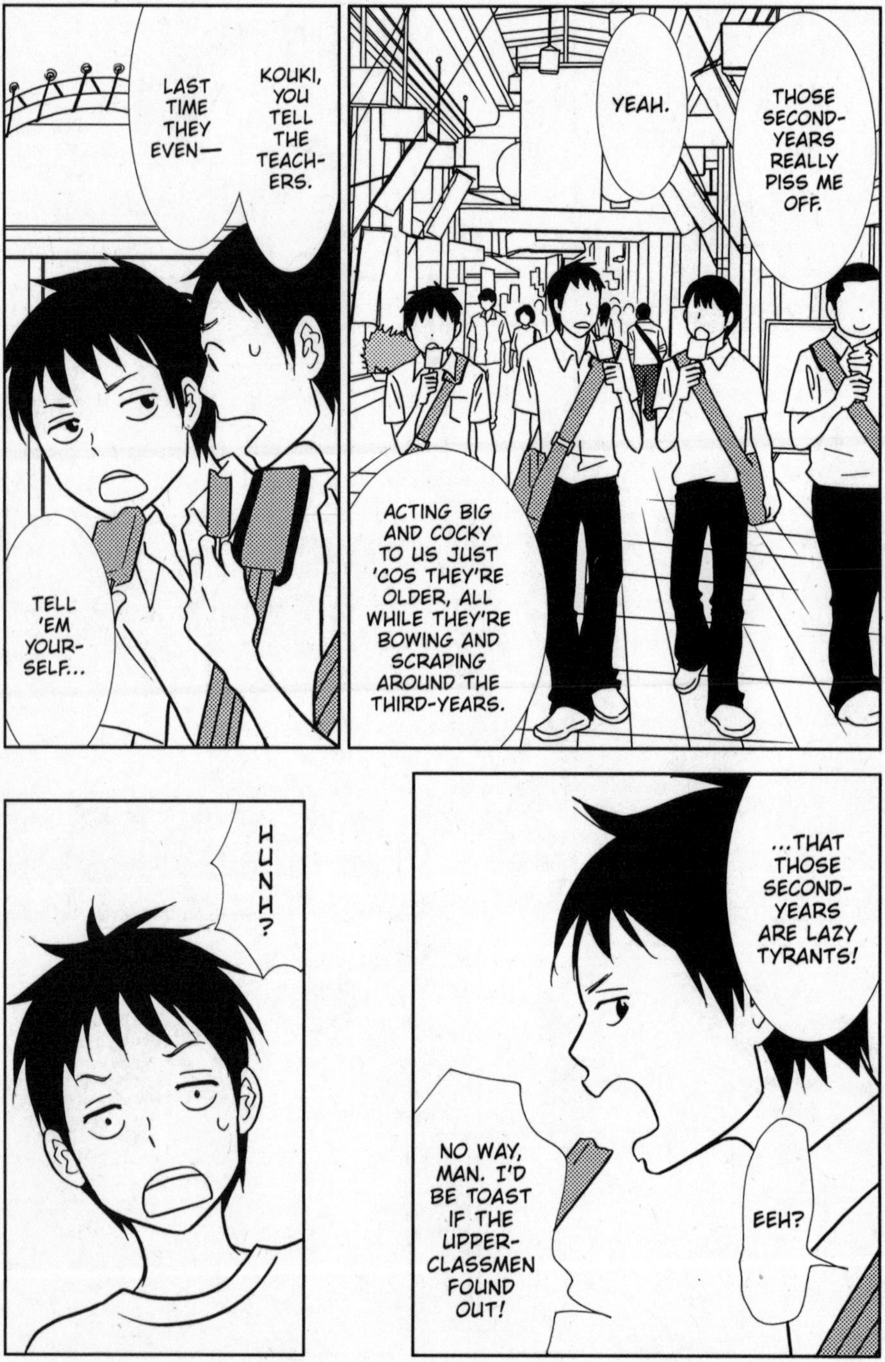
THOSE SECOND-YEARS REALLY PISS ME OFF.
YEAH.
ACTING BIG AND COCKY TO US JUST 'COS THEY'RE OLDER, ALL WHILE THEY'RE BOWING AND SCRAPING AROUND THE THIRD-YEARS.
KOUKI, YOU TELL THE TEACHERS.
LAST TIME THEY EVEN—
TELL 'EM YOURSELF...
...THAT THOSE SECOND-YEARS ARE LAZY TYRANTS!
EEH?
NO WAY, MAN. I'D BE TOAST IF THE UPPERCLASSMEN FOUND OUT!
HUNH?

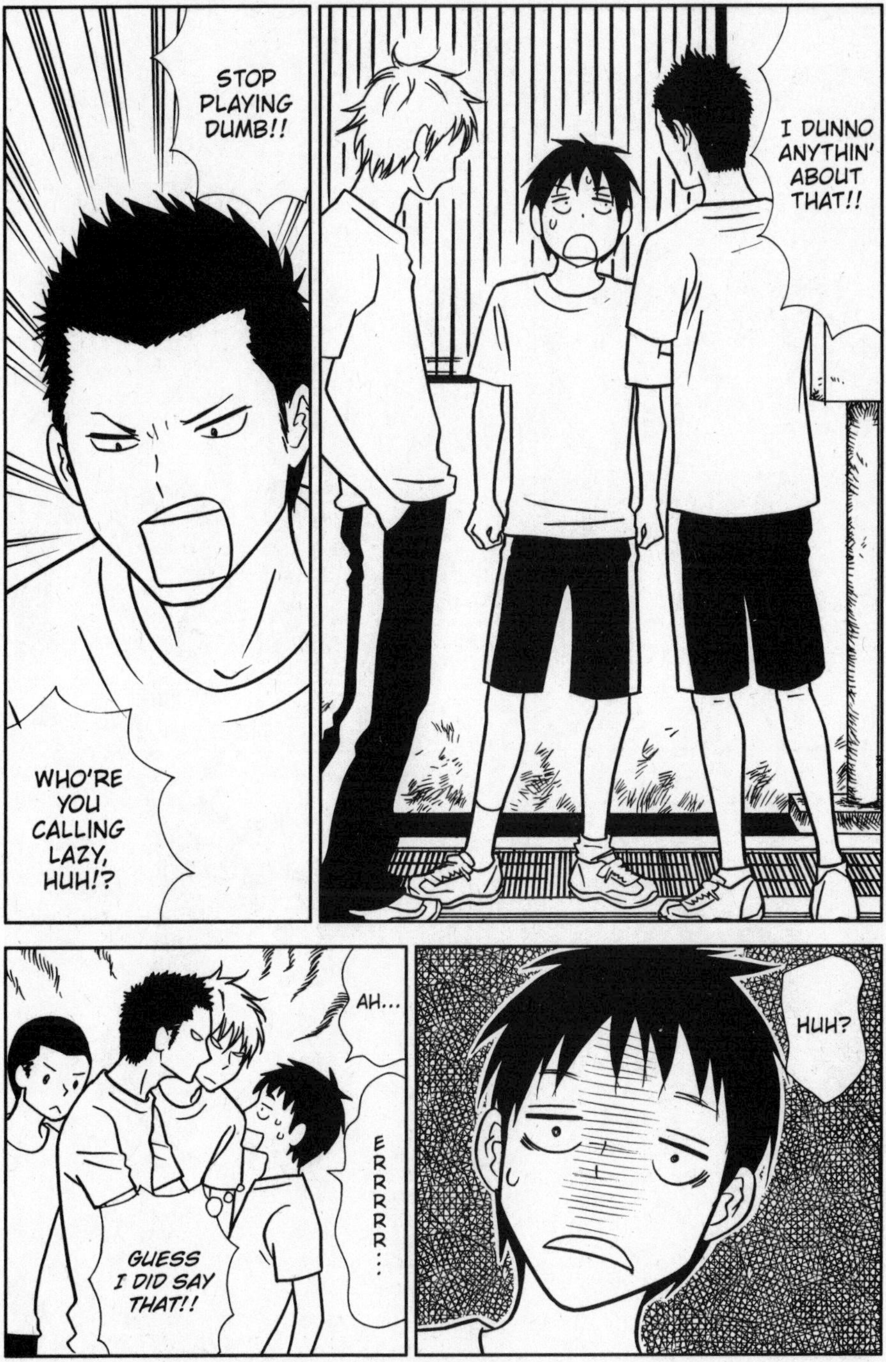
I DUNNO ANYTHIN' ABOUT THAT!!
STOP PLAYING DUMB!!
WHO'RE YOU CALLING LAZY, HUH!?
HUH?
AH...
ERRRRR...
GUESS I DID SAY THAT!!

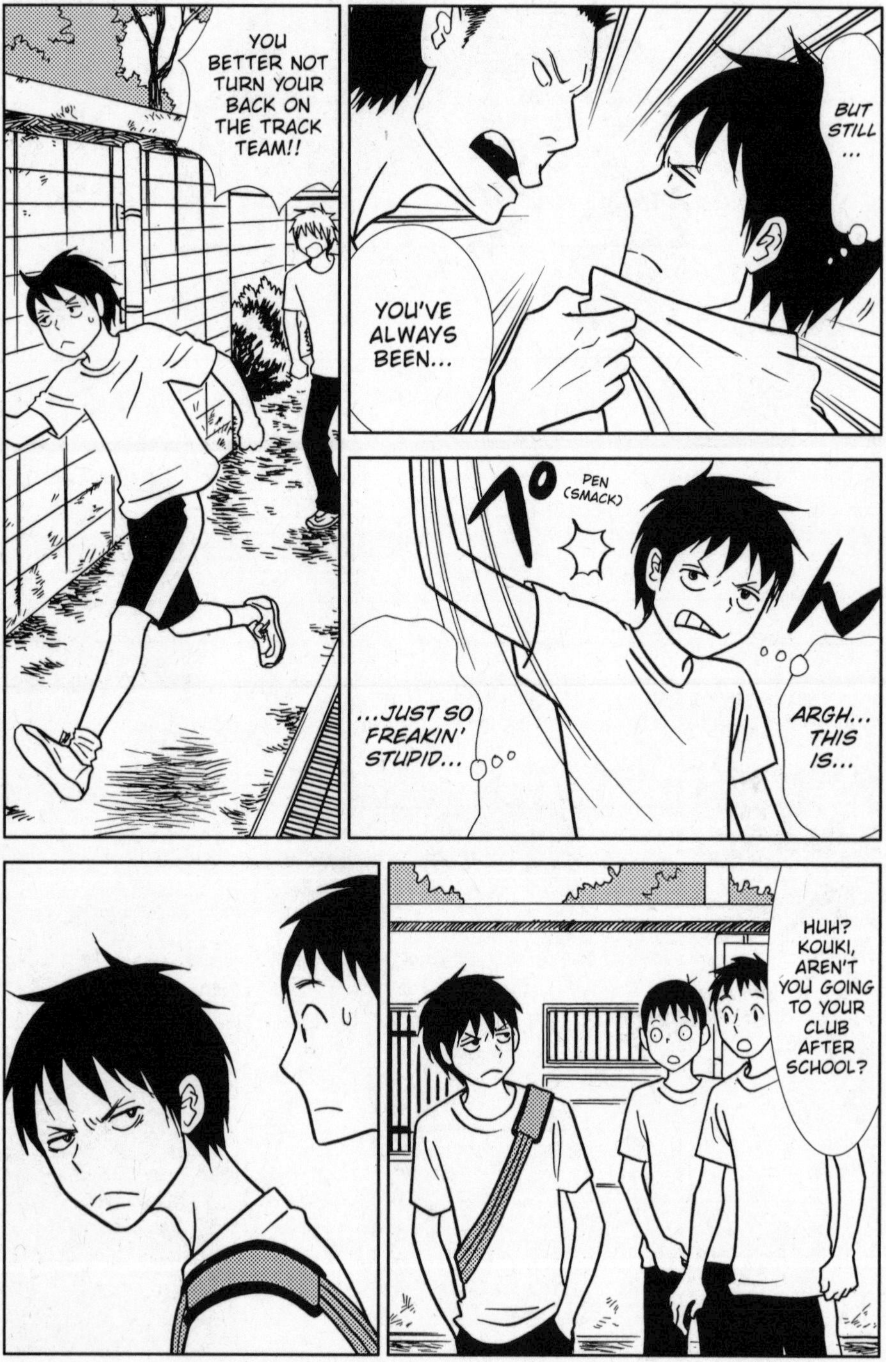

BUT STILL ...
YOU'VE ALWAYS BEEN...
PEN (SMACK)
ARGH... THIS IS...
...JUST SO FREAKIN' STUPID...
YOU BETTER NOT TURN YOUR BACK ON THE TRACK TEAM!!
HUH? KOUKI, AREN'T YOU GOING TO YOUR CLUB AFTER SCHOOL?

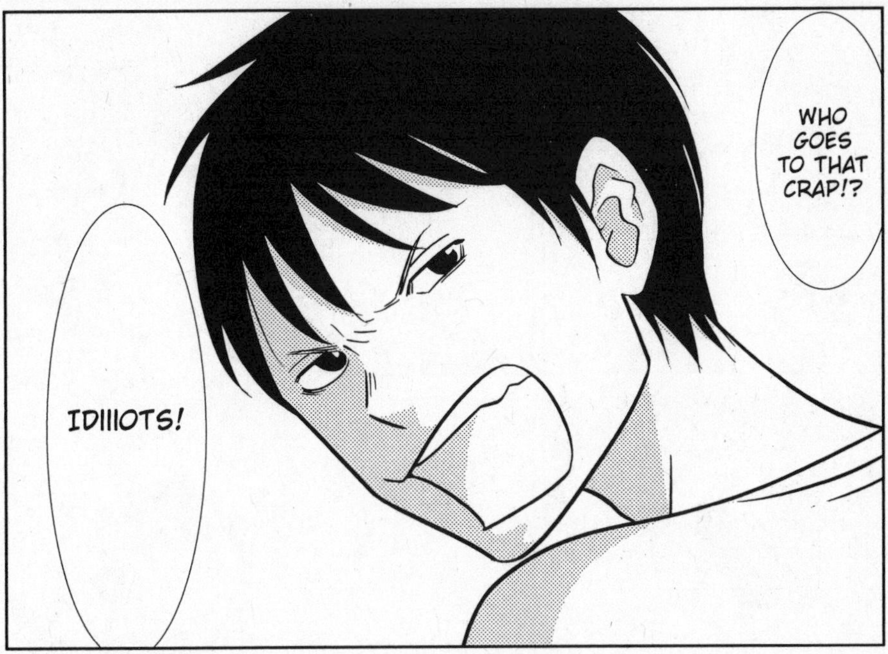
WHO GOES TO THAT CRAP!?
IDIIIOTS!

SIGN: GAME CENTER ONE-UP

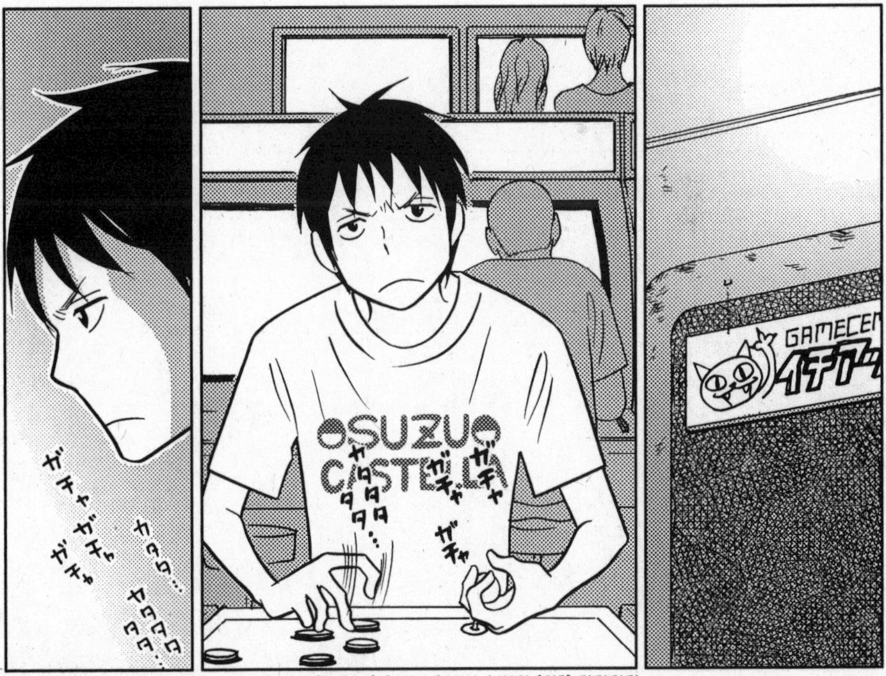
GAMECEN
OSUZU CASTELLA

SFX: KATATA KATATATATATA GACHA GACHA GACHA

SFX: GACHA (RATTLE) GACHA GACHA / KATA (TAP) TATATATA

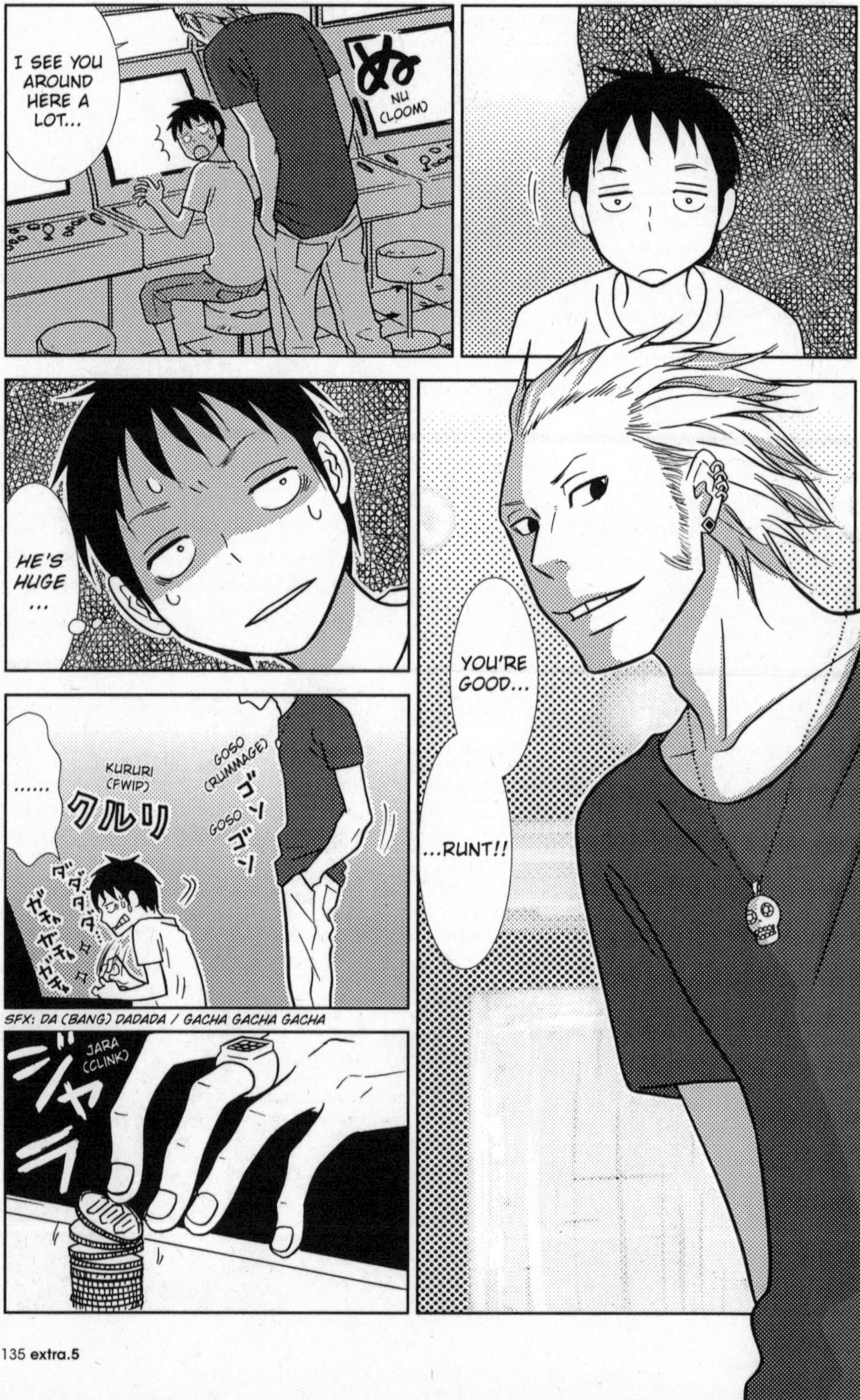
ぬ
NU (LOOM)
I SEE YOU AROUND HERE A LOT...
YOU'RE GOOD...
...RUNT!!
HE'S HUGE ...
GOSO (RUMMAGE)
ゴソゴソ
GOSO
KURURI (FWIP)
クルリ
......
ダダダダ
ガチャガチャガチャ
SFX: DA (BANG) DADADA / GACHA GACHA GACHA
JARA (CLINK)
ジャラ

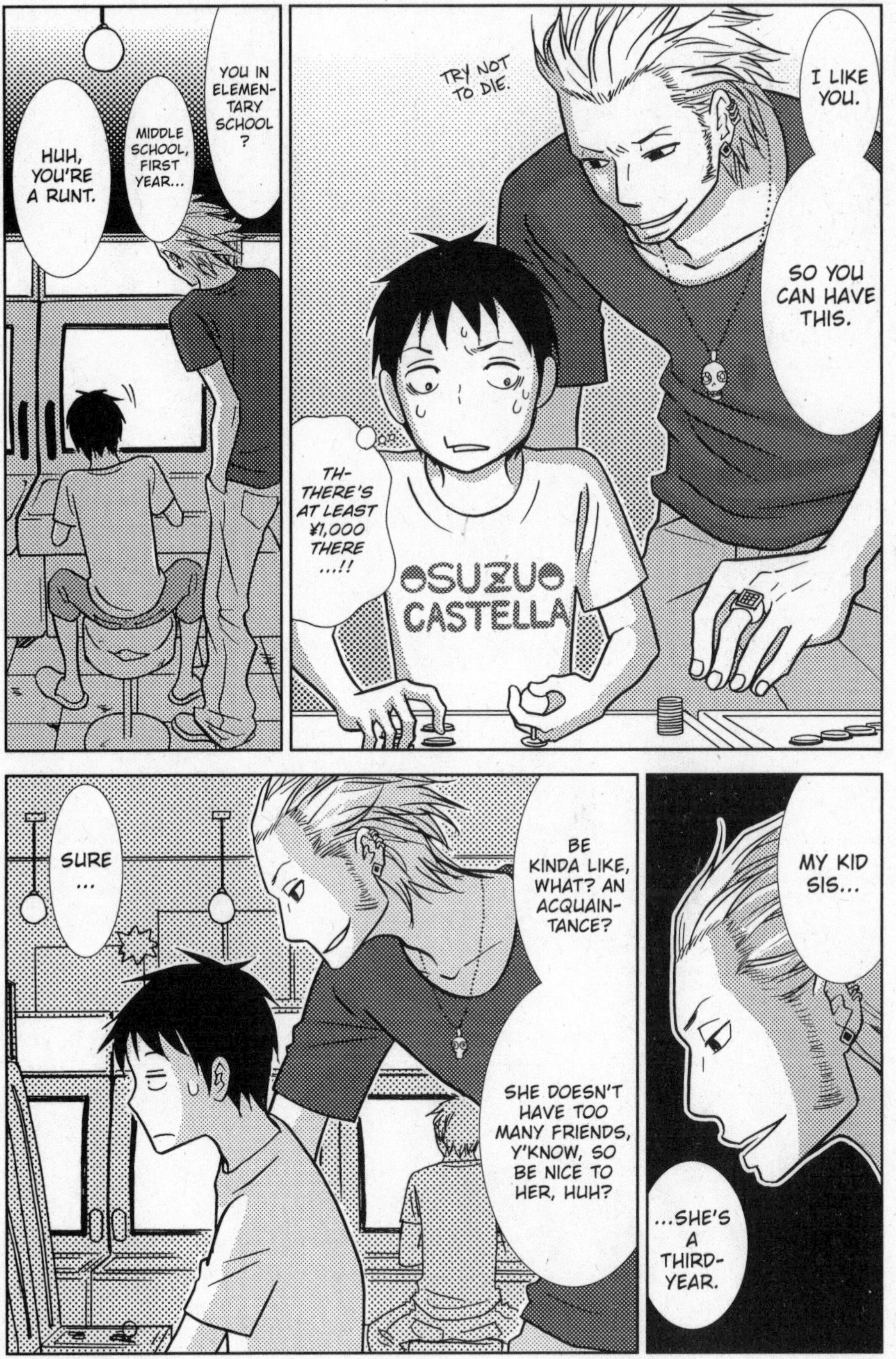
I LIKE YOU.
SO YOU CAN HAVE THIS.
TRY NOT TO DIE.
TH-THERE'S AT LEAST ¥1,000 THERE ...!!
OSUZUO CASTELLA
YOU IN ELEMENTARY SCHOOL?
MIDDLE SCHOOL, FIRST YEAR...
HUH, YOU'RE A RUNT.
MY KID SIS...
...SHE'S A THIRD-YEAR.
BE KINDA LIKE, WHAT? AN ACQUAINTANCE?
SHE DOESN'T HAVE TOO MANY FRIENDS, Y'KNOW, SO BE NICE TO HER, HUH?
SURE ...

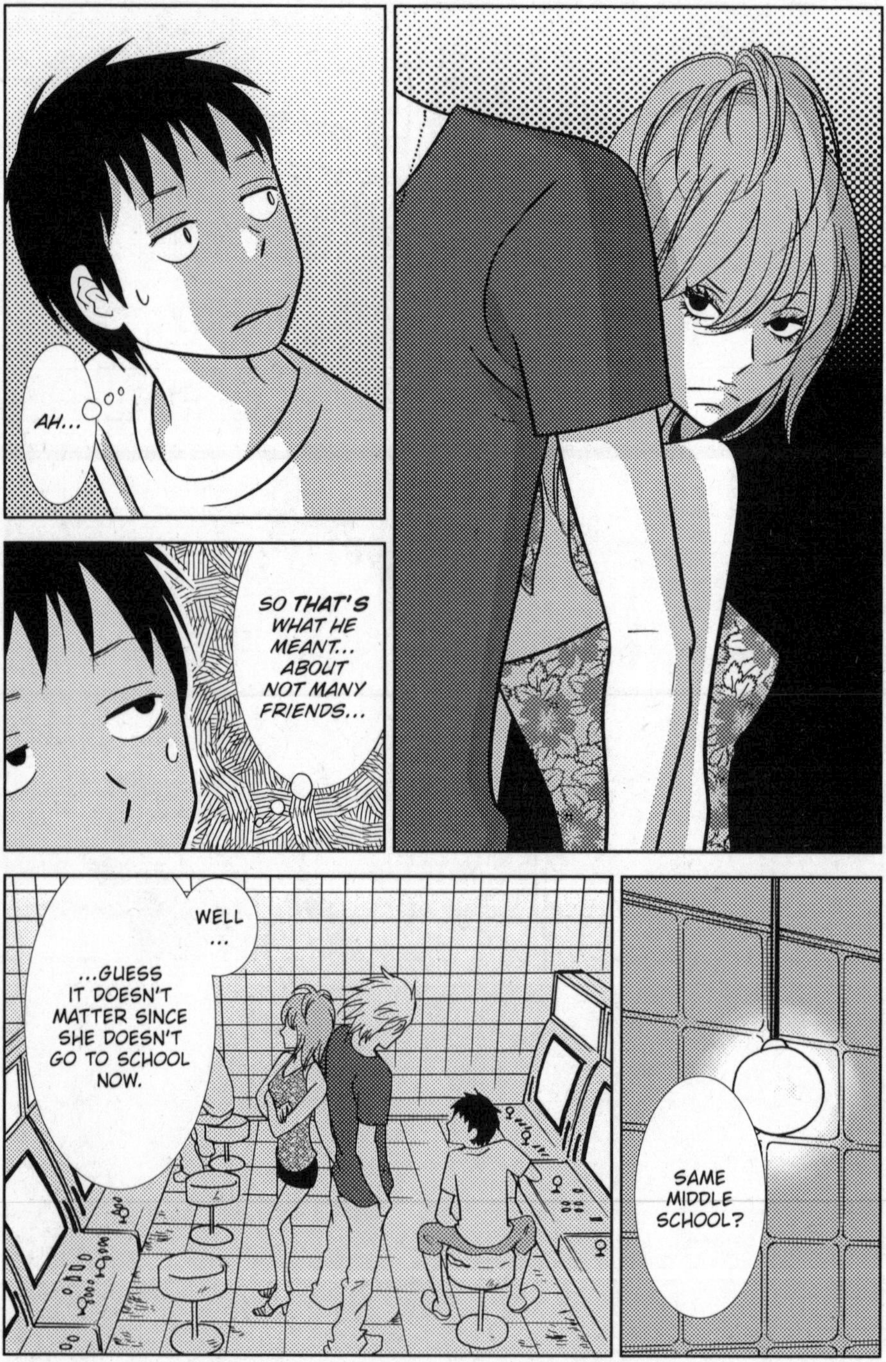
AH...
SO THAT'S WHAT HE MEANT... ABOUT NOT MANY FRIENDS...
SAME MIDDLE SCHOOL?
WELL ...
...GUESS IT DOESN'T MATTER SINCE SHE DOESN'T GO TO SCHOOL NOW.

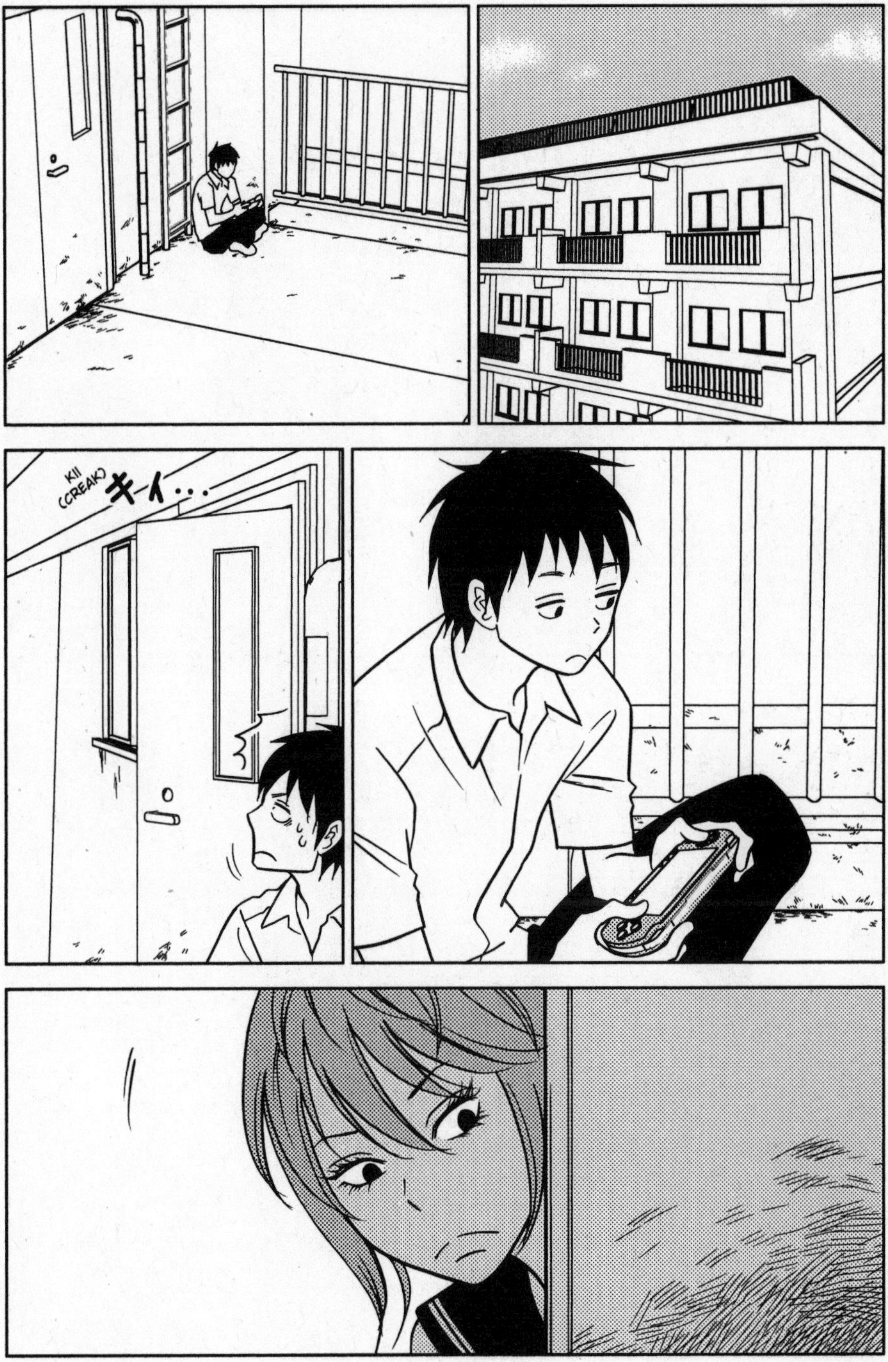
KII (CREAK)
キイ...

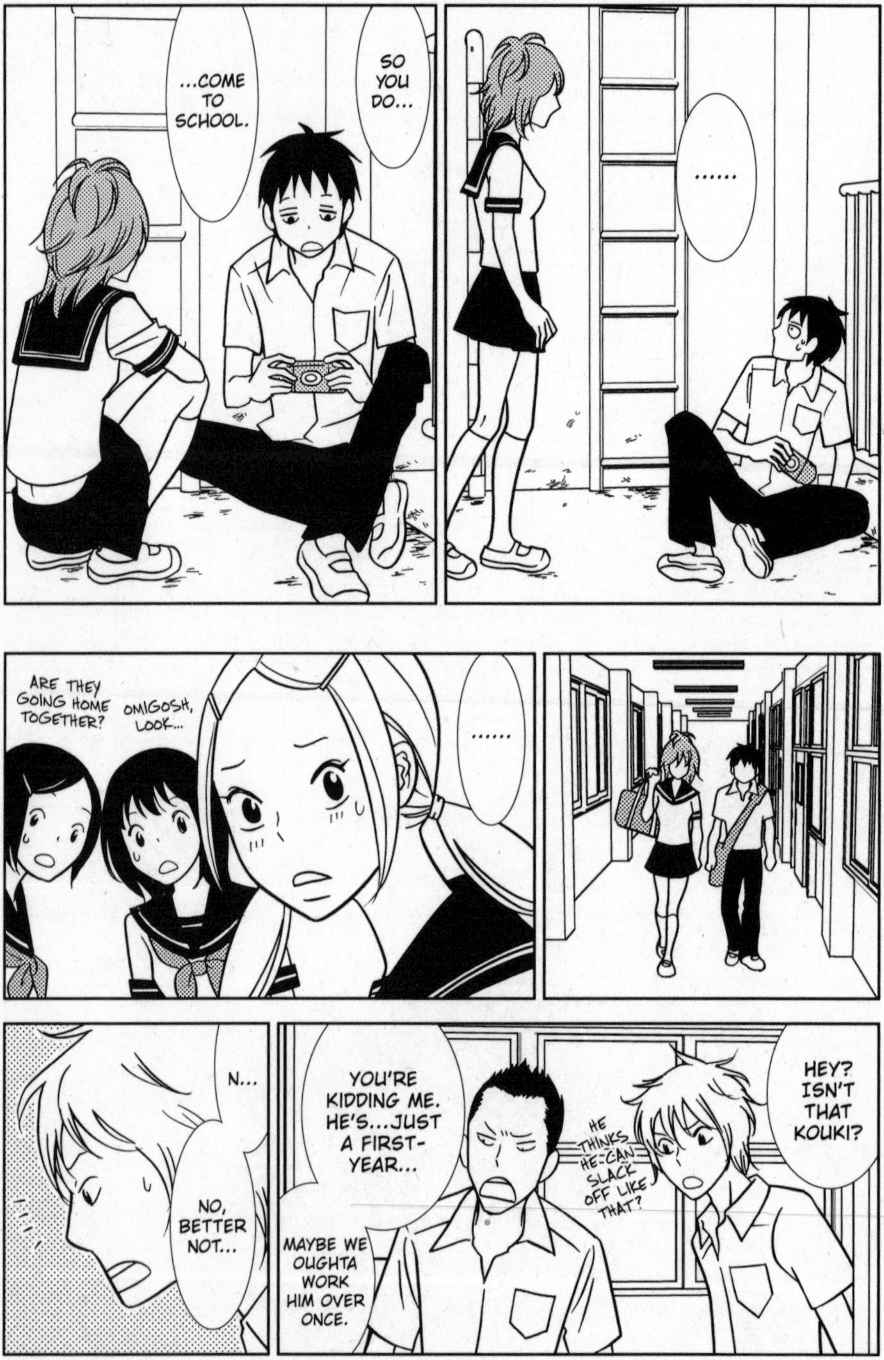
......
SO YOU DO...
...COME TO SCHOOL.
......
OMIGOSH, LOOK...
ARE THEY GOING HOME TOGETHER?
HEY? ISN'T THAT KOUKI?
HE THINKS HE CAN SLACK OFF LIKE THAT?
YOU'RE KIDDING ME. HE'S...JUST A FIRST-YEAR...
MAYBE WE OUGHTA WORK HIM OVER ONCE.
N...
NO, BETTER NOT...

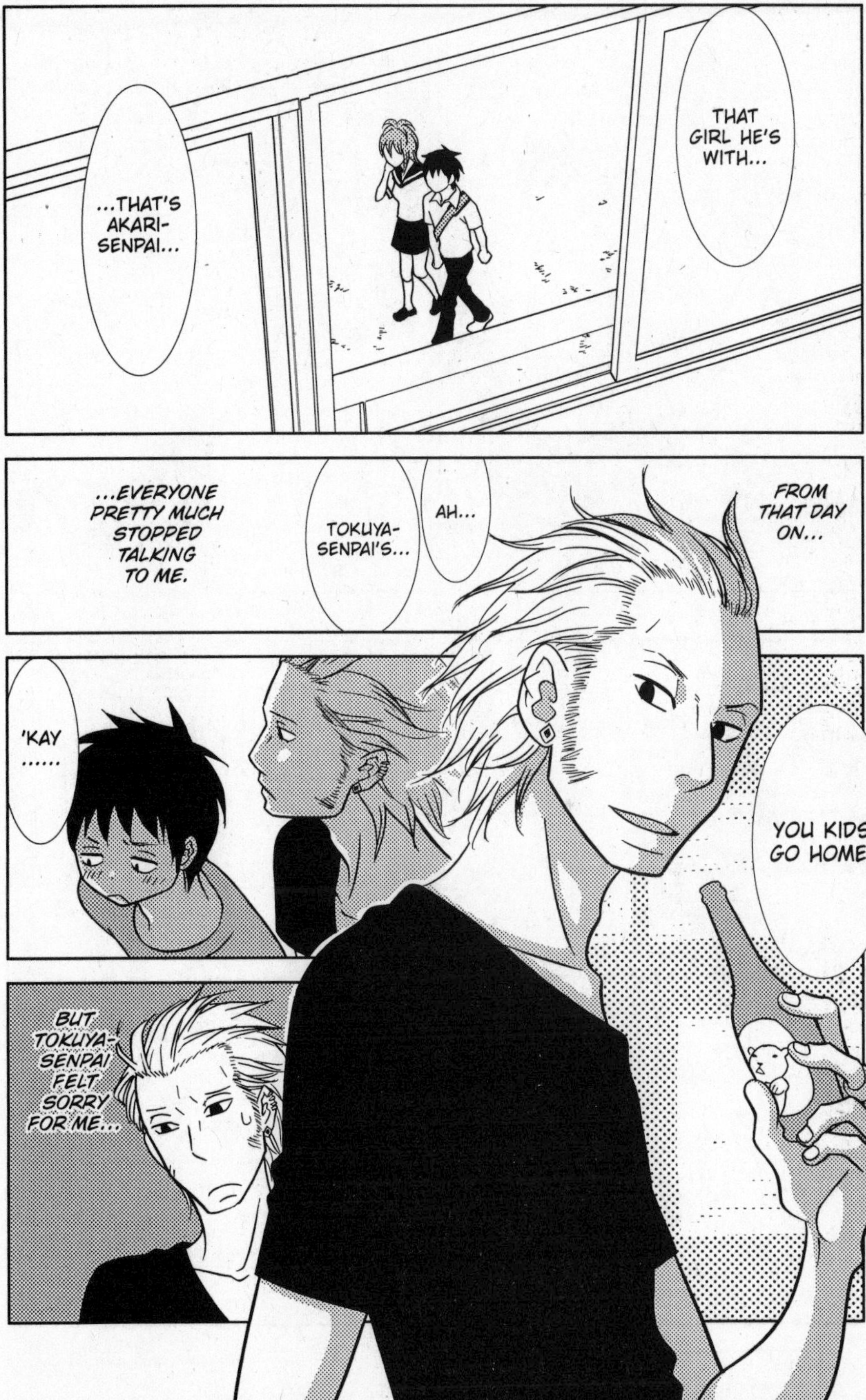
THAT GIRL HE'S WITH...
...THAT'S AKARI-SENPAI...
FROM THAT DAY ON...
AH...
TOKUYA-SENPAI'S...
...EVERYONE PRETTY MUCH STOPPED TALKING TO ME.
YOU KIDS GO HOME.
'KAY ......
BUT TOKUYA-SENPAI FELT SORRY FOR ME...

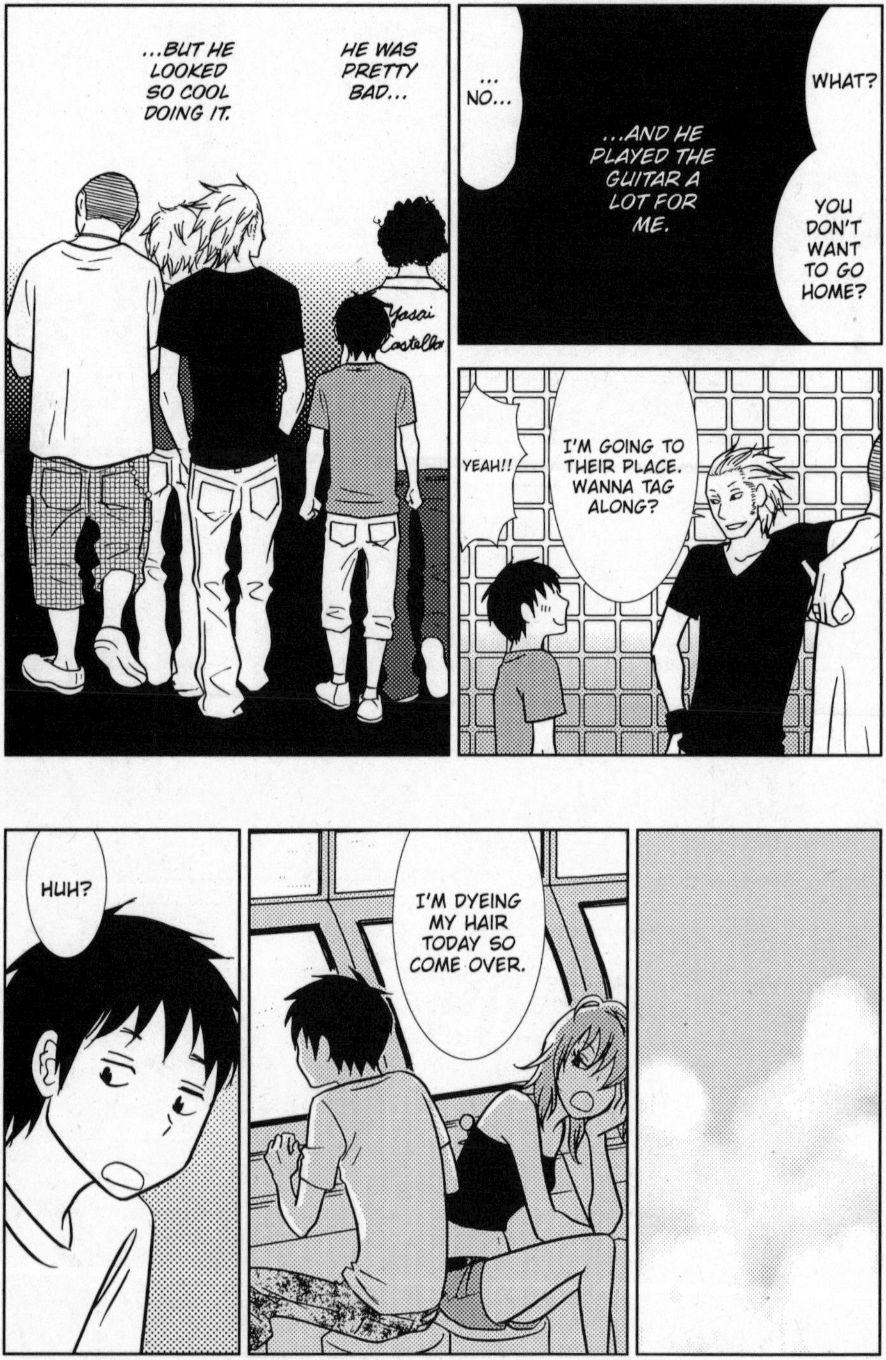
WHAT?
YOU DON'T WANT TO GO HOME?
... NO...
...AND HE PLAYED THE GUITAR A LOT FOR ME.
I'M GOING TO THEIR PLACE. WANNA TAG ALONG?
YEAH!!
HE WAS PRETTY BAD...
...BUT HE LOOKED SO COOL DOING IT.
I'M DYEING MY HAIR TODAY SO COME OVER.
HUH?

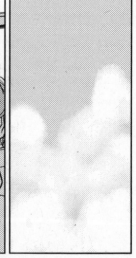

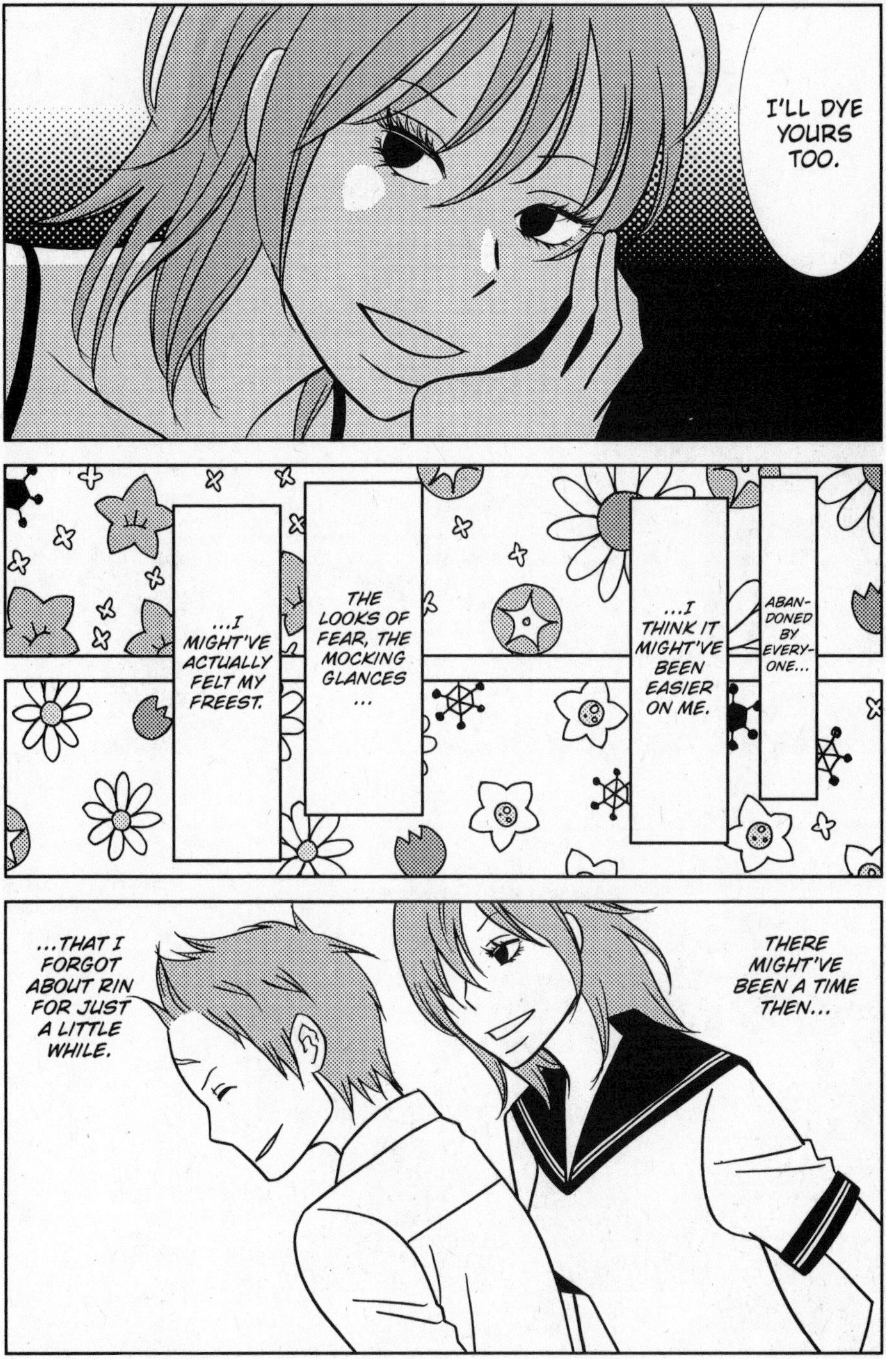
I'LL DYE YOURS TOO.
ABAN-DONED BY EVERY-ONE...
...I THINK IT MIGHT'VE BEEN EASIER ON ME.
THE LOOKS OF FEAR, THE MOCKING GLANCES...
...I MIGHT'VE ACTUALLY FELT MY FREEST.
THERE MIGHT'VE BEEN A TIME THEN...
...THAT I FORGOT ABOUT RIN FOR JUST A LITTLE WHILE.

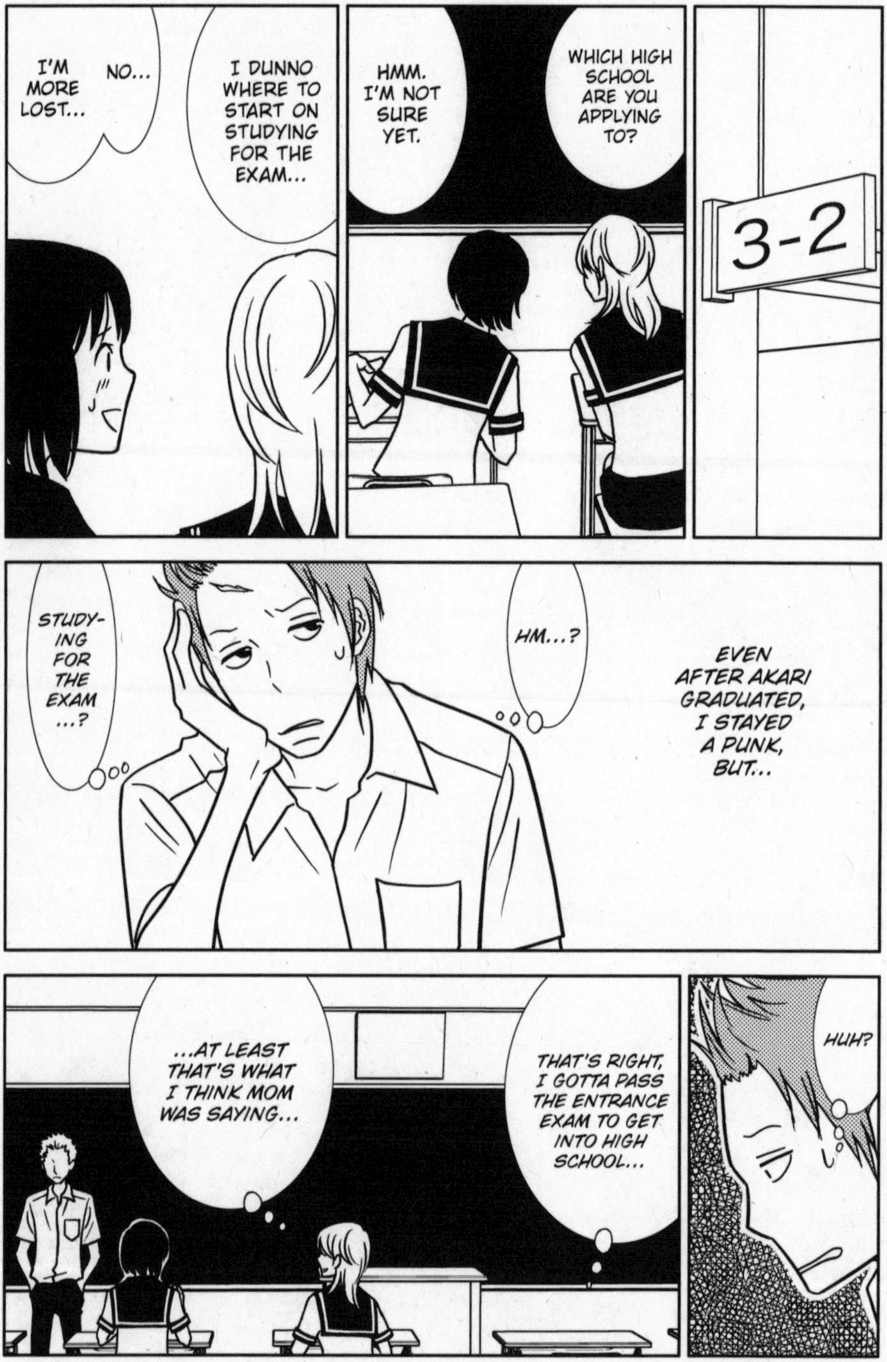
3-2
WHICH HIGH SCHOOL ARE YOU APPLYING TO?
HMM. I'M NOT SURE YET.
I DUNNO WHERE TO START ON STUDYING FOR THE EXAM...
NO...
I'M MORE LOST...
EVEN AFTER AKARI GRADUATED, I STAYED A PUNK, BUT...
HM...?
STUDY-ING FOR THE EXAM ...?
HUH?
THAT'S RIGHT, I GOTTA PASS THE ENTRANCE EXAM TO GET INTO HIGH SCHOOL...
...AT LEAST THAT'S WHAT I THINK MOM WAS SAYING...

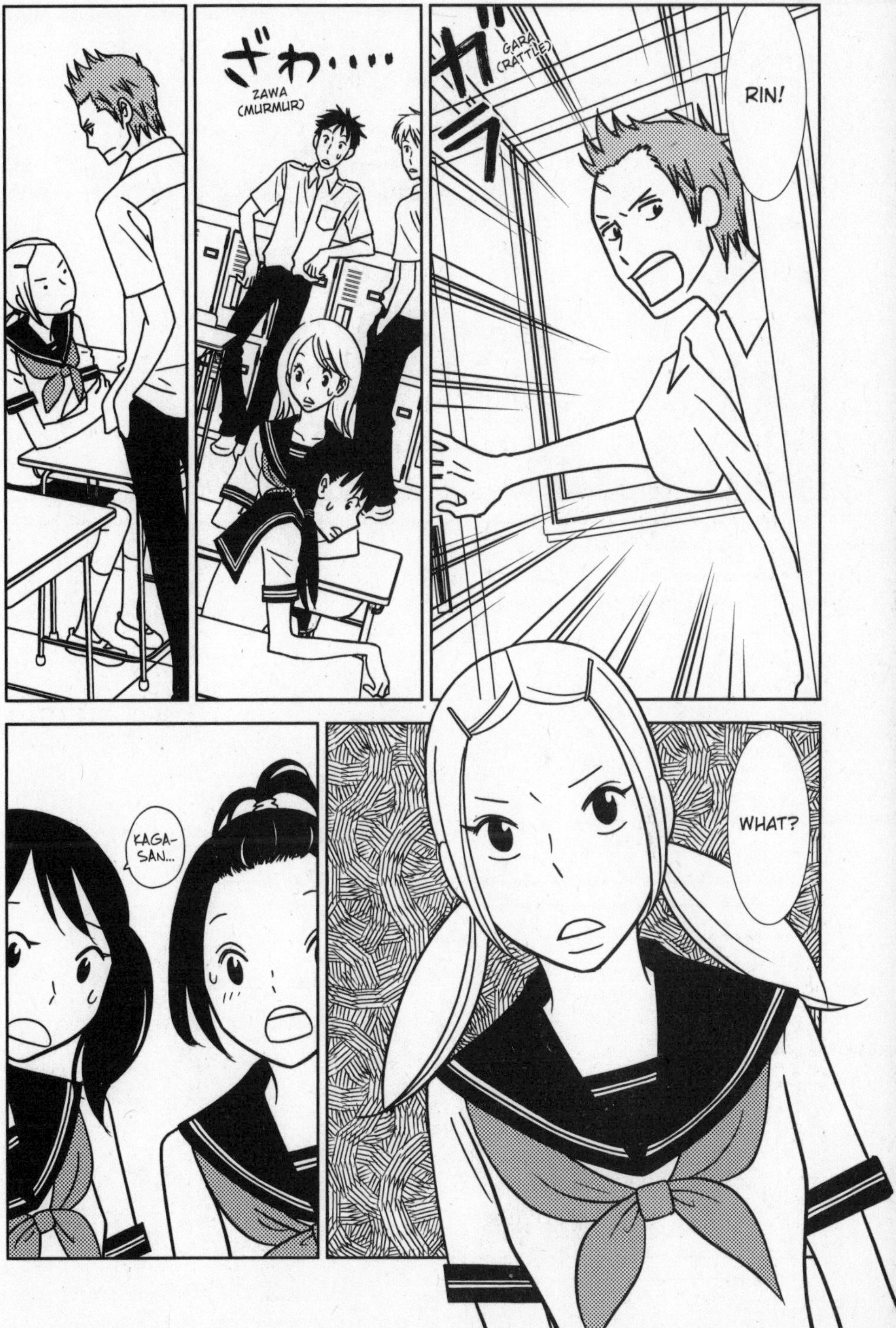
ガラ
GARA (RATTLE)
RIN!
ざわ……
ZAWA (MURMUR)
WHAT?
KAGA-SAN...

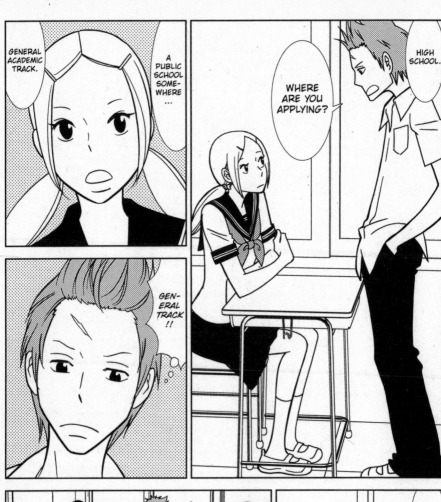

GENERAL ACADEMIC TRACK.

A PUBLIC SCHOOL SOME- WHERE...

WHERE ARE YOU APPLYING?

HIGH SCHOOL.

GEN- ERAL TRACK!!

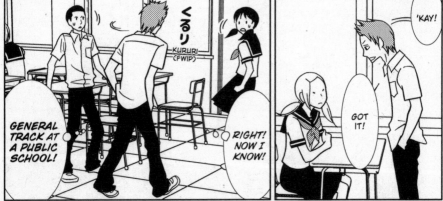

GENERAL TRACK AT A PUBLIC SCHOOL!

くるり
KURURI
(FWIP)

RIGHT! NOW I KNOW!

'KAY!

GOT IT!

*SENIOR HIGH SCHOOLS ARE DIVIDED INTO TWO MAJOR TRACKS INSTITUTIONALLY: GENERAL ACADEMIC TRACK AND VOCATIONAL TRACK. THOUGH STUDENTS WHO GRADUATE FROM ANY TYPE OF HIGH SCHOOL ARE QUALIFIED TO ADVANCE TO HIGHER EDUCATION,
STUDENTS GRADUATING FROM GENERAL ACADEMIC TRACKS HAVE AN ADVANTAGE IN ACCESS TO HIGHER EDUCATION.

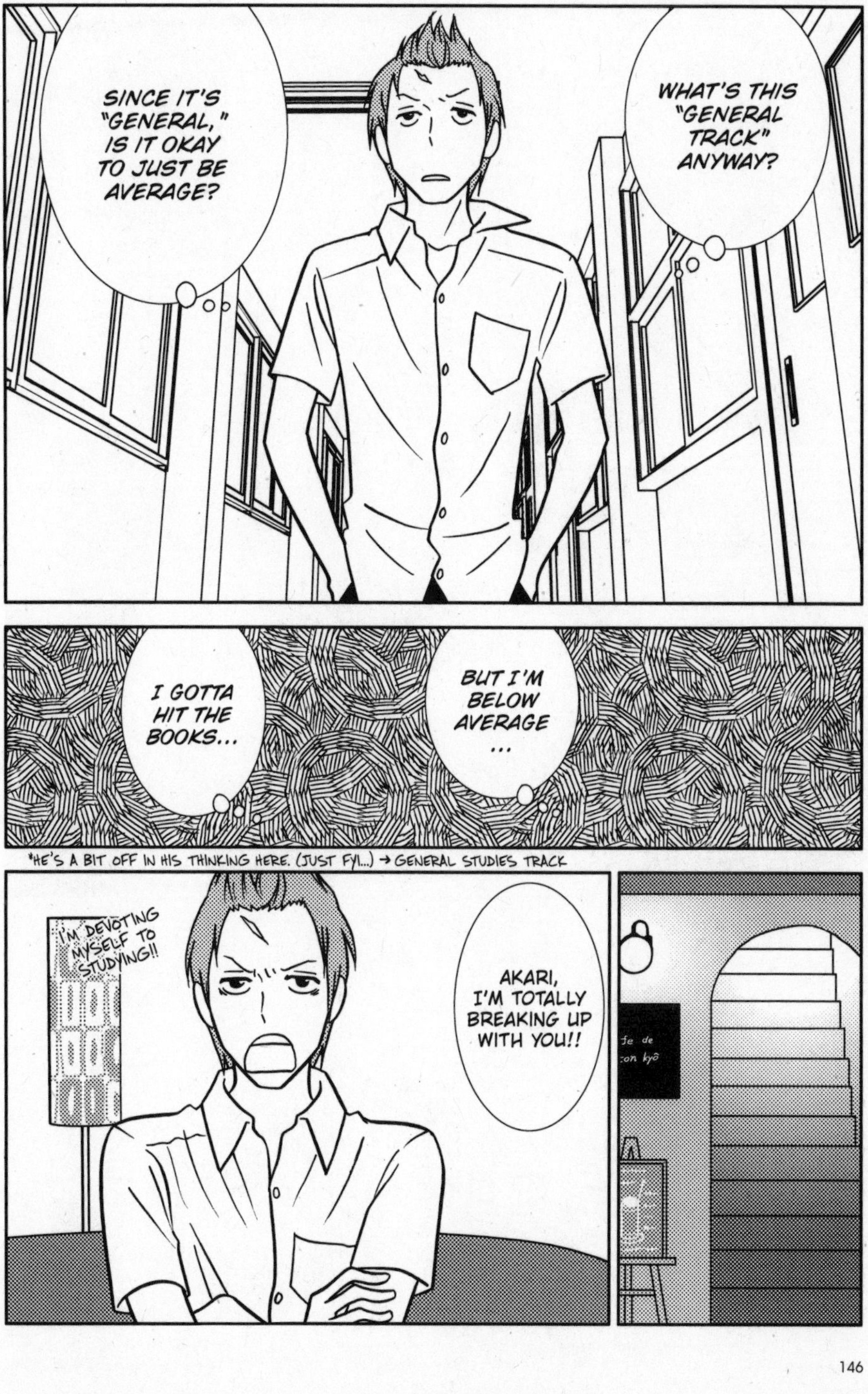
WHAT'S THIS "GENERAL TRACK" ANYWAY?
SINCE IT'S "GENERAL," IS IT OKAY TO JUST BE AVERAGE?
BUT I'M BELOW AVERAGE ...
I GOTTA HIT THE BOOKS...
*HE'S A BIT OFF IN HIS THINKING HERE. (JUST FYI...) → GENERAL STUDIES TRACK
AKARI, I'M TOTALLY BREAKING UP WITH YOU!!
I'M DEVOTING MYSELF TO STUDYING!!

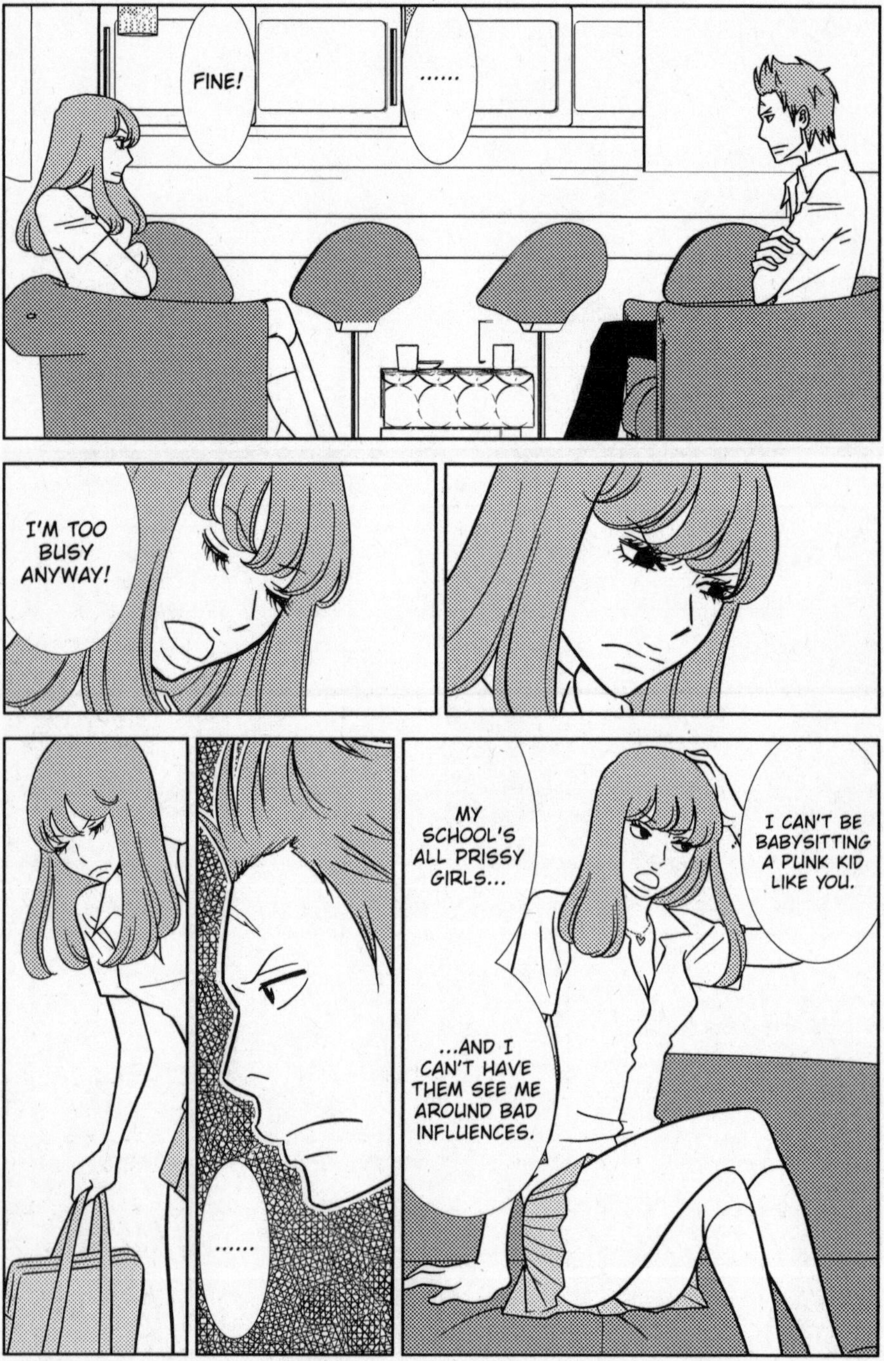
......
FINE!
I'M TOO BUSY ANYWAY!
I CAN'T BE BABYSITTING A PUNK KID LIKE YOU.
MY SCHOOL'S ALL PRISSY GIRLS...
...AND I CAN'T HAVE THEM SEE ME AROUND BAD INFLUENCES.
......

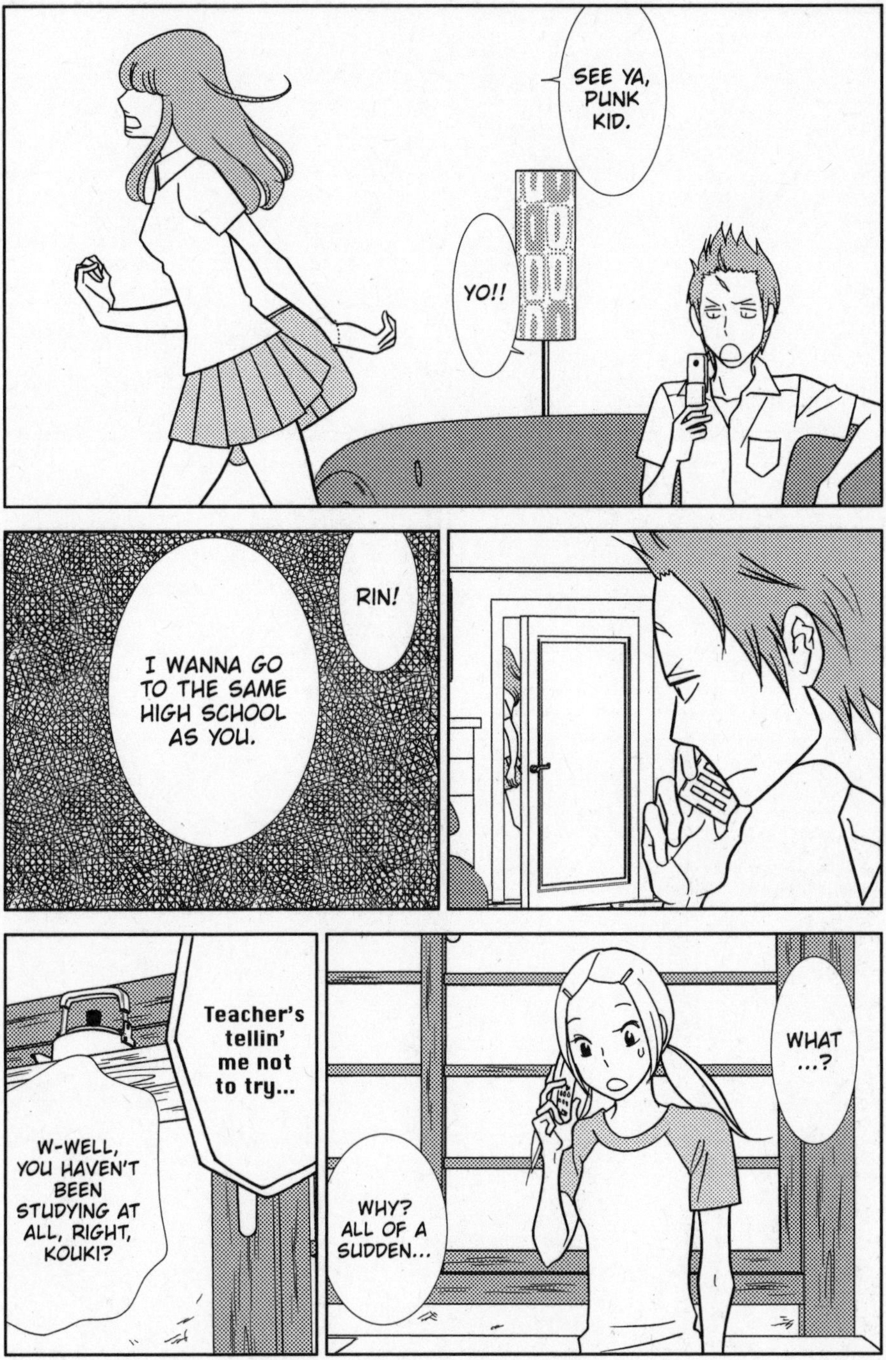
SEE YA, PUNK KID.
YO!!
RIN!
I WANNA GO TO THE SAME HIGH SCHOOL AS YOU.
WHAT ...?
WHY? ALL OF A SUDDEN...
Teacher's tellin' me not to try...
W-WELL, YOU HAVEN'T BEEN STUDYING AT ALL, RIGHT, KOUKI?

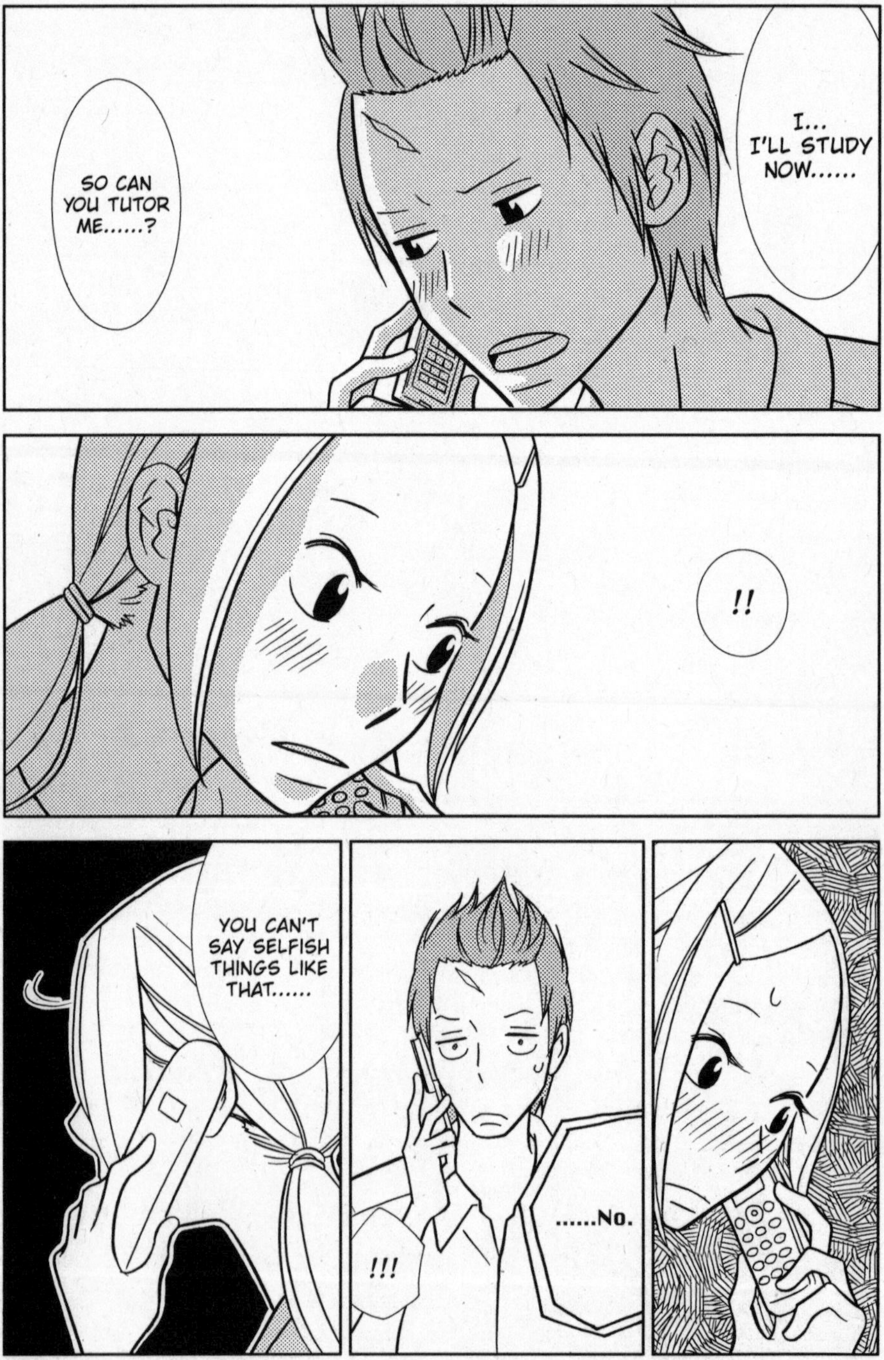
I... I'LL STUDY NOW......
SO CAN YOU TUTOR ME......?
!!
......No.
!!!
YOU CAN'T SAY SELFISH THINGS LIKE THAT......

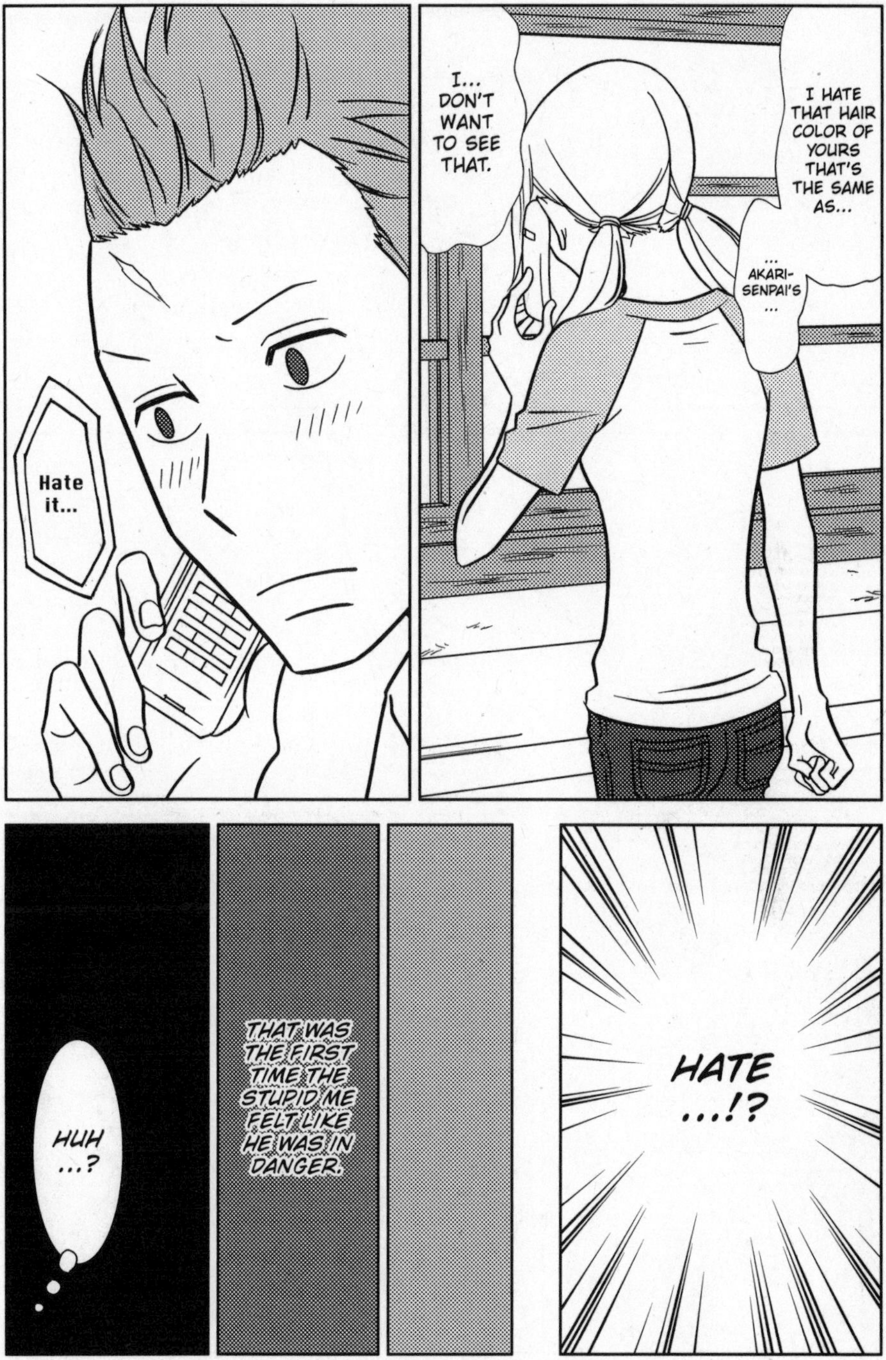
I HATE THAT HAIR COLOR OF YOURS THAT'S THE SAME AS...
...AKARI-SENPAI'S...
I... DON'T WANT TO SEE THAT.
Hate it...
HATE ...!?
THAT WAS THE FIRST TIME THE STUPID ME FELT LIKE HE WAS IN DANGER.
HUH ...?

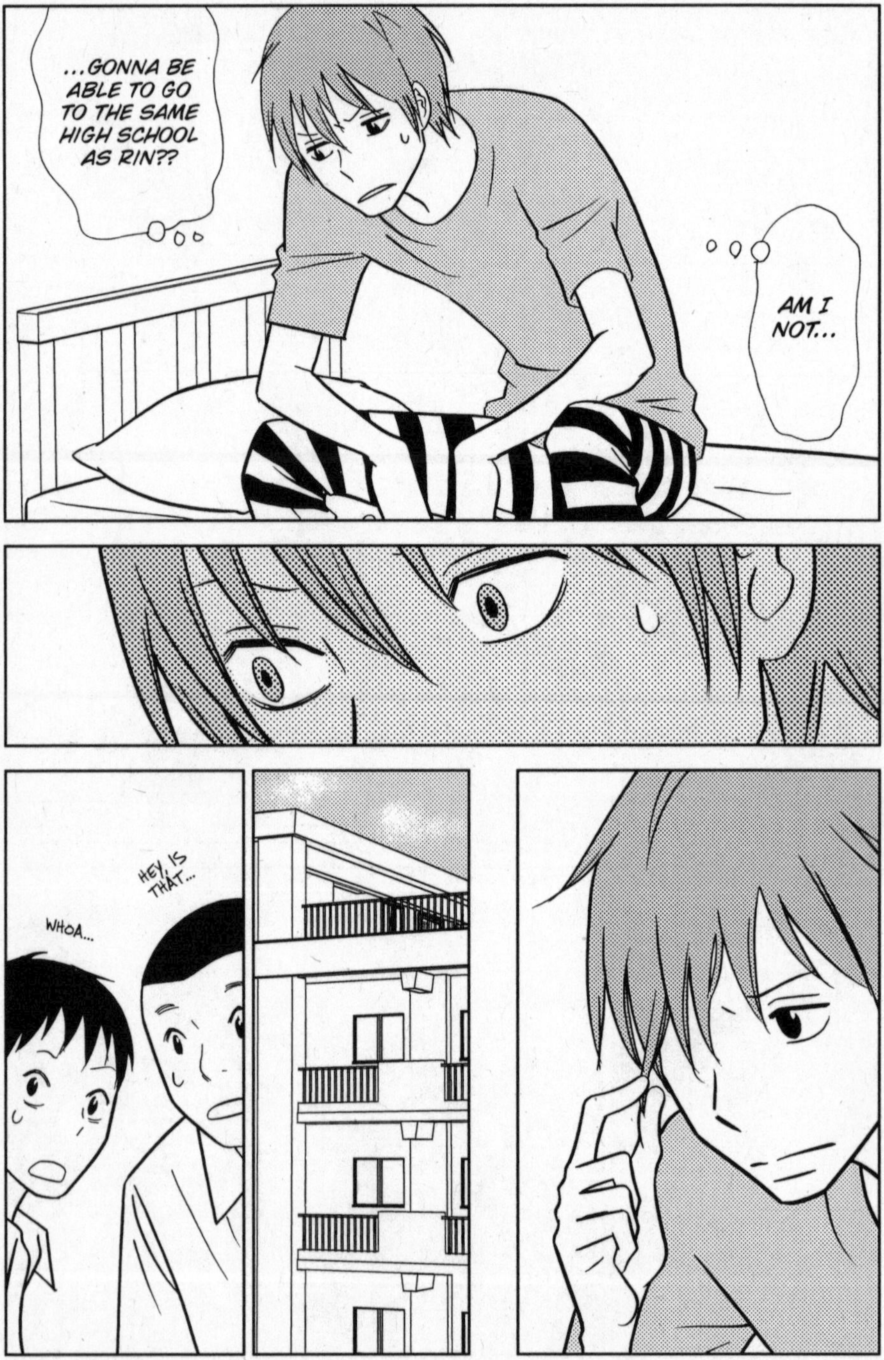
AM I NOT...
...GONNA BE ABLE TO GO TO THE SAME HIGH SCHOOL AS RIN??
HEY, IS THAT...
WHOA...

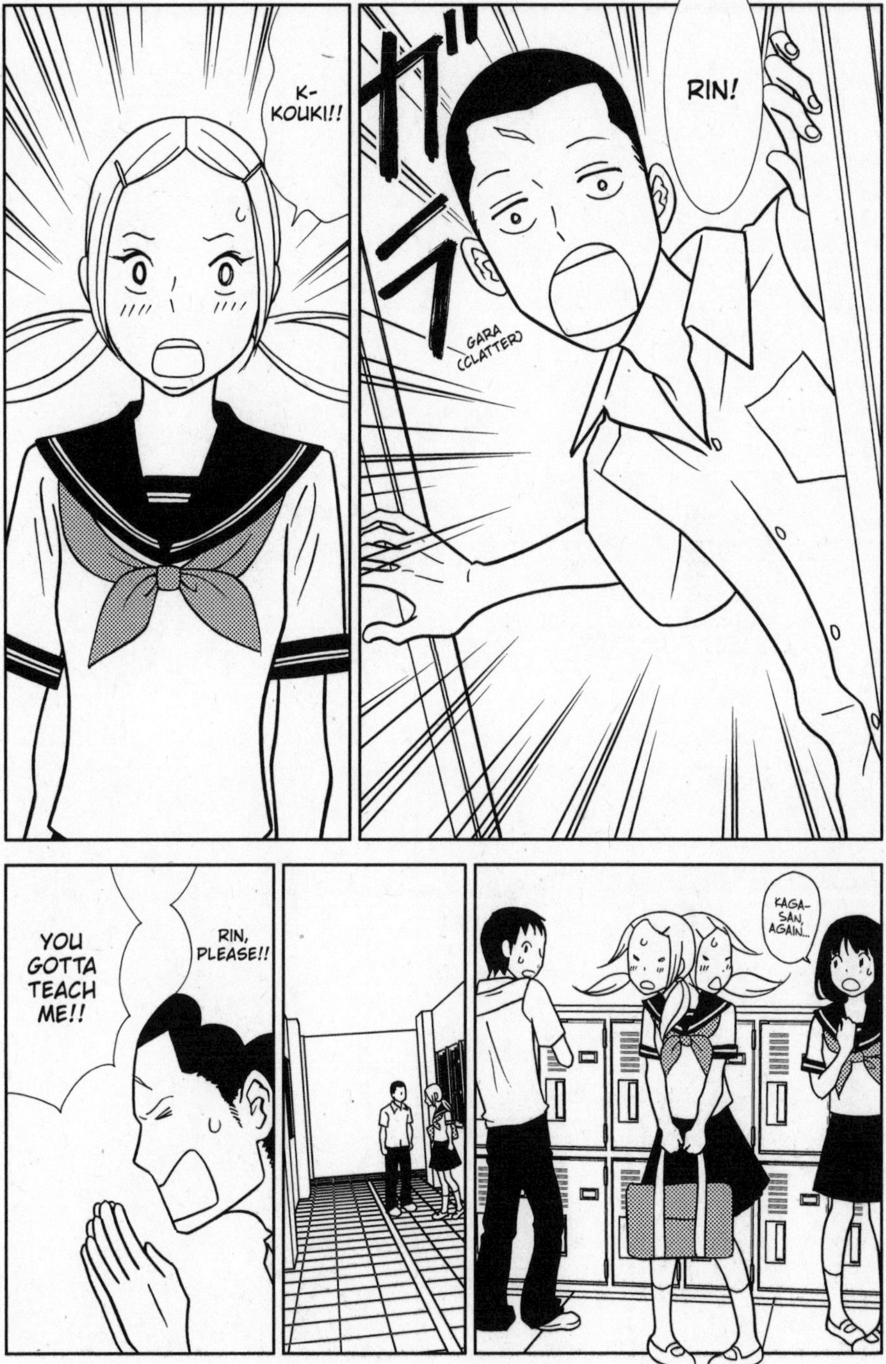
RIN!
ガラ
GARA (CLATTER)
K-KOUKI!!
KAGA-SAN, AGAIN...
RIN, PLEASE!!
YOU GOTTA TEACH ME!!

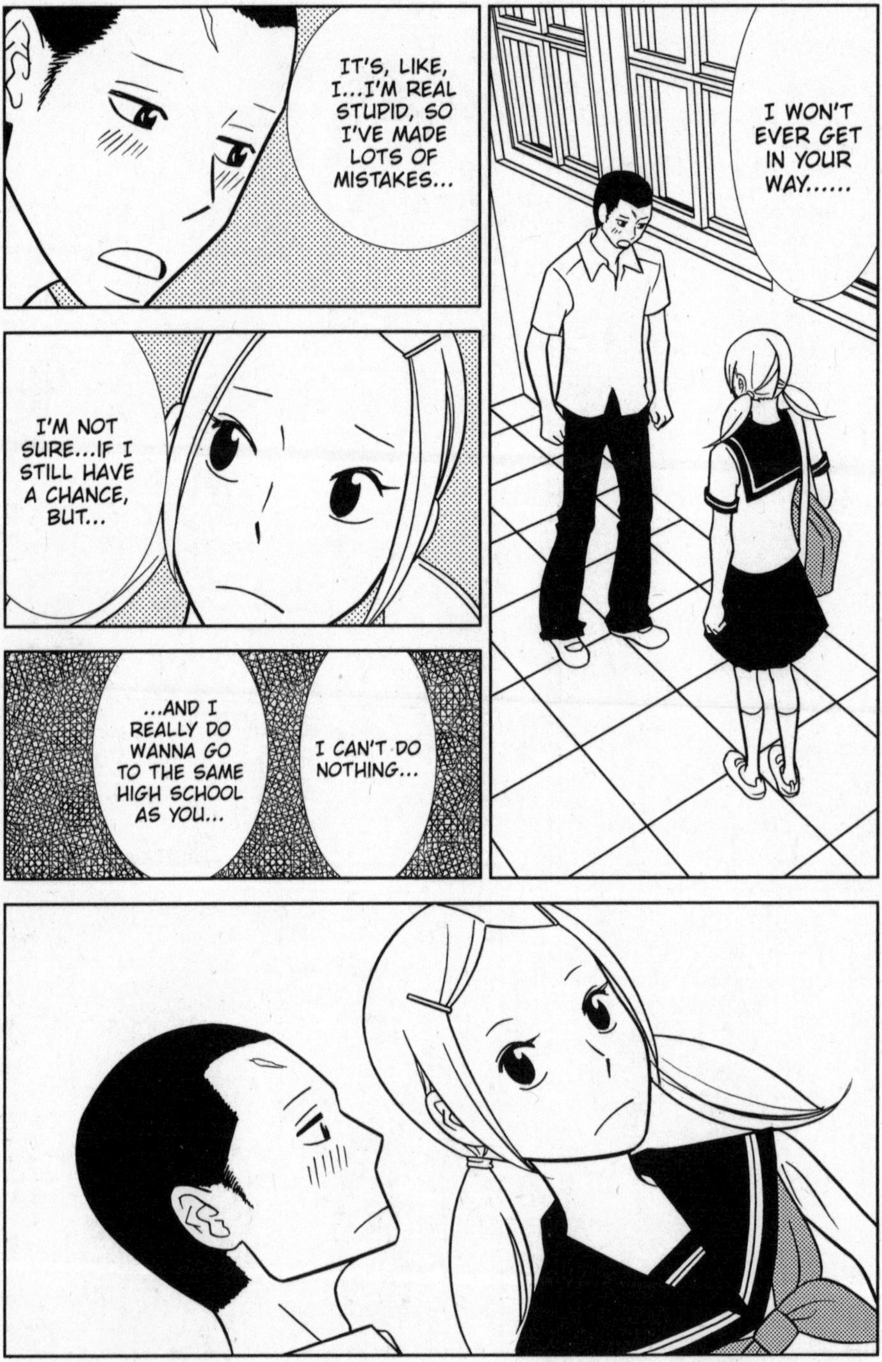
I WON'T EVER GET IN YOUR WAY......
IT'S, LIKE, I...I'M REAL STUPID, SO I'VE MADE LOTS OF MISTAKES...
I'M NOT SURE...IF I STILL HAVE A CHANCE, BUT...
I CAN'T DO NOTHING...
...AND I REALLY DO WANNA GO TO THE SAME HIGH SCHOOL AS YOU...

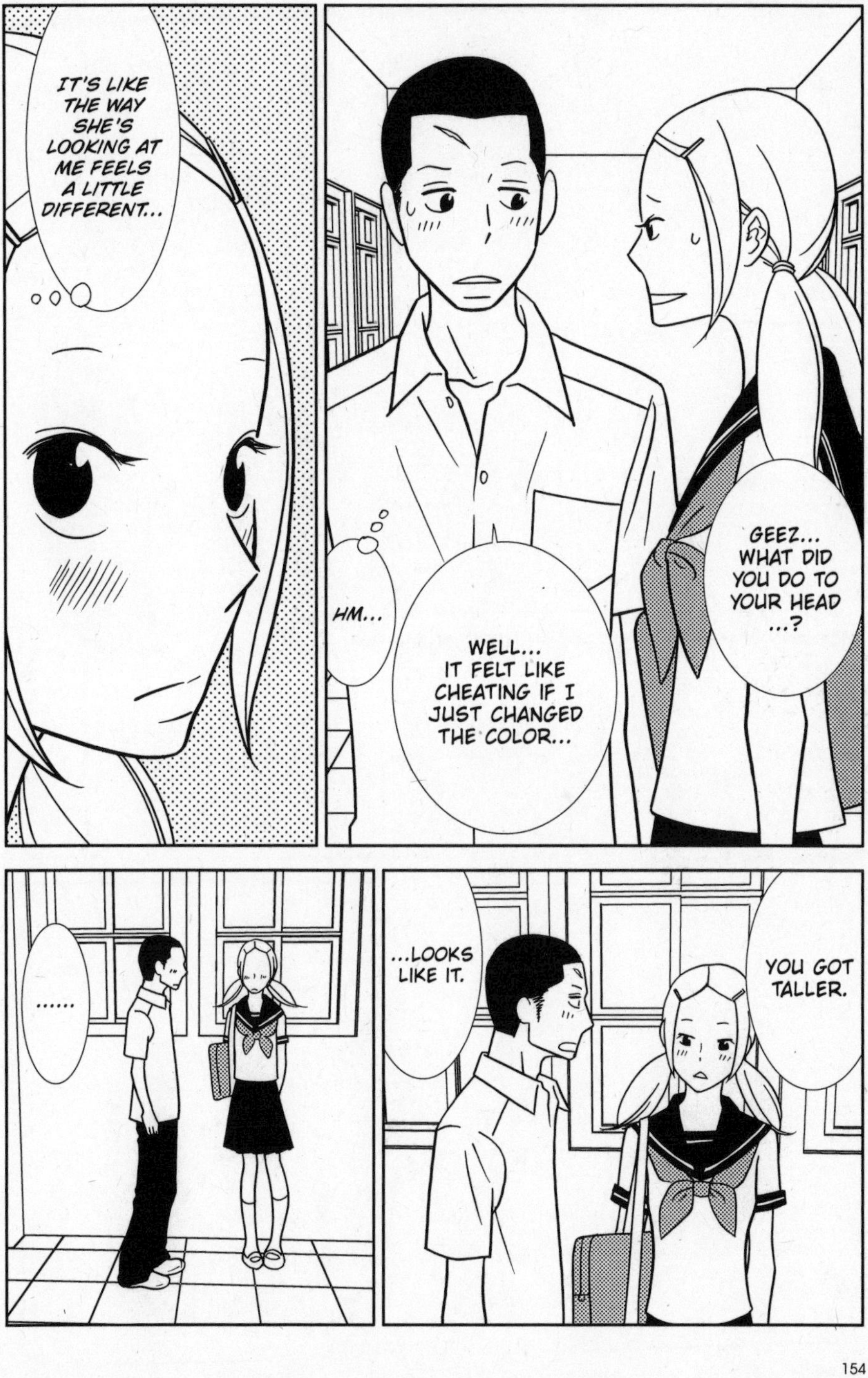
GEEZ... WHAT DID YOU DO TO YOUR HEAD ...?
WELL... IT FELT LIKE CHEATING IF I JUST CHANGED THE COLOR...
HM...
IT'S LIKE THE WAY SHE'S LOOKING AT ME FEELS A LITTLE DIFFERENT...
YOU GOT TALLER.
...LOOKS LIKE IT.
......

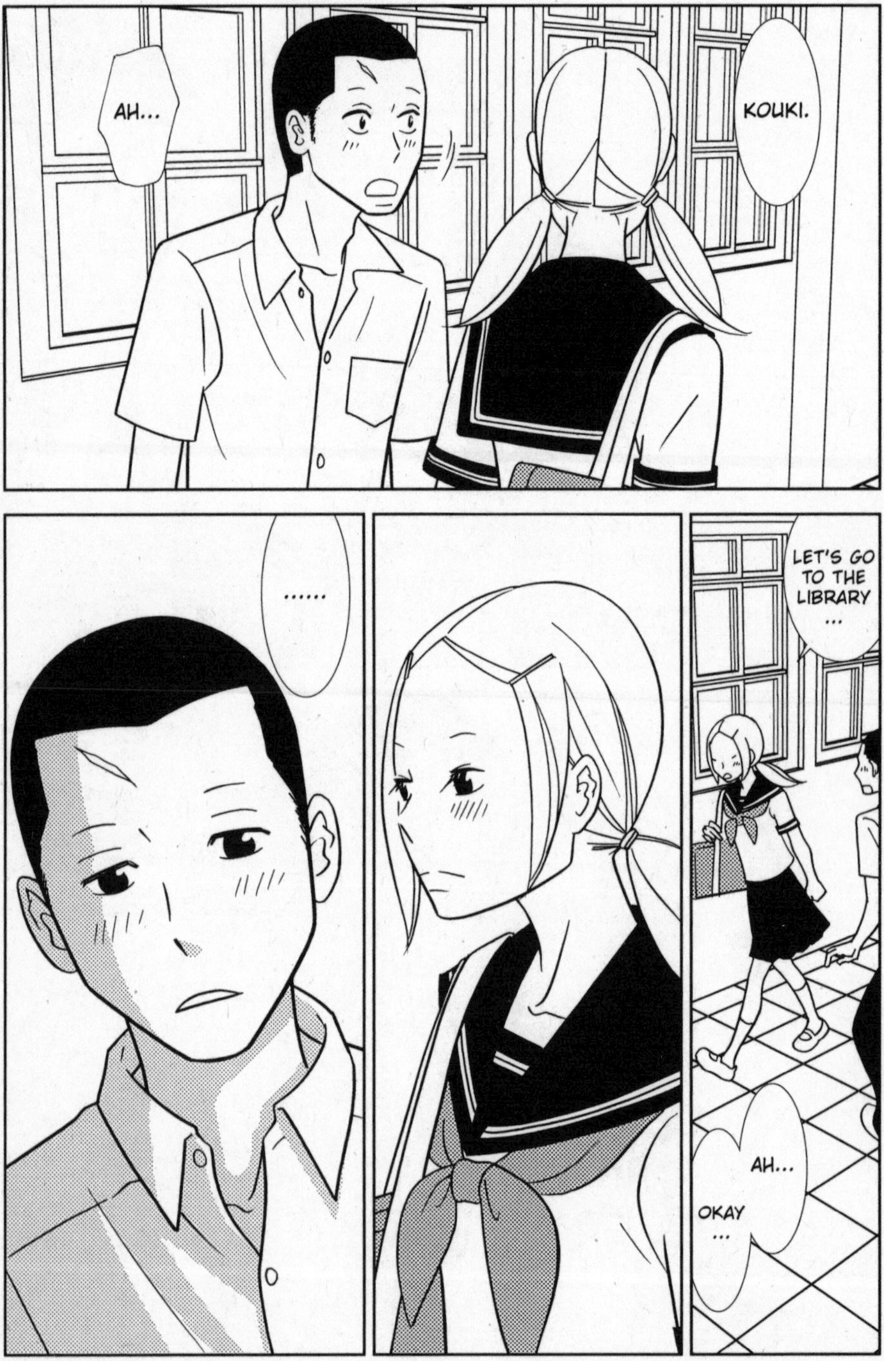
KOUKI.
AH...
LET'S GO TO THE LIBRARY ...
AH... OKAY ...
......

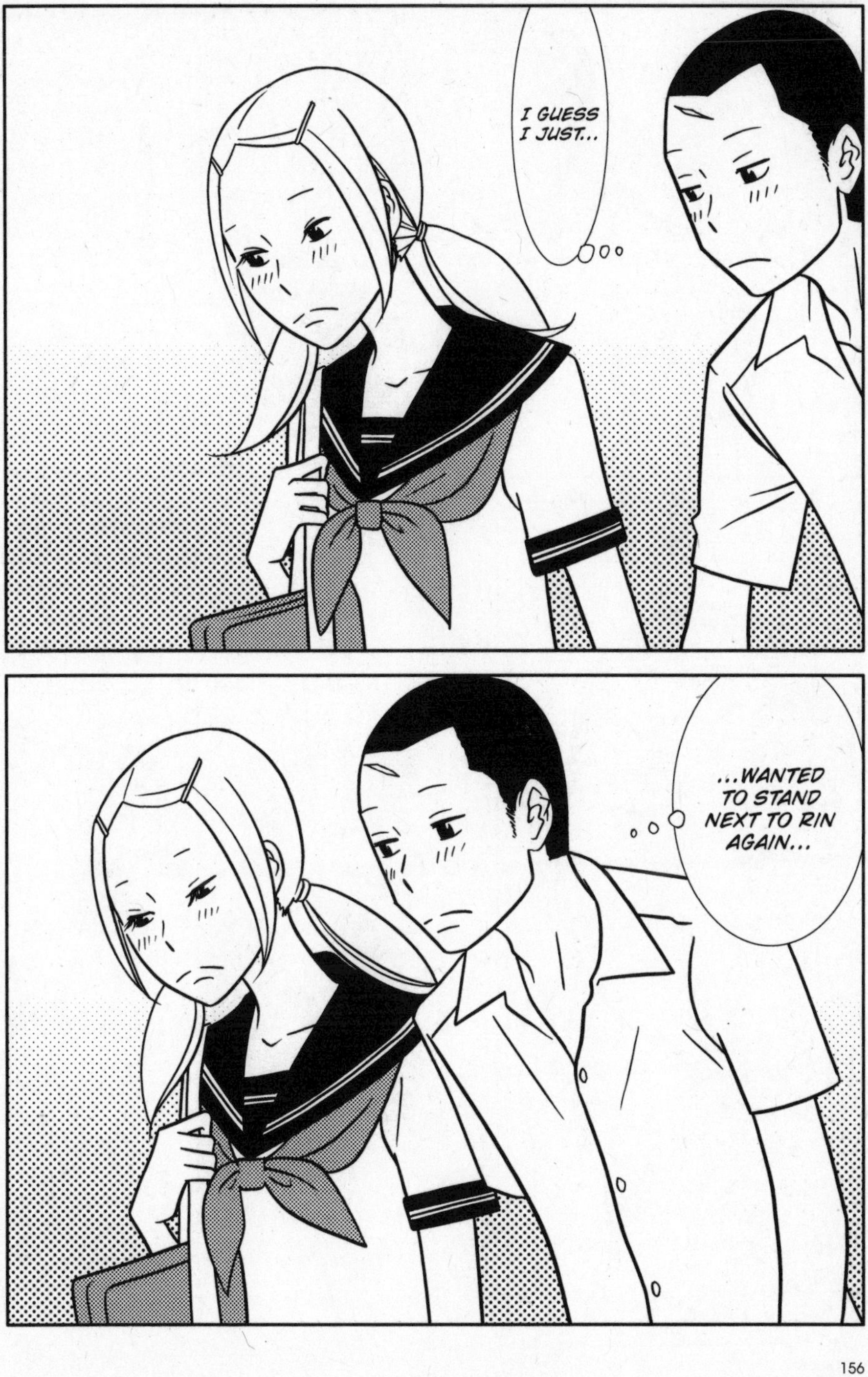
I GUESS I JUST...
...WANTED TO STAND NEXT TO RIN AGAIN...

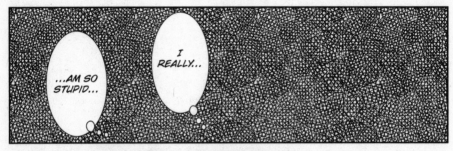

...AM SO STUPID...

I REALLY...

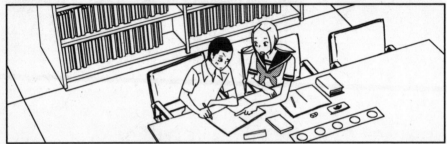

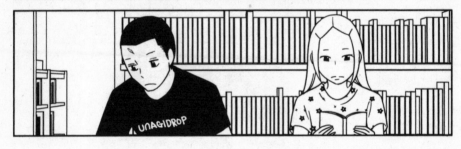

SIGNS: ENTRANCE CEREMONY / HIGH SCHOOL

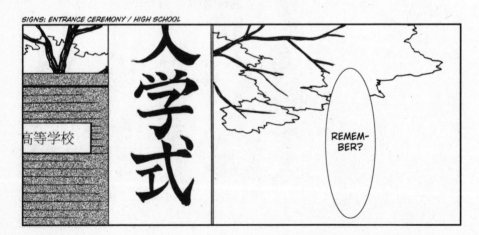

REMEM-BER?

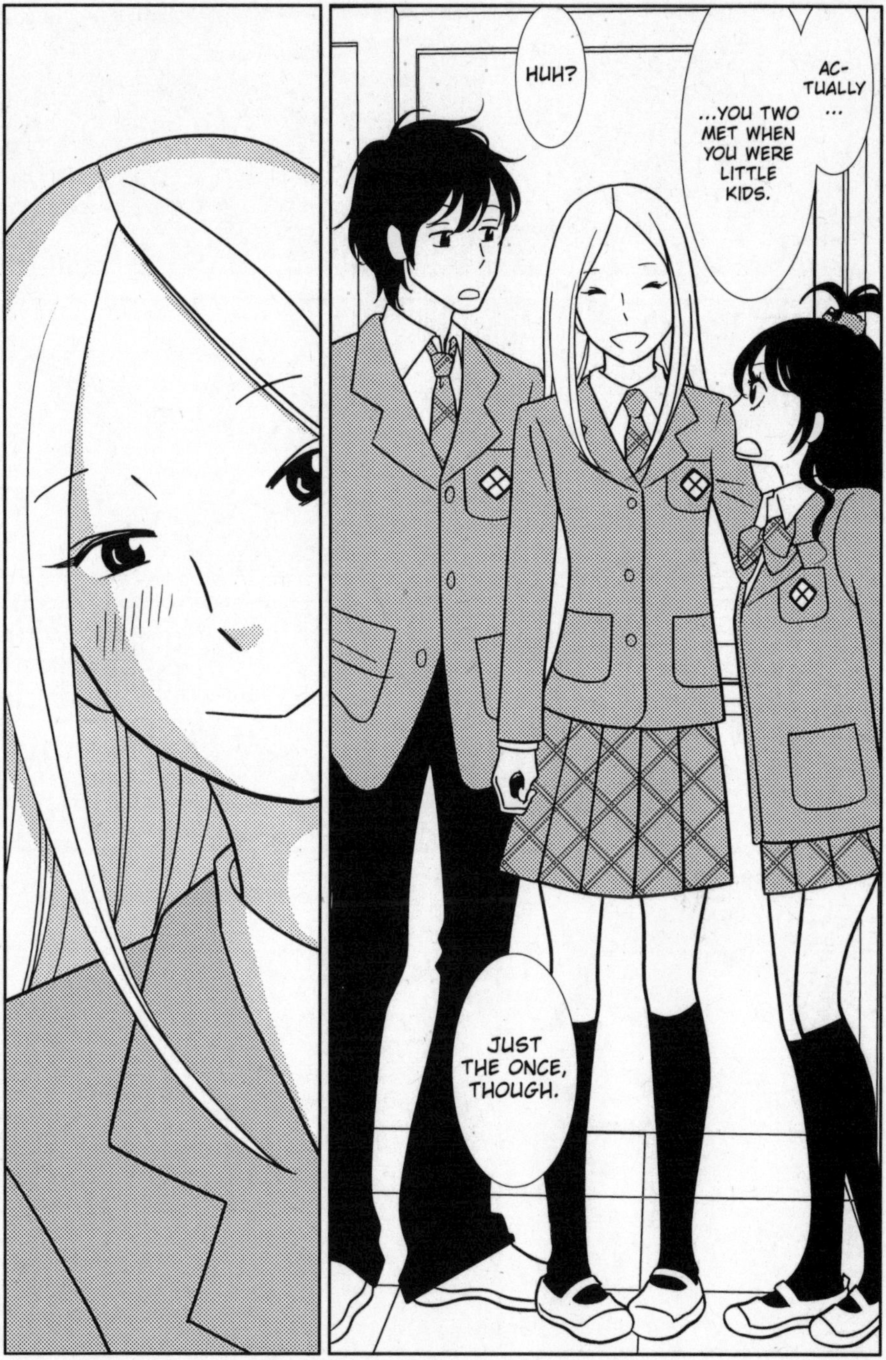
ACTUALLY...
...YOU TWO MET WHEN YOU WERE LITTLE KIDS.
HUH?
JUST THE ONCE, THOUGH.

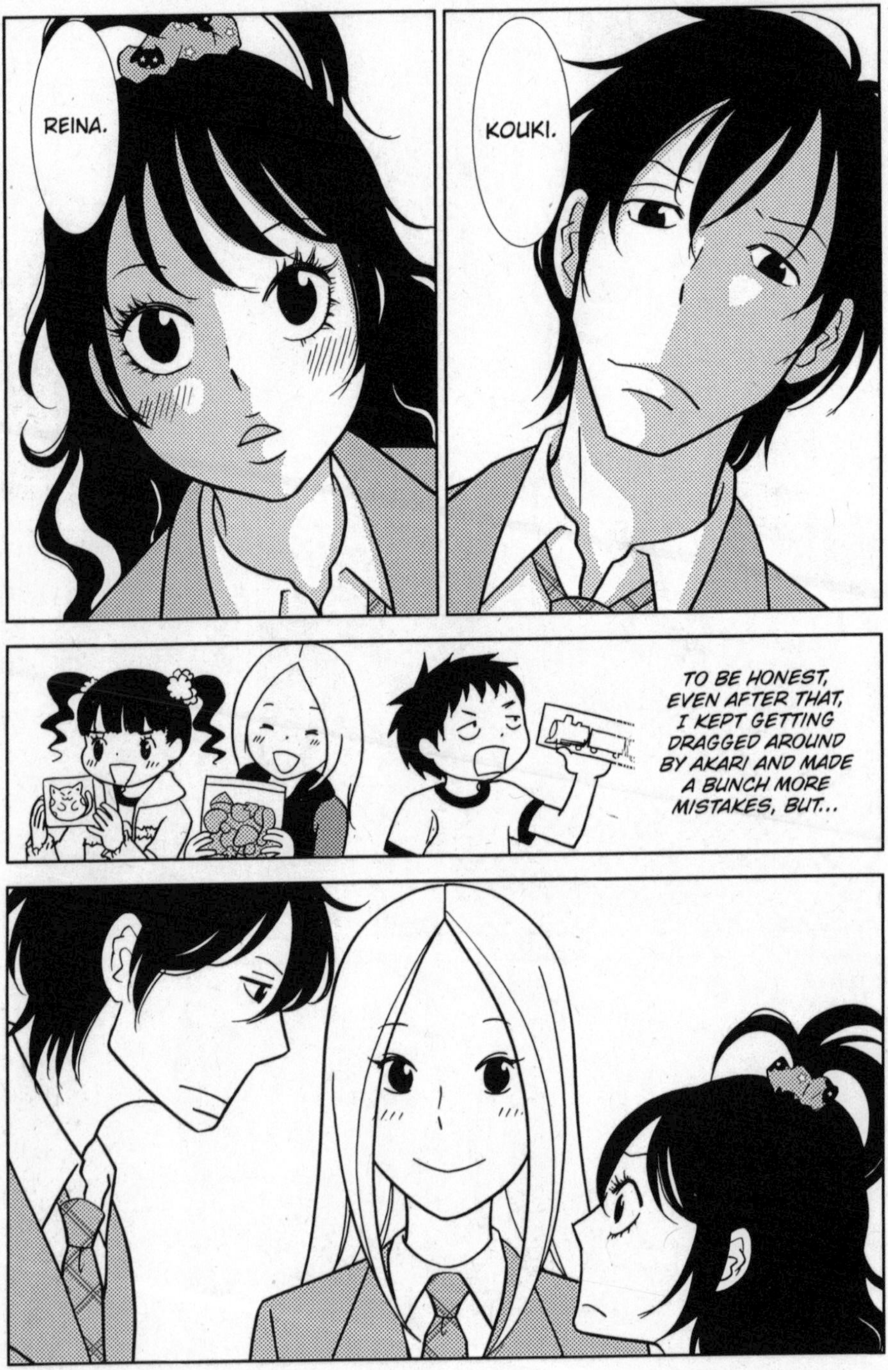
KOUKI.
REINA.
TO BE HONEST, EVEN AFTER THAT, I KEPT GETTING DRAGGED AROUND BY AKARI AND MADE A BUNCH MORE MISTAKES, BUT...

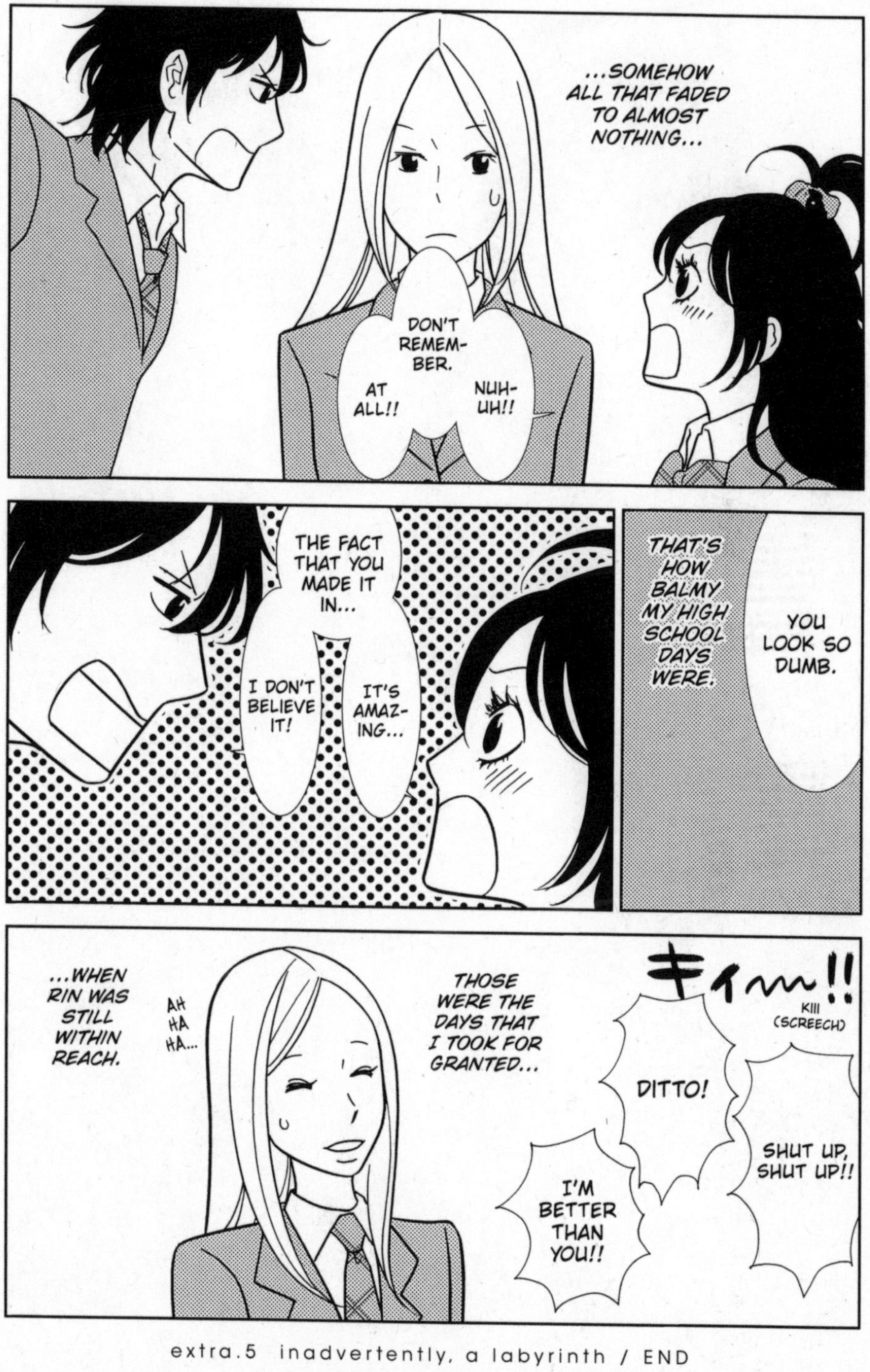
...SOMEHOW ALL THAT FADED TO ALMOST NOTHING...
NUH-UH!!
DON'T REMEMBER.
AT ALL!!
YOU LOOK SO DUMB.
THAT'S HOW BALMY MY HIGH SCHOOL DAYS WERE.
THE FACT THAT YOU MADE IT IN...
IT'S AMAZING...
I DON'T BELIEVE IT!
キィー!!
KIII (SCREECH)
SHUT UP, SHUT UP!!
DITTO!
I'M BETTER THAN YOU!!
THOSE WERE THE DAYS THAT I TOOK FOR GRANTED...
AH HA HA...
...WHEN RIN WAS STILL WITHIN REACH.

extra.5 inadvertently, a labyrinth / END

last extra

and then

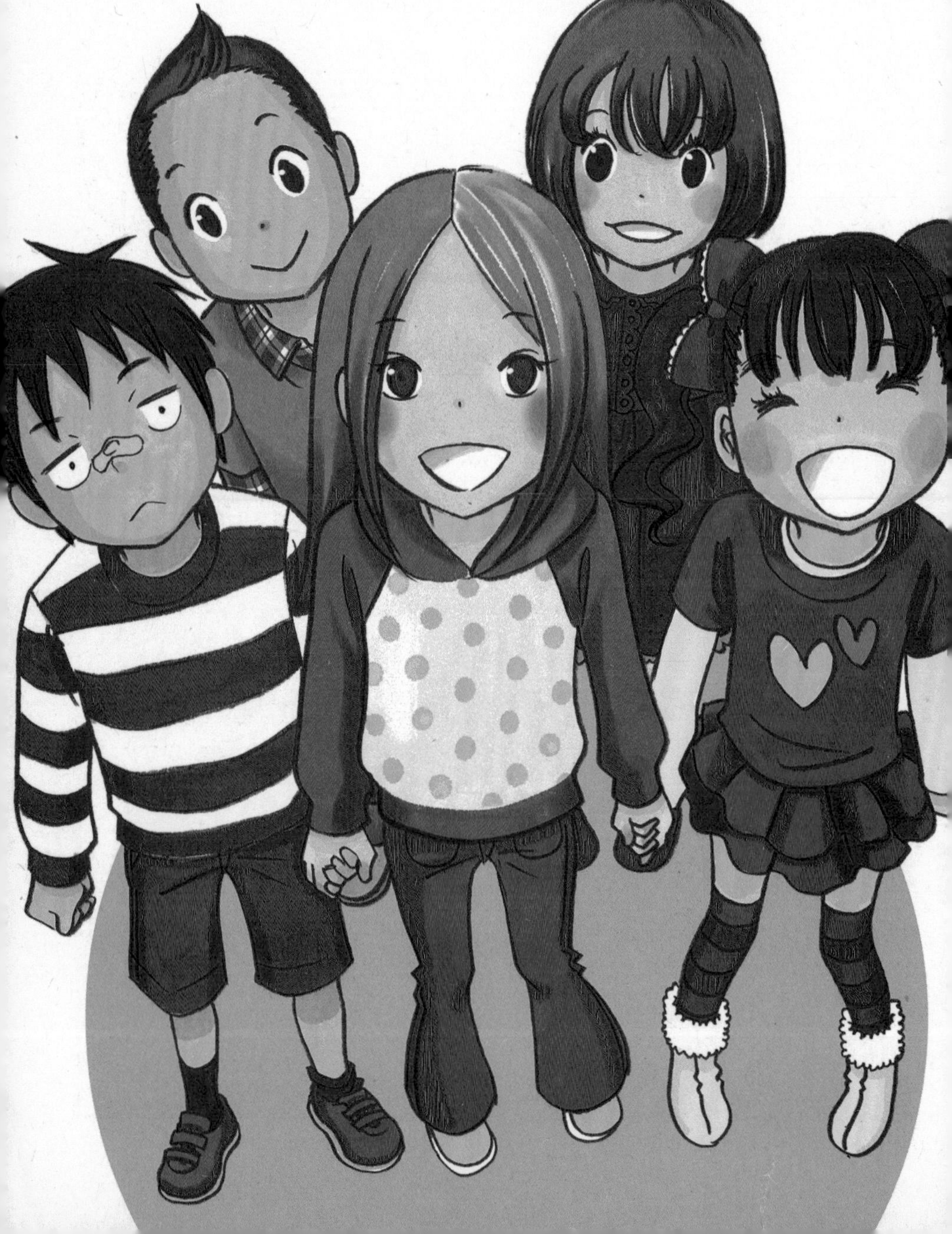

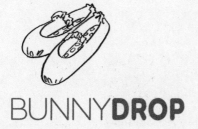

BUNNY**DROP**

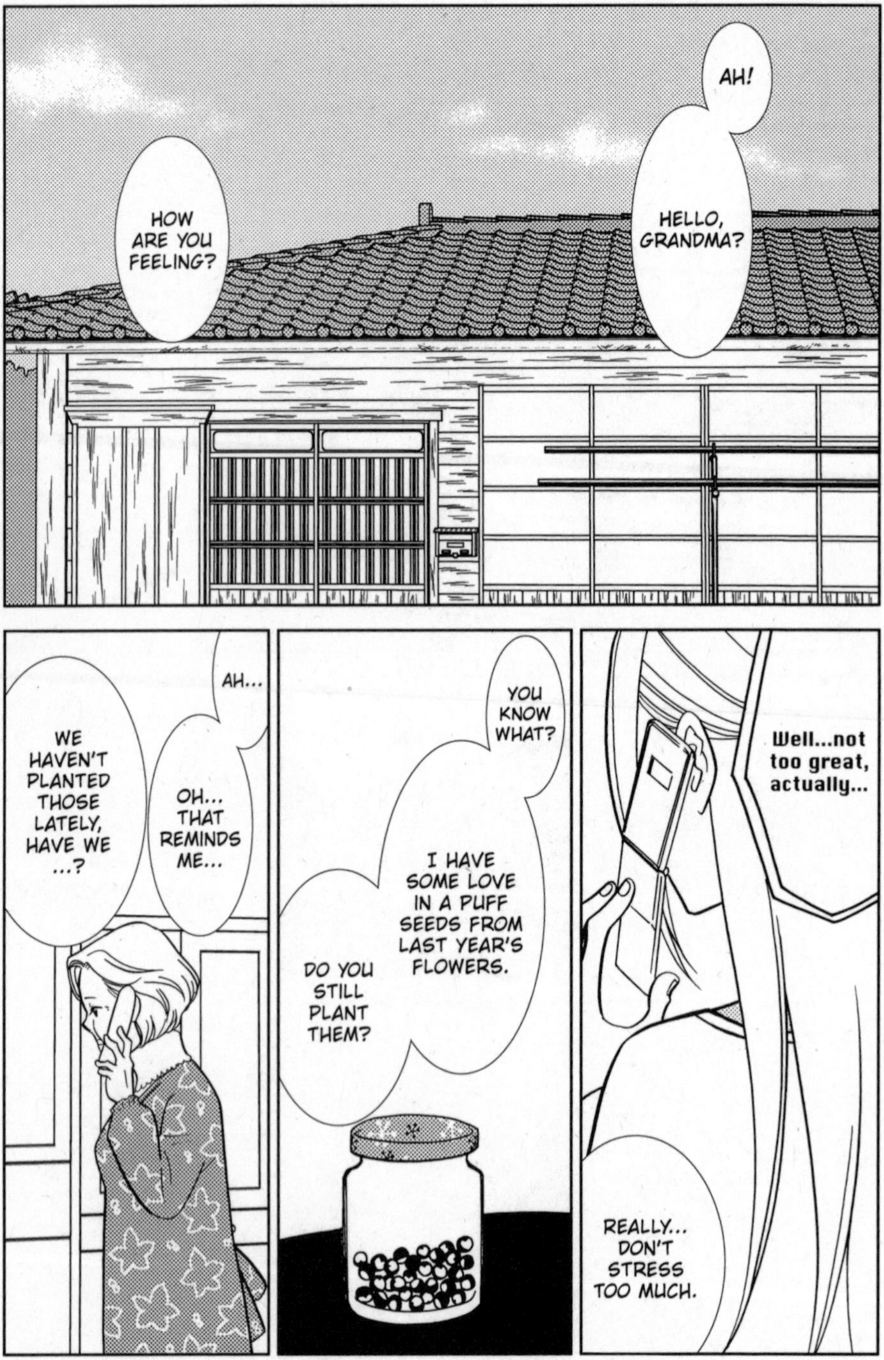
AH!
HELLO, GRANDMA?
HOW ARE YOU FEELING?
Well...not too great, actually...
REALLY... DON'T STRESS TOO MUCH.
YOU KNOW WHAT?
I HAVE SOME LOVE IN A PUFF SEEDS FROM LAST YEAR'S FLOWERS.
DO YOU STILL PLANT THEM?
AH...
OH... THAT REMINDS ME...
WE HAVEN'T PLANTED THOSE LATELY, HAVE WE ...?

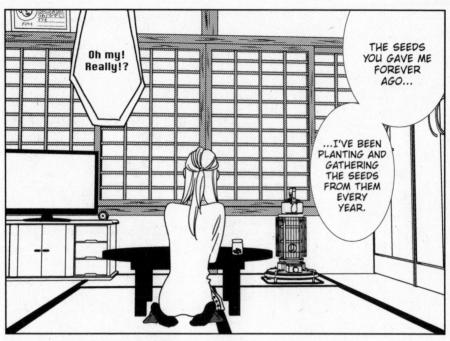

Oh my! Really!?

THE SEEDS YOU GAVE ME FOREVER AGO...

...I'VE BEEN PLANTING AND GATHERING THE SEEDS FROM THEM EVERY YEAR.

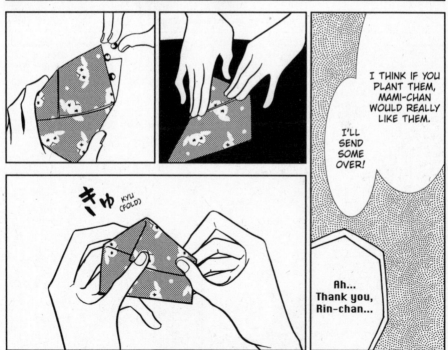

I THINK IF YOU PLANT THEM, MAMI-CHAN WOULD REALLY LIKE THEM.

I'LL SEND SOME OVER!

Ah... Thank you, Rin-chan...

きゅ KYU (FOLD)

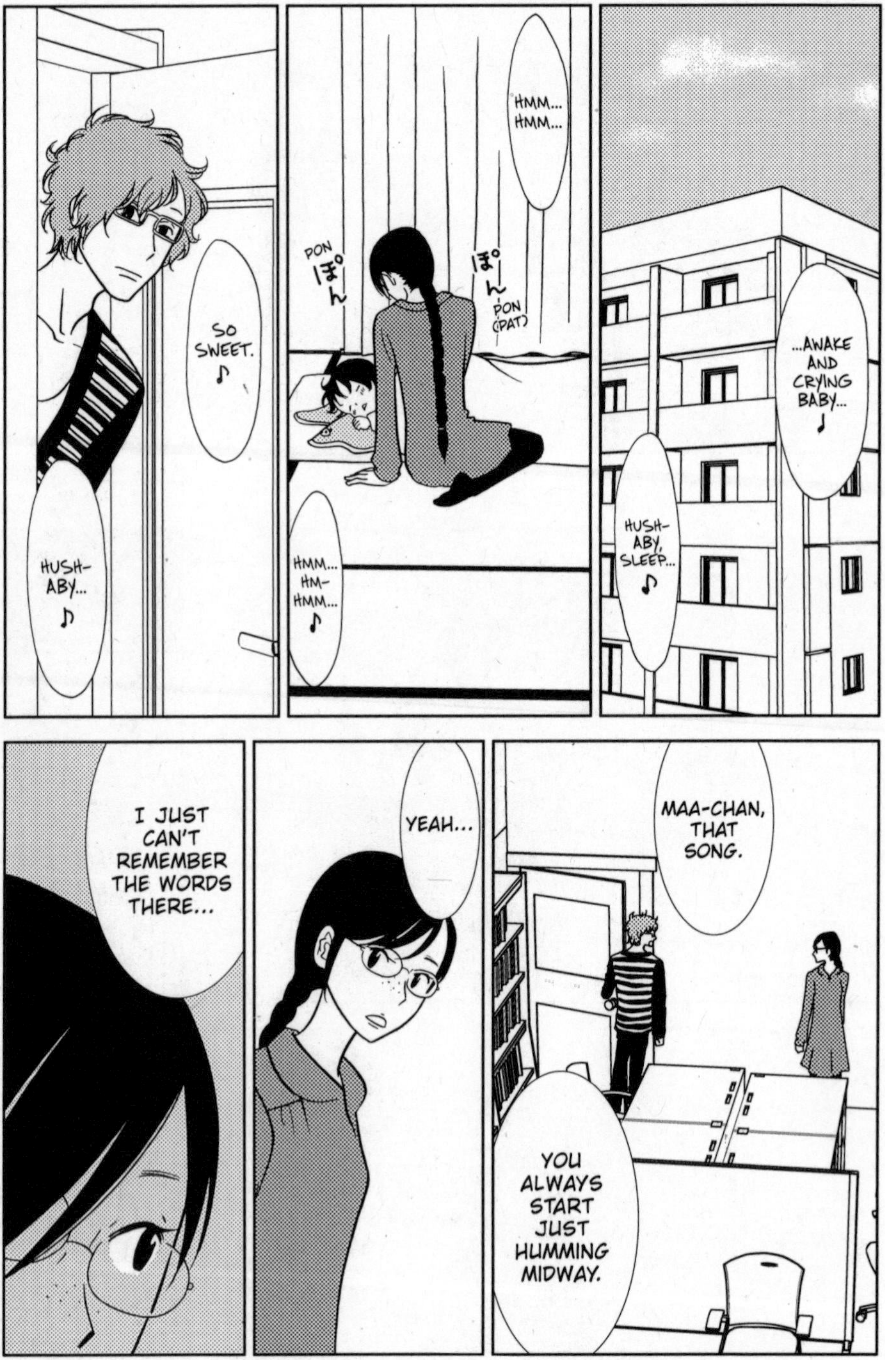
...AWAKE AND CRYING BABY... ♩
HUSH-ABY, SLEEP... ♪
HMM... HMM...
PON ぽん
ぽん PON (PAT)
HMM... HM-HMM... ♪
SO SWEET. ♪
HUSH-ABY... ♪
MAA-CHAN, THAT SONG.
YOU ALWAYS START JUST HUMMING MIDWAY.
YEAH...
I JUST CAN'T REMEMBER THE WORDS THERE...

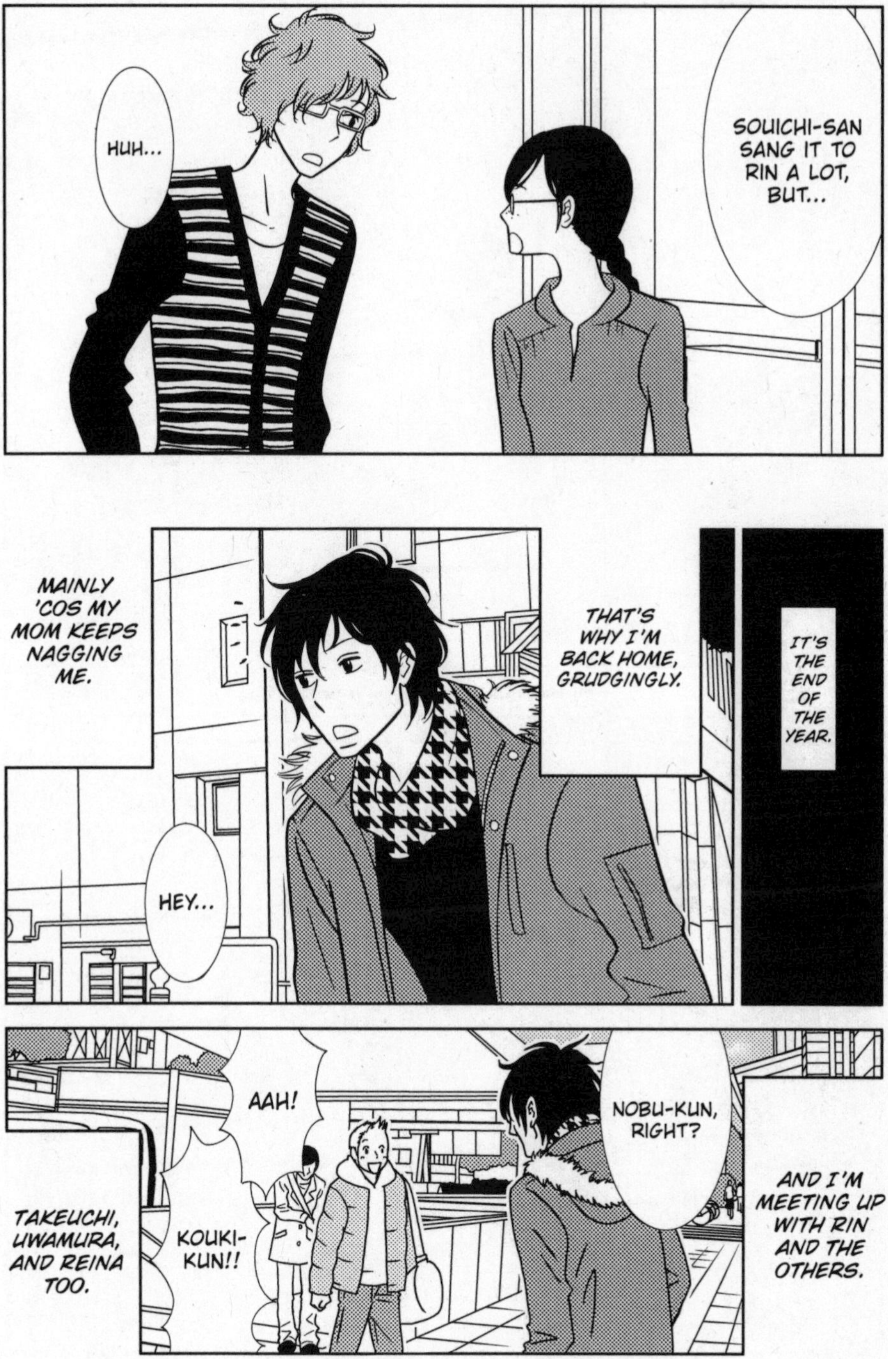
SOUICHI-SAN SANG IT TO RIN A LOT, BUT...
HUH...
IT'S THE END OF THE YEAR.
THAT'S WHY I'M BACK HOME, GRUDGINGLY.
MAINLY 'COS MY MOM KEEPS NAGGING ME.
HEY...
AND I'M MEETING UP WITH RIN AND THE OTHERS.
NOBU-KUN, RIGHT?
AAH!
KOUKI-KUN!!
TAKEUCHI, UWAMURA, AND REINA TOO.

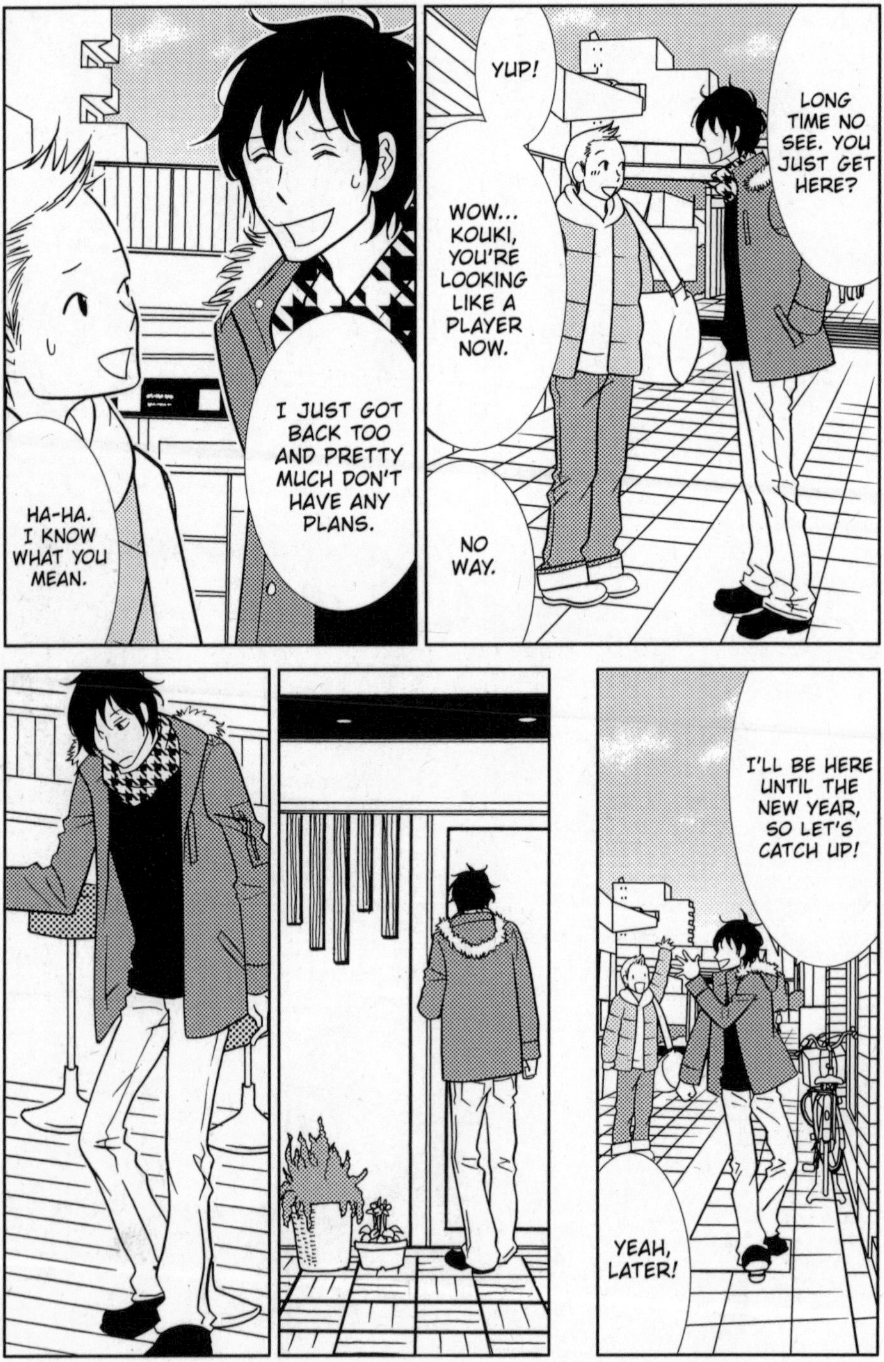
LONG TIME NO SEE. YOU JUST GET HERE?
YUP!
WOW... KOUKI, YOU'RE LOOKING LIKE A PLAYER NOW.
NO WAY.
I JUST GOT BACK TOO AND PRETTY MUCH DON'T HAVE ANY PLANS.
HA-HA. I KNOW WHAT YOU MEAN.
I'LL BE HERE UNTIL THE NEW YEAR, SO LET'S CATCH UP!
YEAH, LATER!

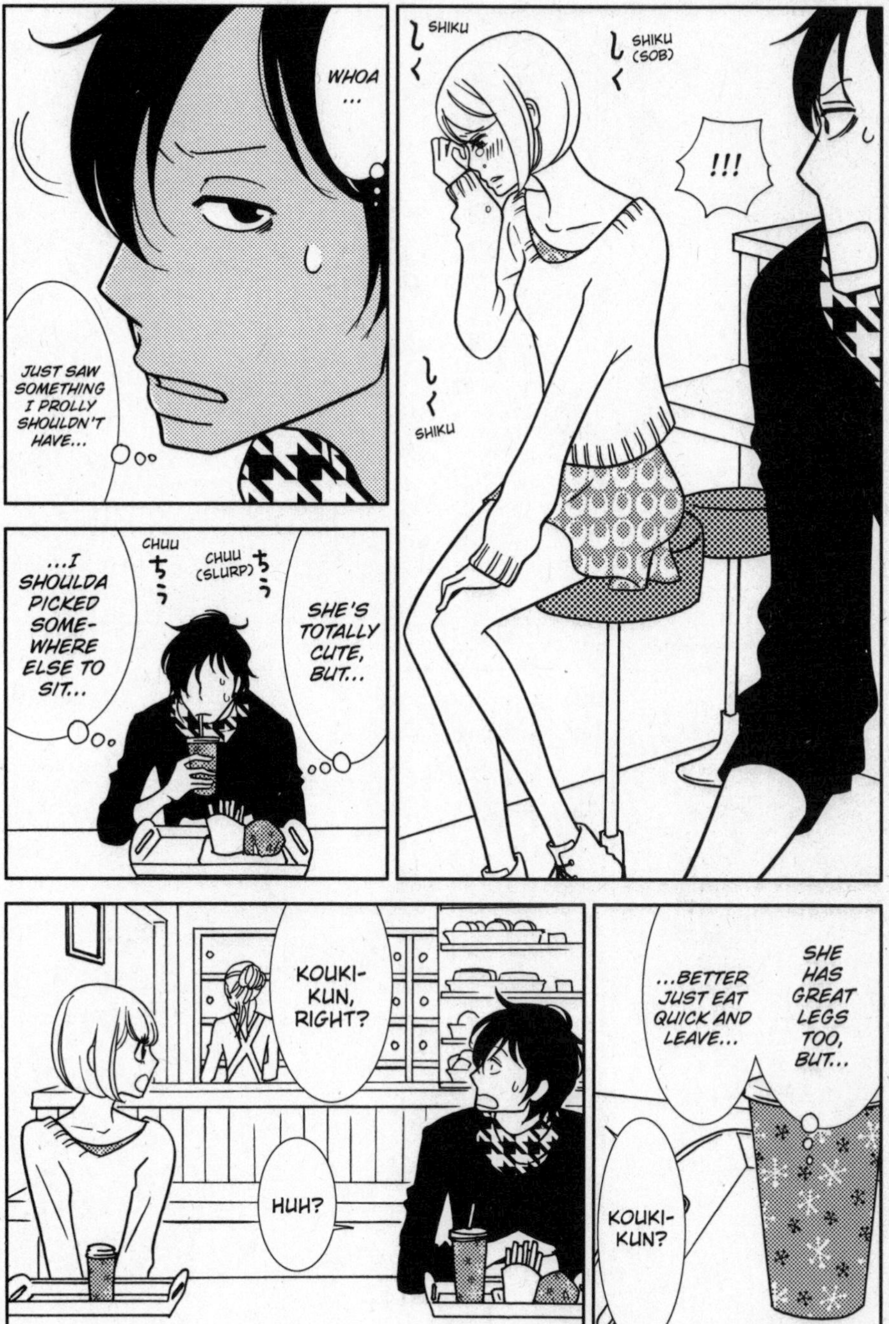
SHIKU (SOB)
しく
!!!
SHIKU
しく
しく
SHIKU
WHOA...
JUST SAW SOMETHING I PROLLY SHOULDN'T HAVE...
SHE'S TOTALLY CUTE, BUT...
CHUU (SLURP)
ちぅ
CHUU
ちぅ
...I SHOULDA PICKED SOME-WHERE ELSE TO SIT...
SHE HAS GREAT LEGS TOO, BUT...
...BETTER JUST EAT QUICK AND LEAVE...
KOUKI-KUN?
KOUKI-KUN, RIGHT?
HUH?

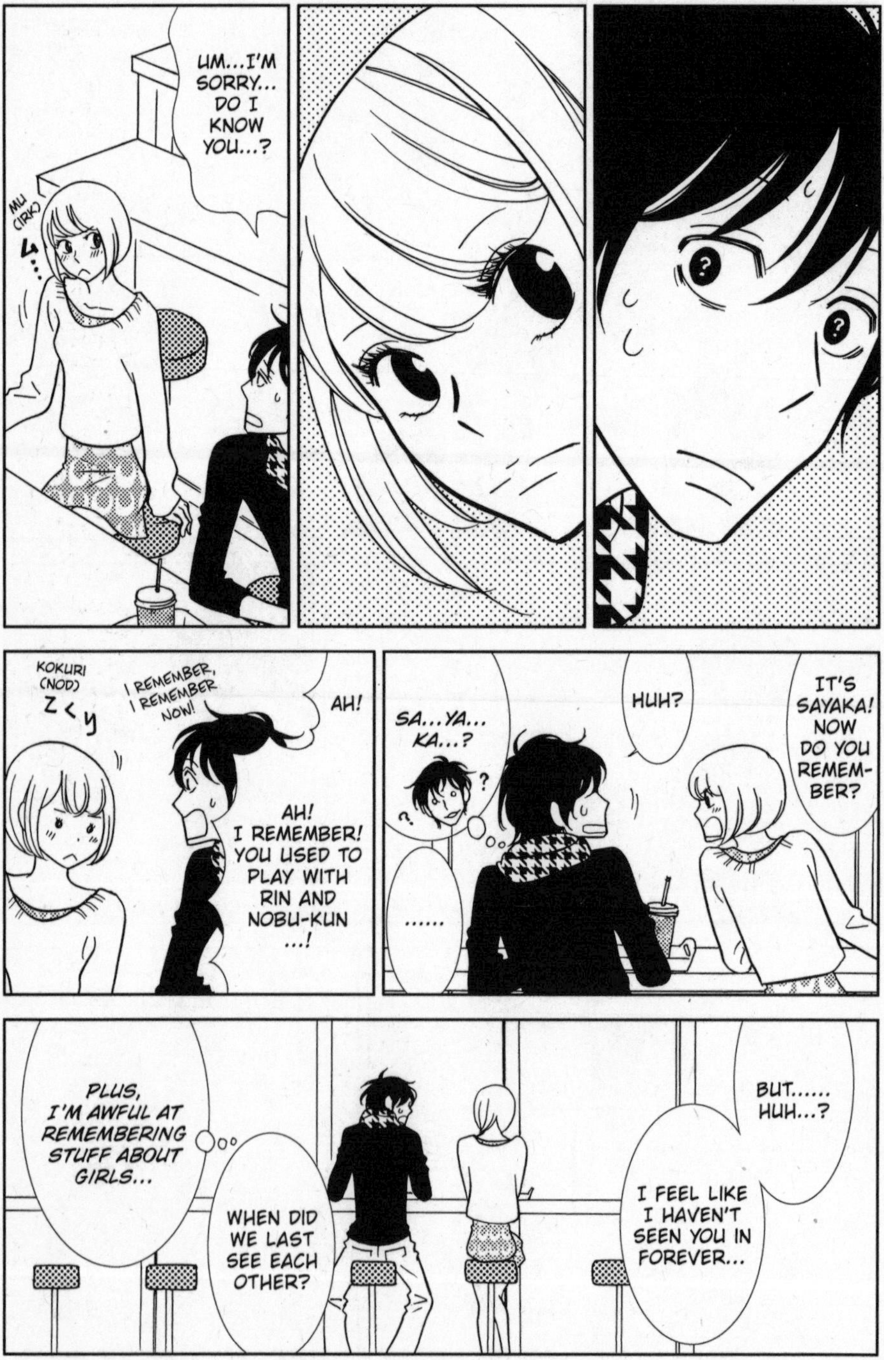
UM...I'M SORRY... DO I KNOW YOU...?
MU (IRK)
IT'S SAYAKA! NOW DO YOU REMEMBER?
HUH?
SA...YA...KA...?
......
AH!
I REMEMBER, I REMEMBER NOW!
AH! I REMEMBER! YOU USED TO PLAY WITH RIN AND NOBU-KUN ...!
KOKURI (NOD)
BUT...... HUH...?
I FEEL LIKE I HAVEN'T SEEN YOU IN FOREVER...
WHEN DID WE LAST SEE EACH OTHER?
PLUS, I'M AWFUL AT REMEMBERING STUFF ABOUT GIRLS...

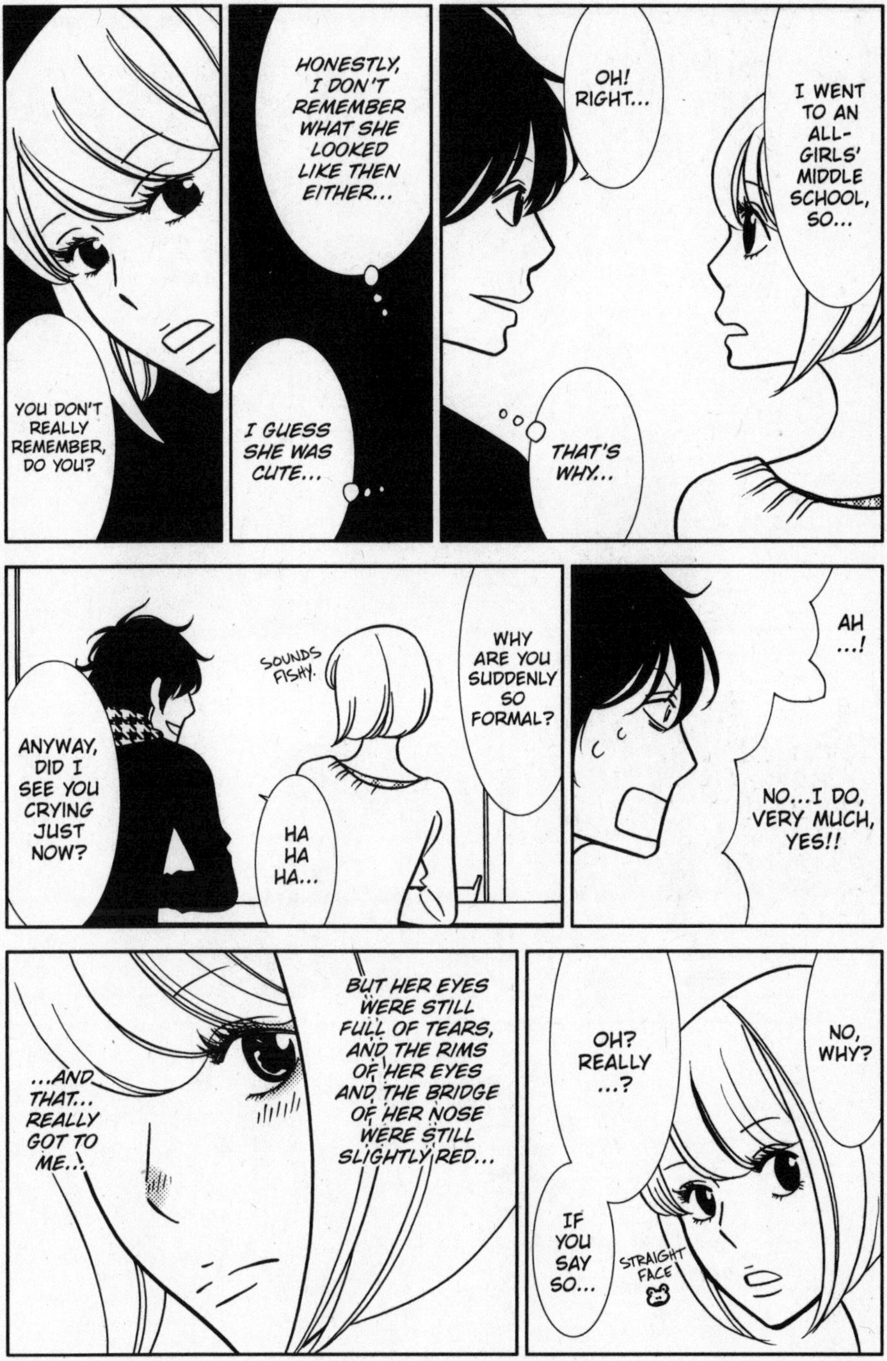
I WENT TO AN ALL-GIRLS' MIDDLE SCHOOL, SO...
OH! RIGHT...
THAT'S WHY...
HONESTLY, I DON'T REMEMBER WHAT SHE LOOKED LIKE THEN EITHER...
I GUESS SHE WAS CUTE...
YOU DON'T REALLY REMEMBER, DO YOU?
AH ...!
NO...I DO, VERY MUCH, YES!!
WHY ARE YOU SUDDENLY SO FORMAL?
SOUNDS FISHY.
HA HA HA...
ANYWAY, DID I SEE YOU CRYING JUST NOW?
NO, WHY?
OH? REALLY ...?
IF YOU SAY SO...
STRAIGHT FACE
BUT HER EYES WERE STILL FULL OF TEARS, AND THE RIMS OF HER EYES AND THE BRIDGE OF HER NOSE WERE STILL SLIGHTLY RED...
...AND THAT... REALLY GOT TO ME...

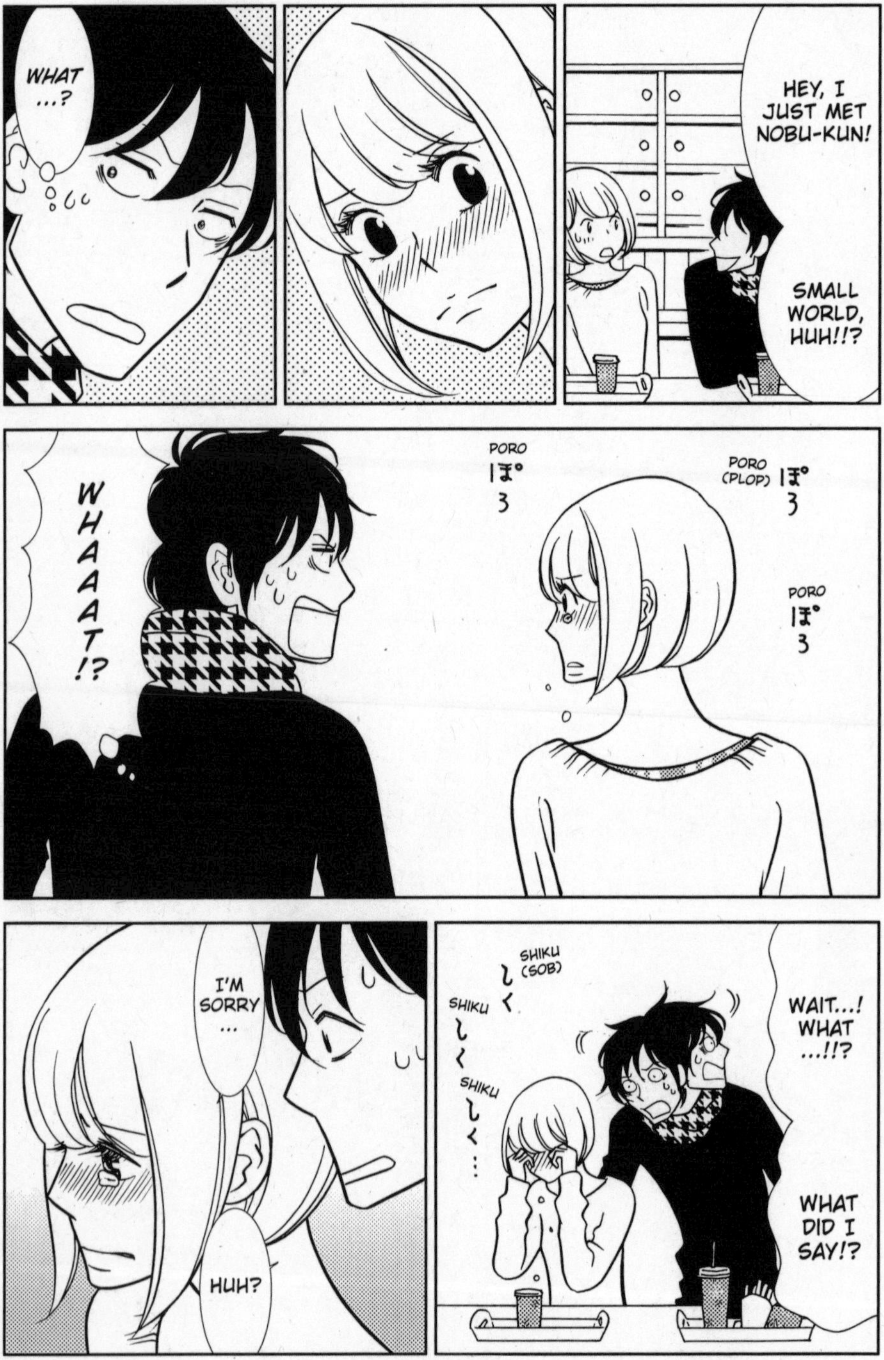
HEY, I JUST MET NOBU-KUN!
SMALL WORLD, HUH!!?
WHAT ...?
PORO (PLOP) ぽろ
PORO ぽろ
PORO ぽろ
WHAAAAT!?
WAIT...! WHAT ...!!?
WHAT DID I SAY!?
SHIKU (SOB) しく
SHIKU しく
SHIKU しく...
I'M SORRY ...
HUH?

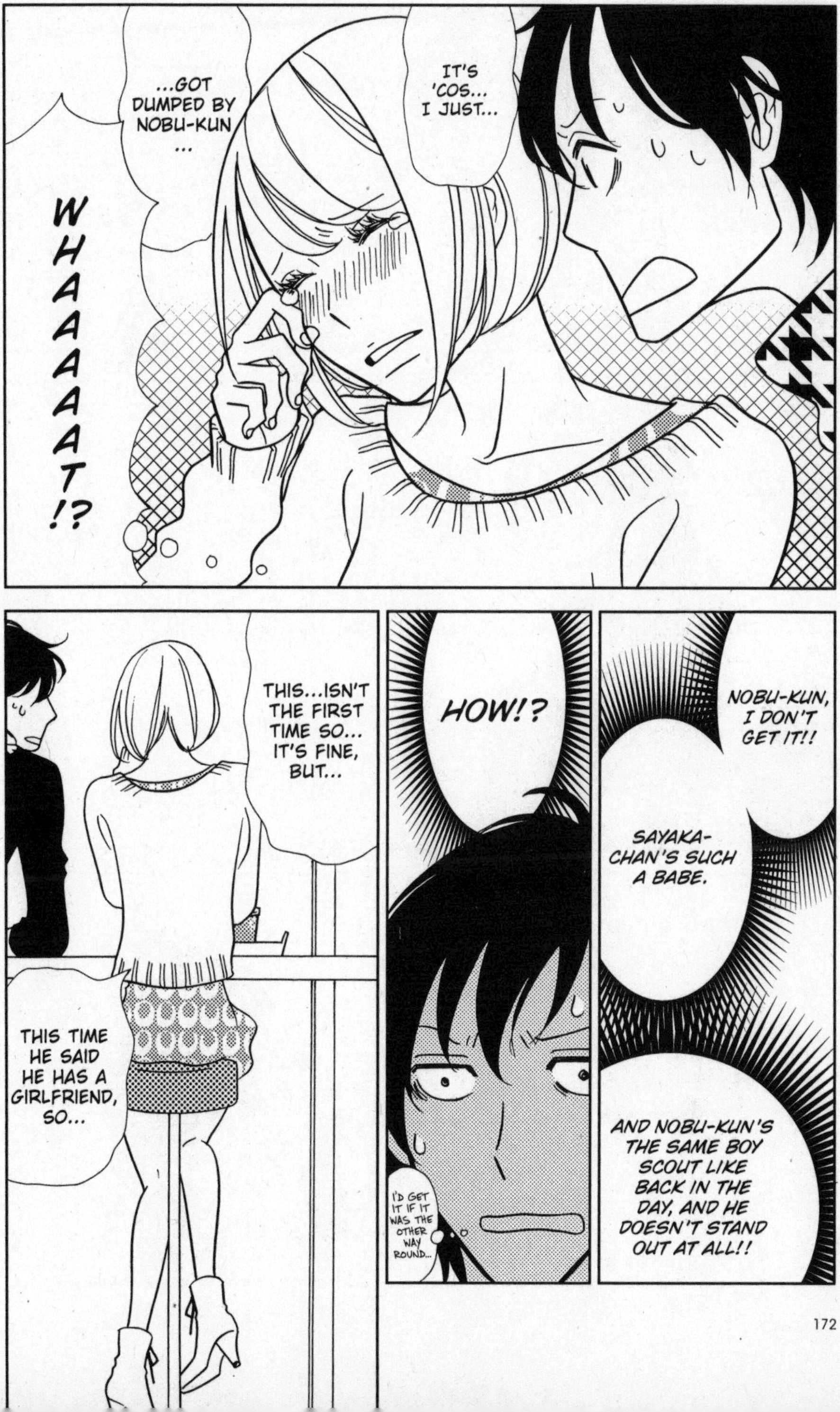
IT'S 'COS... I JUST...
...GOT DUMPED BY NOBU-KUN ...
WHAAAAAAT!?
NOBU-KUN, I DON'T GET IT!!
SAYAKA-CHAN'S SUCH A BABE.
AND NOBU-KUN'S THE SAME BOY SCOUT LIKE BACK IN THE DAY, AND HE DOESN'T STAND OUT AT ALL!!
HOW!?
I'D GET IT IF IT WAS THE OTHER WAY ROUND...
THIS...ISN'T THE FIRST TIME SO... IT'S FINE, BUT...
THIS TIME HE SAID HE HAS A GIRLFRIEND, SO...

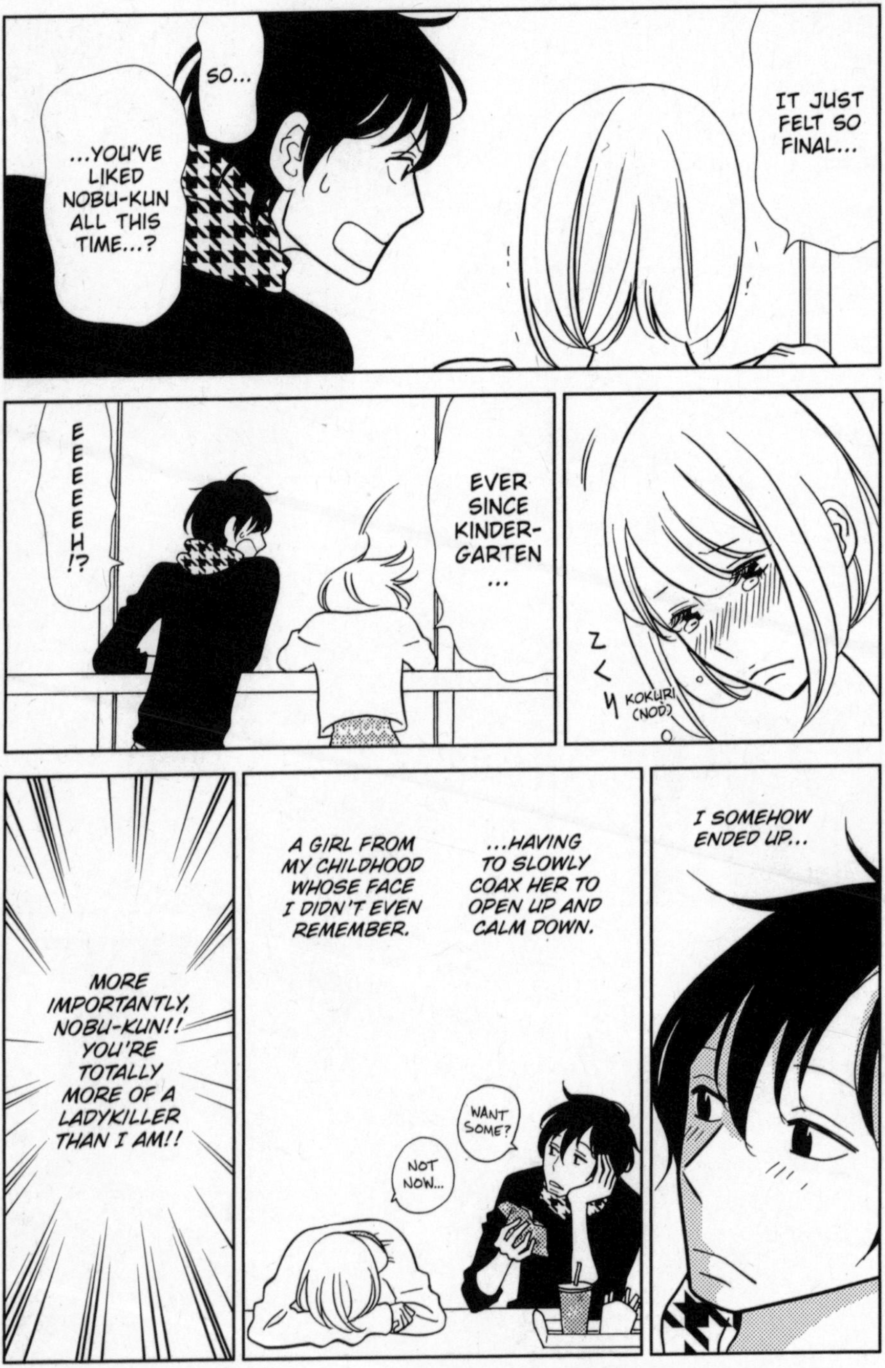
IT JUST FELT SO FINAL...
SO...
...YOU'VE LIKED NOBU-KUN ALL THIS TIME...?
KOKURI (NOD)
EVER SINCE KINDER-GARTEN...
EEEEEEH!?
I SOMEHOW ENDED UP...
...HAVING TO SLOWLY COAX HER TO OPEN UP AND CALM DOWN.
A GIRL FROM MY CHILDHOOD WHOSE FACE I DIDN'T EVEN REMEMBER.
WANT SOME?
NOT NOW...
MORE IMPORTANTLY, NOBU-KUN!! YOU'RE TOTALLY MORE OF A LADYKILLER THAN I AM!!

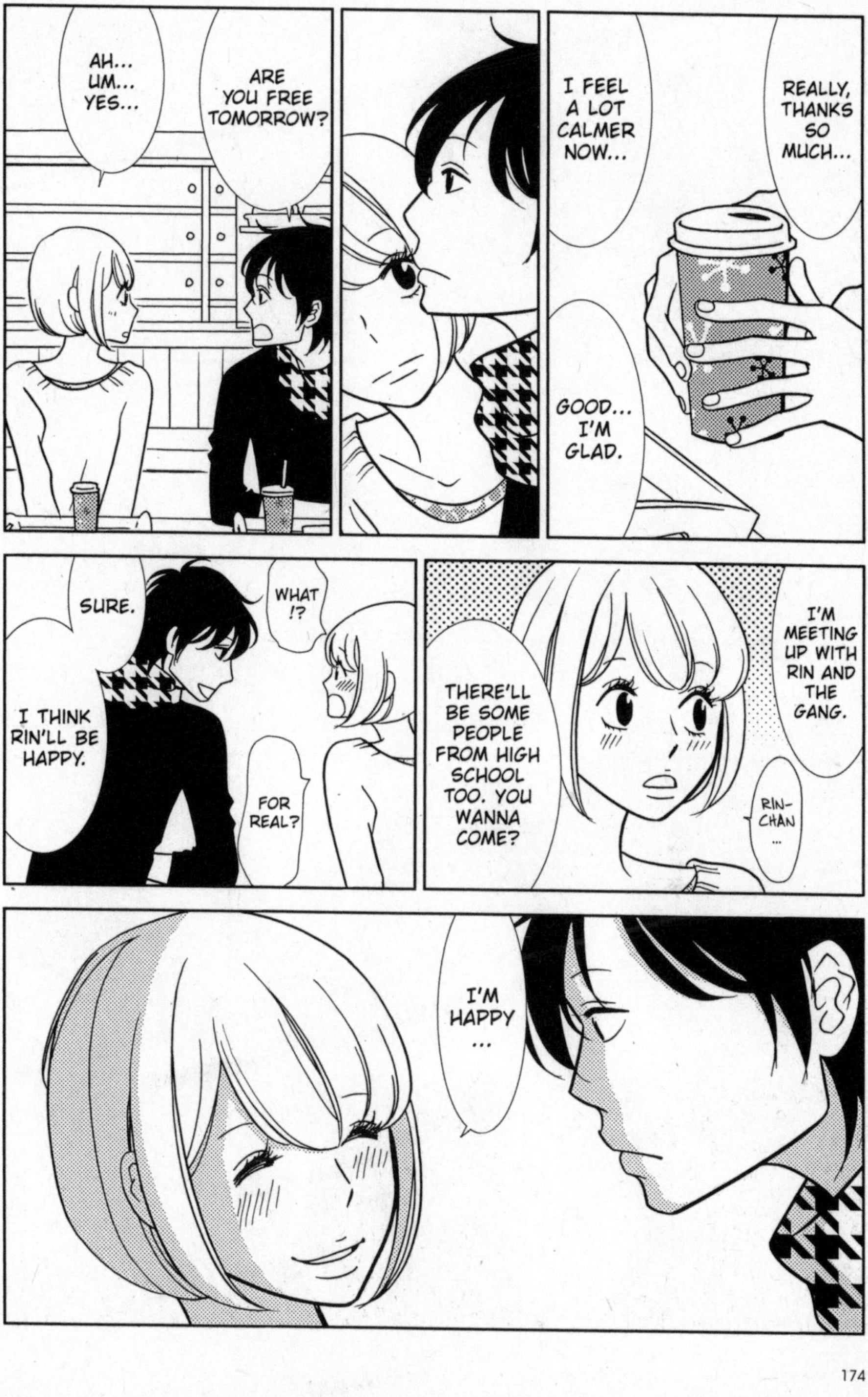
REALLY, THANKS SO MUCH...
I FEEL A LOT CALMER NOW...
GOOD... I'M GLAD.
ARE YOU FREE TOMORROW?
AH... UM... YES...
I'M MEETING UP WITH RIN AND THE GANG.
THERE'LL BE SOME PEOPLE FROM HIGH SCHOOL TOO. YOU WANNA COME?
RIN-CHAN ...
SURE.
WHAT !?
I THINK RIN'LL BE HAPPY.
FOR REAL?
I'M HAPPY ...

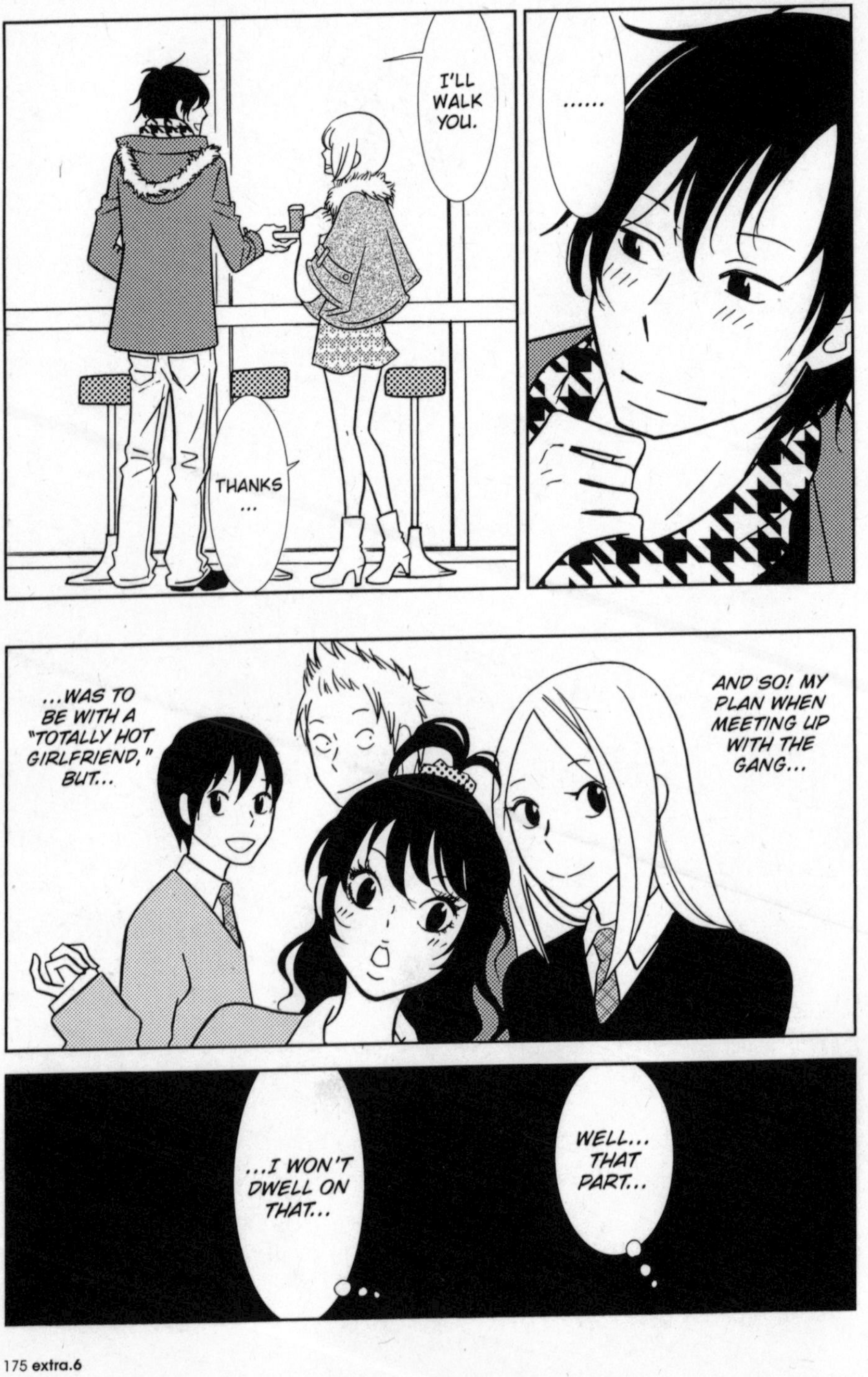
......
I'LL WALK YOU.
THANKS ...
AND SO! MY PLAN WHEN MEETING UP WITH THE GANG...
...WAS TO BE WITH A "TOTALLY HOT GIRLFRIEND," BUT...
WELL... THAT PART...
...I WON'T DWELL ON THAT...

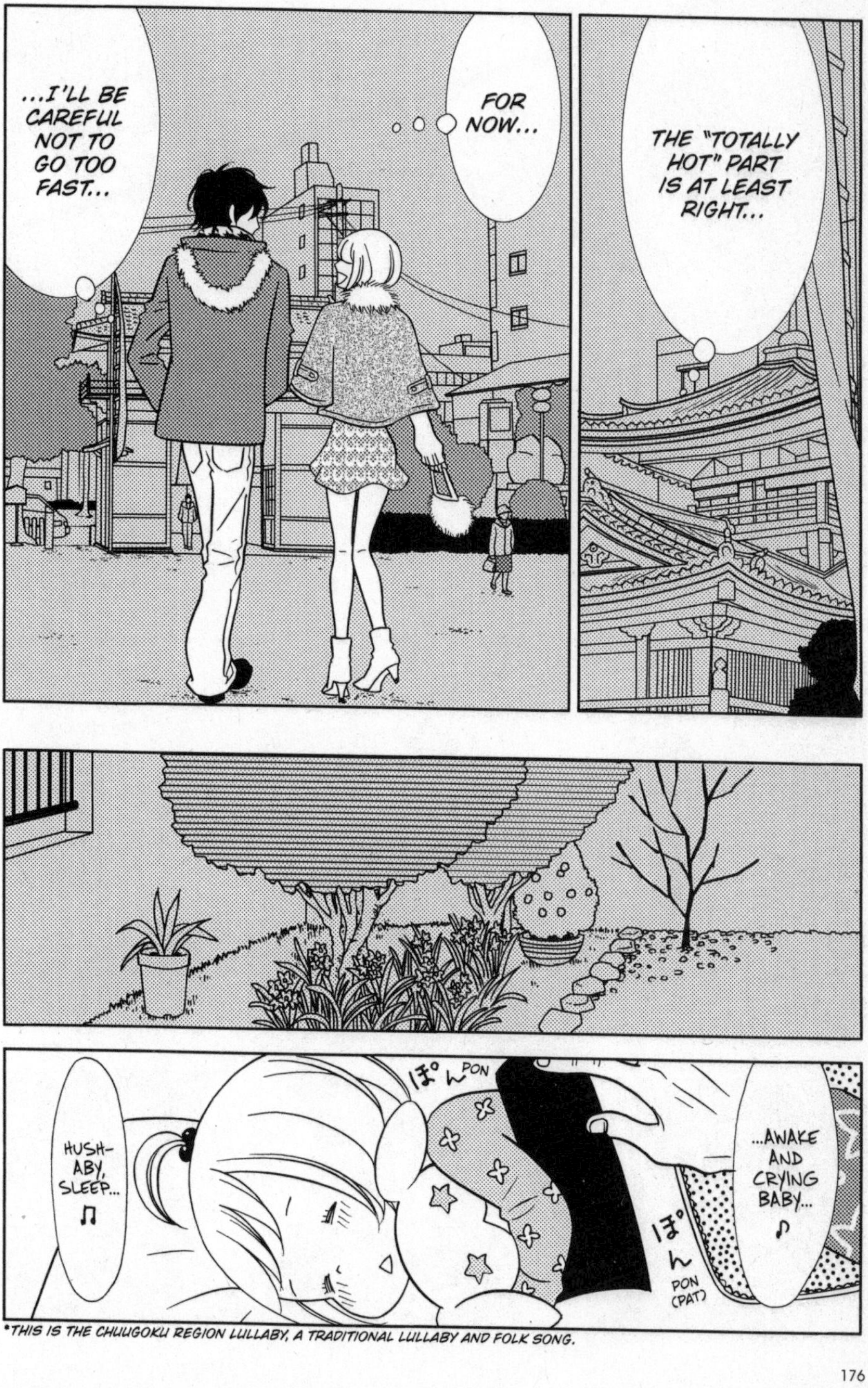
THE "TOTALLY HOT" PART IS AT LEAST RIGHT...
FOR NOW...
...I'LL BE CAREFUL NOT TO GO TOO FAST...
...AWAKE AND CRYING BABY... ♪
ぽん PON
ぽん PON (PAT)
HUSH-ABY, SLEEP... ♫

*THIS IS THE CHUUGOKU REGION LULLABY, A TRADITIONAL LULLABY AND FOLK SONG.

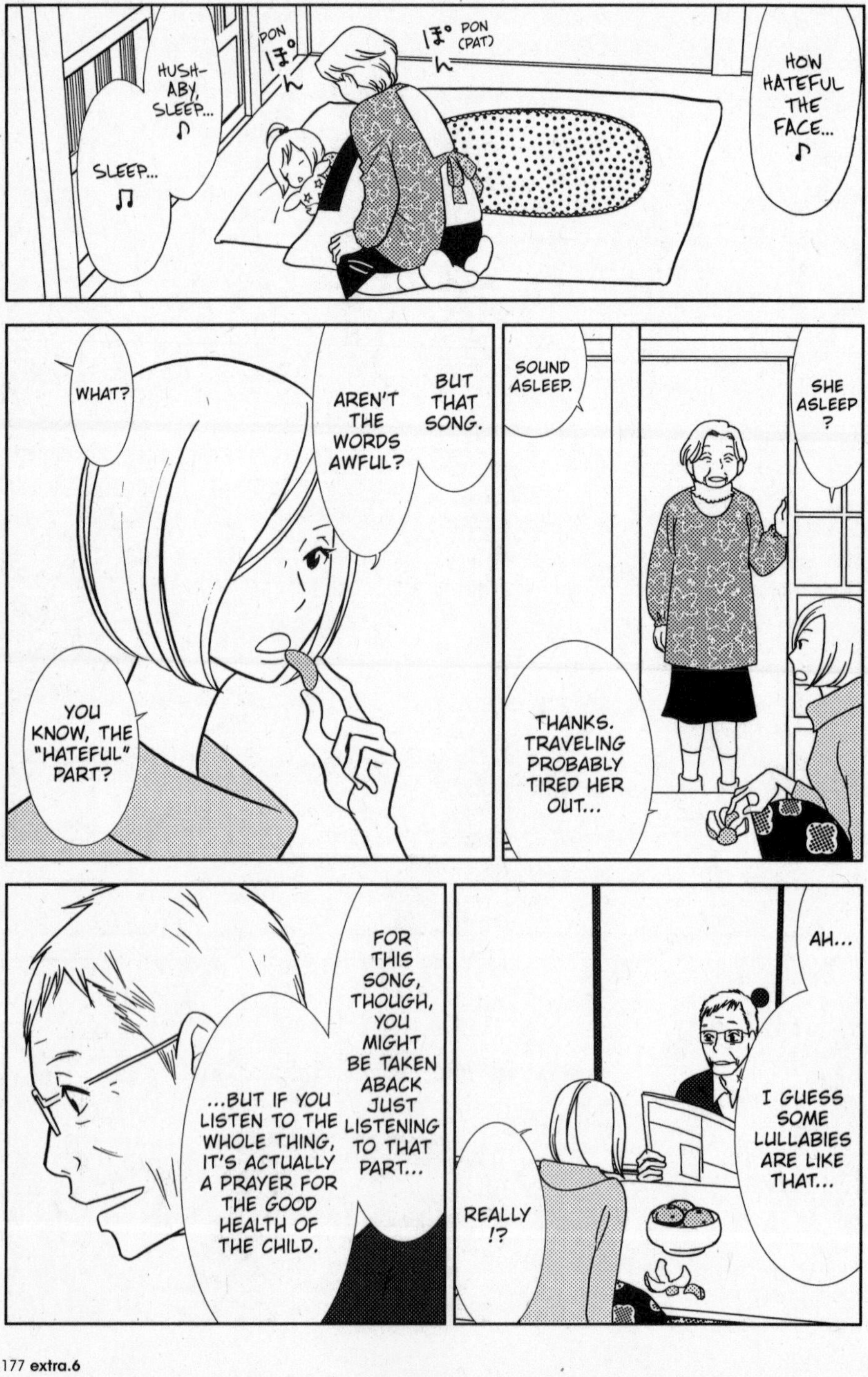
HOW HATEFUL THE FACE... ♪
PON ぽん (PAT)
PON ぽん
HUSH-ABY, SLEEP... ♪
SLEEP... ♫
SHE ASLEEP?
SOUND ASLEEP.
THANKS. TRAVELING PROBABLY TIRED HER OUT...
BUT THAT SONG.
AREN'T THE WORDS AWFUL?
WHAT?
YOU KNOW, THE "HATEFUL" PART?
AH...
I GUESS SOME LULLABIES ARE LIKE THAT...
REALLY!?
FOR THIS SONG, THOUGH, YOU MIGHT BE TAKEN ABACK JUST LISTENING TO THAT PART...
...BUT IF YOU LISTEN TO THE WHOLE THING, IT'S ACTUALLY A PRAYER FOR THE GOOD HEALTH OF THE CHILD.

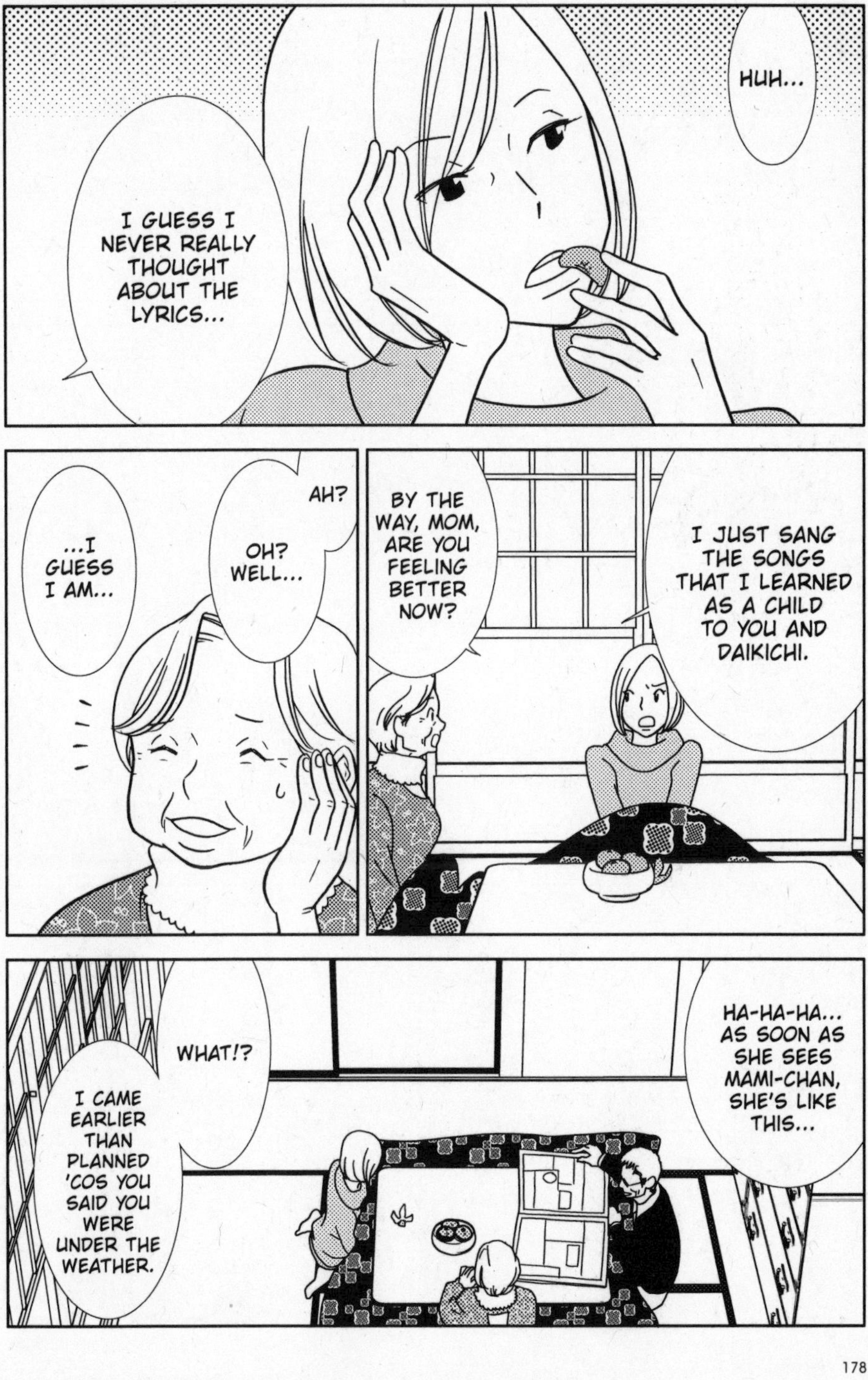
HUH...
I GUESS I NEVER REALLY THOUGHT ABOUT THE LYRICS...
I JUST SANG THE SONGS THAT I LEARNED AS A CHILD TO YOU AND DAIKICHI.
BY THE WAY, MOM, ARE YOU FEELING BETTER NOW?
AH?
OH? WELL...
...I GUESS I AM...
HA-HA-HA... AS SOON AS SHE SEES MAMI-CHAN, SHE'S LIKE THIS...
WHAT!?
I CAME EARLIER THAN PLANNED 'COS YOU SAID YOU WERE UNDER THE WEATHER.

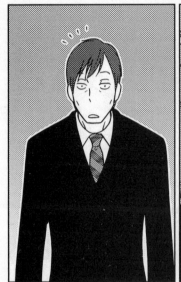

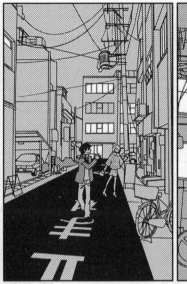

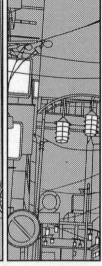

STREET: STOP

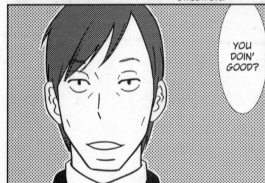

YOU DOIN' GOOD?

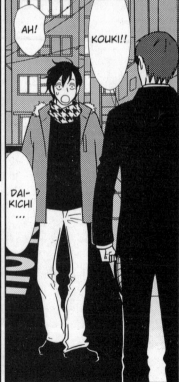

AH!

KOUKI!!

DAI-KICHI...

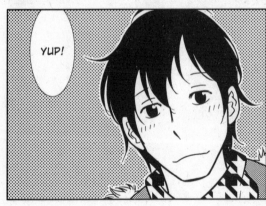

YUP!

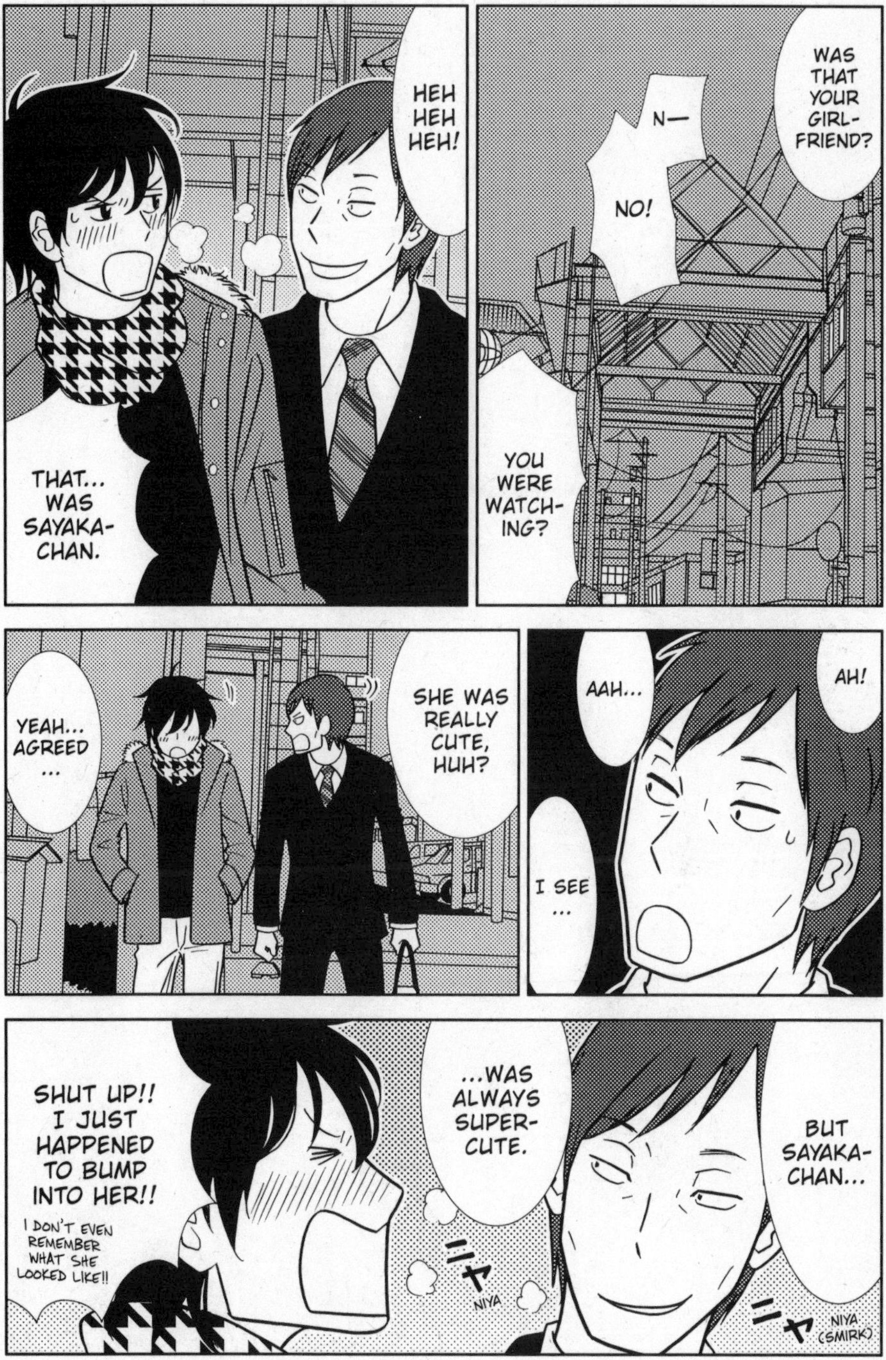
WAS THAT YOUR GIRLFRIEND?
N— NO!
YOU WERE WATCHING?
HEH HEH HEH!
THAT... WAS SAYAKA-CHAN.
AH!
AAH...
I SEE ...
SHE WAS REALLY CUTE, HUH?
YEAH... AGREED ...
BUT SAYAKA-CHAN...
...WAS ALWAYS SUPER-CUTE.
ニヤ NIYA (SMIRK)
ニヤ NIYA
SHUT UP!! I JUST HAPPENED TO BUMP INTO HER!!
I DON'T EVEN REMEMBER WHAT SHE LOOKED LIKE!!

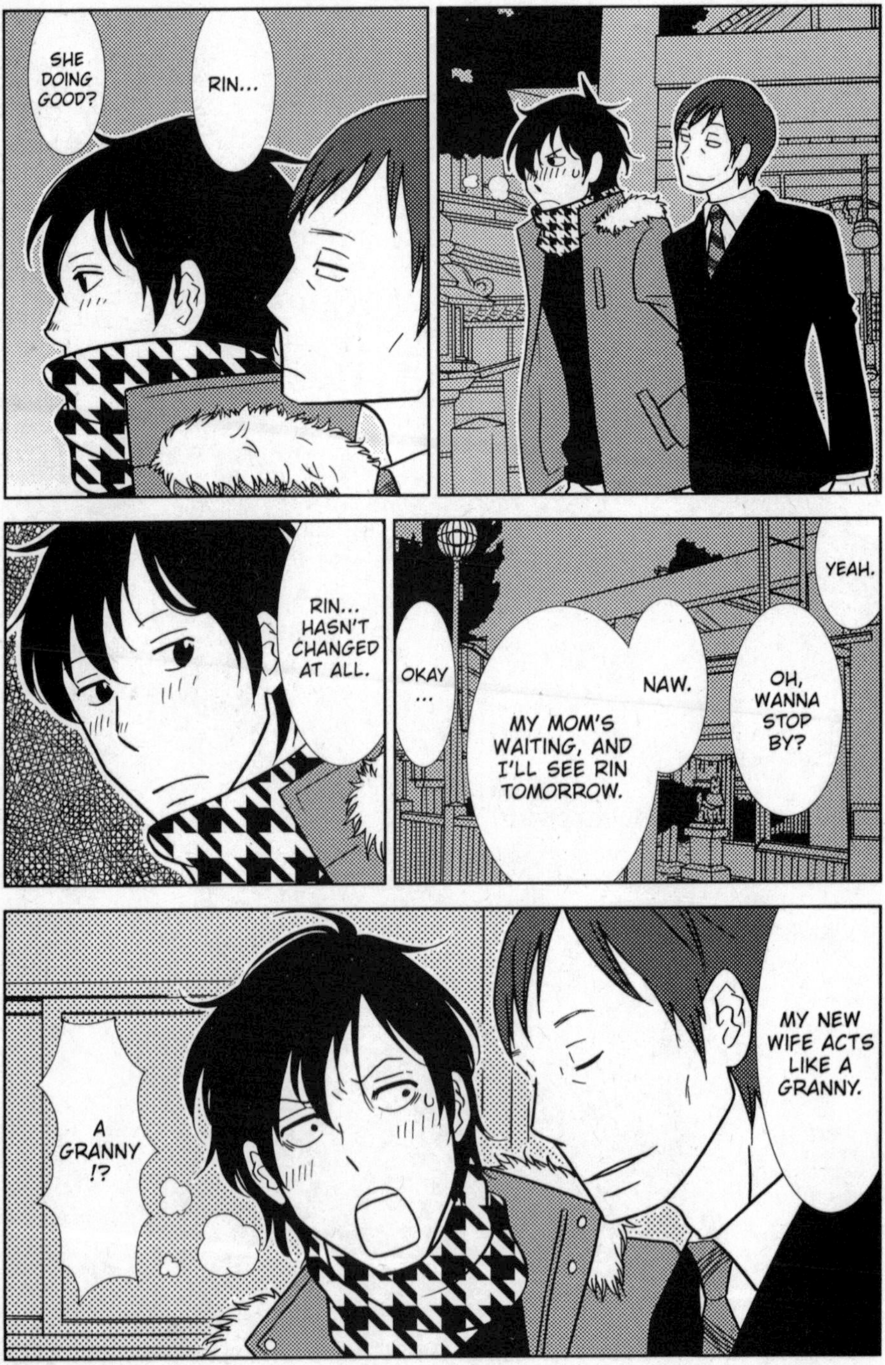
RIN...
SHE DOING GOOD?
YEAH.
OH, WANNA STOP BY?
NAW.
MY MOM'S WAITING, AND I'LL SEE RIN TOMORROW.
OKAY ...
RIN... HASN'T CHANGED AT ALL.
MY NEW WIFE ACTS LIKE A GRANNY.
A GRANNY !?

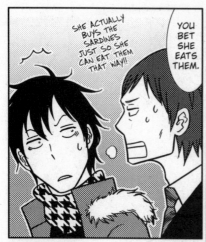

YOU KNOW, BEFORE ...
...I NEVER EVEN DATED SOMEONE WHO ATE THE DRIED BABY SARDINES AFTER USING THEM FOR SOUP...
WHAT? RIN EATS THAT STUFF?
YOU BET SHE EATS THEM.
SHE ACTUALLY BUYS THE SARDINES JUST SO SHE CAN EAT THEM THAT WAY!!
AND...
...BESIDES MY MOM...
...SHE'S THE ONLY OTHER PERSON I KNOW WHO PUTS KAMABOKO IN NIMONO.
HA HA HA!
EVEN MY MOM DOESN'T DO THAT... NIMONO AND KAMABOKO...

*KAMABOKO IS MOLDED FISH CAKE. NIMONO IS A SIMMERED JAPANESE DISH CONSISTING OF VEGETABLES, TOFU, AND/OR FISH THAT HAVE ABSORBED ALL OF THE BROTH IN WHICH THEY ARE COOKED.

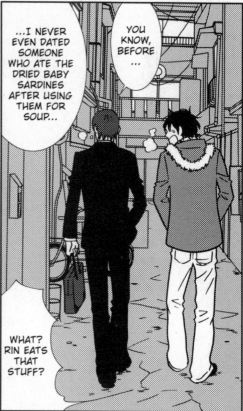

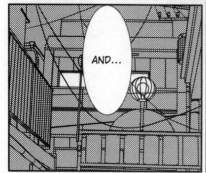

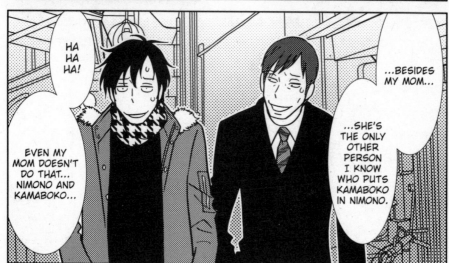

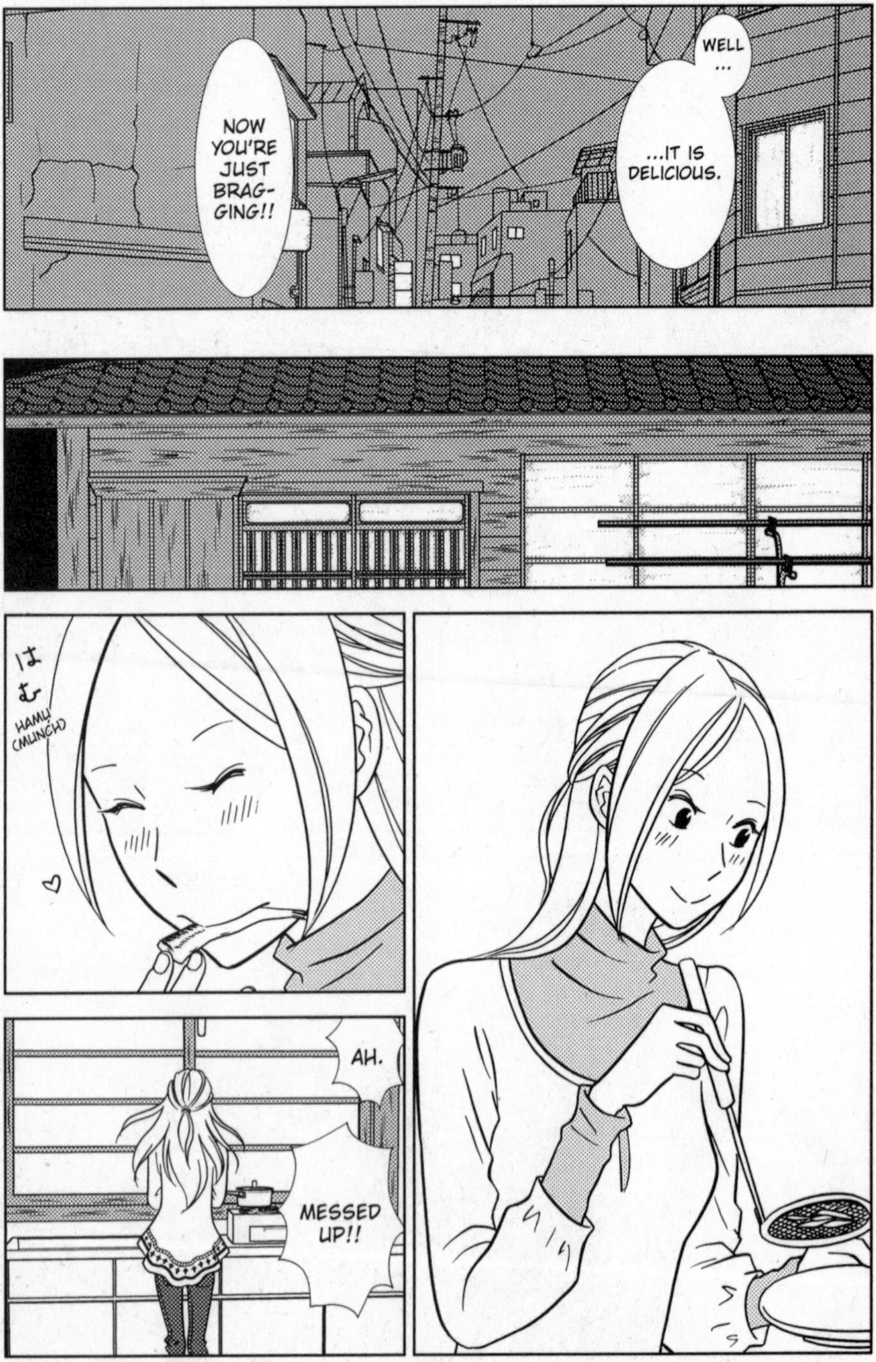
WELL ...
...IT IS DELICIOUS.
NOW YOU'RE JUST BRAG-GING!!
はむ
HAMU (MUNCH)
AH.
MESSED UP!!

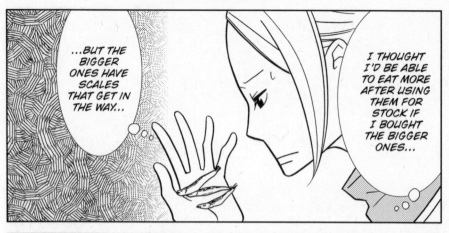

I THOUGHT I'D BE ABLE TO EAT MORE AFTER USING THEM FOR STOCK IF I BOUGHT THE BIGGER ONES...
...BUT THE BIGGER ONES HAVE SCALES THAT GET IN THE WAY...
I'M HOME.
DAIKICHI, WELCOME BACK.
THANKS.
HEY.
I JUST BUMPED INTO KOUKI.
REALLY?
WE'RE ALL GETTING TOGETHER TOMORROW.

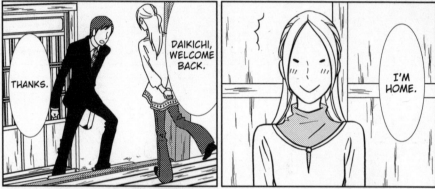

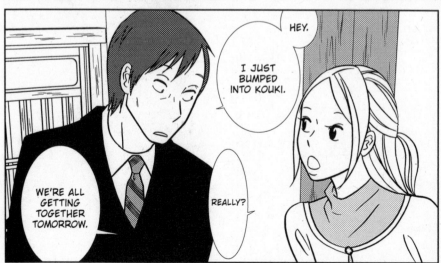

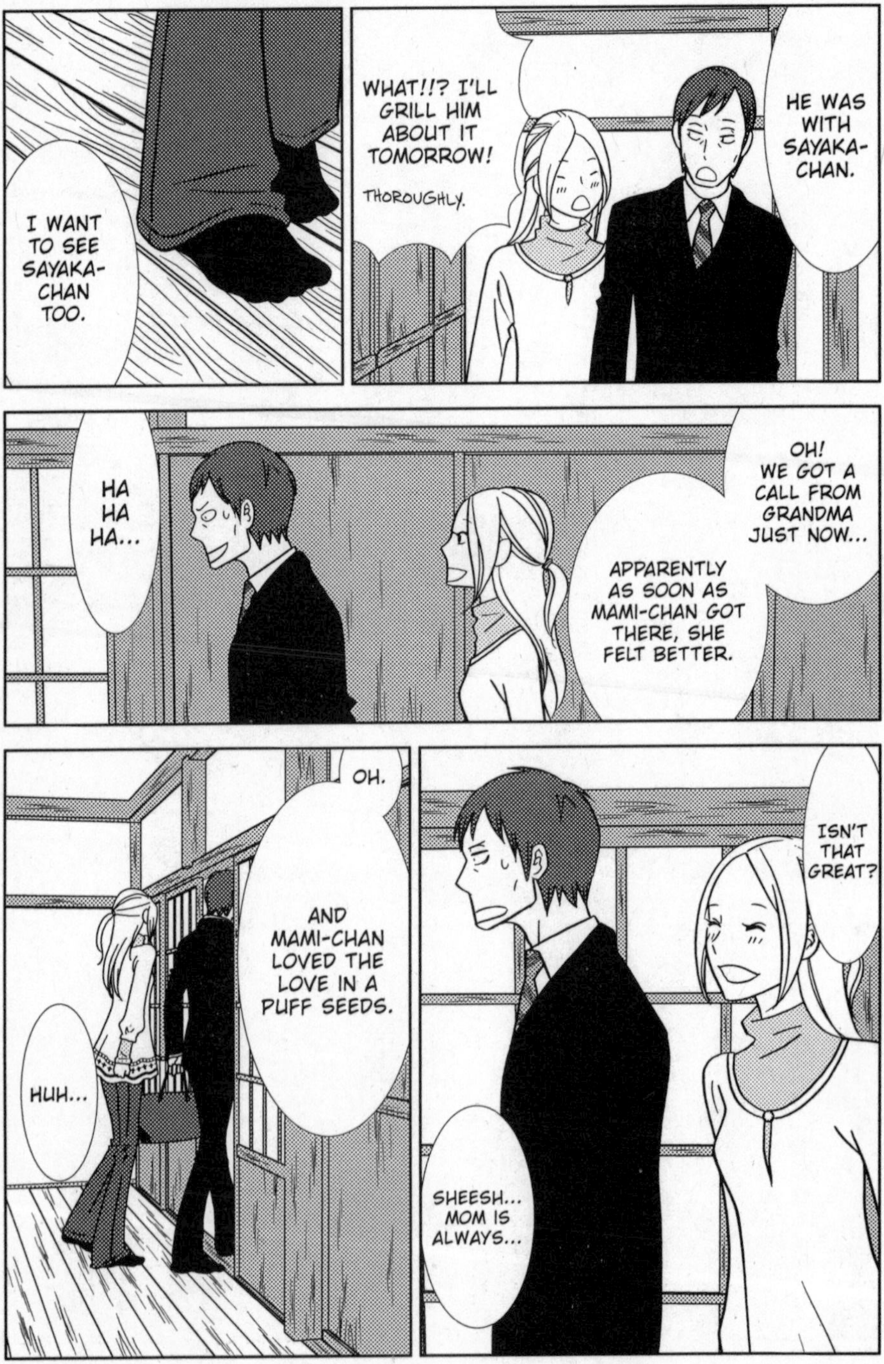
HE WAS WITH SAYAKA-CHAN.
WHAT!!? I'LL GRILL HIM ABOUT IT TOMORROW!
THOROUGHLY.
I WANT TO SEE SAYAKA-CHAN TOO.
OH! WE GOT A CALL FROM GRANDMA JUST NOW...
APPARENTLY AS SOON AS MAMI-CHAN GOT THERE, SHE FELT BETTER.
HA HA HA...
ISN'T THAT GREAT?
SHEESH... MOM IS ALWAYS...
OH.
AND MAMI-CHAN LOVED THE LOVE IN A PUFF SEEDS.
HUH...

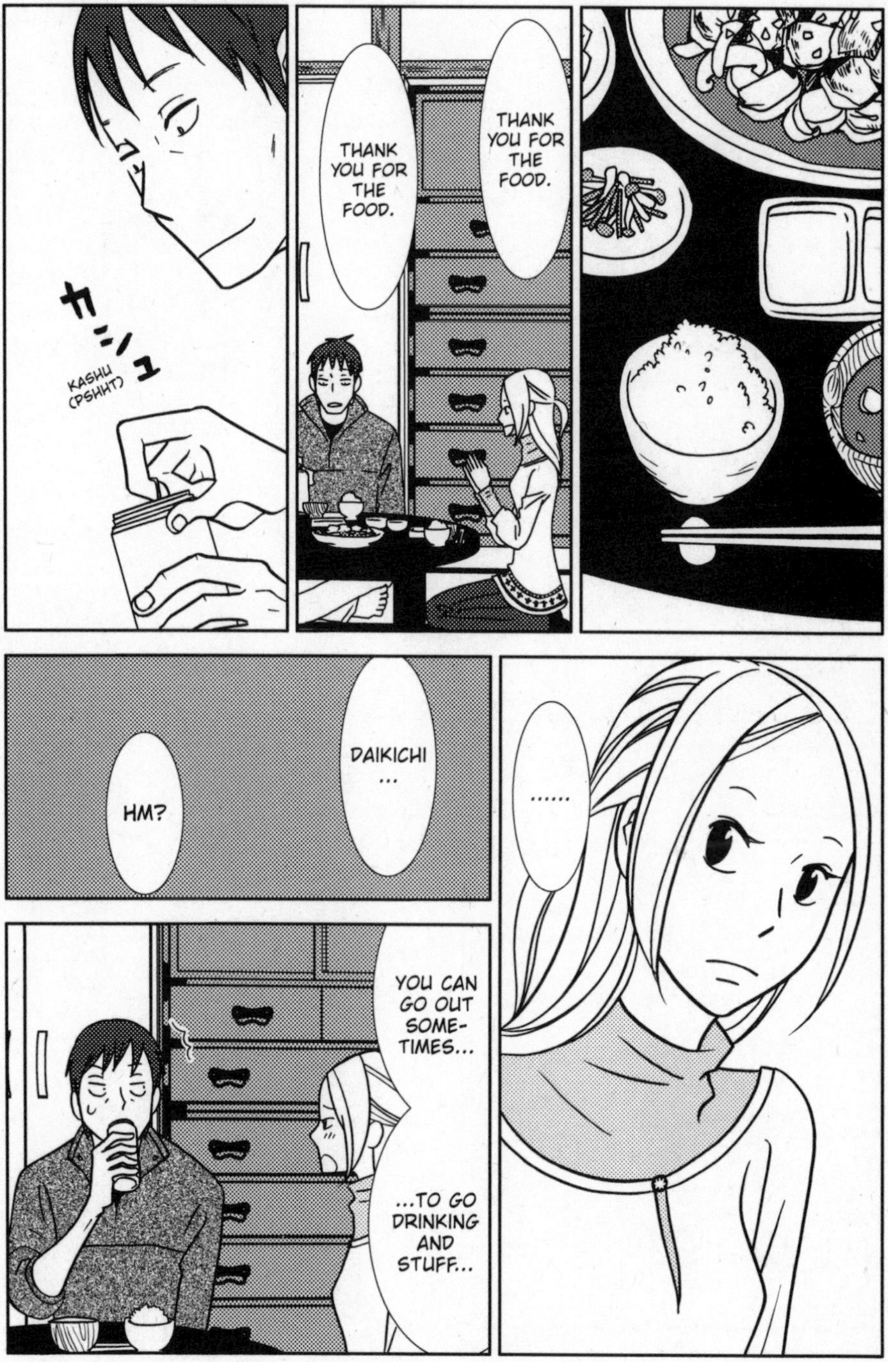
THANK YOU FOR THE FOOD.
THANK YOU FOR THE FOOD.
カシュ
KASHU (PSHHT)
......
DAIKICHI...
HM?
YOU CAN GO OUT SOME-TIMES...
...TO GO DRINKING AND STUFF...

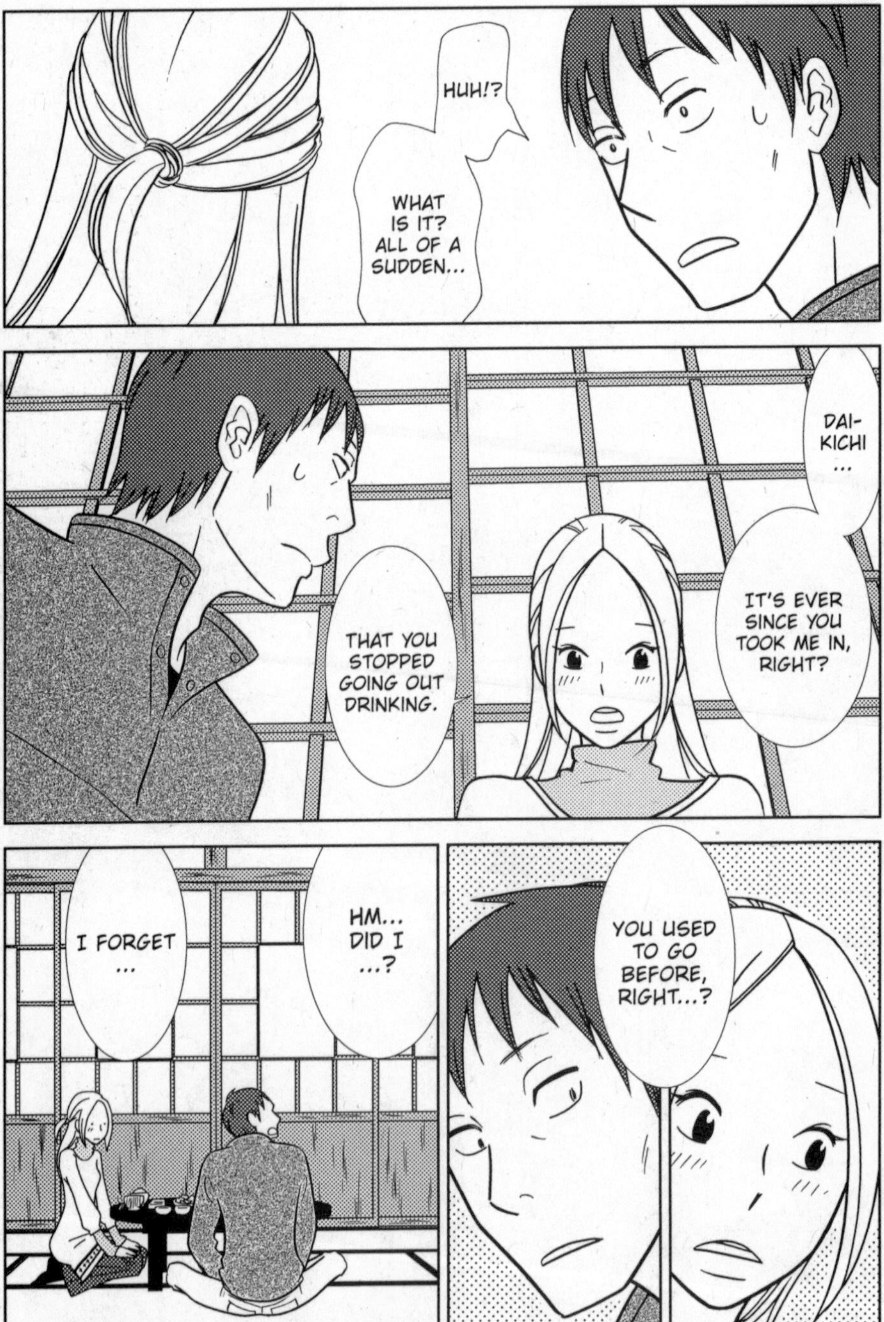
HUH!?
WHAT IS IT? ALL OF A SUDDEN...
DAI-KICHI ...
IT'S EVER SINCE YOU TOOK ME IN, RIGHT?
THAT YOU STOPPED GOING OUT DRINKING.
YOU USED TO GO BEFORE, RIGHT...?
HM... DID I ...?
I FORGET ...

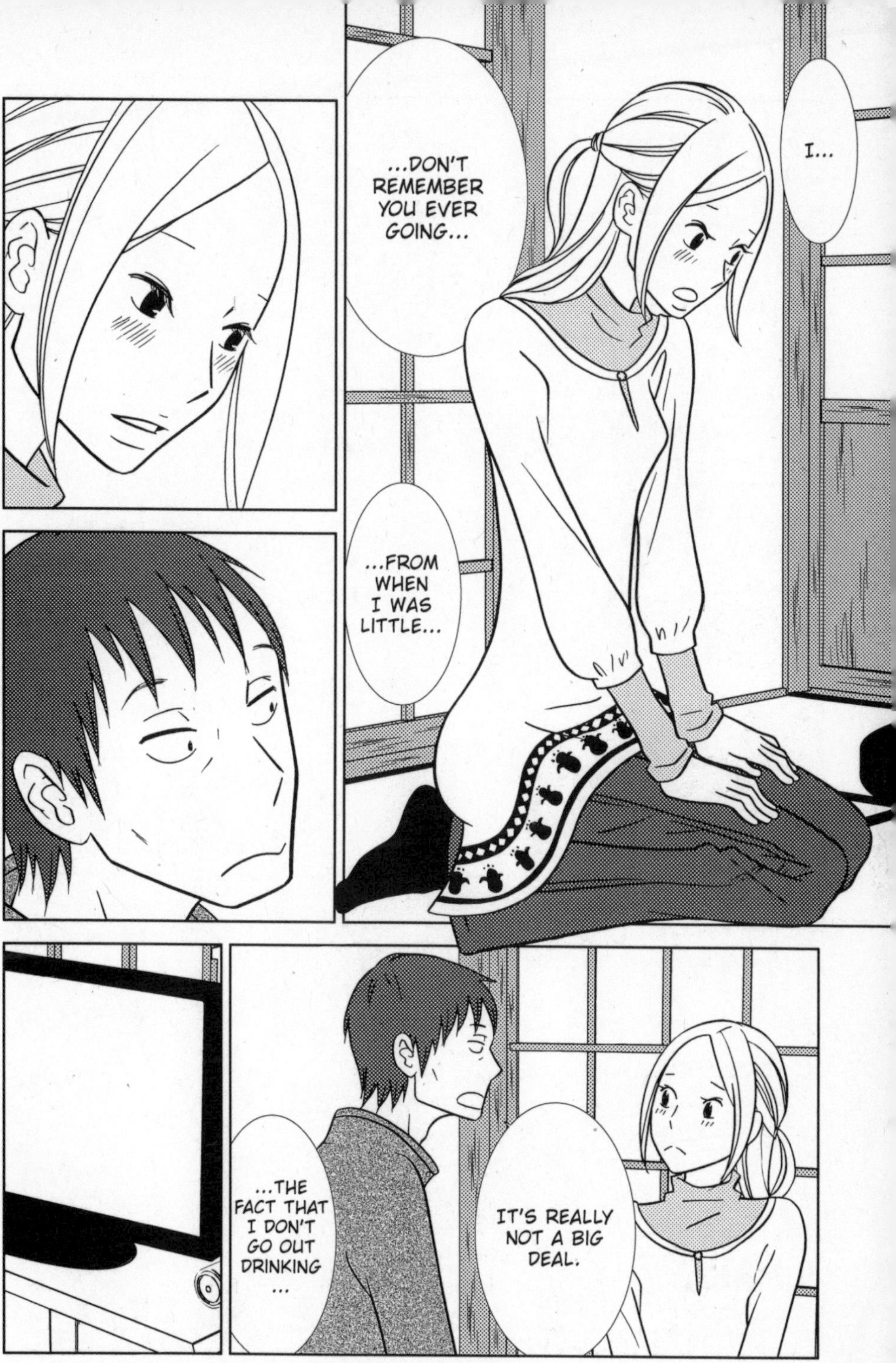
I...
...DON'T REMEMBER YOU EVER GOING...
...FROM WHEN I WAS LITTLE...
IT'S REALLY NOT A BIG DEAL.
...THE FACT THAT I DON'T GO OUT DRINKING ...

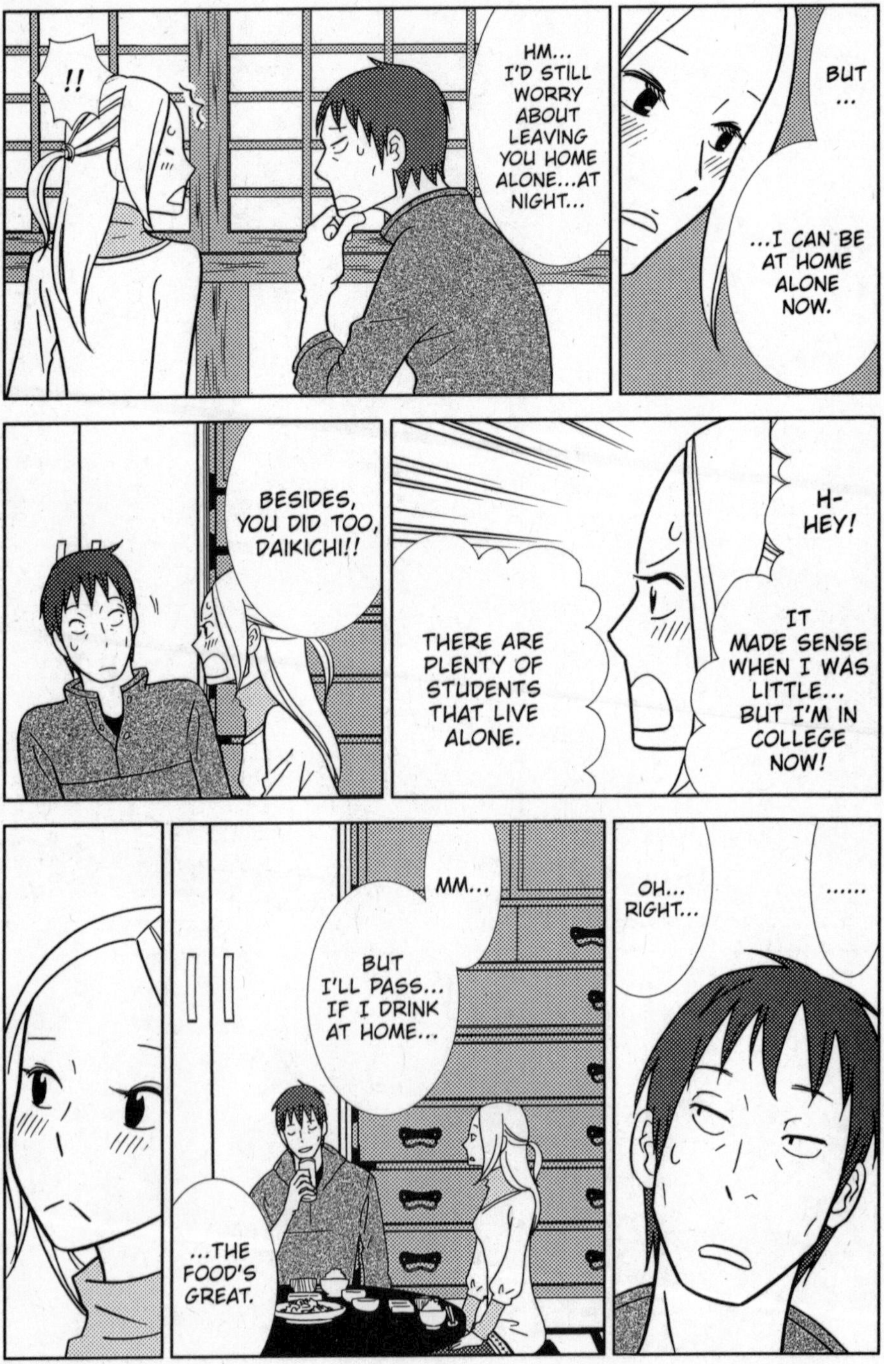
BUT ...
...I CAN BE AT HOME ALONE NOW.
HM... I'D STILL WORRY ABOUT LEAVING YOU HOME ALONE...AT NIGHT...
!!
H- HEY!
IT MADE SENSE WHEN I WAS LITTLE... BUT I'M IN COLLEGE NOW!
THERE ARE PLENTY OF STUDENTS THAT LIVE ALONE.
BESIDES, YOU DID TOO, DAIKICHI!!
......
OH... RIGHT...
MM...
BUT I'LL PASS... IF I DRINK AT HOME...
...THE FOOD'S GREAT.

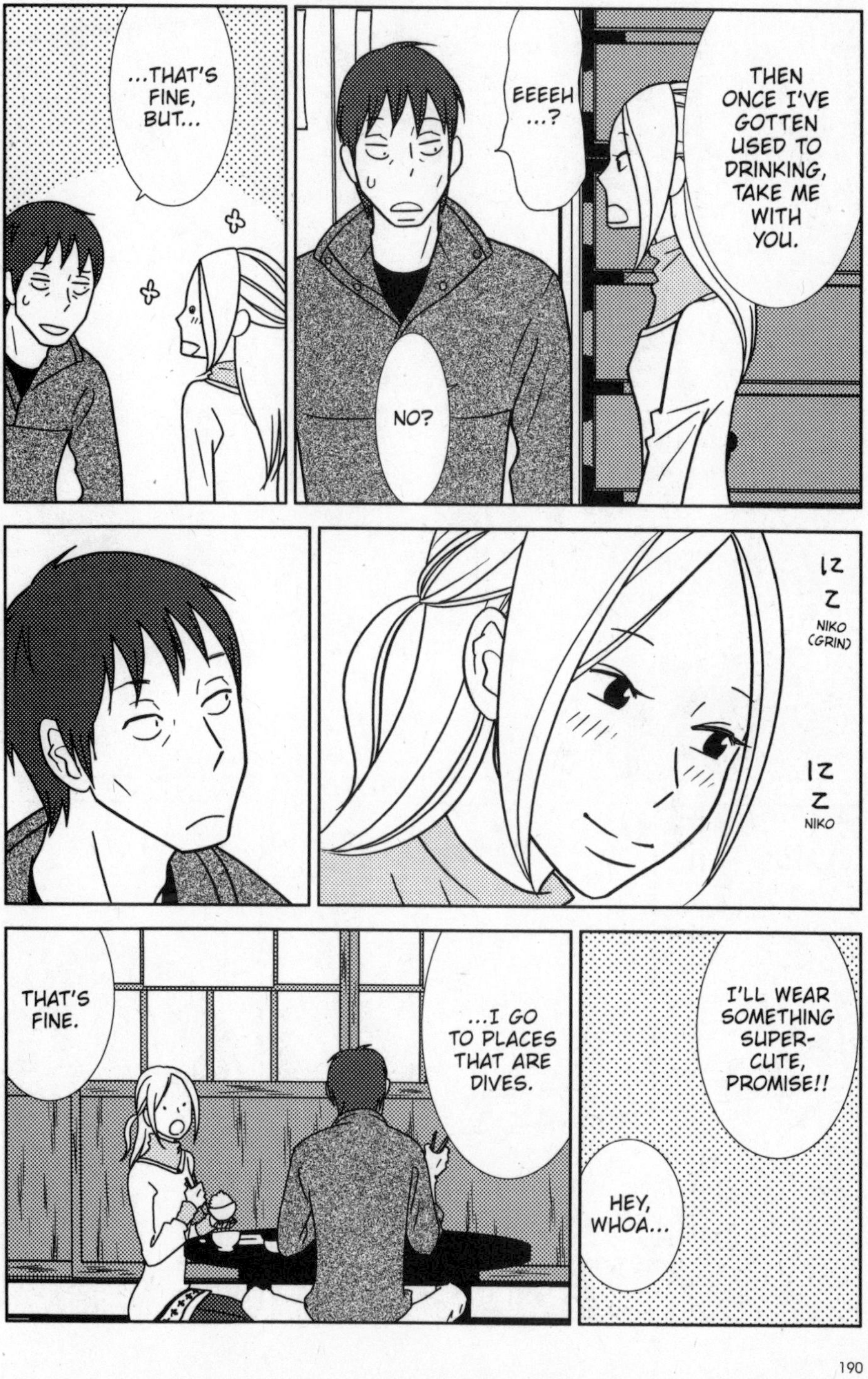
THEN ONCE I'VE GOTTEN USED TO DRINKING, TAKE ME WITH YOU.
EEEEH ...?
NO?
...THAT'S FINE, BUT...
NIKO (GRIN)
NIKO
I'LL WEAR SOMETHING SUPER-CUTE, PROMISE!!
HEY, WHOA...
...I GO TO PLACES THAT ARE DIVES.
THAT'S FINE.

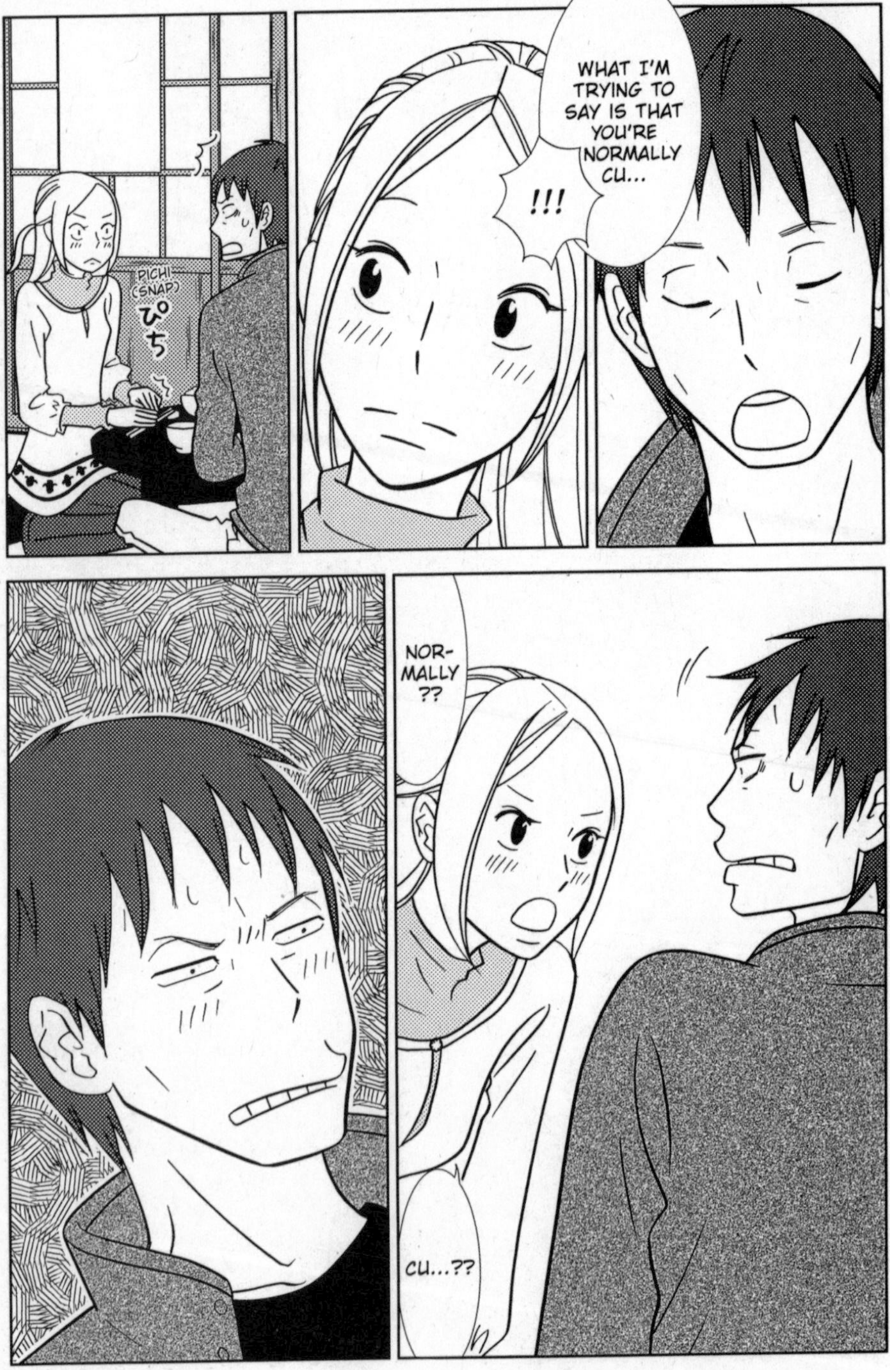
WHAT I'M TRYING TO SAY IS THAT YOU'RE NORMALLY CU...
!!!
PICHI (SNAP)
ぴち
NOR-MALLY ??
CU...??

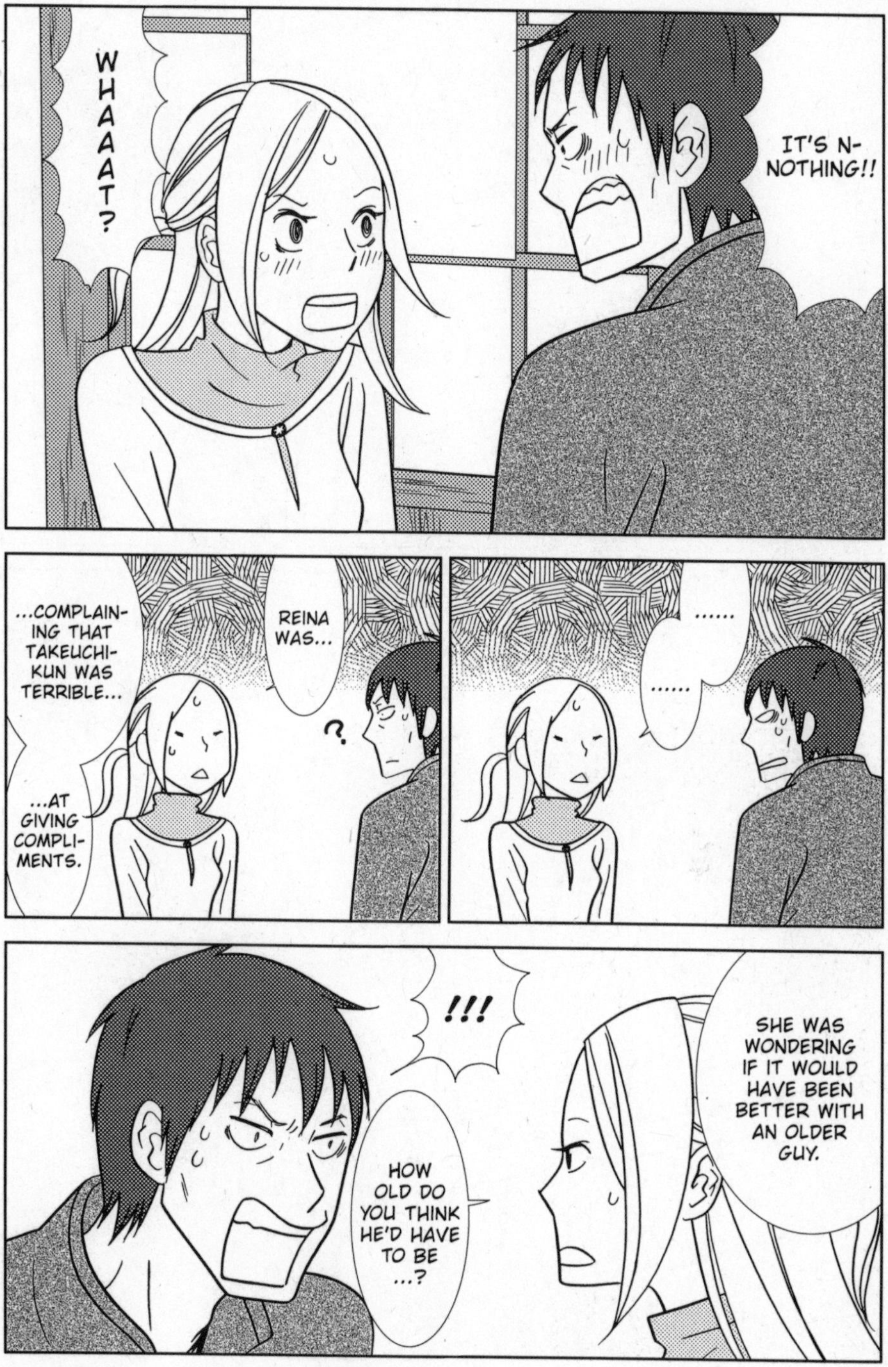
IT'S N-NOTHING!!
WHAAAT?
......
......
REINA WAS...
...COMPLAINING THAT TAKEUCHI-KUN WAS TERRIBLE...
?
...AT GIVING COMPLIMENTS.
SHE WAS WONDERING IF IT WOULD HAVE BEEN BETTER WITH AN OLDER GUY.
!!!
HOW OLD DO YOU THINK HE'D HAVE TO BE ...?

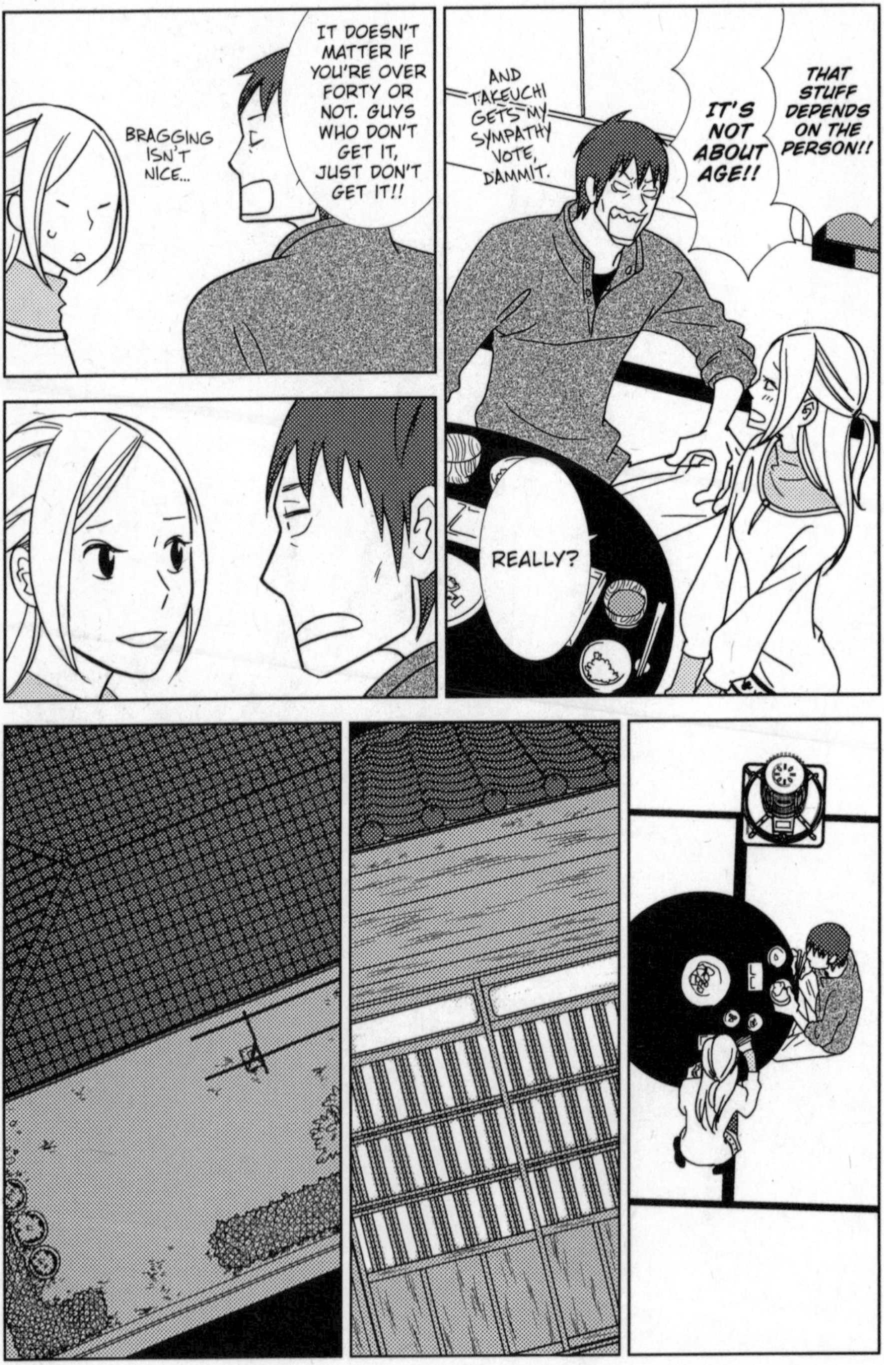
THAT STUFF DEPENDS ON THE PERSON!!
IT'S NOT ABOUT AGE!!
AND TAKEUCHI GETS MY SYMPATHY VOTE, DAMMIT.
REALLY?
IT DOESN'T MATTER IF YOU'RE OVER FORTY OR NOT. GUYS WHO DON'T GET IT, JUST DON'T GET IT!!
BRAGGING ISN'T NICE...

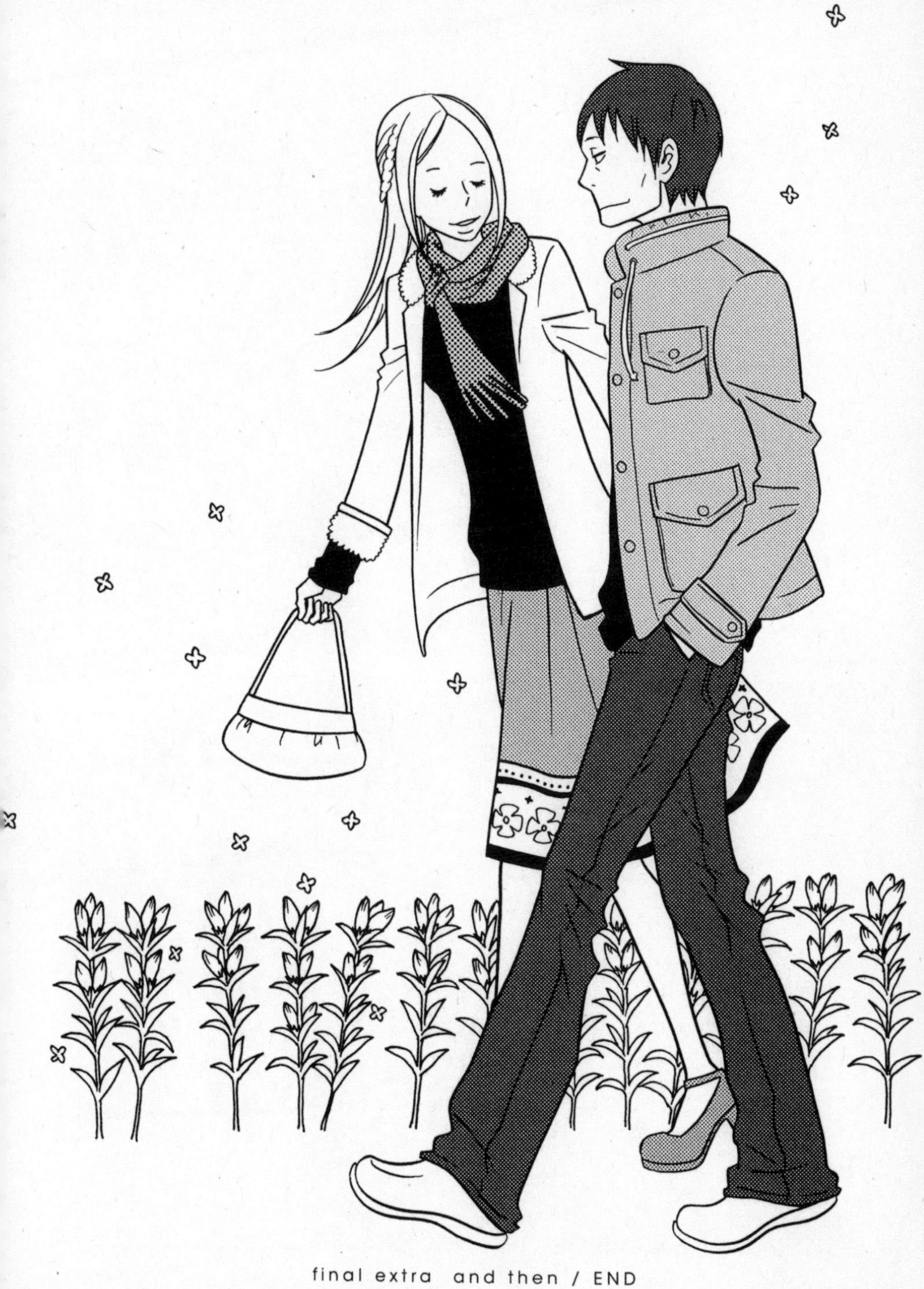

final extra and then / END

BUNNY**DROP**
END

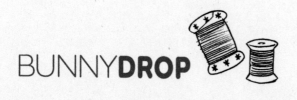

BUNNY**DROP**

Yumi Unita's **BUNNY DROP** Interview!

"It's been tempestuous, but it's a precious and heartwarming work to me."

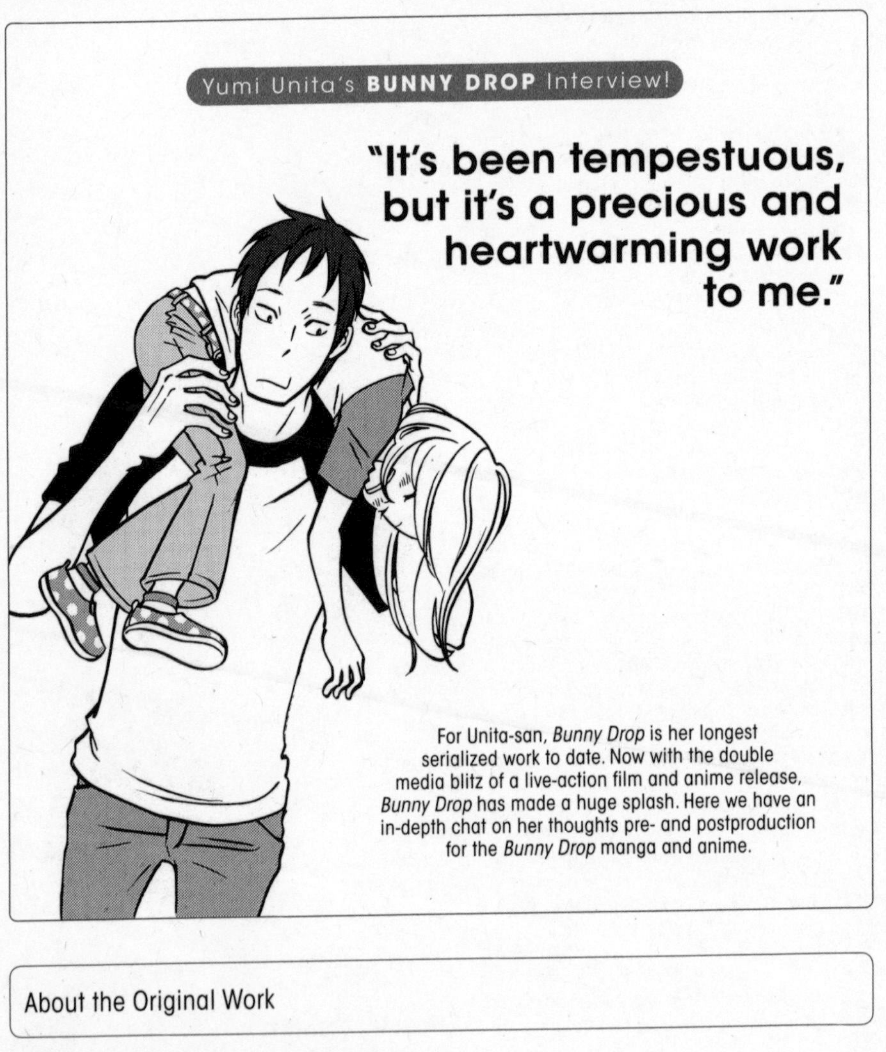

For Unita-san, *Bunny Drop* is her longest serialized work to date. Now with the double media blitz of a live-action film and anime release, *Bunny Drop* has made a huge splash. Here we have an in-depth chat on her thoughts pre- and postproduction for the *Bunny Drop* manga and anime.

About the Original Work

THE ROAD TO *BUNNY DROP*

How did the story concept come about?

My editor at the time made a suggestion, "What about a story about a single guy raising a little girl?" From there, I envisioned how to Yumi Unita-ize it. I was already doing a family-themed work called *The Four of Us* (*Yoningurashi*) with another publisher (Takeshobo) at the time, so I wanted it to contrast with that as well. The *Feel Young* manga anthology didn't have any child-centered stories back then, so even now I think that my editor's decision was a great leap of faith.

Which character was fleshed out first?

That would be Rin. Initially when I began drawing her, I envisioned her a little younger actually, about four years old, but as I mulled over some of the story details, I thought maybe six would be better, especially for her to be able to more realistically process her grandfather's death. Conversely, if she were much older, the fun of having a child character would have been greatly diminished.

At the rough sketch stage, Rin was much younger.

What were you most conscious of when drawing Rin?

She's a very easy character to draw, so there wasn't anything in particular, but...I did take care to show a progressive change in her hair. It's wildest in the beginning. After living with Daikichi for a little while, her hair starts to calm down. By the time she gets to middle school and high school, she's taking good care of her hair, so it's nice and silky.

Was there anything you were particular about when writing Rin's inner voice?

In the beginning, I wanted to concentrate on drawing from Daikichi's perspective, so I rarely wrote out Rin's inner monologues and had the reader infer from her "words and actions," which were few to begin with. That's how it seems to be in real life, when interacting with kids anyway. Kids actually tend not to say and do things that adults want them to say or do, right...? Plus, I wasn't really confident in my ability to write a believable inner monologue for a six-year-old.

What part of drawing Daikichi were you particular about?

Daikichi was a really easy character to draw too. But with his face being a bit, you know...and since it was a story running in a women's magazine, I wanted to give him at least a good physique. But then if I drew him too slender in a shoujo manga style, that would have made things difficult in sizing compared to the child characters. Rin would come out too small, or her head would be larger than Daikichi's, things like that... So I was particularly careful about the size proportion between the characters.

......

Similarly, was there anything you stayed conscious of when drawing Daikichi's inner voice?

This was the reverse of Rin's case... I tried not to write out too much of Daikichi's inner dialogue when Rin was in middle and high school. His voice is just here and there. Also, since Daikichi isn't technically her father, it was difficult to put into words his hesitation about Rin becoming an adult.

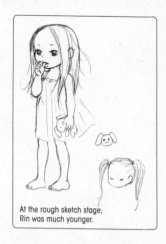

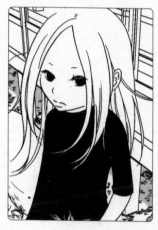

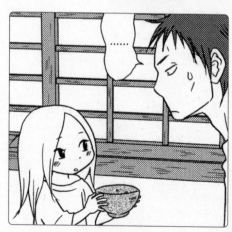

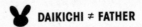

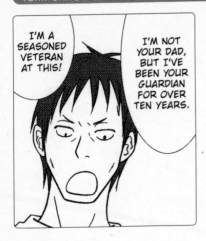

I'M NOT YOUR DAD, BUT I'VE BEEN YOUR GUARDIAN FOR OVER TEN YEARS.
I'M A SEASONED VETERAN AT THIS!

DAIKICHI ≠ FATHER

From beginning to end, Daikichi never wavers from his "guardian" title with respect to Rin. What was the reason and your thoughts on that?

I wanted to show that Daikichi was very serious about his responsibility as a "guardian" and not a "dad," since he was aware that he jumped on the parenting wagon after it had already started moving. It was also his way of giving respect to Masako-san and Souichi-san, not to mention the other fathers and mothers around him.

THE MOST DIFFICULT CHARACTER WAS MASAKO-SAN.

What were the difficult aspects of this story?

In the beginning, the most time-consuming part had to do with Masako-san. It was a pretty hard job, trying to put myself in her head and write her dialogue. I didn't want to write dialogue that just reaffirmed her actions, and I didn't see the point in making her out to be such a villain either... I already knew that readers would hate her, and Daikichi would never forgive her because of his affection for Rin. So I came to realize that at least I and Masako-san's boyfriend needed to love her unconditionally. It was with those thoughts that I was able to persevere. The second section of this story—the middle school years—was also tough. There were a lot of painful storylines during this period, so I took a lot of time thinking about them. Being able to draw a scene where Rin and Kouki are on their cell phones was a bonus. I guess the most difficult part wrapping up the story was Masako-san till the bitter end (laugh). Plus, for the final back and forth between Daikichi and Rin, I tried to be extremely careful, thinking and rethinking it multiple times, stopping to reflect and question everything. Even knowing what the ending was going to be from the very beginning, being a parent myself, I didn't take the road to get there lightly.

Tell us about a character other than Rin and Daikichi who left an impact on you.

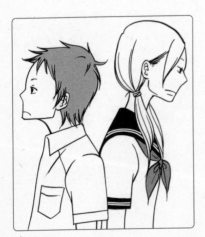

Daikichi's coworkers at the shipping department at the company where he works and Gotou-san were a lot of fun to draw. I drew them with a light heart, so having them as part of the storyline helped when things got too heavy.

What does Bunny Drop *mean to you personally?*

Just by virtue of being my longest series, this title has created a lot of memories for me. It even became a live-action film and an anime series. It's been tempestuous, but it's a precious and heartwarming work that took up most of my thirties. It was almost too much for me to look back on it all. (laugh)

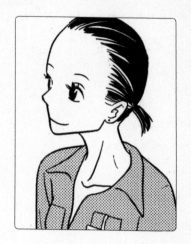

With the movie and anime versions coming out at the same time, and PUFFY singing the theme song (altogether a rare feat), tell me how it made you feel when all that came about.

The movie was decided first and that in itself was shocking. Then on top of that, it went into production as an anime. And PUFFY, who were fans since my debut, were so kind to sing the theme song... I was literally in panic mode every day, it seemed. Panicked in a happy way!

What kind of work would you like to do in the future?

I've always wanted to draw a story about my hometown.

Transformation Into an Anime and a Film

 THE DIRECTOR AND I, OUR THOUGHTS WERE PERFECTLY IN SYNCH.

Did you have any particular requests to make of the production staff?

I think I remember asking them to make it as accessible as possible visually to those who might not normally watch anime, and voice-wise, to make it easy to understand. But the director (anime director Kanta Kamei-san) and I, our thoughts on the work were perfectly in synch. Other than that, I didn't make any requests per se, but I just expanded on their questions and let them know what I considered important when writing the manga... Information-sharing of sorts, I suppose.

Tell us about the moment you saw the storyboard and the character model sheets.

A lot of people worked on the storyboards, so it was fun seeing all the individual touches. At first I didn't know how to follow them, but as they were being shown to me, I somehow got the hang of it, an accomplishment that I'm quite proud of! (laugh) It's interesting how it's similar to, yet dissimilar to, the thumbnailing process in creating manga. When Yamashita-san [character design/chief animation director, Yuu Yamashita-san] first showed me character design roughs for Daikichi and Rin, I remember thinking, "Wow! That's exactly them!" I felt relieved that it was in his hands. Yamashita-san has a great reputation when it comes to drawing main characters, but he's also wonderful with the other characters that are older or guys who look kind of rough. Since *Bunny Drop* is not just a story about Daikichi and Rin, but also about the relationships between them and people of a variety of ages around them, I was really happy in that regard.

Tell us about how you felt when you first read your work as a script.

Kishimoto-san's [story editor/screenwriter, Taku Kishimoto-san] script follows a different order than the original series. They reorganized and incorporated the original four volumes' worth of the manga with all the postscript stories, into an eleven-episode televised animation series. I was really surprised, though, at how there wasn't a disconnect between the manga and the anime. I especially love when Daikichi says, "I'm here!" in that first episode, where he's getting to his grandfather's house. Great, simple, and unassuming words just flow like that.

How did you feel seeing for the first time, Daikichi and Rin actually moving about in the anime?

I was super-duper-ecstatic, of course! I'd been shown the character designs, the storyboards, and the scripts beforehand, but those were at most just a guide, and you can't tell what's going to happen after a lot of people end up working on it. When I saw them finally come alive on the screen, I thought, "Wow...they really made this happen!" I got all choked up. I lost count of how many times I watched the previews.

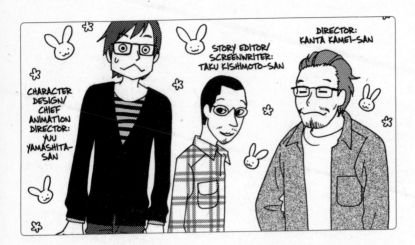

CHARACTER DESIGN/ CHIEF ANIMATION DIRECTOR: YUU YAMASHITA-SAN

STORY EDITOR/ SCREENWRITER: TAKU KISHIMOTO-SAN

DIRECTOR: KANTA KAMEI-SAN

 THEY CAN SERIOUSLY DO ALL THIS IN A TELEVISION SERIES?

How did you watch the first anime episode? Also, what were your thoughts while watching the last episode?

When I saw the first episode, I was amazed. I thought, "They can seriously do all this in a television series?" The opening and ending sequences, the animation, the voice work, the script, the scene development, the music...each and every single component was so fantastic and all worked with each other in harmony. Plus, director Kamei is a bit like a fatherly figure... (Sorry for projecting my own views here...). The director was responsible for the storyboard in the first and last episodes as well, and the Daikichi that he drew had a very fatherly-cool vibe. Very warm and dependable. The actor that portrayed Daikichi, Tsuchida-san [Hiroshi Tsuchida-san] is like that too. That spirit comes through during the very first episode. In fact, I think that's one of the major themes in *Bunny Drop*. Rin's cuteness is a given. I also keenly felt the care with which each word was chosen. It came through in the script and in how the voice actors performed. I believe that was one of the reasons why people of diverse ages appreciated

the final work. But as one cog in this creative process of story-making, I must admit to being extremely proud after I watched the final episode because I had some inkling of how hard and grueling it is to see a project to its completion. It's the same when writing manga, and although it's not the easiest thing to start a project either, somehow with a manga, I figure it'll all work out. To have the discipline to continue a big project and to see it to the end, those are the true bumps in the road on which I travel. Because of this, I'm even more ecstatic and ever more grateful to all the staff that worked on this project.

 THE IMAGE OF THE VOICES CRYSTALIZED AFTER I HEARD THE VOICE ACTORS.

The voice is a major component in animation as well. Did you have voice types in mind from before? What were your impressions after hearing the voice actors?

In a way, yes, I had a vague idea for each character. I wasn't thinking in terms of a specific voice actor but more in a general sense—body type, shape of the jaw, facial characteristics, personality, things like that. When I first heard Tsuchida-san doing the role of Daikichi, the vague idea I had in my mind really crystalized. "Ah! Yes! This is it! This is the voice!" I was blown away by how he really nailed the combination of Daikichi's manliness with his somewhat flat affect. Physically, he's Daikichi too. Ayu-chan in the role of Rin [Ayu Matsuura-san] really got Rin's innocence intertwined with a mature level-headedness. Not only did Ayu-chan have the usual emotions covered, she was able to fully express all the subtle ones so perfectly, I was shocked. To follow acting direction requires a combination of being able to process it in one's mind and the ability to physically carry that process out. It's amazing how, at her young age, Ayu-chan can do it so well.

The premise of *Bunny Drop* is by no means a cheerful one, but Ayu-chan's cute and energetic voice helps you to watch with a happy heart. It's almost a saving grace. Noah-chan, who plays Kouki [Noah Sakai-san] was completely THE boy. In anime, boys' roles are typically done by adult women or boys. So in that sense, I have no reference...I'm still struck with wonder and think it's great how Noah-chan was able to research how to act this part. Since she played such a great boy voice, I was afraid that there were people who wouldn't know about her, so I actually tweeted that Kouki was played by a girl. That got a big response. Oohara-san, who played Kouki's mother [Sayaka Oohara-san], has a voice that feels like a warm embrace and yet is also restrained... It makes even an adult like me want to snuggle up to her. I don't know too much about voice actors, but it just so happened that before it was decided to make the manga into an anime, I was on another project where Oohara-san did a voice, and I was so smitten that I actually looked her up. When I heard that Oohara-san was going to play Kouki's mom, I thought she was the perfect fit. (I totally had a look of triumph on my face!) Of course now, when I work on *Bunny Drop*, I hear the voice of those actors in my head.

Which anime episodes were you most struck by and why?

There are so many that it's hard to choose, but if I had to pick just one...it would be the sixth episode about the commemorative trees. I have an especially strong emotional attachment to this story, so I was particularly happy when the animated version came out wonderfully. I remember feeling a great peace of mind that I was able to write about Daikichi and Rin's "connection."

How did you feel when you visited the production site and the postproduction studio?

I draw for my job so the production site was a dreamland for me. (That said, it must be grueling

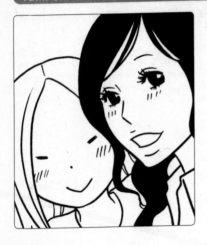

for the people who work there.) A huge difference between creating a manga versus an anime is the sheer number of people associated with an anime production. How everything came together had always been a big mystery to me, so I definitely learned a lot. All the core staffers got along so well and were such a fun bunch of people. The surprises just kept coming at the posproduction studio, one being how they got each episode done in such a short period of time. Seriously...things just kept chugging along. The drive of the hardworking sound director, Wakabayashi-san [Kazuhiro Wakabayashi-san] made an impression on me as well. Wakabayashi-san was a pleasant man of few words who kept things going very smoothly. All the voice actors followed suit, adults and children alike, with that mentality. Everything moved surprisingly quickly. It's truly mind-boggling how many people are involved in an animation... I had a vague sense of what it took, but actually seeing the dedicated hard work put into it and the pressure with my own eyes, I think the director's steering of that kind of ship is truly key to its success.

I understand that you watch a lot of anime, and it was a big surprise to you when you saw in the credits the names of staff members who had worked on some of your favorites?

Anime has a bigger influence on my work than other manga. So when I saw the names in the credits of people who were associated with works that I'd always wanted to emulate, like, "I want to draw like that!" (Of course, it's an honor too, but...) I was sweating buckets! (laugh) I was like, "I'm so sorry!"

Outside of the main story, tell us your thoughts on the special extras on the DVD.

When you're raising a child, I think you become more aware of the seasons. That's why (and this was the same in the book format as well) I was really happy that they portrayed the seasons so well in the extras. In order to be true in portraying the seasons, many things, like uniforms, need to change and with it come lots of design changes amidst the scenery changes. When it comes down to it, it just takes a lot of time and effort...but I think that effort translates into the quality of the work. Suguru Matsutani-san's music also really shines here. I was so, so looking forward to the first special edition extra—a mascot charm of Rin from Volume 2. When they showed me a sample, I was so surprised to see how cute something so small could be! The entire thing, even the back, was totally Rin and so cute.

Tell us how you felt when the DVD went to market for the first time. Your illustrations grace the outside box of the first special edition version, but what did you think of the seasonal illustrations of the inside jackets by Yamashita-san?

I especially love Yamashita-san's illustrations, so when it was decided that I would do the illustrations on the outside of the box, I felt like I might be stepping on toes. I was thinking, "Aww, won't Yamashita-san's stuff be fine?" though it would have been a little immature of me to say that... Looking back, though, I'm glad I did it. It led to the making of a bonus calendar that came with the third volume. Yamashita-san's drawings have a great overall sense of balance (sorry if I sound like a know-it-all...). He has the whole package. The scenery by art director Tatsuta-san [art director/art setting director Ichirou Tatsuta-san] was magnificent each and every episode. I'd like everyone to take a really good look at it. It's the same in book form too, but you don't see backgrounds like that too often these days.

Lastly, has anything been affected by or been changed by having your work reborn through the work (animation, movie) of others?

Both the movie and animation versions were of course an extreme honor, and I had to be careful not to get too full of myself. I knew that I had to focus even more and stay levelheaded and true to my work. So many brilliant people came together and spent an inordinate amount of time and effort to collaborate, and the end product was something I could never even have imagined, it was so wonderful... I just didn't want to let down all of those people and all my fans who saw the movies and animation first and then came to the manga.

Thank you very much!

[Interview first printed in the booklet of
Disc 4 of the Japanese DVD and Blu-ray
Bunny Drop anime release]

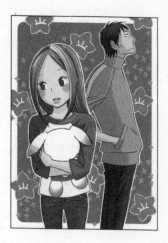

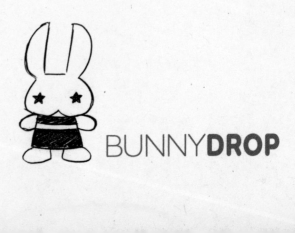

BUNNY**DROP**

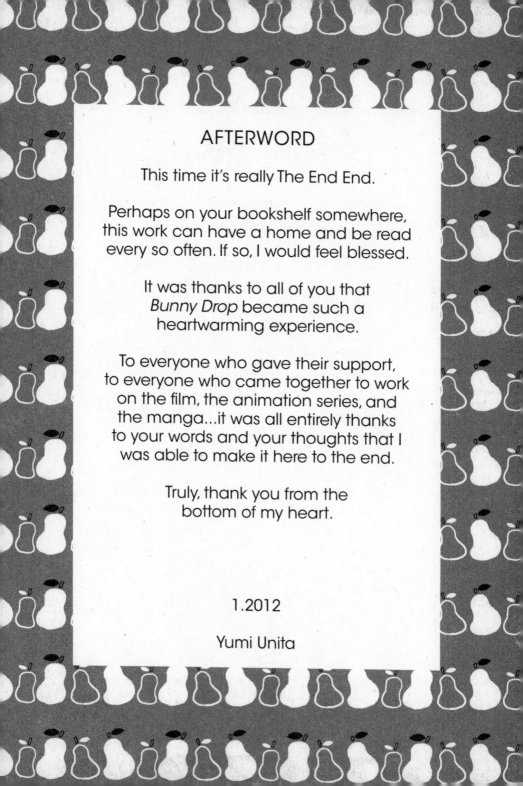

AFTERWORD

This time it's really The End End.

Perhaps on your bookshelf somewhere,
this work can have a home and be read
every so often. If so, I would feel blessed.

It was thanks to all of you that
Bunny Drop became such a
heartwarming experience.

To everyone who gave their support,
to everyone who came together to work
on the film, the animation series, and
the manga...it was all entirely thanks
to your words and your thoughts that I
was able to make it here to the end.

Truly, thank you from the
bottom of my heart.

1.2012

Yumi Unita

SPECIAL THANKS

DIRECTOR SABU KENICHI MATSUYAMA-SAN KARINA-SAN

MANA ASHIDA-CHAN RUIKI SATO-KUN

DIRECTOR KANTA KAMEI-SAN TAKU KISHIMOTO-SAN

YUU YAMASHITA-SAN ICHIRO TATSUTA-SAN GOEN°

DROPS-SAN DOG CURRY THEATRICAL GROUP

HIROSHI TSUCHIDA-SAN AYU MATSUURA-SAN

SAYAKA OOHARA-SAN NOAH SAKAI-SAN

PUFFY AMI ONUKI-SAN YUMI YOSHIMURA-SAN

KASARINCHU TATSUHIRO-SAN KOUSUKE-SAN

SUGURU MATSUTANI-SAN

YOSHIYUKI SEKI-SAN MITSURU KOBAYASHI-SAN

AIZAWA-SAN KAZU-SAN KAJIKAWA-SAN YAMAUCHI-SAN

MIYATAKE-SAN AKIO FUMI

SORRY I COULDN'T WRITE EVERYONE'S NAME...

TO EVERYONE WHO WAS A PART OF *BUNNY DROP*...

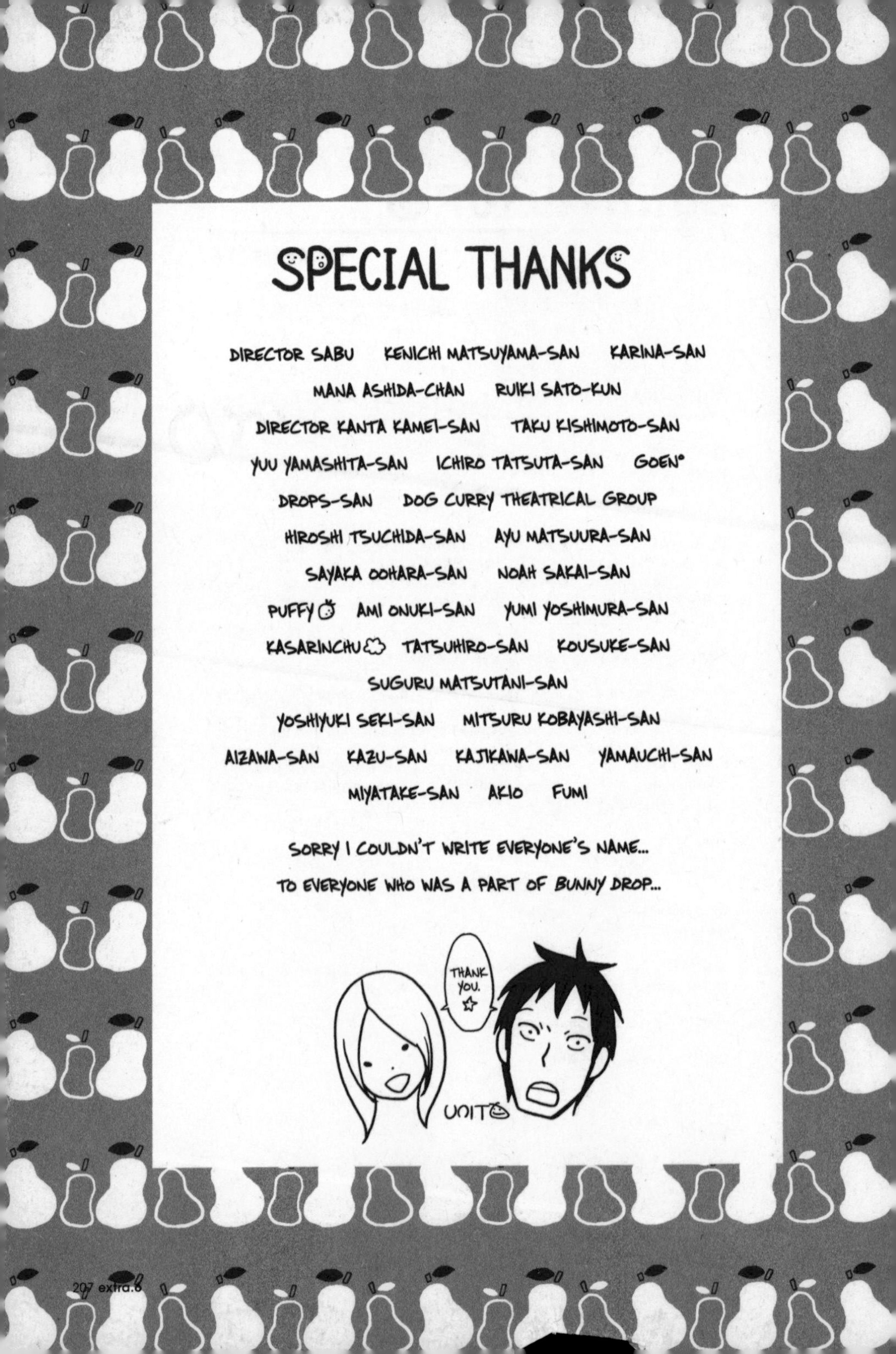

THANK YOU. ☆
UNITA

BUNNY DROP 10

Translation: Kaori Inoue   Lettering: Alexis Eckerman

BUNNY DROP Vol. 10 © 2012 by Yumi Unita. All rights reserved. First
published in Japan in 2012 by SHODENSHA PUBLISHING CO., LTD.,
Tokyo. English translation rights in USA, Canada, and UK arranged with
SHODENSHA PUBLISHING CO., LTD. and Hachette Book Group through
Tuttle-Mori Agency, Inc., Tokyo.

Translation © 2014 by Hachette Book Group, Inc.

Yen Press
Hachette Book Group
237 Park Avenue, New York, NY 10017

www.HachetteBookGroup.com
www.YenPress.com

Yen Press is an imprint of Hachette Book Group, Inc. The Yen Press name
and logo are trademarks of Hachette Book Group, Inc.

First Yen Press Edition: April 2014

ISBN: 978-0-316-40080-0

10 9 8 7 6 5 4 3 2 1

BVG

Printed in the United States of America